THE GREAT IDEAS ANTHOLOGIES

This is a volume in the Arno Press series

THE GREAT IDEAS ANTHOLOGIES

CONTEMPORARY IDEAS IN HISTORICAL PERSPECTIVE
THE HUMANITIES TODAY
THE SCIENCES TODAY
THE SOCIAL SCIENCES TODAY

CONTEMPORARY IDEAS
IN HISTORICAL PERSPECTIVE

Edited by
Robert M. Hutchins and Mortimer Adler

Introduction by John Van Doren

ARNO PRESS
A New York Times Company
New York / 1977

First publication, 1977 by Arno Press Inc.
© 1977 by Encyclopaedia Britannica, Inc.
Published by arrangement with Encyclopaedia
  Britannica, Inc.

THE GREAT IDEAS ANTHOLOGIES
ISBN for complete set: 0-405-07170-1
See last pages of this volume for titles.

Manufactured in the United States of America

———————◆———————

Library of Congress Cataloging in Publication Data
Main entry under title:

Contemporary ideas in historical perspective.

    (The Great ideas anthologies)
    "First printed in The great ideas today."
    Bibliography: p.
    I. Hutchins, Robert Maynard, 1899-   II. Adler,
Mortimer Jerome, 1902-   III. The Great ideas today.
IV. Series.
AC5.C733   081   75-4311
ISBN 0-405-07174-4

INTRODUCTION

Contemporary Issues offers discussions of a controversial nature about matters of common concern by persons whose opinions for one reason or another seemed to carry special weight. It is published along with three other collections — *The Humanities Today, The Sciences Today,* and *The Social Sciences Today* — which bring together the writings of noted authorities on recent developments in the world of learning and ideas, described so far as possible in layman's language, for the benefit of the lay reader.

All of these writings were first printed in *The Great Ideas Today,* an annual publication of the Great Books Division of Encyclopaedia Britannica, Inc., which has appeared every year since 1961. Each issue of this annual, a hard-bound volume of approximately 500 pages, contains a symposium on a topic of current importance, three or four essays devoted to recent developments in the arts and sciences, and an examination of some classic work or traditional subject in contemporary terms. It is intended primarily for readers of Britannica's *Great Books of the Western World* (usually referred to in the pages that follow as GBWW), a 54-volume set of works representing the tradition of western thought from Homer to Freud, and including a topical index, known as the Syntopicon, with references arranged under one or another of what are called the Great Ideas. In offering *The Great Ideas Today* each year to the owners of this set, the editors have in mind that the tradition it embodies accounts for much of what goes on in the contemporary world, and the contributors to the volume, in commenting upon contemporary developments, endeavor to show how that is so. The title of the work reflects a further conviction that it is in terms of the ideas in the Syntopicon that the body of thought comprised by this tradition can be most easily grasped, and that it is by such means that we perceive our connection with the past and bring some coherence to the present.

It is not required, of course, that every reader of these collections be familiar with *The Great Ideas Today,* or that he have *Great Books of the Western World* conveniently at hand. Footnotes occasionally point to such sources, and most of the articles are followed by Notes to the Reader suggesting further study through the Syntopicon, but no special knowledge is assumed. Nor are the pieces to be taken simply as expressions of the editorial purpose with which they were originally commissioned. The views they present are those of their authors, who are mostly men of acknowledged eminence in their chosen fields, and who were offered certain guidelines as to how their subjects should be treated but were left to decide what they should actually say. Each piece therefore stands on its own as a discussion of a current discipline or some aspect of contemporary life, and can be read as such.

Inevitably, many of the pieces show some evidence of the fact that they were written in a particular year, their authors having been asked to summarize developments that concerned them as of that time. This was particularly true in the first issues of *The Great Ideas Today*, when the annual character of the volume was more strictly adhered to than it has been since — which accounts for the fact that fewer pieces have been selected from those early issues than from later ones. Such datedness is mostly superficial, however, and where it is more serious it is apt to be corrected in the course of a later discussion of the same subject by a different contributor. When an essay seemed in some crucial respect to be no longer current, it was left out of these collections, but it was not rejected for its passing references to a year that is now gone by. For those who wish to know what has happened in certain fields since these writings were first published, each collection includes an added bibliography of important works on the subjects covered that have recently appeared.

As the content of the various pieces is partly determined by the annual occasions for which they were written, so their style reflects a concern with the particular audience they were designed to reach. This may be said to comprise not only those persons who receive *The Great Ideas Today* but all who, beyond any special competence they happen to have, take a sober interest in what goes on in the world and are willing to read at substantial length about it. Not a great deal is written for such an audience, whose requirements lie somewhere between journalism and the academic — between, in other words, what is conveyed by those who can write of contemporary developments only as events, not being learned in their subject matter, and those who speak as to the initiate, assuming knowledge of the things they discuss. If most of the contributors to these volumes are themselves academics, and some are journalists, yet they have taken a view of their material and adopted a manner of presenting it which is nowadays untypical of their professions. The result is a series of reports that, while intended for the general reader and avoiding special terminology, provide as comprehensive and detailed an account as such limitations allow of the progress of the disciplines, the development of ideas, and the tendencies of thought in our time.

*　　*　　*　　*　　*　　*

The subjects debated or discussed in the following pages represent certain social and intellectual preoccupations that men everywhere had over the past decade. All of them are still of interest. In many cases, the matters involved were seen as issues, with respect to which positions were taken and disagreements voiced. This is now less likely to be so. If what was said on such occasions in *The Great Ideas Today* is still worth reading, as the editors of this volume presume to think, it is because the developments that were of concern were examined there for the underlying questions they seemed to raise and the permanent importance they might have, rather than for the passing controversy they elsewhere provoked.

For example, at the beginning of the 1960's there was considerable anxiety at the state of affairs in the so-called underdeveloped nations, particularly in Africa, which had only lately emerged from colonial rule and in most cases were in political, social, and economic disarray, if they were not actually at war. The difficulties under which such nations labored and the scanty means they had for dealing with them were clearly seen, particularly in the economic sphere. But their political problem was really the more serious one, and could be stated in terms of the question whether democracy was a sensible or even possible form of government for the condition in which they found themselves. It was this question over which Justice William O. Douglas and Mr. Peregrine Worsthorne, of the London *Sunday Telegraph*, divided, in a debate that is still fresh in what it says about the political arrangements that best serve human dignity and individual freedom.

Since 1963, the discussion of contemporary trends and issues in *The Great Ideas Today* has taken the form of a symposium, rather than a debate, in which various persons with suitable credentials have been invited to participate. The first such symposium was devoted to exploration of space, and the question that was asked was not what the scientific, economic, or military results of this might be, but what were its effects on man — on his conception of himself and the universe he inhabits. Contributors to this symposium, who gave different answers to the question that was asked, were Herbert J. Muller, Aldous Huxley, Hannah Arendt, Paul Tillich, and Harrison Brown.

Among later symposiums, one dealt with the upheaval that had overtaken the Christian church, and considered whether the developments that were occurring might justify a change in the ratio of its concern for the things of heaven and the things of earth — that is, practically speaking, whether it ought to encourage or resist the forces that were pressing it to become secularized, and still are. Participants in the symposium were Harvey Cox, E. L. Mascall, Martin Marty, and M. D. Chenu. Their discussion is followed here by an editorial note of the sort that originally appeared with many of these symposiums, in which the editors recall what is said by the authors of *Great Books of the Western World* on the subject under discussion, in this case the idea of religion.

Two other symposiums are of interest in that they deal with the idea of revolution and the idea of tradition, respectively, and may be read as discussions of opposed tendencies in contemporary life. In the first of these, Arnold Toynbee considers the idea of revolution in historical perspective, Ivan Illich speaks of revolutionary changes that he would bring about in the system of compulsory education, Paul Goodman considers the power that the idea has, or lately had (and will have again), for the young, and William F. Buckley, Jr., reflects upon what he calls "The Sorry Condition of Counter-Revolutionary Doctrine." The subject of tradition is discussed not in its largest and most general sense, which probably is social, but as it affects the arts, sciences, and professions. The interesting fact is that while every discipline and every calling is in some sense a learned undertaking, the attitude toward the theory and practise on which they are based varies a great deal. To reflect, say, upon the different uses that the sciences and the humanities make of their pasts, or that law does, and medicine, is to see at once where the discussion starts. Nor is this of merely academic interest, but raises fundamental questions about the culture of the present day. So at any rate the participants in the symposium suggest, who represent various branches of learning, as theology (Yves Congar), the humanities (Frank Kermode), the sciences (Theodosius Dobzhansky), the law (Harry Kalvan, Jr.), and history (J. H. Plumb).

Last, but not least, will be found a symposium on the hero and the heroic ideal. The question at issue is whether such a figure and such an ideal are any longer possible, and if possible, whether they should any longer be tolerated in the contemporary world. The editorial review of this subject as it is taken up in *Great Books of the Western World* is more than usually long, and rather than following the symposium precedes it, in the manner of an introduction. Contributors to the symposium are S. L. A. Marshall, Ron Dorfman, Josef Pieper, Joy Gould Boyum, Sidney Hook, and Chaim Potok.

John Van Doren

In presenting this volume, as with the collections of writings in the humanities, the sciences, and the social sciences which are being published at the same time, the editors acknowledge the assistance of those who have helped over the years to get out *The Great Ideas Today* — in particular, Peter C. Wolff, Otto A. Bird, and John Van Doren, and in general, the editorial production staff of Encyclopaedia Britannica, Inc. They wish also to thank Wayne Moquin, who for each of these collections prepared the bibliography of recent works that appears at the end.

Recent Books by
Great Ideas Today Authors

Hannah Arendt, *Crises of the Republic* (1972)
    Men in Dark Times (1968)

Harrison Brown, co-author of *Are Our Descendants Doomed:* Technological Change and Population Growth (1972)

William F. Buckley, Jr., *Cruising Speed* (1971)
    Inveighing We Will Go (1972)

M. D. Chenu, *Nature, Man, and Society in the Twelfth Century* (1968)

Harvey Cox, *On Not Leaving It to the Snake* (1968)
    Feast of Fools (1969)
    The Seduction of the Spirit (1973)

Ivan Illich, *De-Schooling Society* (1971)
    Tools for Conviviality (1973)

Martin E. Marty, *Righteous Empire: The Protestant Experience in America* (1970)
    You Are Promise (1973)
    The Fire We Can Light: The Role of Religion in a Suddenly Different World (1973)

E. L. Mascall, *Existence and Analogy* (1967)
    The Openness of Being: Natural Theology Today (1972)

Herbert J. Muller, *Freedom in the Modern World* (1966)
    Adlai Stevenson: A Study in Values (1967)
    Children of Frankenstein: A Primer on Modern Technology and Values (1971)
    In Pursuit of Relevance (1971)
    Uses of the Future (1973)

Paul Tillich, *Systematic Theology,* Vol. 3 (1963)
    My Search for Absolutes (1967)

Arnold Toynbee, *Cities on the Move* (1970)

CONTENTS

WILLIAM O. DOUGLAS

The case for democracy

I   The nature of democracy

The self-governing community
Universal suffrage
Forms of representative democracy

II   Safeguards of democracy

The separation and dilution of powers
Division of legislative powers
Special provisions for special situations
The loyal opposition

III   Freedom

The Honorable WILLIAM O. DOUGLAS, Associate Justice of the Supreme Court, has had a long and varied public career. Born in Minnesota in 1898, he was graduated from the Columbia Law School in 1925. After teaching for several years in the Columbia and Yale law schools, he was appointed to the Securities and Exchange Commission in 1936 and served as its chairman for two years. President Roosevelt nominated him to the Supreme Court in 1939. Mr. Justice Douglas has traveled widely and has written a number of books about his travel experiences. He is also the author of several works on natural life. A lifelong interest in civil liberties is evidenced by a number of works, including the recent *A Living Bill of Rights*.

I THE NATURE OF DEMOCRACY

The self-governing community

Democracy, unlike refrigerators and steel mills, is not an exportable commodity. It is a way of life, contagious among those who have come to see its potentials for the spirit and mind of men. It takes root slowly in new lands. It may take a long, long time for full flowering.

If democracy is to have a steady growth, it needs teachers who can specialize in political education and enlighten the minds of oncoming generations to the perils as well as the opportunities in democratic experiments. The task of educating leaders of these new nations has been long delayed. The task of establishing among those nations institutes of political education so that thousands trained in the philosophy of a free society will be graduated each year has hardly started.

The undertaking is vast and complicated. It will require years, indeed decades, of patient and unremitting work. Yet if the roots of democratic institutions take hold, the ultimate creations will be exciting. Self-government within systems that make room for all minorities and for all the diversities among people is destined to be the achievement of all mankind. Every people must start sometime; and with advanced planning, the start of none need be long delayed.

Montesquieu said: "The people are extremely well qualified for choosing those whom they are to entrust with part of their authority. . . . For though few can tell the exact degree of men's capacities, yet there are none but are capable of knowing in general whether the person they choose is better qualified than most of his neighbours."[1]

My visit to Persian villages in 1950 illustrated the point. Prime Minister Mossadegh passed a law designed to introduce democracy into the villages. Persian villages have never known democracy in their long history, nor have they ever performed municipal functions in the Western sense. They were a species of private property, owned down to the community bathhouse by the landlord. Mossadegh introduced democracy at the grass roots in an indirect way. The Parliament passed the "20 per cent law," under which the rent of each sharecropper was reduced by that percentage. The amount so determined

1 *The Spirit of Laws*, Vol. 38, pp. 4d, 71c

for each village was then divided into two equal parts: one half being remitted to the tenant and the other half being set aside for use by his village. Most landlords evaded the law, but some complied, and those that did set a powerful force in operation. The existence of the village fund made the villagers eager to use it. So they elected from their midst members of a village council – the first in Persian history.

I was present at some of these village meetings. The people were virtually all illiterate. Yet they knew their neighbors; they knew whom to trust; they knew who the ablest in the village were. Their selections of council members were wise ones. The ones chosen would serve the village interests.

Once it occurs to a man that he should actively participate in making the decisions under which he is to live, democracy is on the way. The democratic activist believes that democracy represents a value which should be defended and extended. No attack on democracy can hide the fact that it can be replaced only by a system that substitutes coercion for persuasion, one that replaces the individual's choice with the choice of some ruler.

The habits of most of the world run against active participation in self-government. But those habits are being broken. Our own history is a history of breaking the inner shackles of habit. But our history is not necessarily a unique path.

Outsiders tend to overlook the ties that have long held the people of Asia, the Middle East, and Africa together. Sometimes it was a tribe. It may have been a landlord system or a princely state. In large areas of Asia it was the family. That is true in Vietnam as it was in China. The large majority of Vietnamese – probably 90 per cent – are Buddhists. Their Buddhism fuses several religions – Buddhism, Confucianism, Taoism, and ancestor worship. The cult of the ancestor is the predominant element; it permeates Vietnamese family and social life.

Some say that the familial tradition and the tribal tradition are antidemocratic. But democratic beginnings can be made even where tribe or family is the dominant influence. A national figure is needed – a

PERSIAN VILLAGERS WITH LANDLORD
Though almost all are illiterate, the villagers have acted wisely in public affairs

leader to command loyalties and be the father symbol. Ngo Dinh Diem has filled that role in South Vietnam just as Nehru did in India. Where there is leadership and the mucilage of ties born of custom, religion, race or language, a start toward a democratic society can be made.

People who cannot read have obvious limitations when it comes to being informed about public issues and about candidates for office. Yet modern radio establishes an effective line of communication between candidates and the masses. The mechanics of the ballot present no great obstacle. Election officials can be trained. That was done in India; and it resulted in smoothly operating polling places. Symbols for the separate parties or candidates can be used. In India bullocks were the symbol for the Congress Party, the peepul tree for Socialist, a thatched hut for Praja, a locomotive for Republican, an elephant for Scheduled Castes, etc.

The 1951-52 general election in India was extended over a period of 17 weeks; the one in 1957 was completed in ten weeks. There were 26 parties in the 1951-52 general elections and 25 in the 1957 election. Nearly 200 million people voted. By 1957 there had been many by-elections and several state elections, the experience of the people increasing with each. In 1957 the three leading parties were the Congress Party that polled 48 per cent of the vote, the Praja Socialist that polled 30 per cent, the Communist that polled 9 per cent.

No electorate ever has the comprehension to understand, much less to solve, all problems. A few issues may be understandable, such as war versus peace. Or again, the need of more water in arid lands, food

5

shortages, the lack of doctors, the need of medicines, nurses, hospitals — these are issues that illiterate people may see as clearly as college graduates. The illiterate, of course, do not have the same range of understanding on some issues as the educated citizens have. The nuances of the difference between socialized medicine and medical services rendered on the basis of private enterprise may be more apparent to the educated than to the illiterate. Examples can be multiplied.

Yet, on analysis, the difference in political competence between the educated and the uneducated is one only in degree. Montesquieu says that the people can choose generals and judges for they have "better information in a public forum than a monarch in his palace. But are they capable of conducting an intricate affair, of seizing and improving the opportunity and critical moment of action? No; this surpasses their abilities."[2]

The modern world presents problems too intricate for solution by any but experts. The waste material from nuclear reactors is one example. It is presently being stored in large quantities by those who have mastered nuclear fusion. It has a half-life up to 1,000 years. No vote by any electorate in any country in any world could intelligently resolve the question of its disposal. All that any vote could do would be to express confidence in the ability of one candidate as against the other to solve the problem in a way that would best safeguard the electorate's interests. As Hegel said, even if "the people in a democracy resolve on a war, a general must head the army."[3]

There are many issues on which the electorate in the modern world cannot vote intelligently, e.g., the efficacy of a common market that has no history of actual performance; the damage done to soil, food, and lands by insecticides; the impact of automation and the manner of treating the labor it displaces.

Rousseau said: "Wise men, if they try to speak their language to the common herd instead of its own, cannot possibly make themselves understood. There are a thousand kinds of ideas which it is impossible to translate into popular language. Conceptions that are too general and objects that are too remote are equally out of its range. . . ."[4]

Since modern societies pose problems that only experts can reduce to intelligible form, elections more and more become mere expressions of confidence in a particular candidate, even where the electorate is highly educated and therefore presumably intelligent and well-informed.

Literacy and intelligence are not synonymous. Intelligence and race have no measurable relationship. To return to my Persian village, why leave the management of village affairs to the landlord when the

2 *Ibid.*, p. 4d
3 *Philosophy of History*, Vol. 46, p. 173b
4 *The Social Contract*, Vol. 38, p. 401c

villagers know their needs and can pick from among their own ranks the ones to carry out their desires?

The peoples of newly emerging nations have the capacity to manage their village or municipal affairs. There is no valid excuse for denying them that minimum measure of democracy. At least that much of self-government they should have.

Universal suffrage

Democracy has had able advocates. Thucydides said that "ordinary men usually manage public affairs better than their more gifted fellows" since "those who mistrust their own cleverness are content to be less learned than the laws. . . ."[5] Others have long believed that democracy sires tyranny — the result, Plato said, of drinking "too deeply of the strong wine of freedom. . . ."[6]

The argument *pro* and *con* about democracy is an ancient one. Euripides summed it up in a dialogue:

> *Herald:* A poor hind, granted he be not all unschooled, would still be unable from his toil to give his mind to politics. . . .

> *Theseus:* Naught is more hostile to a city than a despot; where he is, there are in the first place no laws common to all, but one man is tyrant, in whose keeping and in his alone the law resides, and in that case equality is at an end.[7]

Herodotus took up the same debate:

> *Otanes:* The rule of the many . . . is free from all those outrages which a king is wont to commit.

> *Megabyzus:* There is nothing so void of understanding, nothing so full of wantonness, as the unwieldy rabble.[8]

Democracy offers man his only chance of fulfillment — the realization of freedom, justice, and equality. There is, moreover, a flexibility in the concept of democracy which will fit varying needs. It is a form of government which — under built-in controls — any people with resolution can manage.

What do we mean by "democracy"?

The image created in the minds of people of the Western world by the word "democracy" is quite different from what prevailed in the ancient city-states of Greece or from what has sometimes been referred to as the democracy of the mob. Lincoln's democracy, which he extolled in his Gettysburg Address — "government of the people, by the people, for the people" — states the ideal. Lincoln's democracy envisioned that within broad limits everyone had the franchise. Moreover, Lincoln's democracy was not the "town hall" type. The people acted

5 *History of the Peloponnesian War*, Vol. 6, p. 425b
6 *The Republic*, Vol. 7, p. 412a
7 *The Suppliants*, Vol. 5, p. 262a
8 *The History*, Vol. 6, pp. 107d-108a

through representatives. The government was a republic – democratic in principle but representative in form.

The universal franchise and some form of representative government are the ingredients of the "democracy" we talk about when we ask whether it is a form of government that is suitable for the newly emerging nations.

Aristotle discussed the danger of turning the power over to the masses – "for their folly will lead them into error, and their dishonesty into crime" – and the danger of not doing so – "for a state in which many poor men are excluded from office will necessarily be full of enemies."[9] Centuries later – in 1821 – Chancellor Kent spoke much more dogmatically when he expressed the classic position against universal suffrage – the danger of giving the vote to "men of no property" and to "the crowds of dependents connected with great manufacturing and commercial establishments and the motley and undefinable population of crowded ports" and to "every man that works a day on the road or serves an idle hour in the militia."[10]

The principle of universal suffrage does not mean that every person must be entitled to vote. The mentally incompetent are not granted the franchise. Minors are customarily excluded. Most states require voters to be 21 years of age. Alaska lowered the voting age to 19, Georgia and Kentucky, to 18. People convicted of infamous crimes are denied the franchise. Up to the ratification of the Nineteenth Amendment in 1920 – long after Lincoln's Gettysburg Address – the right of women in the United States to vote was not guaranteed by the Constitution. Today twenty states impose some form of a literacy test on voters; and those tests have been sustained against charges of unconstitutionality so long as they are not used as devices to discriminate against classes of voters, e.g., members of a particular race.[11] Many states have had property qualifications for voters. Five states – Alabama, Arkansas, Mississippi, Texas, and Virginia – still have poll taxes. Today nine states in this country bar paupers from voting.

What is the standard by which limitations on the franchise should be tested? It is, I think, a simple one: if – in fact – a person can handle his own affairs, then he should participate in the disposition of public affairs. Exclusion of children and the mentally incompetent is justified. The exclusion of women is based on nothing more than tradition. The perpetual disenfranchisement of felons – allowing no room for rehabilitation – seems unjust.

Literacy tests are often earnestly pressed. The government of Sir Roy Welensky in Rhodesia has long argued for a multi-racial political system based on qualifications in order to vote. That system would

---

9 *Politics*, Vol. 9, p. 479c
10 *The People Shall Judge* (Chicago: University of Chicago Press, 1949), Vol. 1, p. 569. Cf. Kant, *The Science of Right*, Vol. 42, pp. 436d-437c.
11 See *United States Reports*, Vol. 360 (October Term 1958). *Lassiter* v. *Northampton County Board of Elections*, pp. 45-54.

give Europeans a majority at the start. In the end it would give Africans control. It is defended on the grounds of literacy and competency, not race. Literacy tests can be and often are advocated by those who want to maintain the leverage of the *status quo*. But they are difficult to defend except in terms of expediency. In terms of principle they are not warranted.

The exceptions to universal suffrage, diverse and important as they may be in a particular environment, do not destroy the principle stated by Jefferson in the Declaration of Independence:

> We hold these truths to be self-evident, that all men are created equal; that they are endowed by their Creator with certain unalienable rights; that among these are life, liberty, and the pursuit of happiness. That, to secure these rights, governments are instituted among men, deriving their just powers from the consent of the governed . . . .

Those who say that democracy is not appropriate as a form of government suitable for newly emerging nations repudiate the principle of "the consent of the governed." Those who are secure in their own *status quo* usually look askance at those who want a change. Adam Smith stated a jaundiced British point of view concerning our own Founding Fathers:

> The persons who now govern the resolutions of what they call their Continental Congress, feel in themselves at this moment a degree of importance which, perhaps, the greatest subjects in Europe scarce feel. From shopkeepers, tradesmen, and attornies, they are become statesmen and legislators, and are employed in contriving a new form of government for an extensive empire, which, they flatter themselves, will become, and which, indeed, seems very likely to become, one of the greatest and most formidable that ever was in the world. Five hundred different people, perhaps, who in different ways act immediately under the Continental Congress; and five hundred thousand, perhaps, who act under those five hundred, all feel in the same manner a proportionable rise in their own importance.[12]

"Consent of the governed" is an ethical principle. It rests on the dignity and worth of the individual. It assumes there are no inferior people who are to have no voice in the selection of their rulers. It asserts that citizens of these new nations, who have always been under some totalitarian regime, should have a chance to become skilled and responsible in the exercise of the franchise.

"Consent of the governed" is sturdy common sense. It rejects strained metaphors which seek to prove that giving the vote to grown men and women is no different from giving it to children, or that both the poor and the mad are identically incapable of political participation. But the reach of the idea is broader. It looks forward to a time when the free development of each individual is the condition for the free development of all men.

Some new nations have had promising starts under universal suffrage. India—a heterogeneous country of 400 million people—is the conspicuous example. Burma—a smaller nation of 18 million, made up

12 *The Wealth of Nations*, Vol. 39, p. 270c-d

of numerous communities – is another. The literacy rate in these countries is low. In India it averages from 20 to 25 per cent. Yet people, though illiterate, may nevertheless be intelligent. Their choice of Nehru's government in India and of U Nu's in Burma indicates discriminating choices.

The uninformed nature of the electorate is, however, sometimes taken as the excuse for depriving people of voting rights.

In 1958 when Mohammed Ayub seized control of Pakistan, that nation was operating under a written constitution that provided universal suffrage. There were numerous political parties on the national scene. Corruption was common; and many high officials were suspected of using their offices to line their own pockets. Party leaders were also charged with bribing voters. These were the excuses for the dictatorship. Even after the "scoundrels" had been removed from office, democracy was drastically limited. A community was defined as a group of eight to ten thousand people. It was made small so that the members would be likely to know each other and thus be able to make an intelligent choice of the person to represent them in municipal affairs. But the voters were disenfranchised in the selection of all officials above the municipal level. Ayub concluded that the voters had such narrow horizons, such little knowledge of state or national needs that they could not make intelligent choices among candidates running for the higher offices. Municipal officials – elected by the people – select officials for the next higher level; the latter in turn name the officials at the next level, and so on.

ELECTION
REGISTRATION
IN INDIA
*The political
competence
of the largely
illiterate people
has increased
with each election*

In Pakistan it seemed that Plato's formula was being followed: "He who has a mind to establish a State . . . must go to a democracy as he would to a bazaar at which they sell [constitutions], and pick out the one that suits him . . . ."[13] What Ayub did was to select a limited form of democracy; yet it is at least a start toward self-government. And this constitution went further than those of some other new countries.

India followed Thucydides, who endorsed popular rule and said that "if the best guardians of property are the rich, and the best counsellors the wise, none can hear and decide so well as the many; . . . that all these talents, severally and collectively, have their just place in a democracy."[14] This was Nehru's highly principled stand. He reflected the wisdom of John Stuart Mill who emphasized the need through education and experience in community or national affairs of taking people "out of the narrow circle of personal and family selfishness, and accustoming them to the comprehension of joint interests, the management of joint concerns – habituating them to act from public or semi-public motives, and guide their conduct by aims which unite instead of isolating them from one another."[15] These can include

13 *The Republic*, Vol. 7, p. 409c
14 *History of the Peloponnesian War*, Vol. 6, p. 520b
15 *On Liberty*, Vol. 43, p. 320b

10

service on juries, participation in municipal affairs, membership in voluntary groups, and the myriad of activities that add up to the "political education of a free people."

Universal suffrage performs an indispensable function in a republican form of government. "It is *essential* to such a government" Madison said, "that it be derived from the great body of the society, not from an inconsiderable proportion, or a favoured class of it; otherwise a handful of tyrannical nobles . . . might aspire to the rank of republicans, and claim for their government the honourable title of republic."[16]

Forms of representative democracy

Government through representatives is both a necessity in the modern state and the crucial device for the distribution of power. Through it, minority interests, which the majority might not always respect, are safeguarded. The distribution of power is achieved largely by three devices: the separation of powers, the variation of the selection and tenure accorded the various positions, and the absolute prohibition of some action. Before those controls are considered, the forms of representative democracy should be noted.

Most of the newly emerged nations have written constitutions that provide for the direct election of members of the legislature. Some have an upper house whose members are named differently. Malaya has a Senate, a majority of the members being appointed by the Chief Executive. Nigeria has a Senate, some members being appointed but the majority being selected by lower legislative assemblies. The Malagasy Republic (Madagascar) has produced a variant form. Two-thirds of its Senate are elected by "representatives of provincial, municipal and rural authorities" while the rest are elected "from economic, social and cultural groups; selected in part from the most representative groups of this kind and in part for reasons of special individual competence."

Features of the latter kind of representative democracy had counterparts in our own nation. The United States Constitution – as adopted and as it operated until the ratification of the Seventeenth Amendment in 1913 – provided for the selection of Senators by the state legislature, not by the people. The grant to state legislatures to choose our Senators was rationalized on two grounds: it was thought that this device would favor "a select appointment" and give "to the State governments such an agency in the formation of the federal government as must secure the authority of the former, and may form a convenient link between the two systems."[17]

We did not at the beginning have a direct election of a President and Vice-President. Originally, their choice was an independent, uncon-

16 *The Federalist*, Vol. 43, p. 125c-d
17 *Ibid.*, p. 189b

11

trolled act of an Electoral College. The selection of President and Vice-President by an Electoral College was put on several grounds some of which sound familiar when accounts of Pakistan's "democracy" are read. One reason was that "A small number of persons, selected by their fellow-citizens from the general mass, will be most likely to possess the information and discernment requisite to such complicated investigations."[18] Another reason was to "promise an effectual security" against the "mischief" of "tumult and disorder" attendant on popular elections. The integrity of the electors against foreign intrigue or corrupt influence was thought to be assured (1) by making their office dependent on "an immediate act of the people of America"; and (2) by giving the Electoral College a "transient existence." It was thought that this indirect method of election afforded "a moral certainty that the office of President will never fall to the lot of any man who is not in an eminent degree endowed with the requisite qualifications."[19] With the appearance of American political parties, the Electoral College began to perform merely a perfunctory role. The party system itself became a device by which universal suffrage was disciplined. While in law only a few states bind their electors to follow the popular will, in practice and tradition the Electoral College makes no independent choice.

The Constitution of the Malagasy Republic vests the executive function in a President who is elected for a term of seven years. He is chosen by an electoral college composed of (a) members of the national assembly; (b) members of the Senate; (c) members of provincial councils; and (d) delegates of municipal and rural assemblies elected by those assemblies, the number of delegates to correspond "proportionately" to the number of inhabitants.

18 *Ibid.*, p. 205c
19 *Ibid.*, p. 206b-c

12

India's executive power is vested in the President who is chosen for a term of five years by an electoral college composed of (a) elected members of the two Houses of Parliament and (b) elected members of the legislative assembly of the states.

Article II of our Federal Constitution gives the choice of federal judges, not to the people, but to the President with the advice and consent of the Senate. Mill thought that "Of all officers of government, those in whose appointment any participation of popular suffrage is the most objectionable are judicial officers."[20] Only one-fourth of our states vest the selection of state judges in the governor or legislature; the rest of our states provide for the election of judges by the voters. This latter system, however, is not in vogue in the new nations. Under their constitutions judges are appointed by the executive branch; and once appointed they usually are made "irremovable," as the constitutions of the Republic of Cameroun and the Republic of the Ivory Coast state it.

Mill believed that "no executive functionaries should be appointed by popular election: neither by the votes of the people themselves, nor by those of their representatives," because, as he put it, "The business of finding the fittest persons to fill public employments . . . is very laborious, and requires a delicate as well as highly conscientious discernment. . . ."[21]

We leave this function in the federal system to the President, who acts with the advice and consent of the Senate. He names members of the Cabinet, members of various agencies, ambassadors, ministers, consuls, and federal judges. In our states so-called cabinet posts are generally elected. But below that level the executive has the appointing power. In the newly emerged nations the various functionaries of government are named by the executive.

Universal suffrage need not reach down to that level of *expertise*. It is, however, important that the people choose the main officials. For as Aristotle said, "when the democracy is master of the voting-power, it is master of the constitution."[22]

The extent to which the "direct" election of a leader and of legislators by the people will be successful will not necessarily depend on their literacy or prior experience. It will turn on the quality of the leadership that commands their loyalties. Men like Nehru and U Nu have been symbols of honesty and integrity, as well as symbols of national aspirations. Where there is leadership of that quality, people rise to their responsibilities.

Hegel made the point that elected officials represent not a particular interest; they are there to "vindicate the universal interest . . . their assembly is meant to be a living body in which all members deliberate in common and reciprocally instruct and convince each other." That is not always what happens. Yet we know from our own experience

20 *Representative Government*, Vol. 43, p. 413d   21 *Ibid.*, p. 412a
22 *The Athenian Constitution*, Vol. 9, p. 556d

that the lawmaker "acquires and develops a managerial and political sense, tested by his experience. . . ."[23]

Legislative assemblies elected by the people have their evils and spawn their bureaucracies like any form of government. But as Mill pointed out: "The disease which afflicts bureaucratic governments, and which they usually die of, is routine. . . . In the profession of government, as in other professions, the sole idea of the majority is to do what they have been taught; and it requires a popular government to enable the conceptions of the man of original genius among them to prevail over the obstructive spirit of trained mediocrity."[24] Yet "freedom cannot produce its best effects, and often breaks down altogether, unless means can be found of combining it with trained and skilled administration."[25]

Representative democracy through the various forms it can take gives that opportunity at the municipal, the provincial, and the national level.

Even Egypt and Indonesia grant the people the right to vote only in municipal elections. Morocco does the same, though its municipal councils are mainly advisory. In 1960 Morocco let both men and women over 21 years old vote. For villages or municipalities of 7,500 people or less, nine council members were elected. That number increased proportionately until in communities over 225,000 in size, 51 council members were chosen. Above that level, these three governments withhold that right, trusting only a dictatorship.

Vietnam under Ngo Dinh Diem has had municipal elections since its independence. In 1961 it had its first presidential election.

In the Philippines, though the people, since independence, have voted in national elections, they were denied the right to vote in municipal elections until 1960. Under the Spanish regimes, which long ruled the Islands, the people were not trusted to vote at any level of government. The ruler named the governors of the provinces; and they in turn named the members of the village councils. Resistance to the grant of the franchise in municipal elections was great. The conservatives shook their heads, saying the people were not yet ready for that responsibility. But a group of Filipinos (organized as the Philippine Rural Reconstruction Movement and aided by Dr. James Yen of the International Mass Education Committee) had awakened the people in some 100 villages in the Islands to the needs of modern village development. As a result of that awakening, the political pressures for a grant of the franchise mounted.

There has been a similar awakening throughout the underdeveloped continents. The Asian and African experiments show that universal suffrage can be immediately granted to the people at least in municipal elections. Nations that trust only a dictatorship miss a great opportunity to start their people on the path to self-government. Those

23 *Philosophy of Right*, Vol. 46, p. 103b-c
24 *Representative Government*, Vol. 43, pp. 364d-365a
25 *Ibid.*, p. 365b-c

14

who do not trust the people to choose their rulers can always find convenient excuses to withhold the franchise from them.

The difference in viewpoint is age-old. But the principle of "the consent of the governed" will not be long denied in these revolutionary times without setting into operation forces of disintegration within a nation. The ideas of our own Declaration of Independence are so powerful a ferment in underdeveloped areas that an effort to thwart them will only feed the cause which the Communists champion.

The reason for relying on the principle of "the consent of the governed" is not, however, to thwart Communist strategy. It is a sound principle because it places confidence in the people. It expresses the belief that all peoples, given a chance, will have the insight and intelligence to manage their own affairs. It is true, as Mill said, that "the power which is strongest tends perpetually to become the sole power."[26] However, this tendency is no barrier to the inauguration of representative forms of democracy, but merely indicates the problem with which the architects of any new system must deal.

II SAFEGUARDS OF DEMOCRACY

The separation and dilution of powers

The democratic theory is that the majority will have a vision of the common good and act in the best interest of the particular community. The aims and objectives, as well as the procedures for attaining them, will change from time to time as new needs arise and as the wisdom of the people grows. Certainly the wisdom of the people is likely to be a better guide over the years than the vision of a ruler or a family.

Yet the problem is not solved by turning every political decision over to a "town hall" or even to the majority. *The Federalist* spoke of "the confusion and intemperance of a multitude," adding that "In all very numerous assemblies, of whatever character composed, passion never fails to wrest the sceptre from reason. Had every Athenian citizen been a Socrates, every Athenian assembly would still have been a mob."[1]

The sheer weight of numbers in a law-making group creates its own special problems. "In the first place, the more numerous an assembly may be, of whatever characters composed, the greater is known to be the ascendancy of passion over reason. In the next place, the larger the number, the greater will be the proportion of members of limited information and of weak capacities."[2]

But the objection to majority rule strikes even deeper. While the will of the majority is a safeguard against types of tyranny, even ma-

26 *Ibid.*, p. 376a
1 Vol. 43, p. 173a-b
2 *Ibid.*, p. 181b

jorities must be restricted to prescribed procedures where the life, liberty or property of an individual is threatened. A "pure democracy," according to Madison, gives rise to abuses by the majority — "there is nothing to check the inducements to sacrifice the weaker party or an obnoxious individual."[3]

One protection is the separation of powers. The Declaration of the Rights of Man of 1789 (preface to the French Constitution of 1791) said that "Every society in which . . . the separation of powers is not determined has no constitution." Aristotle made the classic statement of separation of powers between the legislative, executive, and judicial branches.[4] Madison referred to the joinder of legislative, executive, and judicial power in the same hands "whether hereditary, self-appointed, or elective" as "the very definition of tyranny."[5] Montesquieu said that all would be lost were "the same man or the same body, whether of the nobles or of the people, to exercise those three powers, that of enacting laws, that of executing the public resolutions, and of trying the causes of individuals."[6]

Madison thought the legislative power more likely than the others to become dominant, *first* because its constitutional powers are most extensive and less susceptible of precise description and *second* because it "alone has access to the pockets of the people. . . ."[7]

Men were often condemned, exiled, imprisoned, or executed, and their property confiscated by a *legislative* act. Such acts are called *bills of attainder* and are proscribed in our Constitution. If penalties are to be fastened on the citizen, the regular *judicial* procedures (with all their safeguards including right to counsel and to jury trial) must be followed. The vicious effects of bills of attainder greatly influenced the provision in the Virginia Declaration of Rights of June 12, 1776, that "the legislative and executive powers of the state should be separate and distinct from the judiciary."

Legislatures were sometimes vindictive and punished an act which, when committed, had violated no ordinance. We ban those laws as *ex post facto*. India's and Malaya's constitutions have comparable provisions. *Ex post facto* laws are engines of tyranny since today's innocent act is tomorrow's crime — should the government have an end to serve by making it such.

A legislature may represent a religious group that uses governmental power to wreak vengeance on religious minorities. Our First Amendment protects the conscience of the individual and his right to worship as he pleases; and it prohibits the "establishment" of any church, such as was done in our colonial days when the Church of England was the official church in some colonies, supported by taxation. The Malaya Constitution has comparable provisions, with the exception

3 *Ibid.*, p. 51c-d
4 See *Politics*, Vol. 9, pp. 498b-502a,c.
5 *The Federalist*, Vol. 43, p. 153d
6 *The Spirit of Laws*, Vol. 38, p. 70a
7 *The Federalist*, Vol. 43, p. 151d

that "propagation of any religious doctrine or belief among persons professing the Muslim religion" may be regulated by law. The Indian Constitution has broad provisions guaranteeing the free exercise of religion and banning the collection of taxes to be spent for religious purposes. Nigeria provides, *inter alia*, that no religious denomination shall be prevented from providing "religious instruction" in any place of education "maintained wholly" by that denomination. Nations that are emerging from French colonial rule usually have less explicit guarantees as to freedom of conscience and religion. But the basic guarantee is usually present. Thus the Constitution of the Republic of the Ivory Coast states that government "shall respect all beliefs." The Republic of Cameroun declares for "separation of Church and State."

Majorities sometimes went on "lynching bees." The rule of law is designed for guilty and innocent alike. The police under majority rule may prove as noxious as police under a dictator or king. Power is a heady thing, even when its source is majority rule. Montesquieu said that "every man invested with power is apt to abuse it, and to carry his authority as far as it will go. . . . To prevent this abuse, it is necessary from the very nature of things that power should be a check to power."[8]

The police have been a notorious example. They tend to become a law unto themselves. Hence we have provided that a person, when arrested, must be taken without unreasonable delay before a magistrate so that his detention, if it continues, is a public affair. In this country that matter is governed by statute; in India and in Malaya it is embedded in the Constitution.

Our Constitution provides for a "speedy" trial of criminal cases. Nigeria requires a judicial hearing "within a reasonable time." By reason of our Fourth Amendment — which is duplicated in most states — police cannot ransack a house or business office or automobile at will. They must first get a warrant from the magistrate. The police throughout history have taken short cuts, using torture and numerous ingenious devices to compel suspects to confess. Since everyone has a breaking point, coercion produces untrustworthy admissions of guilt. Moreover, burning, stretching, beating, abusing defenseless people are affronts to human dignity. Our Fifth Amendment outlaws any compulsion to produce admissions used against the citizen in a criminal prosecution. Most of the newly emerged nations leave this matter to legislative control. A few put protective provisions in their constitutions. Thus Nigeria provides that "no person shall be subjected to torture," and that no defendant in a criminal case shall be compelled to take the stand.

Our Fifth Amendment protects property as well as life and liberty. One man's land cannot be taken by government and granted to another person. The taking must be for a "public purpose." No matter who the

8 *The Spirit of Laws*, Vol. 38, p. 69b-c

property owner is, if his property is taken, he must be paid "just compensation." The Republic of Cameroun has a provision comparable to ours. Like provisions are found in the constitutions of nations that were colonies under England. India has a variation in a recent amendment that makes the amount of compensation depend on a legislative determination not subject to judicial review.

Our Bill of Rights has no "equal protection" clause in it. But the Fourteenth Amendment — forged in the Civil War — has one that is applicable to the states. The racial problems that gave rise to it are reflected in the backgrounds of the newly emerged nations. The principle of "equal protection" is without exception underlined in the new constitutions; and in some, notably Burma, India, and Malaya, the provisions are spelled out in some detail.

The Presidential system used in this country marks a distinct separation of power between the executive and legislative branches. The Constitution provides that "no person holding any office under the United States shall be a member of either House during his continuance in office." Similar provisions for separation of the executive from the other branches are included in the new constitutions for the Republics of Cameroun, Malagasy, and Senegal, each of which was greatly influenced by French precedents.

The cabinet or parliamentary system, in vogue in many new nations, creates a close executive-legislative relationship. That is the system that prevails in England and in most European nations. India followed that example with a slight modification in the creation of an office of President that is largely *sui generis*.

Yet the parliamentary system in young inexperienced hands may prove to be the least desirable. It may result in more turbulence than progress. Even France — wise and experienced in the art of government — abused the parliamentary system so as to make every government temporary. The new French Constitution by strengthening the role of the executive produced what is popularly known in Asia and Africa as *De Gaullism*. That is, however, but one version of the strong executive which we established in our Constitution.

Those who have little faith in popular sovereignty point to Ghana where majority rule under a parliamentary system has led to great abuse. It was doubtless naïve of the British to endow that nation with the Westminster system that requires a high degree of sophistication and discipline for successful operation. A separation of powers with the establishment of a strong executive such as we and the French have would have provided a greater degree of stability and yet assured popular sovereignty.

Hamilton called the "complete independence" of the judiciary essential in a constitution that curbs legislative power as ours does. "Limitations of this kind," he said, "can be preserved in practice no other way than through the medium of courts of justice, whose duty it must be to declare all acts contrary to the manifest tenor of the

person,
The judges
from the ex
ay be advised wi
erform no judiciary
he judges may be remove
is possessed of the judici
again, can exercise no ex
constitutes the supreme exe
ment of a third, can try and
ecutive department.[17]

In some respects the mea
eyes of people who never kn
own. There are guarantees a
ment. Nigeria's Constitution g
tained" a right to compensatior
hibited by many of these new c
usual guarantee as is the "right t
(Madagascar) enshrines in its Co
selective way in which old grieva
provision in the Constitution of th
crecy of correspondence shall be in
in pursuance of a decision by the ju
Hobbes, who made out a case ag
monarchy, said that a legislative ass
and produce a civil war, that orators w
destroy popular assemblies, that demo
against majorities or to use his words
counsel of the major part, be it good
antees in modern constitutions go far
government itself.
These restraints on government reflec
Jefferson reduced to one sentence centur
those values when he wrote in our Dec
"All men are created equal; they are endov
certain unalienable rights; that among these
pursuit of happiness." Man has some rights, J
rive from God. These are rights which no go
withhold nor, having recognized, withdraw.
divine spark that is in every human being.
Our Constitution does not express in specifi
rights which should be protected. After Jefferso
logued the most important ones and put them in ti
added a catchall: "No person . . . shall be depriv
property, without due process of law." This is mo
against procedural irregularities. It declares some

17 *The Federalist*, Vol. 43, p. 154c-d
18 *Leviathan*, Vol. 23, p. 106d

21

A COURT SCENE IN THE IVORY COAST
*"An independent judiciary [can insure] that every man . . .
will receive equal justice under law"*

Constitution void."[9] Hamilton, indeed, proclaimed in favor of judicial
review of the constitutionality of legislative acts long before *Marbury*
v. *Madison* was written by Chief Justice Marshall.[10] Hamilton said
that "the Constitution ought to be the standard of construction for
the laws, and that wherever there is an evident opposition, the laws
ought to give place to the Constitution."[11] It has been said that "The
keystone of the whole structure is, in fact, the system provided for
judicial control—the most unique contribution to the science of government which has been made by American political genius."[12]

One basic requirement for a democratic regime is a judiciary that is
free from manipulation or control by the executive or by the legislature.
An independent judiciary is the rock against which all storms of passion break. It is an assurance that the conscience of the community
will find expression, that every man, no matter how unpopular, will
receive equal justice under law.

Montesquieu sounded the alarm about joining the judiciary power
with either the legislative or executive. If it were joined with the former, he said, "the life and liberty of the subject would be exposed
to arbitrary control; for the judge would be then the legislator." If
the judge were joined with the executive, he stated, "the judge might
behave with violence and oppression."[13]

Judges have been tyrants. The jury that acquitted William Penn of
the charge of committing a nuisance was jailed by the judge. Judges
were often mere instrumentalities to carry out the will of the king or
dictator. The most important control over judges is the jury which
makes its independent determination of guilt or innocence in criminal

9 *The Federalist*, Vol. 43, p. 230d
10 See *United States Reports*, Vol. 5 (December Term 1801), pp. 137-180.
11 *The Federalist*, Vol. 43, p. 238b
12 Charles A. Beard, *An Economic Interpretation of the Constitution of the United States* (New
York: Macmillan Co., 1939), p. 162
13 *The Spirit of Laws*, Vol. 38, p. 70a

19

cases or fin[...]
tions do not[...]
has been Br[...]
jury system b[...]
in these new [...]
education in go[...]

The new con[...]
the judiciary. T[...]
of confrontation [...]
sumption of innoc[...]

In the America[...]
against a gradual c[...]
partment, consists i[...]
the necessary consti[...]
croachments of the o[...]
indeed, marked by a [...]
great masses of power [...]

In this country none [...]
Mr. Justice Brandeis sai[...]

> The separation of the [...]
> completely autonomous. [...]
> others, as it left to each p[...]
> their nature executive, legis[...]
> not secure full execution o[...]
> means of doing so. Full exe[...]
> clines to create offices indis[...]
> gress, having created the offi[...]
> priation. Or, because Congres[...]
> appropriation, prevents, by re[...]
> of officials who in quality and [...]
> execution of the law.[16]

The President with his veto e[...]
gress. Congress can override a [...]
ating authority—exercises a pro[...]
The judiciary—by refusing to en[...]
a check or restraint on both the [...]
These are mere examples. The list [...]
constitutional system is long. Thos[...]
restricted in what they may do. The [...]
Constitution apply in the main to ou[...]
while accepting majority rule throug[...]
limitations on each branch of governm[...]
be honored, so that no branch will ride [...]
Madison summarized the matter as fo[...]

> The magistrate in whom the whole exe[...]
> himself make a law, though he can put a ne[...]

14 *The Federalist*, Vol. 43, p. 163b
15 *Representative Government*, Vol. 43, p. 412c
16 *United States Reports*, Vol. 272 (October Term 1926). *My*[...]

---

as well, *e.g.*, freedom of movement within the country, is[...]
to leave the country.[20]

Specially designed controls over the executive, legisla[...]
judicial branches are available to every new country that a[...]
written constitution. What specific ones may be needful and nec[...]
will depend on the background of the people in question, the he[...]
geneity of their population, religion and custom, the dominance[...]
tribes, and the like.

England's unwritten constitution is a product of 600 years of history. It governs people who are largely homogeneous in race and language and who occupy a rather small, compact area. England's example may be the ideal. But it is not practical for the new nations who
have had no prior experience in self-government. A written constitution with a clear separation of powers is for them a prerequisite. Only
in that way can the reserve powers of the people be protected, the
authority of government restricted, and the rights of minorities defined.
Power needs restraints, qualifications, and conditions. Prescribed
procedures are important, as means are often as important as the ends
themselves. What particular restraints are needed depends in part on
the peculiar problems of the particular nation.

A written constitution filled with guarantees gives no assurance, of
course, that in practice rights will be recognized and proper procedures followed. But a written charter serves as a rallying point in case
of crises; and it establishes necessary guidelines for all departments
of government and for the individual citizen as well.

Division of legislative powers

Lycurgus, the lawgiver of Sparta, instituted as part of his reforms a
senate which had power equal to the King's in matters of great
moment and which gave a balance between royalty and democracy.
Plutarch described this reform as follows:

> For the state, which before had no firm basis to stand upon, but leaned
> one while towards an absolute monarchy, when the kings had the upper
> hand, and another while towards a pure democracy, when the people had
> the better, found in this establishment of the senate a central weight, like
> ballast in a ship, which always kept things in a just equilibrium; the twenty-
> eight always adhering to the kings so far as to resist democracy, and on the
> other hand, supporting the people against the establishment of absolute
> monarchy.[21]

The division of legislative powers between an upper and lower house
in this country served in part a similar purpose. *The Federalist* states
that the Senate "distinct from and dividing the power" with the House

19 See *United States Reports*, Vol. 314 (October Term 1941). *Edwards v. California*, pp. 160-186.
20 See *United States Reports*, Vol. 357 (October Term 1957). *Kent et al. v. Dulles, Secretary of*
   State, pp. 116-143
21 *Lives*, Vol. 14, p. 34d

of Representatives "doubles the security to the people, by requiring the concurrence of two distinct bodies in schemes of usurpation or perfidy, where the ambition or corruption of one would otherwise be sufficient."[22]

The Federalist advances another reason for a Senate—"the propensity of all single and numerous assemblies to yield to the impulse of sudden and violent passions, and to be seduced by factious leaders into intemperate and pernicious resolutions." A legislative body performing these functions, it was thought, should "be less numerous . . . possess great firmness," and "hold its authority by a tenure of considerable duration."[23]

It was believed that a body of men with long tenure would devote more time "to a study of the laws, the affairs, and the comprehensive interests of their country" and thus become better acquainted "with the objects and principles of legislation."[24]

The Federalist emphasized the evils of constant change in government. It also underscored two main evils of a rapidly changing government: the lack of respect for the nation abroad and the lack of confidence at home:

> But the most deplorable effect of all is that diminution of attachment and reverence which steals into the hearts of the people towards a political system which betrays so many marks of infirmity, and disappoints so many of their flattering hopes. No government, any more than an individual, will long be respected without being truly respectable; nor be truly respectable without possessing a certain portion of order and stability.[25]

The authors of *The Federalist* pointed out that "no long-lived republic" failed to have a Senate.[26] The grant of two Senators to each state—no matter what the size of the state—had the virtue of keeping the upper house small; it was also "at once a constitutional recognition of the portion of sovereignty remaining in the individual states, and an instrument for preserving that residuary sovereignty."[27]

The House of Representatives, chosen directly by the people, was designed to have "a common interest with the people."[28] Frequent elections—every other year—was one method of assuring it and of securing the liberties of the people. The standard used by the authors of the Constitution was—"the greater the power is, the shorter ought to be its duration; and, conversely, the smaller the power, the more safely may its duration be protracted."[29] In the House of Representatives the Constitution expressed the democratic ideal by giving each vote "an equal weight and efficacy."[30]

The Senate was given certain powers in which the House did not share: (1) by a vote of two-thirds to agree to treaties made by the President; (2) to pass on nominations made by the President to the major

22 Vol. 43, p. 190a
23 *Ibid.*, p. 190b
24 *Ibid.*, p. 190c, b

25 *Ibid.*, p. 191c
26 See *Ibid.*, p. 193a.
27 *Ibid.*, p. 189c

28 *Ibid.*, p. 165d
29 *Ibid.*, p. 167a
30 *Ibid.*, p. 172a

public offices; (3) to sit as the court that passes on impeachment charges against officials. The Senate, designed to represent "the free-holders and property owners" and other conservative interests in the nation, thus had important controls over executive action.

Offsetting those powers was one exclusive power granted the lower house — "All bills for raising revenue shall originate in the House of Representatives." Montesquieu emphasized the impropriety of the nobles in an aristocracy levying the taxes.[31] When the people lay the taxes, their burdens may be heavy "but they do not feel their weight."[32] The matter was discussed in *The Federalist:*

> The House of Representatives cannot only refuse, but they alone can propose, the supplies requisite for the support of government. They, in a word, hold the purse — that powerful instrument by which we behold, in the history of the British Constitution, an infant and humble representative of the people gradually enlarging the sphere of its activity and importance, and finally reducing, as far as it seems to have wished, all the overgrown prerogatives of the other branches of the government. This power over the purse may, in fact, be regarded as the most complete and effectual weapon with which any constitution can arm the immediate representatives of the people, for obtaining a redress of every grievance, and for carrying into effect every just and salutary measure.[33]

The Constitution of Nigeria has a provision requiring all "money bills" to originate in the lower house. But they may not originate there except on the recommendation of the executive. Yet having been passed by the lower house and having lain before the Senate for at least a month, a "money bill" may become law without Senate approval. A similar provision governs all other bills passed by the House in consecutive sessions but not passed by the Senate.

Malaya's Constitution also bars revenue measures from being introduced in the Senate. And only a Minister can introduce or move such a bill in the House. Enactments into law of a "money bill" may be made by the House alone under provisions comparable to those in Nigeria's Constitution.

Burma has a legislative body composed of two chambers. One is the Chamber of Deputies. The other — approximately half the size of the Chamber of Deputies — is the Chamber of Nationalities drawn from the five states and the several territories that are included in the Union of Burma. These two chambers in Burma act conjointly. Yet restrictions are placed on the Chamber of Nationalities. It may not initiate a "money bill"; and "money bills" sent by the Chamber of Deputies to the Chamber of Nationalities are sent only for advice and recommendations which can be accepted or rejected by the former. Thus is control of revenue matters kept out of the hands of minorities that have presented separatist and other acute problems to the central government.

31 See *The Spirit of Laws*, Vol. 38, p. 24a-b.
32 *Ibid.*, p. 143b
33 Vol. 43, p. 180d

In this regard, India's Constitution is similar to Burma's. No "money bill" may be introduced in the upper house (Council of States); and the lower house (House of the People) may accept or reject any recommendations concerning a "money bill" made by the Council of States.

India has another innovation. As already noted, the executive power is in a President, chosen by an electoral college. The government, parliamentary in form, is headed by a Prime Minister who is appointed by the President. A Council of Ministers, presided over by the Prime Minister, advises the President in the exercise of his functions. Yet, though the President is the executive, he has certain legislative powers. When the two houses are not in session and "the President is satisfied that circumstances exist which render it necessary for him to take immediate action, he may promulgate such Ordinances as the circumstances appear to him to require." Any law that Parliament cannot pass, the President cannot promulgate; and the laws that he promulgates must be laid before the Parliament. They cease to operate at the end of six weeks from the reassembling of Parliament, unless Parliament erases them earlier.

There is no one formula for division of legislative power that will fit every nation. Tribes, blocs, minority groups, the fragile quality of a particular society—these may suggest not only restrictions on legislative authority but also the assignment of one kind of legislative power to one group, another kind to a different group. Local requirements may, indeed, lead to a grant, as in India, of limited lawmaking authority to the executive. The constitutional devices are so varied and flexible that a wide range of controls over legislative procedures is available.

The problem is not whether newly emancipated people should start down the path to self-government. The question is what particular formula for the division and control of legislative power best fits the genius of a particular people.

Special provisions for special situations

Federalism is an imperative necessity for some new nations. Wherever there is a large land mass under central control, federalism is a *sine qua non*. If the outlying areas are far removed from the center, local affairs must be entrusted to local management. No government, no matter how mature, how wise, how experienced, can administer all affairs from the center if the geographical area is as large as Australia, Canada, India, Russia, or the United States. Local problems can be intelligently managed only at a state, county, or municipal level.

Moreover, a variety of races, cultures, religions, or languages may necessitate political divisions that might not otherwise occur. Language has led to some regrouping of states within India. Religion— which resulted in Pakistan's being torn from the original India—is at

25

times a force that clamors for political divisions within one nation. There are Muslim, Christian, and pagan communities in many African nations. Political expediency may require the drawing of state or provincial lines within one nation so as to recognize these separate religious groups. That policy—though not ideal by democratic standards—may nonetheless be pursued within the general framework of a democratic form of government. When such diversities combine with a large land mass, some form of federalism is almost inevitable.

Madison said that in a federal system composed of "republican members, the superintending government ought clearly to possess authority to defend the system against aristocratic or monarchical innovations." He cites Montesquieu for the proposition that governments of "dissimilar principles and forms" are less adapted to "a federal coalition of any sort than those of a kindred nature . . . . 'Greece was undone,' he [Montesquieu] adds, 'as soon as the king of Macedon obtained a seat among the Amphictyons.' "[34]

These considerations led in this country to a guarantee by the Federal Government of "a republican form of government" for each state. As Madison said, "Whenever the States may choose to substitute other republican forms, they have a right to do so, and to claim the federal guarantee for the latter. The only restriction imposed on them is that they shall not exchange republican for anti-republican Constitutions . . . ."[35]

The central government (in this country) guarantees the constituent members of the federation against invasion. It manages foreign affairs as well as defense. It provides a uniform coinage, a postal service, and protection for commerce moving between the members of the federation as well as protection in the free movement of people. The central government also retains power to put down insurrections within the federation. Madison laid great emphasis on the latter:

> In cases where it may be doubtful on which side justice lies, what better umpires could be desired by two violent factions, flying to arms and tearing a State to pieces, than the representatives of confederate States not heated by the local flame? To the impartiality of judges they would unite the affection of friends. Happy would it be if such a remedy for its infirmities could be enjoyed by all free governments; if a project equally effectual could be established for the universal peace of mankind!
>
> Should it be asked, what is to be the redress for an insurrection pervading all the States, and comprising a superiority of the entire force, though not a constitutional right? the answer must be, that such a case, as it would be without the compass of human remedies, so it is fortunately not within the compass of human probability; and that it is a sufficient recommendation of the federal Constitution, that it diminishes the risk of a calamity for which no possible constitution can provide a cure.[36]

The division of powers between the central government and the states cannot be determined by one formula. The minimal requirements

34 *Ibid.*, p. 141b
35 *Ibid.*, p. 141c-d
36 *Ibid.*, p. 142c

PRESIDENTS MODIBO KEITA OF MALI, KWAME NKRUMAH
OF GHANA, AND SÉKOU TOURÉ OF GUINEA
SIGN A PACT CREATING AN ECONOMIC UNION
Forms of confederation can help the new nations meet many of their problems

have been stated. In the United States the grant of power to the central government was much more limited than what the central government enjoys in India. The difference is in terms of history. In this country the states created the Federal Government; they existed as living political entities prior to the Constitution. In India the Constitution created the states and accordingly relegated them to an inferior position.

Loose forms of confederation sometimes serve special needs. In 1959 the Republic of Niger joined the Republics of the Ivory Coast, the Upper Volta, and Dahomey in organizing the Council of Entente. It meets semiannually and is presided over in turn by each of the heads of state of the four nations. It has established a customs union and a fund for financial assistance to the member states; and it concerns itself with coordination of development plans for the four countries. A similar loose federation was worked out in 1959 between the Republic of the Congo (French), the Central African Republic, and the Republics of Chad and Gabon. By 1960 a charter had been adopted by the Central African Republic, the Republic of the Congo (French), and the Republic of Chad granting the federal government jurisdiction over foreign affairs, defense, postal and telecommunication departments, currency, and coordination of economic matters. This federation became known as the Union of the Republics of Central Africa.

The stability in the Belgian Congo may eventually be found in a form of federalism built along tribal lines.

27

Whatever form of federalism is used—whether the American type, the Indian type, or a looser form—the constitution should include schedules which specify in some detail the matters assigned to the states and those assigned to the federal government.

Federalism is no cure-all; it creates difficult problems of its own. Yet it is often one way—perhaps the only way—whereby, to use Hegel's words, "the constitution adopted by a people makes one substance —one spirit—with its religion, its art and philosophy, or, at least, with its conceptions and thoughts—its culture generally; not to expatiate upon the additional influences, *ab extra,* of climate, of neighbors, of its place in the world."[37]

Federalism can be put in a democratic framework by the newly emerged nations, as Burma, India, and Nigeria illustrate. Federalism may not fit other areas which though large in land mass are torn by tribal or religious animosities. For as Mill said, "Governments must be made for human beings as they are, or as they are capable of speedily becoming . . . ."[38]

Several types of controls, not products of the Western experience, show how versatile the democratic procedures can be once there is a will to walk that path.

Singapore, formerly England's Crown Colony, is an island off Malaya. It is largely Chinese and its future—whether a part of Malaya or an independent nation—is still in balance. There are turbulent forces; and the Communists, always well organized, stand ready with a united front to take over. The spirit of independence from any foreign control is, however, strong. The British have worked out a solution which some suspect, but which in essence provides an orderly transition. Full self-government is granted the people of Singapore; and they in recent years have developed a multi-party system. But England retains control of defense and of foreign affairs. This is an interim arrangement; but it shows how with gradual approaches a beginning of self-government can be made. It is a striking demonstration that neither Franco's Spain nor Russia's Hungary is the alternative we need face.

Cyprus is a more dramatic illustration of the flexibility of democratic procedures once that way of life is chosen. Cyprus is composed of a Greek community representing about 80 per cent of the people and a Turkish community representing about 15 per cent. The Greeks are largely urban people; the Turks, agricultural. The animosities between the two groups have been long-standing. The prospect the Turks faced of being under Greek rulers seemed a gloomy one. The prospect the Greeks faced of either partition of the island between the two peoples or the maintenance of a Greek regime over a rebellious Turkish minority was not encouraging. The result was the negotiation of a constitu-

37 *Philosophy of History,* Vol. 46, p. 174b
38 *Representative Government,* Vol. 43, p. 368c

tion which made a viable democratic system—though not the ideal one—out of two antagonistic groups.

This 1960 Constitution recognizes both languages as "official"; and each community is given the right to celebrate its national holiday. A particularized Bill of Rights is included, a declaration that enumerates the rights of the citizen in much more detail than our own. There are provisions disqualifying the President or Vice-President from being either a minister in the cabinet or a member of the legislature. The President is to be a Greek; the Vice-President a Turk. The executive power of the President is described with particularity. So is the executive power of the Vice-President. There is also a list of powers that the two exercise "conjointly." Some powers of "veto" are to be exercised either separately or conjointly. The executive powers not assigned to the President or Vice-President are exercised by a Council of Ministers, designated by the two with the stipulation that seven shall be Greeks and three Turks.

Universal suffrage is provided for; and 70 per cent of the House of Representatives is to be elected by the Greek community; 30 per cent by the Turkish community. The members of the House are elected for five years; the President of the House is a Greek, elected by the Greek community; the Vice-President of the House is a Turk, elected by the Turkish community. The House has all legislative power, except that granted to two Communal Chambers, also elected by universal suffrage. It has legislative power over religious matters; educational, cultural and teaching matters; personal status, etc. Its Greek members are chosen by a Greek electoral list; its Turkish members, by a Turkish electoral list. The President has the right to veto any law or decision of the Greek Communal Chamber; the Vice-President, any law or decision of the Turkish Communal Chamber.

The representation of the two communities appears throughout the Constitution. Even the Attorney General and the Deputy Attorney General may not belong to the same community. Neither may the Governor and Deputy Governor of the Issuing Bank nor the Accountant General and Deputy Accountant General. The public service, at all levels and in all grades, is composed of 70 per cent Greeks and 30 per cent Turks. The same percentage governs the composition of the Public Service Commission that supervises the public service.

The army must be 60 per cent Greek and 40 per cent Turkish. The same is true of the security forces. Forces stationed in a Greek community must be Greeks; and Turks must be stationed in Turkish communities.

An independent judiciary is provided, the Supreme Constitutional Court being composed of one Greek, one Turk, and one neutral. Next in the hierarchy is the High Court of Justice, to be composed of two Greeks, one Turk and one neutral, the last having two votes. As to trial courts, if plaintiff and defendant belong to the same community, only judges of that community shall sit. The same is true in criminal suits where the accused and the injured person belong to the same community. If the persons mentioned are of different communities, the judges shall belong to both also. Separate Turkish municipalities are created in five of the largest towns. In a Turkish municipality the council is elected by the Turkish electors; in a Greek municipality the Greek electors make the selection.

Other like provisions maintain the legal and constitutional identity of each community, establish safeguards for it and offer assurance that its special interests will not be overridden by the other. The two main groups are Greeks and Turks. There are other groups also — Armenians, Maronite Catholics, and Latins. They can join either the Greek or the Turkish electoral list. But in all events they enjoy constitutional protection against discrimination both as individuals and as groups. The Cyprus experiment in democracy shows how a start toward self-government can be made and a separation of powers achieved, even when racial animosities and suspicions run high.

A third device of utility to newly emerging countries has been written into the Indian Constitution. It was feared that some communities might be so fragile, so lacking in leadership, so swept by passions as to bring their early experiments in democracy to disastrous ends. So the Indian Constitution provides in Articles 356 and 357 that the President, when "satisfied that a situation has arisen in which the government of the state cannot be carried on in accordance with the provision" of the Constitution, may take over the administration of the affairs of that state as though it were an enclave of the national government. He may not, however, suspend the courts nor exercise any judicial function. During the declared emergency, the federal parliament takes over all the legislative functions of the state.

India has found it desirable or necessary to exercise that power several times since her independence. The most recent was in 1959. Kerala had elected a Communist government in 1957. By 1959 that regime had operated Soviet-style to produce great cleavages in the state and to siphon off public funds into party programs. So the central government took over Kerala's affairs until a new election could be held. A 1960 election put a coalition of Congress Party-Praja Socialist Party in power.

A further device is the electoral register system that England used in India. When the people chose representatives in their local government, they voted only for a Muslim in a district predominantly populated by people of that belief, a Hindu where that faith was in the majority, and so on. This system was carried so far as to apportion available space in universities and colleges not only among religious groups but among the various castes. If the incoming class was 100, only specified numbers could be drawn from the several groups. Thus even though by scholastic standards the first 100 applicants were all Hindus or all Muslims or all Brahmans, the best had to give way for more mediocre students from other religious groups or castes.

THE MULTI-RACIAL GOVERNMENT OF TANGANYIKA
*Governments can be so organized that all important racial
and religious groups are represented*

Old habits are hard to break; and when independence came there was a great impetus to continue the former practices. The old apportionment of students, however, is now prohibited by the Indian Constitution. The Supreme Court of India has maintained that if there are 100 openings in a college class, the best 100 must be taken though they all be Untouchables, Muslims, etc. And the same democratic principle prevails in choosing men and women to the state and federal parliaments.

The system of the electoral register, however, has been used and is being used elsewhere. Lebanon, the small country on the Phoenician coast lying just north of Israel, is composed of three religious communities: the Muslims (Sunni and Shi'a), the Druses, and the Christians (mostly Maronites). The Christians have a slight majority; and the Constitution requires that the President be a Maronite; the Prime Minister must be a Sunni Muslim; and the Speaker of the Chamber of Deputies must be a Shi'a Muslim. The country is divided into election districts, each one being assigned to one of the three religious groups. No one not a member of that group can represent that district. A person organizing a socialist party—as did Kamal Jumblatt, a Druse— cannot run socialists in each district unless they are members of the required religious faith. For example, a Muslim district may be teeming with Christians who are socialists. But the problem is to find a Muslim who thinks the same way. None may exist; or if one is found he may be weak and ineffective. Thus the difficulty of building a new party or maintaining an old one is compounded. The candidate who qualifies by the religious test may lack the qualities to win on economic or social issues.

The electoral register system is being applied in modified forms in Africa. In Kenya the Africans outnumber all other races 24 to 1. Pending independence from British rule, the law provides for a 65-man Assembly. Of these, 33 are elected on a common roll; that is, all races vote for that number. The Africans took those 33 seats in the 1961 election. Ten seats are reserved for the whites, eight for Asians, and two for Arabs. All voters—Africans included—select these 20. Thus only those candidates most favorable to the Africans are chosen.

The remaining 12 members of the 65-member Assembly are four whites, four Africans, three Asians, and one Arab. These twelve are selected by the Assembly. When the Assembly sits as an electoral college, there are 33 Africans and 20 non-Africans. So the other 12 meet the specifications of the African majority.

There is a Council of Ministers in addition to the Assembly. It is the executive branch under a British Governor and is visualized as a temporary stop-gap to give the British residual control until the people are ready for full independence. It is composed of four colonial office officials, four Africans, three white settlers, and one Asian. Thus the 65,000 whites who own the great wealth of Kenya, who produce 80 per cent of Kenya's exports, and who have long had their way in Kenya affairs are being given more votes than the formula "one man—one vote" would allow them. The old electoral register system has been modified to protect the position of a small group in Kenya but one which may be vital to its economic life. Whether this device—which is anti-democratic in some ways—will create a stabilizing influence in a difficult transitional period is as yet wholly speculative.

There is but one time to start self-government, and that is now, no matter how illiterate, how inexperienced the people. Even though it may be limited in form and qualified by many safeguards, it will give the people a chance to acquire experience. Democracy cannot be legislated; it can only be acquired. But it can never be acquired unless some opportunity to practice it is afforded.

The loyal opposition

Faction is an acute problem in some new nations. Its causes, as Madison said, are "sown in the nature of man."[39] It can be, as Hobbes observed, "contrary to the peace and safety of the people, and a taking of the sword out of the hand of the sovereign."[40] The forces of faction can set back the progress of promising young nations. "In a society under the forms of which the stronger faction can readily unite and oppress the weaker, anarchy may as truly be said to reign as in a state of nature, where the weaker individual is not secured against the violence of the stronger . . . ."[41]

39 *The Federalist*, Vol. 43, p. 50c
40 *Leviathan*, Vol. 23, p. 121d
41 *The Federalist*, Vol. 43, p. 164c-d

Most new nations have been viewed with alarm by defenders of the *status quo*; and faction has been a chief target for those who want rebellions put down. Some in 1776 thought that continued union with Britain was the only thing that would save America from rancórous and virulent factions which have disrupted democracies.[42]

Yet faction presents not only danger but opportunity as well. Madison said: "Liberty is to faction what air is to fire, an aliment without which it instantly expires. But it could not be less folly to abolish liberty, which is essential to political life, because it nourishes faction, than it would be to wish the annihilation of air, which is essential to animal life, because it imparts to fire its destructive agency."[43]

It is inevitable that different political schools of thought will develop in every nation, Madison noted. "As long as the reason of man continues fallible, and he is at liberty to exercise it, different opinions will be formed. As long as the connection subsists between his reason and his self-love, his opinions and his passions will have a reciprocal influence on each other; and the former will be objects to which the latter will attach themselves. The diversity in the faculties of men, from which the rights of property originate, is not less an insuperable obstacle to a uniformity of interests."[44]

The problem is to provide channels through which faction becomes a stabilizing force. Mill said that "it is almost a commonplace, that a party of order or stability, and a party of progress or reform, are both necessary elements of a healthy state of political life . . . ."[45]

When that stage is reached in the evolution of a democratic society, there emerges a party or parties of the "loyal opposition."

One of the most difficult problems of a new nation—long under colonial rule or dictatorship—is the development of a two-party system.

The road is usually a rocky one. A good example is Turkey. Both men and women vote there; in the 1957 election, 85 per cent of the eligible voters went to the polls. Adnan Menderes won. His Democrat Party obtained 4,427,368 votes. The votes of the other parties were as follows:

Republican People's Party	3,752,861
National Republican Party	603,759
Freedom Party	357,796

After the election, Menderes clamped down hard. He forbade political meetings except at election time. He leveled a law at state employees (a majority of whom had been appointed by his Republican rival) making their retirement effective after 25 years of service, rather than 30, or at 60 years of age rather than 65.

42 See Adam Smith, *The Wealth of Nations,* Vol. 39, p. 420c.
43 *The Federalist,* Vol. 43, p. 50b
44 *Ibid.*
45 *On Liberty,* Vol. 43, p. 289c

Menderes also continued a restrictive law governing the press. It was a crime to print any article or any cartoon that was "insulting to the government." One cartoon (that resulted in the closing of the paper and the conviction and imprisonment of the cartoonist) depicted a policeman arresting a burglar near a safe. The policeman tells the burglar, "Of course you would come out empty-handed. Don't you know there are bigger thieves than you?" The label on the safe suggested that it was the national treasury.

Editors were also sent to jail and fined after trials that were secret. University professors were suspended, one for stating to a newspaper reporter that he believed some of the new rules of the Turkish Parliament were unconstitutional. Freedom of speech and of press suffered in Turkey even more than it did in this country under the Alien and Sedition Laws that John Adams sponsored and that Thomas Jefferson opposed.

Menderes might have survived the persecutions of editors, cartoonists, and professors. But he went so far as to suppress his political opposition represented by the leader of the Republicans, Ismet Inönü, collaborator of Atatürk, who founded modern Turkey. A committee was appointed to look into the "destructive and illegal activities" of the Republicans. Inönü was dogged by the police on his campaigns. His meetings were broken up. Army officers who protested and resigned were arrested. The debates in the parliament were so acrimonious that one day Inönü said: "If you go on like this, even I shall not be able to save you."

Students, restless under Menderes, began to parade and protest. They poured through the streets of Istanbul. In retaliation, Menderes put Istanbul under martial law and closed the universities. A group of 60 Turkish lawyers put on their robes and marched the streets of Istanbul in protest of Menderes. They, too, were stopped and some were arrested. When representatives of the North Atlantic Treaty Organization foregathered in Istanbul in May, 1960, they found tanks guarding the building where they conferred. Facing the tanks were hundreds of students shouting "Freedom." This was the stuff which generated the military *coup d'état* of May, 1960.

Leaders of nations that are young in the ways of democracy often resent criticism. Criticism is considered a personal affront. Unlimited criticism carried so far as to label the opposition a "party of treason" leads to a breakdown of democratic processes in any country. Tolerance of criticism and debate—the maintenance of a loyal opposition—is one first and hard lesson the newly emerging nations must learn.

Practices similar to those of Menderes on the part of the Nkrumah government in Ghana have been much publicized.[46] Excesses can be

46 See Rothschild, "On the Application of the Westminster Model to Ghana," *Centennial Review*, Vol. 4 (Fall 1960), pp. 465-583.

expected in other nations. People without experience and traditions in self-government need time to develop them. They do not evolve overnight or quickly. But without a start no progress can be made. Political maturity is acquired only with experience in political affairs.

The multiplicity of parties is a phenomenon common to most new nations. People tend to rally around special causes, forming parties to serve one particular end. Thus in Indonesia, 45 political parties appeared, serving very special needs.

Until Sukarno dissolved Parliament in 1960 and took control, Indonesia's splinter parties produced many cabinet changes. Since World War II, French cabinets changed on the average six times a year until De Gaulle took office. The rate in Indonesia was one every eight months. The result was great instability. For while France had an effective civil service that carried on whatever happened, Indonesia had a paucity of experienced personnel.

Sukarno's most vociferous critics were the large Masjumi Party (which wanted an Islamic state) and the small but elite Socialist Party—both dissolved by Presidential decree in 1960. The Socialist Party was headed by Sjahrir who went about his work in a scholarly way. For 500 years under the Dutch, political parties were non-existent. Sjahrir felt it important to formulate a program covering all aspects of Indonesian affairs—agriculture, currency and banking, exports and imports, foreign policy, unemployment, land distribution, and so on. He conceived his role as that of an educator. Year after year he produced pamphlets on a wide range of subjects with the aim of (a) educating the intelligentsia and (b) forging an over-all program that would command support. But his efforts have now ceased. Neither his efforts nor the efforts of other Indonesian parties reached fruition because no national elections have been permitted since 1955 out of fear (perhaps only an excuse) that the Communists would gain control.

Dialectical materialism has given the Communists a discipline that other parties lack. The leaders are trained to select issues that capitalize on discontent. Never do they go to the people with a program that reveals the nature of communism and the regimentation which will be fastened on the nation if the Communist Party wins. That is one reason why that party does not serve the role of the "loyal opposition." It does not reveal the true choice that the electorate has; it seeks strength through tactics that are utterly devious. The classical Communist tactic is to infiltrate parliamentary governments, getting if possible at the start the ministries of defense, communication, and education. That was what the Tudeh Party in Iran did under the Ghavam government in 1946.[47] They almost succeeded in that respect in Iraq in 1959. Once some such foothold is gained, the Communist

47 See Douglas, *West of the Indus* (Garden City, N.Y.: Doubleday & Co., 1958), pp. 241-242. Cf. Lenin, *Selected Works* (London: 1938), Vol. 10, pp. 97, 100-105; Stalin, *The Road to Power* (New York: 1937), p. 41.

Party proliferates its control. It seeks power "for keeps"; and once it acquires the reins of government it does not tolerate opposition. That may in time change. In Yugoslavia the Communist Party tolerates an opposition; but it is only a token, not a true, opposition in the Western sense.

The "multiplicity of interests" is sometimes said to give the individual security for civil rights just as the "multiplicity of sects" helps underwrite religious rights.[48]

Communist political strategy, however, is astute and capitalizes on the presence of splinter parties. It places its candidates selectively, running them only in those districts where victory is probable. That is the way it won the 1957 election in Kerala, India. By 1960, however, the opposition parties (Congress, Praja Socialist, and Muslim League) had grown in political wisdom, united forces, and ran candidates on a selective basis. The result was that this coalition beat the Communists.

The workings of the Communist Party are becoming more and more evident to political leaders on all continents. The episodes of Hungary and Tibet have made a deep impression on the minds of even illiterate people. Communist strategy will continuously aim at capitalizing on situations where numerous splinter parties exist and in every electoral district where poverty, disease, slum conditions, illiteracy combine to create volatile situations. But to date Communism has made no significant progress in areas where popular sovereignty is exercised. The presence of the Communist Party is therefore an excuse—not a valid cause—for withholding the franchise from the people.

The other extreme from splinter parties is the presence of one party that commands most of the votes. A "loyal opposition" has then little chance to develop. Mill asked: " . . . is it not a great grievance that in every Parliament a very numerous portion of the electors, willing and anxious to be represented, have no member in the House for whom they have voted?"[49] Puerto Rico has a system for remedying this defect. It derives from a system for minority representation designed by Thomas Hare in 1859 and discussed by John Stuart Mill.[50]

Down to 1950, the Governor of Puerto Rico was appointed by the President of the United States. In 1951 Puerto Rico acquired a constitution and the right of self-government in most of its internal affairs. The Chief Executive is a Governor; the legislature is made up of a Senate and a House.

Numerous parties have competed for popular support. The most popular has been the Popular Democratic Party headed by Muñoz Marín. He and other Puerto Ricans of influence and wisdom decided that in the long run the Commonwealth would thrive only under a regime in which opposition parties had a voice in legislative matters.

---

48 See *The Federalist*, Vol. 43, p. 164c.
49 *Representative Government*, Vol. 43, p. 371c
50 See *Ibid.*, pp. 372 ff.

Accordingly, a provision was included in the Constitution whereby a certain number of candidates of each minority party are declared elected, if one party elects more than two-thirds of the members of either the Senate and the House.[51] The size of the legislature is increased, within those limits, so that each minority party obtains representation equal to the proportion of votes received by their respective candidates for Governor.[52]

In the 1956 election this article operated as follows in the Senate:

Popular Democrats elected 23 to the Senate
Republicans elected   2
Independence Party elected 2

The Republicans were granted four *adicional* Senators and the Independence Party, one, as a result of the popular vote for Governor.

In the 1956 election, the Popular Democrats won 47 seats in the House. The Republicans won three and the Independence Party one. As a result of the popular vote for Governor, 13 additional members were added to the House. Of these the Republicans obtained 8 (making a total of 11) and the Independence Party 5 (making a total of 6).

In selecting the candidates to fill the *adicional* slots in the Senate and House, the names are chosen first from the list of at-large candidates in declining order of total votes received. If any places remain to be filled, they go to the district candidates who have polled the highest percentage of votes in their home districts.

In the British tradition, the loyal opposition has acquired important status. Canada, following the British practice, has a law which makes the "Leader of the Opposition in the House of Commons" a full-time office. The occupant receives not only the sessional allowance, which every member receives, but a salary of $15,000 a year in addition.

The Canadian philosophy conceives the powers of government as powers in trust; and it supplies the mechanism to scrutinize the manner of their exercise. Those out of power become as important as those in power. The people make the leader of the group out of power a salaried guardian. His protests may come to naught. But his presence on a full-time basis sobers those in power.

While young nations usually do not have the tradition of a "loyal opposition," India and Burma have it to a degree. They reflect the British heritage. The Dutch and the French left no such legacy in their colonies. Neither did the Belgians nor the Germans. This means that the "loyal opposition" will have difficulty getting roots in many new nations. Yet there is only one way to develop that tradition and that is to create the opportunities for its growth. Only self-government gives a people the chance to experience criticism, to develop parties, to learn respect for minorities, to become skilled in dealing with those

---

51 See Article III, 7.
52 The Senate has 16 directly elected members from eight districts and 11 elected at-large. The House has 40 chosen from single-member districts and 11 elected at-large.

37

who use power oppressively. What people need is the chance to become skilled both in electing leaders and in choosing those who will lead the opposition.

III FREEDOM

Winning independence is the bare beginning of the struggle for freedom. Countries that are not colonies are not necessarily free, as Cuba under Batista, Spain under Franco, the Congo under Lumumba, and China and Russia under the Communists illustrate. Rousseau noted: "Liberty, not being a fruit of all climates, is not within the reach of all peoples."[1] We do not need to accept such counsel of despair, but we must realize that the requisites of freedom are not available on a pushbutton basis.

What are the forces opposing freedom in new nations? One factor is that many of them are not nations except in name. Joseph Ileo, the new Premier of the (formerly Belgian) Congo said: "Congolese unity does not exist. The Congo is not a people. It is a collection of large ethnic groups and each of them is a people." The group that commits itself to self-government must have the basic ingredient of a viable society, whether it be economic or commercial, racial or religious, linguistic or cultural. The fact that various groups were under the same colonial regime may be wholly irrelevant. As Aristotle said, " . . . A state is not the growth of a day, any more than it grows out of a multitude brought together by accident."[2] The Ottoman Empire that ended with World War I held vast areas together from Iraq to Egypt. Once colonial ties end, centrifugal forces often tend to separate people into new groupings.

Foreign machinations constitute a second factor inimical to freedom. They can be utterly destructive of a nation's independence. Laos was torn asunder by the power plays of Soviet Russia and the United States. The most important role of the United Nations in the days ahead may indeed be to afford new nations protection from such power plays.

Perhaps the strongest factor opposing freedom is the very lack of freedom itself. People who have had no prior experience in self-government need preparation for it. Educational foundations need to be laid for any experiment in government, and they need projection into a long future, for liberty is nurtured slowly. Yet, prior to 1959, no Congolese had ever cast a ballot or participated in any political decision. Not one Congolese had been trained as a lawyer, doctor, army officer, or senior civil servant. Few Congolese had ever attended college; and most of them had not completed their studies. The Bel-

---

1 *The Social Contract*, Vol. 38, p. 415b
2 *Politics*, Vol. 9, p. 504d. Some thought the union of Rome with the allied states of Italy ruined the Roman Republic. See Adam Smith, *The Wealth of Nations*, Vol. 39, p. 271a.

gians planned to turn their Congo loose in fifty years. But when the French across the river gave independence to their Congo, the fever of nationalism assumed a virulent form in the Belgian Congo. The Belgians, who refused to talk of independence in May, 1959, decided in October, 1959, to grant it in eight months. Their feverish activities to produce a constitution led to the inauguration of a parliamentary system which is so sophisticated as to be singularly unsuited to a people without any prior experience in government.

Viewing these acknowledged difficulties, some say the new nations cannot have freedom because of their illiteracy and inexperience. But they are putting a false case. The question is not whether all nations should be free; it is merely how much freedom a new nation can enjoy.

Each people must be given as much freedom as it can cope with — no less. This means that some nations should enjoy the full extent of freedom as it exists in the Western democracies, while others must for the time being get along on less. In some areas — particularly in Africa — the Western ideal of freedom is still distant. Here the true unit of government is the tribe, not the nation. Any attempt to fit democratic structures to tribal groups will be difficult and long drawn out. Tribal governments, being totalitarian, are more readily susceptible to Communist management than to democratic influence. Yet even there modest starts can be made. A flow of teachers to those areas can be established; leaders can be trained abroad in Western philosophy.

And it is important that a start, no matter how modest, be made. The lack of preparation for democracy can only be overcome by giving people a measure of self-government. Ability to govern itself well and responsibly will not suddenly spring up in any nation; it must be encouraged to grow. But the first step must be taken or there cannot be any progress. Just as children learn to walk by walking, so young peoples learn to govern themselves by actually being given the opportunity to vote and to decide their own affairs.

Of course, this involves risks. The risks can be minimized by making use of the many safeguards that are available to the maker of democratic constitutions. Not the least of these safeguards is the adaptability of democracy to local conditions. Democracy in the Malagasy Republic need not — and indeed must not — be identical with democracy in Great Britain or the United States.

With careful nurturing, countries will develop their own leadership. One man who has the vision of a free society may be sufficient — one man like Thomas G. Masaryk, Nehru, U Nu, or even an Atatürk. Men of that character can be found and educated in the new nations. There are no peoples who cannot develop the dispositions for democratic government.

WOMAN VOTING
IN GUINEA
*Giving people
the opportunity
to vote
is a way
of preparing them
for democracy*

STUDENTS
IN A
SECONDARY
SCHOOL
IN NIGERIA
*Education is
the best method
cquainting people
democratic ideals
and practices*

What are these dispositions? Irving Kristol answers:

> This is a large question, and any short answer will be inadequate. But it is not too gross an over-simplification to say that included among them must be: a veneration for the rule of law as against the rule of men; a reliance on common reason as the dominant human motive, as against superstition or passion; a sense of community that transcends class divisions and the recognition of a common good beyond individual benefits; a scrupulous use of liberties towards these ends for which those liberties were granted; a distribution of wealth and inequalities according to principles generally accepted as legitimate; moderation in the temper of public debate and public demeanour.[3]

Freedom involves discipline, "the spirit of obedience to law."[4] The discipline that is essential to freedom is the discipline that comes from "internal constraint" as Harry D. Gideonse has put it.[5] Freedom requires acceptance of moral responsibility.

In no nation will all of these qualities be found at all times. Mobs break loose whatever the degree of development a nation may boast. Some people seem to take longer than others to develop these dispositions. A chart of British evolution from William I to Elizabeth II would be an uneven one. Setbacks and reverses wipe out advances; even a century may show little progress. Hence we do not advance the discussion to say, as many do, that Ghana in 1961 is no farther along than England was under Henry II. Government is built both on education and experience; and there is no short cut to either.

Certain it is that many years will pass before people, not yet freed from tribal patterns of life, will acquire the maturity, constraint, and practical wisdom for management of full-fledged democratic institu-

3 "High, Low and Modern," *Encounter*, August, 1960, pp. 38-39
4 Aristotle, *Politics*, Vol. 9, p. 509d
5 "The Literature of Freedom and Liberal Education, Measurement and Research in Today's Schools" (American Council of Education, Washington, D.C.)

tions. We of the West have been preoccupied with arming new nations and with trying to provide them with technicians and industrial plants. There is, however, nothing ideological about machine guns or cement plants; and a man who can read the instruction book that comes with a tractor can also read the Communist Manifesto.

Technicians and industrial plants, as well as armies, are necessary for underdeveloped nations. But education needs top priority. For only through education can the theory, ideals, and practical problems of a free society be made known to people who have not yet heard of Aristotle, Jefferson, or Madison. In this respect we of the West have largely wasted the years since World War II.

What Dr. Johnson called the "fund of virtue and principle to carry the laws into due and effectual execution" will be sadly missing in some areas.[6] Yet the "community of families and aggregation of families in well-being," of which Aristotle spoke, are present to some degree in every society.[7]

Jefferson's dictum that representative democracy requires "an aristocracy of virtue and talent" sets a far-distant goal for some new nations, perhaps for most of them.[8] Yet self-government at some levels provides a people with the only opportunity they can ever have to develop their own particular "aristocracy of virtue and talent." It is never too early to start.

One distinctive contribution of America to the development of democracy is insight into how the two strains of the belief in "consent of the governed"—common sense and visionary—run together in life. Lincoln summed up the entire matter on June 26, 1857, when he spoke of the Declaration of Independence:

I think the authors of that notable instrument intended to include *all* men, but they did not mean to declare all men equal *in all respects.* They did not mean to say all men were equal in color, size, intellect, moral development or social capacity. They defined with tolerable distinctness in what they did consider all men created equal—equal in certain inalienable rights, among which are life, liberty, and the pursuit of happiness. This they said, and this they meant. They did not mean to assert the obvious untruth, that all were then actually enjoying that equality, or yet, that they were about to confer it immediately upon them. In fact they had no power to confer such a boon. They meant simply to declare the *right,* so that the *enforcement* of it might follow as fast as circumstances should permit.

They meant to set up a standard maxim for free society which should be familiar to all: constantly looked to, constantly labored for, and even, though never perfectly attained, constantly approximated, and thereby constantly spreading and deepening its influence and augmenting the happiness and value of life to all people, of all colors, everywhere.[9]

What Lincoln said in 1857 should be our goal today.

---

6 See Boswell, *Life of Johnson,* Vol. 44, p. 178c.
7 See *Politics,* Vol. 9, p. 478c.
8 See *Writings of Thomas Jefferson* (Mem. ed.; 1903), Vol. 1, p. 54.
9 Roy P. Basler (ed.), *The Collected Works of Abraham Lincoln* (New Brunswick, N.J.: Rutgers University Press, 1953), Vol. 2, pp. 405-406

PEREGRINE WORSTHORNE

The case against democracy

Primitive democracy

Historical conditions suitable to democracy

Industrialization

Education

The importance of indigenous development

Parliamentary procedures

The dangers of radical reform

Dangers of premature democracy

PEREGRINE WORSTHORNE was born in 1923, and was educated at Oxford and Cambridge universities. Since World War II, in which he served as a commissioned officer in the British Army, he has been a member of the editorial staffs of several leading British newspapers. He became Assistant Editor of the *Sunday Telegraph* (London) this year. He has traveled extensively in Africa, Europe, and America, and is a frequent contributor to British and American magazines.

Primitive democracy

The purest form of democracy that I have ever experienced was in the most primitive society that I have ever visited — an ancient tribe living in the volcanic belt of northern Kenya. The members of the tribe were quite illiterate, lacked even a system for measuring time, and had scarcely ever had contact with a white man. Yet as I listened to the chief and elders discussing some vexed fishing problem — whether or not to extend their spearing activities further westward along Lake Rudolph — it struck me that their system of government corresponded very closely to the democratic ideal.

Democracy, we are told, consists of institutional arrangements for arriving at political decisions which realize the common good by making the people itself decide issues through the election of individuals who are to assemble to carry out its will.[1] Admittedly, the chiefs and elders, as they sat on their logs debating, would not have described their activity in quite these terms. Yet they had been chosen by the people, were assembling to discover and determine the popular will, quite as much as, if not more than, does the United States Congress or the British House of Commons.

Indeed, never before or since have I seen the theory of democracy so accurately carried out in practice. The chief himself did little of the talking, but listened sagely to the elders putting forward different points of view. The arguments, expressed with great passion and excitement, lasted for some hours. Only when the elders had exhausted their disagreements did the chief speak, and then only to express what he conceived to be the sense of the meeting. Once he had spoken the elders nodded their assent and the meeting passed on to the next business.

But I was left in no doubt that if the chief had misconstrued the middle way, or had delivered himself of a decision that had not represented the lowest common denominator of agreement among the elders, he would not have enjoyed his position of *primus inter pares*. His authority, in short, sprang from his skill at discovering the general will. He was the very model of a democratic leader, quite as much as President Kennedy or Mr. Macmillan.

---

1 See Montesquieu, *Spirit of Laws*, Vol. 38, pp. 4a-6b; Kant, *Science of Right*, Vol. 42, p. 451c; and *The Federalist*, Vol. 43, p. 125c-d. Eighteenth-century philosophers used the term "republic" when discussing representative government.

So long as a society remains small, cohesive, and primitive, government, if it can be called such, has few incentives and little opportunity to flout the will of the people. In the first place, the minds of both ruler and ruled are so dominated and circumscribed by custom and superstition that virtually all political decisions determine themselves, since they simply grow out of the past. There is an organic parallelism between the individual will and the general will. If everybody wants to do what everybody else wants to do, because nobody can think of doing anything differently, government by the people, of the people, for the people presents no problems. Rulers and ruled are truly one.

Moreover, the sheer physical condition of a primitive, subsistence economy means that it just does not pay a ruler to subjugate the ruled. What is the point of enslaving another man if he cannot physically produce an appreciable surplus over and above what is indispensable to maintain himself? If the ruler tries to take any appreciable part of the fruits of other men's labor for his own use, he soon finds himself in the position of the French peasant who complained that just as he had taught his donkey to live without eating, the wretched animal died. It is not until society advances to a certain stage of technical *expertise,* which enables individuals to produce far more than they need to consume, that the temptations of government really begin to operate.

But even then, the chances of maintaining some form of popular or representational government remain bright, for it is difficult, physically speaking, for primitive rulers to govern for long without the consent, or against the will, of the people. That is to say, even when they develop the will to do so, they lack the means. If one-man-one-vote is the guarantee of democracy in advanced societies, one-man-one-spear does the job just as well in backward societies.

46

It is, in short, no part of my thesis to argue that the underdeveloped countries are *per se* unsuited to democracy because they are underdeveloped. In many ways Africa, for example, during the last thousand years has experienced more widespread popular participation in government than have the other more advanced continents. I very much doubt whether the naked savage of my northern Kenyan tribe plays a smaller role in determining his own affairs than does a citizen of New York or London. On the contrary, he probably plays a very much more active role. The question that needs to be asked today, therefore, is not whether the backward peoples can enjoy primitive democracy. We already know that they can. What is in question, however, is whether backward peoples can enjoy sophisticated democracy of the kind which the colonial powers have chosen to leave behind. While democracy is ideally suited to very primitive societies, which have yet to be faced with complicated political problems — and also perhaps to very sophisticated societies like Britain and America, most of whose complicated political problems have already been solved — is it going to prove suitable to primitive societies seeking to become advanced industrial states?

Historical conditions suitable to democracy

W hat I believe, and what this essay is intended to show, is that the historical experience of Europeans and Americans has been such that democracy and progress have been able to advance hand-in-hand, whereas the kind of conditions with which the Afro-Asians are now faced makes it unlikely that they will enjoy the same good fortune. This has nothing inherently to do with the threat of Communism, which for the underdeveloped countries is largely a problem of geographical accident, depending on whether or not their borders happen to march with those of Russia or China. Communism merely adds to and deepens the problem, but it does not create it.

Just imagine that the Romans, before leaving ancient Britain, had established a unified nation, which they had left in charge of a cadre of trained native administrators who, by some miracle, could call upon all the twentieth-century techniques of government — rapid communications, armed forces equipped with modern weapons, mobile police, a functioning bureaucratic machine; and that, in addition, the Romans had been clever enough to develop by that time the know-how of industrialization, so that the tribes, instead of being driven mad by cold and hunger, could be clothed and fed; and that, moreover, the native rulers subsequently had the good sense to enlist into their ranks any bright young tribesmen who grew up with any talent either for administration or industry. Can it seriously be believed that under these conditions the kind of representative institutions which are now Britain's pride and joy would ever have evolved? Even if the Romans had done us a further miraculous service, and made available

47

whole libraries of democratic literature, so that the ruling cadre were steeped in the works of Locke, Montesquieu, and Thomas Jefferson, and had further anticipated history by clothing the infant body politic with the gloriously ponderous garments of parliamentary government, it still does not seem to me at all likely that the political course of British history would have led us in the direction which it actually took. Unless the ruling group had wrecked the whole show by quarrelling among themselves, or industrialization had failed and the tribes had risen up through starvation, or had been fired to passionate resentment by supression of some cherished custom like the right to paint their bodies with woad, the result would have been at best a protracted authoritarian system of government which the rulers felt no real need to impose with undue cruelty and against which the ruled felt no need to rebel.

What primarily saved Britain from such a fate, and what has been the basic condition out of which freedom has evolved in the classical democracies of the past, is that the opportunities for rulers to oppress and the opportunities for the ruled — or those of them that wished to — to oppose oppression have been roughly speaking kept in balance.

In Africa and Asia today, however, this crucial balance has been fundamentally upset by the colonial legacy, which has created an educated elite (in whose hands twentieth-century power is now invested) in the midst of still primitive, illiterate masses whose means of resistance has scarcely advanced since the stone age.

AN AFRICAN
BUSH VILLAGE
*Within a few miles
of the modern
capitals
are primitive mud
or rush hut
communities*

In the capitals can be found ministers, civil servants, large, modern government buildings, army barracks, central banks, etc. – all the instruments and paraphernalia for ruling a modern state. Within a few miles of the capital cities, however, will be mud or rush hut communities in much the same primitive condition of social and economic organization as they were at the beginning of time – except that, in some cases, the inhabitants now have the vote. So far as the primitive masses are concerned, the rulers of today in the underdeveloped countries enjoy a superiority of sheer physical and administrative power which makes the greatest tyrants of old seem like impotent weaklings. One of the primary brakes on absolutism – technical incompetence – is, thanks to the colonial powers, sadly lacking in Africa and Asia today.

Another brake, which the intervention of the colonial powers has also removed, is the inhibiting presence of traditional or religious restraint. One of the most important limitations on governmental power in the past has been a tacit understanding between ruler and ruled that certain actions, although not prohibited by law, were contrary to immemorial custom or forbidden by conscience. No institutions, for example, existed to thwart the will of the absolute monarchs who ruled by divine right in Europe until the French Revolution. Yet they voluntarily accepted certain moral restraints, which were regarded as heinous to ignore, and, out of respect for immemorial custom, refrained from extending governmental power into areas like conscription or direct taxation. It was not until after the French Revolution had introduced the theory of the general will that governments felt free to extend their activities irrespective of traditional restraints.[2] Fortunately for Britain and the United States, this democratic doctrine of the general will, which places such immense power in the hands of majority government, emerged only after the people's basic individual liberties were firmly entrenched and powerful nongovernmental organizations and institutions existed to defend them. Moreover, in these countries, this revolutionary doctrine of the general will had to cohabit with an equally strong tradition and faith in personal liberty. But where it did not, as in Russia and Germany, disaster soon ensued.

No similar historic traditions or religious scruples, however, inhibit the governments of the underdeveloped countries today, since the new states have sought to make a clean sweep of their primitive or colonial past. The President of Ghana would not be at all impressed, when considering whether or not to lock up some opponent, if he were told: "This is not how we used to behave in the jungle," or "This is not what the British used to do." In any case, the economic, political, and social revolution transforming the new states today has been so dramatically rapid that continuity with the past has been decisively broken.

The lack of these traditional or religious restraints among the rulers would not matter so much if there existed a widespread spirit of liberty

2 The theory of the general will was originally developed by Rousseau. See *The Social Contract*, Vol. 38, pp. 392a, 395a-398b.

TRIBAL
DANCING
IN
WEST AFRICA
*To create
national unity,
the governments
will have to disrupt
ancient tribal
and communal
patterns of life*

among the ruled or if it was likely soon to develop. But this is far from
being the case. The whole concept of freedom is quite alien to very
primitive peoples. Take, for example, freedom of conscience or freedom of speech, which are so central to the meaningful practice of democracy.[3] Why should primitive peoples cherish such rights, which are
only valuable to a man who is capable of independent thought. For the
great majority of the people of Asia and Africa, whose lives are still
circumscribed by custom, convention, and superstition, independent
thought is virtually out of the question. They lack the intellectual
capacity as much to believe as to doubt, both of which are relatively
sophisticated intellectual processes. Primitive peoples do not obey the
rules of their communities because they *believe* them to be right, or
disobey them because they *believe* them to be wrong. They obey them
out of habit, because it is easier to do so; and they disobey them only
out of passion or self-interest. It is difficult to believe that such communities will be inspired to do battle with arbitrary government in the
name of freedom of speech or conscience.

For the same reasons it is improbable that any large body of opinion
in the underdeveloped countries will wish to oppose their governments
very passionately on any of the other issues which advanced democ-

3 For J. S. Mill's views on the importance of such liberties to a free society, see *On Liberty*,
Vol. 43, pp. 272d-274a.

racies regard as important, like due process of law, freedom to associate, *habeas corpus,* etc.[4] For the time being, at any rate, the popular will is quite unable to grasp these concepts.

What the people would be prepared to do battle with government about is any attempt to wean them of their superstitions, or disrupt their ancient tribal or communal patterns of life, or change their languages. These are the kind of catalysts around which genuine popular movements could be formed.

That they will be so formed is, unfortunately, highly unlikely, since the constitutions of these new countries are usually expressly designed to stifle these few genuine expressions of the popular will. They are regarded either as threats to national unity — which of course they are — or as threats to modernity, which is also true. Governments, therefore, can claim the backing of the constitution in stamping them out. It is difficult, however, to feel very confident about the growth of representative institutions in societies where the only things that mean anything to the great majority of the people have to be, for reasons of state, regarded as treason or, if not as treason, as archaic obstructions to progress.[5]

Even the concept of national freedom, which sparked the struggle for independence from colonial rule, can be said to affect only a small minority — the educated elite. The proportion who feel passionately involved with individual liberty — an infinitely more subtle concept — is far smaller, since those few who have the education and background to understand the arguments intellectually are almost all connected with government, and are therefore more fascinated with authority than freedom. The rest, as I say, are either too poor or too ignorant to care.

Seldom, therefore, in history have governments had such opportunities to rule arbitrarily, and so few objective or subjective reasons for restraint, as they have today in the underdeveloped countries of the world; and seldom, if ever, have the ruled been so powerless to resist.

The picture, however, is even less promising than that. For not only are the rulers in a position to oppress, and the ruled in a position to be oppressed, but there exists today a justification for the oppressor and a consolation for the oppressed which between them have almost made it impossible to think about freedom as an Afro-Asian concept at all. "Give me liberty or give me death," said Patrick Henry. But to the famished millions of Asia and Africa, death may not be the alternative to liberty, but its consequence; and slavery, instead of being equivalent to death, may be the means of life. For it may well be that dictatorship is the only method of raising the Afro-Asian standard of living so that it keeps pace with expanding population rates; that speedy in-

---

4 See *Constitution of the United States*, Amendments 1-10, 14, 15, and 19, Vol. 43, pp. 17a-19d.
5 "Representative institutions necessarily depend for permanence upon the readiness of the people to fight for them in case of their being endangered" (J. S. Mill, *Representative Government*, Vol. 43, p. 350d).

dustrialization cannot be forced through fast enough by any other means. No former tyrant in history has ever enjoyed so plausible an excuse. Even more baffling, no oppressed peoples have ever had such good reason to suppose that their rewards for suffering in silence will be in this world rather than the next.

If the debate about freedom, which has raged through the centuries in the classical democracies, had started off in this context; if the great formulators of democratic doctrine had come to the subject at a time when it presented itself in these terms, instead of, for example, about the rights and wrongs of religious toleration,[6] would they have reached the conclusions which they did? But this *is* the context in which the politically articulate people in Afro-Asia are reaching their political conclusions. While there is no reason to suppose that it will necessarily make communists of them — power politics will really decide that — it strikes me as puerile to suppose that it will make them into ardent democrats. A few, like Mr. Nehru, reared in the great liberal tradition, may maintain their democratic faith, as well as maintaining power. But Mr. Nehru is an exception who certainly proves no rule, as anybody who has talked to the younger generation of Afro-Asian leaders cannot fail to have learned.

Industrialization

It may be objected that all I have done so far is to point out the obvious, namely, that conditions among the *masses* in the underdeveloped countries today are not conducive to freedom. But will not the prospects be radically improved once industrialization has raised the general standard of living and education has raised the general standard of knowledge? These particular hopes spring eternal in the Western breast. My own view, however, is that industrialization and education are just as likely — indeed more likely — to lead in the opposite direction. Far from helping to create independent and powerful interests prepared and able to counterbalance the power of government they will tend, in the particular circumstances of the underdeveloped countries, to strengthen further the government's hands.

It is perfectly true that in Britain, and in the other classical democracies, the growth of an industrial bourgeoisie, and that of a commercial bourgeoisie before, played an immensely valuable role in bringing absolute government under democratic control. But they did not do so because of any abstract faith in the virtues of representative government. The bourgeoisie fought for political representation and for some measure of control over the government because the ruling groups of the time refused to allow them the freedom they needed to trade and produce.[7] Feudal rule in Europe, for example, rigidly excluded aspiring

6 See Locke, *Letter Concerning Toleration*, Vol. 35, pp. 1a-22d.
7 For Marx-Engels' account of the role played by the *bourgeoisie*, see *Manifesto of the Communist Party*, Vol. 50, p. 420a-c.

merchants from the circle of governmental influence and saddled them with restrictions and difficulties which prevented them from trading to the maximum advantage.

It is difficult to exaggerate the role which the commercial requirements of the trading groups in England in the eighteenth century had on the development of British politics.[8] Commerce instills in those who practice it the arts of negotiation, bargaining, honoring agreements, respect for law. Its interlocking relationships preclude any clear chain of command and cut across strict hierarchies. The commercial ethos

BRITISH
MERCHANTS
AT LLOYD'S
OF LONDON
...e commercial
...geoisie played
...mportant role
... development
of English
democracy

makes regimentation anathema. Toleration, flexibility, mutual trust, and a sensitive feel for every change in social trends — these are the qualities that make commerce flourish. They are also the qualities that are peculiarly conducive to the successful practice of parliamentary government. It was no accident that Britain's commercial bourgeoisie should have developed a taste for democratic institutions, for an independent judiciary, and even, in time, for an incorruptible civil service. Arbitrary government, erratic implementation of the law, and corrupt administration made it impossible for them to ply their trades.

I do not mean to suggest that the battle against absolutism fought by Britain's commercial interests, which played so superb a part in winning British liberties, was strictly a matter of economic self-interest. There was, of course, also a magnificent body of doctrine evolved to lend rational justification to the cause. Economic self-interest provoked intellectual argument to justify that self-interest which in turn sparked genuine idealism, so that by the time the circle was completed,

---

8 For an illuminating discussion of this theme, see Henry A. Kissinger, *The Necessity for Choice* (New York: Harper & Bros., 1961).

the bourgeoisie and the professional interests, like the law associated with them, were prepared to sacrifice life and limb, welfare and prosperity, for a political doctrine initially designed to justify their making money. But this, of course, is how all reform comes about — through a subtle blend of selfishness and idealism so interwoven that it is never quite clear which is the chicken and which the egg.

So far as Britain was concerned, nineteenth-century industrialists certainly continued the struggle to limit the power of government. It is much less clear, however, whether the actual processes of industry really favor the diffusion of power, in the way that commerce does. The governing principle of an industrial society is efficiency, which ordains that all its component parts — including the human beings involved — be reduced to manipulatable quantities. A strict chain of command or hierarchy is an essential condition for efficient production. Whereas in commerce the arts of negotiation, bargaining, and compromise determine success, in industry it is more the capacity to command, regiment, manipulate. There is, in short, nothing in the ethos of industry which helps to create a democratic attitude to politics.

The growth of industry in Britain helped to promote democratic institutions not because the industrialists wanted democracy but because the ruling order of the day did not want industry. It was because the land-owning ruling class sought to place restrictions on the growth of industry, so as to protect their own agricultural interests, that the industrial groups espoused the cause of freedom against an unsympathetic government. What they were fighting against was governmental obstruction and what they were fighting for was industrial autonomy.

The difficulty facing the underdeveloped countries is that they are attempting to jump virtually from a condition of mere subsistence straight to industrialization, without lingering in that intermediate period of slow commercial growth during which, in the classical democracies, the habits and attitudes of democracy and parliamentary government took root. What is more, the impulse for industrialization, far from meeting governmental obstruction, is actually coming from the government itself. Whereas in the classical democracies industry had a vested interest in curbing the power of government, because it was being used to obstruct their aims, in the underdeveloped countries industry has a vested interest in supporting governmental power, because it is being used to promote their aims.

History, as I say, certainly does not encourage the view that there is anything in the industrial process itself which favors a free society, or encourages industrial managers to wish necessarily to control government. So long as the process of industrialization coincides with a government well disposed to this development, which does not seek to obstruct, past experience suggests that industry is prepared to stand aside from politics. This was certainly true in Germany and Japan, where industrialization took place with the support and active encouragement of the landed ruling class. In both these cases the industrial

managers were quite happy to barter political participation for economic autonomy, and insofar as they developed any interest in politics at all, it was to encourage nationalism rather than liberalism.

I cannot myself see why industrialization should have different results in the underdeveloped countries. Why should the new class of industrial managers there, whom the governments will do everything in their power to cosset and favor, and who presumably will have little cause to complain against, and every reason to praise, the government of the day — why should they insist on any active participation in ruling the country? Since their prime interest will be in maintaining the stability of the government, it is more likely that all their influence will be concentrated on increasing rather than decreasing its powers. The truth is that democracy can be slowed down by governments giving people too much of what they want too early as much as by granting them too little too late.

Contrary, therefore, to the optimistic assumptions that industrialization will be the ally of democracy in the underdeveloped countries, it seems to me more likely to be a powerful force operating in the opposite direction. A frustrated industrial bourgeoisie, which happens to evolve in a country where parliamentary institutions have taken root, can prove a supremely effective dynamo for setting the wheels of democracy in motion. This was the situation which Britain was lucky enough to enjoy. But a satisfied bourgeoisie, basking in the sunshine of governmental patronage, which evolves in a country where parliamentary institutions have no roots, is likely to be an equally effective brake preventing the wheels of democracy from ever getting into motion.

But if industrialization is unlikely to throw up a radical bourgeoisie, or one determined to curb the power of government, is it not possible that the workers in Africa and Asia will develop the taste for free in-

55

stitutions? This seems extraordinarily unlikely. Uprooted from their tribal lands, cut off from their customs and traditions, and subjected to the atomization of industrial life in city slums, it is difficult to see how they can be expected to stand up to a combination of government and management. But even if in time they are in a position to do so, it is highly unlikely that their objective would be the creation of a liberal democracy.

Insofar as they influence politics at all, they will tend in the direction of extremism rather than moderation, since it will be prompted more by the agonies of hunger in their bellies than the passion for liberty in their hearts. Working-class revolutions, provoked by hunger and poverty, seldom enlarge the field of freedom, since this is not their aim. British political liberties were won, not by the masses fighting for bread, but by particular groups and interests fighting for the right to pursue their own ends without government interference. If the hungry masses in Asia and Africa seek to intervene in politics, their prime object will be to create a government which will do more for them rather than less. They will not be asking for the right to do what they want, but rather to get what they need. While this is an absolutely proper political demand, it is not one that has anything to do with liberty. If it is made after the establishment of liberal political institutions, and is satisfied because of the existence of these institutions—as was the case in the classical democracies—then it strengthens them, by demonstrating that they work. But in the underdeveloped countries, worker intervention in politics is likely to lead either to outright repres-

SLUM SCENE
IN LAGOS,
NIGERIA
*Poverty and hunger
are almost certain
to lead to demands
for stronger
governments
—at the expense
of personal
freedoms*

sion by the government or to the establishment of some form of popular tyranny along Communist or Peronist lines.

Most of the new underdeveloped states, it should be noted, have started their lives under moderate left-wing governments led by men claiming to espouse democratic socialism. All the miseries of early industrialization and population expansion will, therefore, be visited on the heads of the moderates. It seems to me rather unfortunate that these new states should begin their life, politically speaking, in the middle of the road, since if things go wrong, they must move either to the right or to the left. Some have already moved far to the right; others are all too likely to move very much further to the left. What is surely very improbable is that a country which starts at the center of the political spectrum, before it has yet to face all its agonizing growing pains, will survive the experience without toppling one way or the other.

Education

After industrialization, Western optimists place the highest hopes in education as the process which will do most to encourage the growth of free institutions in the underdeveloped countries. This is certainly a possibility, since once men begin to think, everything becomes possible.

Except in this very general sense, however, it does not seem to me that education is likely to have the desired effect. People have a vague idea that education will produce inquiring minds who bring rational thought to the problems of society. When there are enough inquiring minds bringing enough rational thought to bear, democracy is expected to appear.

But when one examines the effect of education in practice today in the underdeveloped countries, the picture is rather different. For the overwhelming majority it is, at best, simply a matter of learning to read and write. The tiny minority who pass through universities, and who constitute the inquiring minds, are swiftly absorbed into the machinery of government, since the demand of administrative posts still greatly exceeds the supply. In other words, the opinion formers who are meant to act as watchdogs on governmental propriety, and maintain the people's side of the argument which goes on eternally between rulers and ruled, are almost to a man in some way connected with, or dependent on, the government itself. In time, of course, their numbers will increase. But the other main source of livelihood for the educated elite will be industry, which is not likely, as I have sought to show, to encourage any great independence of thought. The trouble is that for the foreseeable future there will be so much room on the governmental bandwagon for the educated elite that there will be no need for any of them to worry about its speed and direction. Of course, if industrialization fails to keep pace with educational plans, and there are very

57

many more graduates produced than there are jobs for them to fill, the situation will be very different. Unemployed graduates today do not sit around reading Thomas Jefferson, or studying the Westminster rules of parliamentary procedure. Their inquiring minds tend to travel Marxwards by the fastest route.

It seems highly unlikely, therefore, that the processes of education and industrialization will of themselves produce organized private interests determined enough and strong enough to impose restraint on the arbitrary exercise of public power. The reason is horribly simple. Without governmental backing, no private interest will be able to prosper.

The importance of indigenous development

What the West finds so difficult to appreciate is that all the activities now proceeding in Asia and Africa, which have the creation of modern industrial states as their aim, almost entirely lack indigenous momentum. Of course, the masses want the benefits of industrialization and want to be rid of disease, famine, drought, and flood. But this is quite different from wanting to make the sacrifices which would enable these blessings to be realized. While there is widespread popular demand for the ends, there is virtually no support at all for the means.

It might be argued that this was also true initially in the Western democracies, where industrialization, for example, provoked the mob to break up the machinery with sticks and staves. The great difference, however, is that because Western advances in techniques, skills, and knowledge were almost all indigenous developments, they inevitably created their own body of informed support. Clearly, industrialization could not take place until there were enough industrialists to make it possible; modern techniques of agriculture could not become widespread until there were enough farmers to understand them; modern ideas of hygiene and medicine could not be generally practiced until

58

enough doctors recognized their importance and enough patients were prepared to risk them. Since the Western peoples were their own pace-setters, throwing up their own pioneers, the speed of advance never exceeded the capacity for at least some sizeable section of society to keep up with it. Progress, moreover, depended on private citizens discovering new techniques, organizing themselves to give effect to them, and persuading others to tolerate or support their activities. Governments could assist this process, but clearly could not initiate it. The result has been the gradual growth over the centuries of innumerable professional associations, corporate bodies, seats of learning, and interest groups, rich in pride and achievement, whose voices carry great weight with government because their roots are deeply based in public approval and respect.

No equivalent developments can be observed in the new states of Africa and Asia. Progress in these countries is almost exclusively imported from abroad. In most cases the process of importation was initiated by the former colonizing powers and can be maintained only by the most strenuous efforts of government operation, since the people themselves are almost wholly unable to initiate and invent.

Take, for example, medical science. If the progress of medicine in the underdeveloped countries depended on the wit and inventiveness of the local medical professions, it could not possibly keep pace with modern requirements. That it can do so at all is made possible only by the intervention of government, which decides to import the necessary drugs, etc., or to send local doctors abroad to learn modern techniques. The same is true in all the other fields of modern knowledge. In the underdeveloped countries, in short, it has to be the government that sets the pace and pioneers the new frontiers, since the people are themselves unable to do so. It seems to me quite absurd to imagine that in these areas there are likely to develop those professional and private concentrations of power and influence, over and above government, which have been so crucial in establishing Western freedoms. All the forces of initiative, invention, imagination, and drive which in the West arose from the private sector, and therefore nourished and strengthened the private sector, are having to come in the underdeveloped countries from government, and are likely to strengthen and nourish the claims of government.

The West should be able to understand this today, since to some extent the classical democracies are themselves beginning to experience a comparable difficulty. The greatest advance in modern science — nuclear fission — seems to defy democratic control, precisely because it was very largely a product of governmental rather than private enterprise. As a result, no private or professional body exists that can altogether understand its immense complexity. Parliaments find it difficult to discuss the problems it raises; the people recoil in baffled horror, willing to accept the security advantages it offers, but quite unable to feel that its future is their private responsibility.

AN ELECTION SCENE
IN KENYA
*Many of the important
government posts are still held
by expatriate Europeans*

In the underdeveloped countries, however, virtually every aspect of modern society presents the public with the same kind of difficulty which nuclear fission today poses for Britain and America. It is as difficult for Afro-Asian public opinion to grapple with the problems of industrialization and modernization, and to develop means of controlling governments in these respects, as it is difficult for Anglo-American public opinion to do the same in respect to nuclear power.

Fortunately for the West, however, democratic institutions evolved and took root before the advent of nuclear power. The relationship between ruler and ruled was formed in conditions where the latter had more than enough cards to hold its own in the game. Unfortunately, the opposite is true of the countries of Asia and Africa.

The position is even further complicated in many of the underdeveloped countries by the presence of large numbers of expatriate Europeans who, in the absence of an adequate local elite, still fill many of the crucial professional, executive, and university posts. In some cases they even occupy high rank in the civil service, in the police and armed forces. Most of the capital invested, too, is foreign, and in Ghana by far the best and most modern newspaper is British-owned. To a dangerous extent, in short, the elite, which should be bringing informed criticism to bear on government, is made up of what in effect are foreign mercenaries whose continued presence in the country can always be revoked by governmental fiat. Many of these foreign expatriates are, no doubt, men of high principle, who stayed on to help the new states through their post-independence difficulties. But clearly their status as former colonial masters is highly invidious, and the one thing they cannot allow themselves is to get in any way involved in politics. The same is even more clearly true of foreign business firms, whose economic interest must prompt them to do everything possible to keep the government sweet. The British-owned Ghana newspaper solves its problems by rigorously eschewing all political controversy. As a result, however, the very groups which, in a healthy democracy, bring informed criticism to bear on government, and provide the raw material of ideas and argument for the public to feed on, tend in many of the underdeveloped countries to be reduced to the role of political eunuchs. In some fields the position will, of course, improve as more native talent is trained to take over the jobs now done by expatriates. So far as foreign capital is concerned, however, the problem may well become worse, particularly in those areas where stable and strong government is established. For the stronger the government becomes, and the less the area concerned seems subject to the instabilities of democracy, the more attractive it will be to the foreign investor. The fact must be faced that there is here a direct clash between the economic health of the underdeveloped countries and their prospect of democratic growth.

For all these reasons, therefore, it seems to me that the prospect of organized concentrations of private power being able to control arbitrary government is exceedingly remote. Yet without them I cannot see how parliamentary democracy can hope to work. Merely dispensing the vote does little of itself to strengthen the ruled against the ruler, since the vote is only useful to a citizen who, as well as being a head to count at election times, is also an interest which counts at all times.

This basic fact of democratic life is easily forgotten in the West, which likes to think that its own liberties arose from the franchise. This, however, is a dangerous half-truth. For while it is true that in Britain and America individual liberties are today protected by the vote, they were not created by the vote. They were created by dint of various interests, one after the other, so organizing themselves that they were in a position to fight for their rights. The vote, so to speak, is the flower that springs from liberty, not the root, and to create parliaments in the underdeveloped countries, as the colonial powers have done, without first creating interests to be represented in them, is as nonsensical as fabricating cups in a desert before first discovering water.

Parliamentary procedures

However much, therefore, the governments of the underdeveloped countries may wish to be democratic, in the sense of wanting to govern according to the will of the people, they have no way of discovering what the people's will may be, since parliamentary institutions can give them no guidance.

But that, it may be argued, is surely the job of the political parties. The political parties, however, can only express the needs and wants of the people if there exist organized interests and groups who have translated these needs and wants into precise and politically meaningful terms. For the parties simply to offer the people a vague choice of programs at election times is a singularly ineffective way, by itself, of either discovering what the people want or of committing the victorious party to any particular course. Unless this electoral process is also accompanied by all the subterranean bargaining between the political parties and the various sectional interests which go on in the classical democracies, it amounts to little more than a somewhat undignified struggle between various groups of ambitious politicians to get their hands on the levers of power, and has little more to do with the will of the people than the intrigues and plots by which one dictator gets rid of another. The role of the opposition in such circumstances scarcely extends beyond that of making government awkward for the ruling party, without in any way helping to give effect to the desires of the ruled.

This, however, is the situation in which parliamentary government has to operate in the underdeveloped countries. No wonder, therefore, that in one state after another, parliamentary institutions are increasingly regarded as a nuisance by the governments and as an irrelevance by the peoples. Since they simply hinder the former without helping the latter, they can be swept aside without any loss to either.

Indeed, it may well be better that they be swept away, since it is much better that undemocratic government should not masquerade under a false name. More important, it is infinitely more promising if those opposed to government policies in the underdeveloped countries, instead of prematurely concentrating on parliamentary representation — when they have nothing yet to represent except their own personal ambitions — should concentrate their energies on organizing, not political parties, but genuine pressure groups which reflect genuine interests.

Failing this it seems virtually unavoidable that those governments in underdeveloped countries which continue to espouse democracy will remain absolutist in fact, while democratic in name, which is the worst result possible, because it subjects the body politic to all the agony of the poison of tyranny while at the same time discrediting and corrupting the cure. Unpleasant as it is to recognize it, there can surely be little doubt that in the underdeveloped countries no political system could be more likely to strengthen those in power and weaken those in opposition than classical parliamentary government on the Westminster model.

The only obstacle which democracy erects against abuse of power is the electorate's right to reject an unpopular government at the next election. All the unwritten, subterranean limitations that exist in primitive autocracies are eliminated in favor of this single major democratic sanction; since if sovereignty is derived from the people, a popularly elected government must remain sovereign until it is replaced by its successor. Any attempt to limit its power while it is in office would contradict the basic assumption on which democratic theory rests; namely, the absolute sovereignty of the popular will. [9] In theory, majority rule is the most tyrannical form of government conceivable — absolutism tempered only by impermanence. [10] In practice, of course,

9 Rousseau: "The general will alone can direct the State according to the object for which it was instituted, i.e., the common good . . . . Sovereignty, being nothing less than the exercise of the general will, can never be aliented . . ." (*The Social Contract*, Vol. 38, p. 395a).
10 See *On Liberty*, Vol. 43, p. 269a-c.

in the classical democracies, the knowledge that if a government misuses power the opposition will win the next election acts as an incomparably efficient brake. But in underdeveloped countries it is extraordinarily difficult for this brake to work, or if it does work, for it not to lead to a fatal political skid.

It is difficult for the brake to work because the party in power has at its disposal all the modern techniques of propaganda which spring from possession of the reins of government. By this I do not mean simply the brute instruments of corruption and intimidation, although these are certainly very formidable. Nor do I refer merely to the more subtle forms of patronage, although these too are numerous and almost irresistible. In Ghana, for example, it is possible to tell how an area is expected to vote at the next election or how it voted at the last election by whether it boasts a new school or welfare center. But even more important in binding the electorate to the ruling party is the fact that, for the most part, the ruling party is made up of the men who actually fought and won independence and who, therefore, are surrounded by an almost legendary aura of glory, which all the organs of the state inevitably seek to amplify and maintain. It is difficult, if not impossible, for an opposition to compete against such advantages.

But if the opposition did win—that is to say, if the brake did work —it is equally difficult to see how this would not put the state into a dangerous skid. For in these newly independent states, which lack all natural cohesion, made up as most of them are of conflicting tribes with no common interest in the present or tradition of co-operation in the past (except for the single objective of getting the colonial power out), without a common culture or language, and with unresolved economic rivalries between region and region, it is often only by the President's or Prime Minister's building himself up as a demi-god that any loyalty to the central government and any national unity at all can be created and maintained.

The realities, in short, demand that the leader should build himself up as indispensable. But the whole theory of democracy requires that the Prime Minister should be *dispensable.* If the opposition cut him down to parliamentary size, it might well be an act of treason against the state, in the sense that in fulfilling their constitutional role they may be endangering national unity. Not only does this inhibit the opposition, but, in a way more dangerous, it justifies a government's use of every method to limit and weaken their opponents.

These difficulties have, of course, already done grievous damage in many new states seeking to establish parliamentary government. Either the ruling party consists only of a coalition of politicians, without organization in depth, and is therefore easily broken up over differences in policy or personalities, which was the case with Pakistan's Muslim League; or it is so strong and so deeply entrenched that no other party can hope to dislodge it from power, as is the case with the Convention People's Party in Ghana. What is required, however, if parliamentary government is to work at all successfully, are two large parties, both representing a multiplicity of interests. One of them must always be content to remain out of office for some ten years, while the other treats it with all the respect due to a loyal opposition.

These sophisticated requirements, however, are not likely to be realized in the underdeveloped countries, but rather in societies where government is not the only basis of power; in societies, that is to say, where there are a great many concentrations of private power through which influence can be exerted — a condition which is singularly absent in the underdeveloped countries. The British habits of parliamentary life evolved in the eighteenth century, under an aristocratic system, when it did not make all that difference to those contending for office whether they got it or not. Victory at Westminster meant patronage and power, but defeat was by no means unpleasant, since not only did it enable one to spend more time in the hunting field or in the library but it also meant that, being freed of office, one could concentrate better on running local affairs. Whoever won, the aristocratic system continued, which was all that really mattered. The important thing was not to win elections, but to be born into the aristocracy or to win the King's favor.

No wonder, therefore, that the whole activity of parliamentary contest evolved on civilized lines. There was really no great danger in anybody's rejecting the four governing assumptions of party rule: (1) when a party forms a government, it shall govern by consent instead of coercion; (2) it shall itself consent to surrender the government to the direction of a rival party; (3) when this exchange takes place it shall be in a peaceful way; (4) the changes in existing relations in the whole community shall be of a moderate instead of a drastic sort.

These sophisticated constitutional habits, formed during the aristocratic period when they did not really require much of a sacrifice, acquired such momentum and became so deeply ingrained that they have continued unimpaired into Britain's present state of universal suffrage and popular sovereignty. Indeed, it can almost be said that Britain's particular form of democracy has been fashioned so as to conform to the cherished habits of a bygone age. The difficulty bedevilling the new countries of Asia and Africa is that they need to develop an aristocratic attitude to politics in a democratic age: to show an eighteenth-century sophistication without ever having lived through the eighteenth century.

The truth is that in these countries politics do matter quite desperately. Here there is no aristocratic class or capitalist class whose basic position in society is determined by considerations other than electoral victory. In the new states, the popular mandate is the only source of honor and power.

This is not simply a personal problem, involving loss of patronage and physical amenities, although this aspect is real enough. (The difference in mode of life between being Prime Minister and being Leader

of the opposition in most of these countries is almost inconceivably wide: for the former, world-wide travel, luxury and pomp, hobnobbing with the world leaders as equals, all of which must be infinitely intoxicating to men who, for the most part, have risen from nothing, which in these areas really means nothing; and for the latter, total futility.)

Far more important, in these countries the only way of shaping events is through politics. There are no other tempting concentrations of power — economic or social — through which events can be influenced. Yet these nations are, in most cases, either wholly new, on the very threshold of their national history, or are undergoing vast transformations — religious, social, economic, and cultural. Probably never again in their history will their governments be called upon to make such crucial decisions, affecting the very basis and structure of society; decisions which in Europe were decided only by force. It seems to me quite insane to suppose that any group of politicians, faced with the prospect of being out of office for ten years at such a time, and understandably aware of all the methods their opponents can use to keep them out of office forever, will show the necessary sophistication and restraint to make the parliamentary system work.

The dangers of radical reform

It may well be argued, of course, that these difficulties are only temporary growing pains as the new states get under way. Dr. Nkrumah, for example, may see himself as doing consciously to Ghana what the Tudors did unconsciously to sixteenth-century Britain — forging a cohesive nation strong enough, at a later date, to survive the strains of parliamentary government.

This comforting parallel, however, is vitiated by one striking difference in the situation between the new, underdeveloped states and that of the classical democracies, which have also gone through the experiences of absolutism. Britain evolved into a democracy by way of monarchy and even dictatorship. The underdeveloped countries, however, are evolving into dictatorship by way of parliamentary government. Having, so to speak, started from the top, and descended to the bottom, it may prove far more difficult to make the ascent a second time. What is so disturbing about so many of the newly independent countries is that the necessary growing pains are taking place in bodies politic whose outward forms are already fully grown. While a young body politic is expected to behave wildly, and to kick and scream, it is difficult to smile indulgently when instead of being swathed in the swaddling clothes of autocracy, it is dressed up in the venerable uniform of a mature democracy. More important, by tripping and tearing this incongruous adult uniform in childhood, it will have been reduced to shreds and tatters by the time the new states might with luck have been ready to wear it. In other words, by the time the underdeveloped countries are ready for democracy, the institutions of parliamentary government will have been damaged beyond repair.

This, I think, is what worries me most about the way things are going in the underdeveloped countries—the dreadful double talk which must be so lethally confusing to the simple, primitive peoples whose futures are at stake. Reduced to its stark outline, what is happening to these peoples in Asia and Africa is that the majority are being either coaxed or dragooned into giving up their ancestral ways and customs, the ways of their forefathers, and to adopt values and pursue activities which the minority believe to be good for them. They are being refashioned in the most radical sense, almost recreated.

In the Communist countries, like China, this process is being done with great cruelty and speed; in the non-Communist countries it is being done very much more slowly and with gentler methods. But it is being done in one way or another in all the underdeveloped countries. In the non-Communist countries, however, it is being done in the name of democracy and freedom, since these are the slogans used. It is being done, moreover, through the instruments normally associated with democracy and freedom — popularly-elected governments, legal process, trade unions, etc. The masses are not being forced to be free, as they are in the Communist countries. [11] They are being invited to be free, conditioned to be free, seduced into freedom by material rewards, or the promises of material rewards.

To study this process at work in India, where it is being conducted with exemplary patience and humanity, is even more frightening than it is in those countries where it is being forced through with brutality. In China the concept of freedom is being destroyed. In India, however, it is being castrated. The masses are being accustomed to associate freedom with a passive acquiescence, while the elite in power are becoming accustomed to interpret freedom as a restraint on the speed with which they push through reforms designed to improve the people's lot. But there is nothing in this relationship which we in the West can regard as appertaining to democracy and freedom. While we can

---

11 The notion that men must sometimes be coerced into freedom can be traced to Rousseau. See *The Social Contract*, Vol. 38, p. 393a-b.

be thankful that the Indians are not using Communist methods to industrialize the country and should pray that they will succeed in raising the material standard of living, so that the Communists will have no excuse to step in and do the job for them, we surely cannot argue that what is happening there is democratic or that the spirit abroad in India today is that of freedom, as that idea is understood in the West.

Freedom in the West is an active, creative force. A free people is one in which each group has fought for its rights and feels strong enough and organized enough to protect them. But for the overwhelming majority of Indians, freedom has no such connotation. It is a gift, which they are pleased to accept, but which, because they have not made it for themselves, could be easily taken away from them if another set of rulers, less civilized than the present lot, should choose to do so. It seems to me a great error for the West to pretend otherwise since, if this gift of freedom *is* taken away from them, it is better that the West should be on record as saying that it was only *ersatz* anyhow. If the Indians think that what they have got now is freedom, not only may they not mind terribly losing it but also, far worse, they may never be inclined to look for it again.

In one very important sense, therefore, it seems to me that the long-term prospects for freedom are better in Pakistan than they are in India. In Pakistan, there is no attempt by the junta of generals to pretend that the transformation of the country from a primitive pastoral community to a modern industrial society is being achieved through democratic means. It is being done quite openly and frankly by dictatorship. [12] President Ayub does not claim to represent the popular will, or bother to carry through meaningless elections. The political atmosphere is one of unashamed aristocratic tutelage, with the educated elite justifying their right to give the orders on the rational ground that they can read and write whereas the masses cannot. While this may not make Pakistan a favorite at the United Nations, this uninhibited disregard for contemporary double talk at least has the crucial advantage that when the masses do become educated and do want to organize their own rights, they will be able to do so in the name of democracy, since the democratic theory will not have already been pre-empted by an oligarchy flying false colors.

Put it another way. Frank recognition by the Pakistan oligarchy that they are not a democratic government leaves the field free for later generations of Pakistani democrats to justify their claim to a share in government on democratic grounds. Nor is this possibility merely academic. The encouraging aspect of the Pakistani rulers today is that, although they are not democrats, they are very much liberals – liberal aristocrats, if you will, educated in Britain and deeply imbued with the liberal tradition.

12 "There are . . . conditions of society in which a vigorous despotism is in itself the best mode of government for training the people in what is specifically wanting to render them capable of a higher civilisation" (J. S. Mill, *Representative Government*, Vol. 43, p. 436b).

PRESIDENT AYUB
OF PAKISTAN
TAKING THE OATH
OF OFFICE.
*The cause of freedom
may be better served
by avowed dictators like Ayub
than by demagogues who claim
to represent the people*

While it is perfectly true that they are subject to no objective or in-stitutional brake on their absolute power, since they have abolished the franchise and rule by decree, they have not denied the subjective and personal limitations which come from the liberal conscience. In the long run this is surely a more promising situation than what is hap-pening in those other underdeveloped countries where the rulers claim to be operating according to the popular will, and go through the mo-tions of acquiring an electoral mandate which, for reasons already mentioned, present no great difficulty.

In these democratic countries the rulers, by claiming to respect the democratic brake on absolutism − which cannot work − in fact acquire a tremendously powerful new accelerator towards tyranny. Backed by an electoral mandate which allows them to claim that what they want to do is what the people want them to do, they are able to ignore all restraints, private as well as public. If you believe, as they do, that the voice of the people is the voice of God, and if you can control the voice of the people − as they can − then your voice be-comes the voice of God, and any dissident, oppositionist voice be-comes the voice of the Devil, to be treated accordingly. On balance, therefore, it would seem that the prospects of eventual freedom are better in the countries that espouse dictatorship openly, like Pakistan, than in those which dress it up in all the hideous garments of Jacobin democracy.

Dangers of premature democracy

Paradoxical as it may sound, therefore, what is perhaps most wor-risome about the political prospects of the underdeveloped coun-tries is not the absence of democracy but its premature presence. The democratic doctrine has been fruitful of freedom in the West because, when it was initially propounded in its modern form in the eighteenth century, there was no possibility whatsoever of its being actually im-plemented. European society even then was far too complicated, and made up of far too many partially conflicting interests, for the idea of the "general will" to be taken at all literally. Nobody studying society as it actually existed could suppose that on any particular issue, king, nobles, priests, peasants, and artisans would all agree as to the common good, which is why, of course, the great propounders of the democratic doctrine were compelled to postulate the existence of some idyllic primitive society populated by noble savages.[13] So far as Europe was concerned, therefore, one thing was clear from the start: either society had to be revolutionized to make it fit democratic theory or democratic theory had to be revolutionized to make it fit society.

The French Revolution, in its disastrous Jacobin phase, was an attempt to do the former. By destroying all the established feudal institutions—monarchy, church, and aristrocracy—it hoped to remove all the obstacles to a people's government based on the general will. The result was democratic dictatorship. The Russian revolution made the same attempt with even more disastrous results. European experience suggests, therefore, that the more strenuously countries seek to revolutionize society to make it fit democratic doctrines, the blacker are the prospects for freedom. Only in those countries, like Britain, where circumstances encouraged a gradual compromise between democratic ideals and undemocratic reality, where, in other words, it has been *unnecessary* to carry democracy to its logical conclusion, has freedom tended to grow. What fostered freedom in Britain was that the anti-democratic forces—monarchy, aristocracy, and church—were sufficiently strong and sufficiently flexible to be able at once to satisfy the democratic urge without abdicating to it unconditionally.

The ancient feudal institutions of monarchy, aristocracy, and church still continue to play important parts in British government, without in any way having to justify their role on democratic grounds. In other words, the democratic doctrine has never gained undisputed sway over the British body politic. There are still tests for governmental legitimacy other than the claim to represent the general will, as the continued existence of the House of Lords and the Monarchy suggest. The result, of course, has been to dilute the full force of democratic government. Minority views, even if they are clearly unable to command majority support, can still find protection, since the will of the majority is not the only force built into the public structure of the state. The same result has been brought about in the United States, where a whole battery of institutional checks on the general will, headed by the Supreme Court, exist to protect the individual citizen from the tyranny of the majority.

There can be little doubt that these safeguards against unqualified majority rule have brought about a revolutionary change in the theory of democracy as it is understood in the Anglo-Saxon world. The democratic theory, in short, has been revolutionized to fit reality. No longer can it seriously be argued that power to decide political issues is actually invested in some abstraction called "the people," since it is rec-

---

13 Rousseau describes the state of nature inhabited by "noble savages" in the *Discourse on the Origin of Inequality*, Vol. 38, esp. pp. 362a-366d.

ognized that trying to do so leads either to chaos or tyranny. Either the government never acts at all, because it is always searching for a non-existent "general will," or it acts arbitrarily on behalf of a fictitious general will which, in practice, is merely its own will masquerading as that of "the people."

Under the Anglo-Saxon tradition of democracy, therefore, all "the people" do is decide who is to do the deciding, which simply means that every few years the individual elector can cast a vote in favor of one individual rather than another. Instead of governing themselves, therefore, the people merely choose who should do the governing on their behalf. This is certainly a far cry from Rousseau's ideal of government somehow magically reflecting the general will. But this, of course, is precisely its virtue. In return for abdicating a fictitious right to self-government, the people gain a real right of electing those who are to do the governing. The Anglo-Saxon tradition, in short, takes all the divine right nonsense out of democracy. Acts of government cease to be endowed with the magic of the "general will" and become merely executive decisions on which the people can express an opinion every four or five years or so.

Conditions in the underdeveloped countries, however, are such that the divine right nonsense is the only aspect of democracy that does make any sense at all. Take, for example, that north Kenyan tribe which I described at the outset of this essay. As I sought to show, its chief did in a real sense represent the "general will." Indeed this almost instinctive communion between leader and led was the natural method for reaching any decisions. This tribe, in short, represented precisely the kind of society that the eighteenth-century formulators of the democratic doctrine had in mind as their prototype. Insofar, therefore, as the primitive tribes of the underdeveloped countries are concerned, pure democracy can be taken very literally indeed. However, whereas the ruled are still at the "noble savage" level, and therefore ideal material for pure democracy, the rulers are skilled in all the guile and sophisticated techniques of impure democracy, as it has developed to suit the advanced societies of the West. The combination could hardly be more disastrous. Not only do the rulers have all the advantages of primitive democracy, in being able to argue that they represent "the general will," but they also have at their disposal all the techniques of twentieth-century electioneering to prevent any challenge to this claim from ever emerging. The underdeveloped countries, in short, have the worst of both democratic worlds. As in primitive democracy, the masses are accustomed to feel an instinctive solidarity with governmental decisions — a solidarity which the governments are too sophisticated to share; and, as in advanced democracy, the governments know how to exploit demagoguery, corruption, and gerrymandering, while the masses have no idea how to make the most of their votes.

Just imagine that, in the eighteenth century, some absolute monarch in Europe had had the imagination to see how democratic doctrine could be exploited to buttress his throne, and had exploited all the instinctive popular respect and devotion for the crown to win election after election, and to weaken and destroy any middle-class opposition to the royal prerogative. Fortunately for Europe, the monarchies were slow off the mark, and by the time democracy became the accepted method of government, it had already been established as the even more effective method of limiting government. In Asia and Africa, however, the reverse is true. It is the governments who, while still enjoying the instinctive support of primitive peoples, have embraced democracy from the start, while the great majority of those over whom they govern are quite ignorant of their democratic rights. Democracy, in short, has begun as a method of government, before establishing itself as a method of limiting government.

It seems highly doubtful, therefore, whether the Afro-Asian world will be able to look to democracy as the fountainhead of freedom which it has proved in the West. The conditions, as this essay has sought to show, are almost wholly different. I well realize that this is a profoundly pessimistic conclusion. Yet for the West to reach any more optimistic conclusion on the basis of the present evidence would be even more pessimistic, since it would suggest that Africa and Asia were being judged by quite different standards from those by which the West would judge its own prospects.

The best service the West can give to the cause of freedom in the underdeveloped countries is to refuse to debase its own understanding of what freedom means. It has never been part of the Western thesis that freedom can be easily achieved. Its whole history, right up to the present—as Spain and Turkey exist to show—suggests that freedom is, even in advanced countries, as elusive as it is precious. Far better, therefore, that the West should be frankly pessimistic about the prospects of freedom in Africa and Asia than that it should accept double standards, which will confuse its own peoples without helping those in other lands.

NOTE TO THE READER

The reader who wishes to make an effort to resolve the issue posed in the Great Debate will find it helpful to consult the *Syntopicon* and *Great Books of the Western World*.

The reader should first turn to the introductory essays to the *Syntopicon* chapters on DEMOCRACY and LIBERTY. These essays discuss many of the problems raised in the preceding pages. In addition, useful references to *Great Books of the Western World* will be found in the *Syntopicon* under the following topics:

For the suitability of democracy to all nations and all peoples, see

DEMOCRACY

4d. The suitability of democratic constitutions to all men under all circumstances: conditions favorable to democracy; progress toward democracy

PROGRESS

4c. The growth of political freedom: the achievement of citizenship and civil rights

SLAVERY

6c. The transition from subjection to citizenship: the conditions fitting men for self-government

For the need to have an educated citizenry before democracy can be expected to flourish, see

CITIZEN

6. Education for citizenship

DEMOCRACY

6. The educational task of democracy: the training of all citizens

For the safeguards which democracy needs, see

CONSTITUTION

7b. The safeguards of constitutional government: bills of rights; separation of powers; impeachment

DEMOCRACY

4c. The infirmities of democracy in practice and the reforms or remedies for these defects

5c. The distribution of functions and powers: checks and balances in representative democracy

For the dangers inherent in democracy, see

DEMOCRACY

2. The derogation of democracy: the anarchic tendency of freedom and equality

2a. Lawless mob-rule: the tyranny of the majority

2b. The incompetence of the people and the need for leadership: the superiority of monarchy and aristocracy

OPINION

7b. Majority rule, its merits and dangers: protections against the false weight of numbers

TYRANNY

2c. The corruption of democracy: the tyranny of the masses or of the majority; the rise of the demagogue

For the benefits of democratic government, see

DEMOCRACY

4. The praise of democracy: the ideal state

4a. Liberty and equality for all under law

(1) Universal suffrage: the abolition of privileged classes

(2) The problem of economic justice: the choice between capitalism and socialism

4b. The democratic realization of popular sovereignty: the safeguarding of natural rights

A Symposium on Space

HAS MAN'S CONQUEST OF SPACE
INCREASED OR DIMINISHED HIS STATURE?

HERBERT J. MULLER

ALDOUS HUXLEY

HANNAH ARENDT

PAUL TILLICH

HARRISON BROWN

INTRODUCTION

In setting up the symposium that follows, the editors deliberately took an approach to space exploration different from that common in newspapers and magazines. The question asked here does not have to do with the scientific, economic, or military results of space exploration, but rather with its effects on man. The editors asked the five participants in the symposium what, in their opinion, the exploration of space is doing to man's view of himself and to man's condition. The question does not concern man as a scientist, nor man as a producer or consumer, but rather man as *human*. We therefore invited non-scientists as well as a scientist to participate in the symposium. Our panel includes a historian, a novelist, a political philosopher, a theologian, and a physical scientist. We gave them free rein to express their opinions, but asked them particularly to consider whether, from their special perspectives, space exploration is a desirable pursuit for the human race in general and for the American people in particular. In brief, we hope that this symposium will give a new focus to the discussion about the American efforts in space.

The space race already has lost some of its novelty. At a time when neither the Russians nor the Americans have launched more than a handful of persons into orbit, a feeling is already beginning to develop that too much is being made of astronauts and cosmonauts, and that a mere circling of the earth in a space vehicle hardly warrants much excitement. Thus, the enthusiasm about men in space—whether they be Americans or Russians—appears to have waned. For the first time, questions are being asked about the desirability and utility of the space enterprise. Initially, when the Russians appeared to have all of the technical advantages and all the luck in their space efforts, there was wide support in the United States for the American attempts to catch up. The question of whether we *ought* to try to conquer space was bypassed as unworthy of further consideration, because the answer, it was felt, was so obviously affirmative.

As long as the conquest of space was (and is) considered merely in the light of a race between the U.S. and U.S.S.R., the only problems concerning it worth discussing were whether we were going about this conquest in the right way, whether the nation was getting its money's worth, and whether the Americans would succeed in beating the Russians. In this spirit, expenditures for rocketry and all the other appurtenances needed to send men and instruments, first to the moon and then to the planets, were approved with alacrity by the Congress as well as by the general public.

In recent months, however, either because the American achievements seem more nearly to match those of the Russians, or because the mere passage of time seems to make adventures in space less exciting, some doubts about the American space program are beginning to be voiced. Most criticism is directed against the efforts to send men to the moon (Project Apollo). "Anybody who would spend 40 billion dollars in a race to the moon for national prestige is nuts," said former President Eisenhower. Some critics question other aspects of the space program. What may we expect to learn about the moon and the planets by visiting them? What more can we learn about these heavenly bodies from human observers than can be learned by sending up highly sophisticated instruments? What are the costs which the United States is going to have to bear during the next few decades in order to reach its goals? Are these costs commensurate with the expected results? How are the expenditures, in money, in manpower, and in technological resources, going to affect other national goals of the United States? These are just a few of the questions raised.

Our symposium concerns the desirability of space exploration, but it deals only indirectly with many of the scientific and economic questions. It is directed to the basic principles behind all human enterprise, and asks: Should men engage in the conquest of space? Indeed, can they be kept from it? What are the long-range results of this enterprise? What effect will success in conquering space have on mankind? What effects would result from failure? Are the gains worth the risk? Our symposium tries to evaluate man's ventures into space from this point of view.

Technological considerations cannot, of course, be entirely eliminated from any debate about space exploration, and so they find their way into these essays. But they play a subordinate role here, the central question always being—Is space exploration good for man? Conversely, some consideration of the value of the space effort to mankind, not based on military or technological grounds, also finds its way into discussions dealing with the scientific and engineering principles behind the effort. Thus, in Part III of this book, in the article dealing with the year's advances in physical sciences and technology, we have one physicist questioning the U.S. Man-in-Space program, while another one defends it. This discussion, as well as the more technical matters concerning rockets and satellites, will be found on pp. 279-357.

HERBERT J. MULLER, one of America's best known historians, was born in Mamaroneck, New York, in 1905. Educated at Cornell University, he has taught at Cornell and Purdue, and is now Distinguished Service Professor at Indiana University. He is the author of several widely read works on history, including *The Uses of the Past* and *The Loom of History*. At present, he is completing a three-part history of freedom. The first volume, *Freedom in the Ancient World*, won the 1962 Phi Beta Kappa award for the best work in history, philosophy, and religion. The second volume, *Freedom in the Western World*, appeared in February, 1963, and the third, *Freedom in the Modern World*, is in preparation.

To a good positivist, I suppose, the question whether man's conquest of space has increased or diminished his stature is simply meaningless. This kind of "stature" is wholly subjective, any speculation about it is unverifiable, and the question is only another distraction from the serious business of thought. Or so I was told, with some irritation, by a distinguished mathematician whose opinion I asked.

To a historian, however, the question is quite meaningful, all the more important because it cannot be answered with assurance. Man's stature has been a live issue ever since the rise of modern science, which has profoundly transformed his thought and feeling about himself. Today it brings up the very difficult but still practical problem of keeping abreast of our knowledge, trying to understand the extraordinary history we have been making. And to me the irritation of the positivist suggests the most extraordinary thing about the conquest of space—that apparently it does not strike most Americans as really extraordinary. They were obviously excited by the feats of our astronauts, but my impression was that they felt essentially like spectators at a sporting event or another Hollywood super-feature. Rocketing around the earth was only the latest wonder in an age for which wonders have become routine. Ordinary Americans might be baffled by the question we are discussing here, or consider it merely academic.

More precisely, what excited them was not the feats of Man—it was the feats of Americans. We were catching up with those Russians. The godless Russians seem much prouder of the conquest of space as a purely human triumph, but otherwise it is chiefly another incident in the Cold War—the really important affair of our time. How the rest of the world feels about the triumph I cannot be sure, except for one thing: Men everywhere are not simply throwing out their chests. Whatever pride they may take in the latest demonstration of the fantastic power that the human race has achieved is mingled with dread of the uses men may make of this power. Such possibilities bring up what I assume is our main concern. The pertinent question is not so much how men in general *do* feel about this feat as how they *ought* to feel, in view of the past history and the possible future of the human race.

Now, only one who is certain of the future, or of the meaning of man's history, can give a simple, positive answer. For the rest of us nothing would seem more obvious than the complexities and ambiguities of modern history; but nothing is harder to keep clearly, steadily in view. The conquest of space plainly does heighten the stature of man by a crowning demonstration of his amazing capacities and of achievements that writers are now disposed to slight—apparently because they are not plain enough. It is also a striking demonstration of mighty forces that have tended to belittle man, and now threaten to end his history— though most ordinary Americans and Russians seem not to have been sufficiently struck by these tendencies. On both counts the oversights suggest a want of historical sense, especially because our age is supposed to be very historical-minded. So I think it might help to begin with a backward look.

Let us go all the way back to the magic of prehistoric man. His artifacts indicate that it grew more elaborate, and seemingly compulsive, as his culture developed. Although we can never be sure of his mentality, his belief in magic most likely had an ambivalent effect, confirming at once his fear of the unknown and his confidence that he knew it well enough to bend it to his own purposes. At least these dual tendencies became more marked with the rise of civilization. By this time men had learned a great deal, they had achieved remarkable technological feats, and presumably they felt bigger, as certainly they built bigger; yet they also developed a still more elaborate magic, which they failed to distinguish clearly from their empirical knowledge, and their monumental architecture testified to their belief in their utter dependence on the gods. The Greeks stand out as the first people to arrive at a clear conception of natural causes and a conscious faith in man's own powers of mind, without benefit of magic or supernatural aid—a faith that to early Christians seemed the deadly sin of pride, since they knew that only by the grace of God had man any stature. Even so, the pride of the Greeks was not overweening by modern standards. Their poets constantly warned them of the dangers of *hubris;* in their classical prime they took it for granted that man was a mortal animal, and they added no divine cubit to his stature by endowing him with an immortal soul. At no time did they entertain visions of earthly progress or indefinite improvement of the human condition.

Hence in this respect, too, the rise of modern science in the seventeenth century signified a revolution in thought. But because it most obviously heightened men's confidence in their own powers, we should note that their possibly sinful pride was still rather different from that of most Americans and Russians today. Although Francis Bacon trumpeted the power that science could give man over nature, and foresaw the wondrous inventions that would come from it, men in general were not dazzled by visions of its practical utility and did not at once set about applying their new knowledge to technology. Enthusiasm was stirred rather by a purely intellectual feat, an apparent growth in mental or spir-

FIDEL CASTRO EMBRACING RUSSIAN COSMONAUT GAGARIN
*The godless Russians seem much prouder of the conquest of space
as a purely human triumph, but otherwise it is chiefly another incident in the cold war*

itual stature, symbolized by Newton's grand theory. It was summed up in Alexander Pope's well-known couplet:

> Nature and Nature's law lay hid in night:
> God said, *Let Newton be!* and all was light.

The new confidence in man's powers of mind bred the singular idea of progress, a faith such as no previous society had ever had, that by virtue of man's own efforts the future would be ever better than the past; but again men were not yet thinking primarily of a material progress. Rather they conceived a progress in civility, through reason and knowledge, by the standards of their "Age of Enlightenment." With this faith came more optimistic ideas about the nature of man that are especially pertinent for us, since they had much to do with the rise of democracy. Man was conceived as an essentially rational animal, or at least rational enough to be capable of self-government; by the same token he was no longer essentially a fallen creature of Original Sin but naturally good, or at least good enough to be fit for freedom. From the ancient doctrine of "natural law," a universal principle of justice that in the Enlightenment seemed confirmed by Newtonian law, thinkers now drew the corollary of "natural rights," the rights of all men to life, liberty, and the pursuit of happiness. Thomas Jefferson, the foremost champion of common men, most clearly indicated how much their increased political stature owed to science, in particular to his "great Trinity"—Bacon, Newton, and Locke.

We must now add that few men really understood the work of Newton, which for ordinary men was only a more difficult form of magic, and that the whole optimistic faith of the Enlightenment rested on a good deal of confusion. I believe that all of us who still hold to the ideals of a free society are logically and morally committed to the essentials of this faith, but for this reason we need at once to discount it. From the beginning modern science has bred persistent, often wild misunderstanding. Bacon had a crude idea of the inductive method that he expected would work all the miracles described in *New Atlantis*, his essay in science fiction. (See Vol. 30, pp. 199-214.) The spreading idea that human history was a progress was not based on a critical, empirical study of history, but was supported by a contempt as well as an ignorance of most of the past before God had decided—it would seem arbitrarily—to let Newton be. There was no logical connection between natural law as formulated by Newton and the rights of man, which hardly looked natural in view of man's history. The universe that he made so beautifully clear was due to get more mysterious than it had ever been before. Pope's couplet would inspire one by a modern poet:

> It did not last: the Devil, howling *Ho!*
> *Let Einstein be!* restored the status quo.[1]

But in particular we have now to deal with the basic ambiguities or paradoxes involved in the triumph of science, the modern counterpart of the ambivalence of prehistoric magic. These did not become fully apparent until the nineteenth century. Applied science then spurred the astounding development of technology, the immense increase in material wealth and power—the meaning of progress to most Americans. The idea of progress became a commonplace in all the advanced Western countries. For many men it was supported by the theory of evolution, from which they drew the inference that progress was the law of nature as well as of history, and therefore in effect automatic, guaranteed. "Always toward perfection is the mighty movement," Herbert Spencer proclaimed. Yet the theory of evolution depressed many other men, even apart from the initial emphasis on the endless, bloody struggle for survival. It suggested that man had not been specially created as the lord of this earth, but was only an advanced form of ape, a latecomer on the animal scene. It recalled the pessimistic implications of modern science from the outset, the reasons why it might lessen the stature of man by making him feel insignificant in the cosmos it revealed. Churchmen who attacked the heretical faith in science and in progress still

1 Reprinted by permission from *Collected Poems* by J. C. Squire, Macmillan and Company Ltd.

upheld the very proud belief that the universe had been created primarily for the sake of man; but since the Copernican theory had been established, man no longer lived at the center of the universe, and he found it harder to maintain so exalted an idea of his importance.

In the seventeenth century Pascal most eloquently expressed the paradoxes of the human condition in the light of the new knowledge. Man was not simply insignificant or vile; though he was "but a reed, the most feeble thing in nature," he was nevertheless a "thinking reed" (*Pensées,* 347; Vol. 33, p. 233b); he knew the universe that crushed him, he alone was aware of the immensities that dwarfed him. But therein lay his curse, a torment unknown to the rest of the creation. Pascal himself was the more tormented because, while he believed that thought made the dignity of man, he had the most vivid awareness of the limitations of reason. The human mind was always liable to error and folly; it could not really comprehend the extremes of the infinitely great and the infinitely small between which men lay, or the mysterious mixture of spirit and clay in his own nature; it could never know the final, absolute truth it always sought. In particular, reason could not prove what for Pascal was the all-important truth—the existence of God. So he devoted his own brilliant mind to combating the skepticism that was spreading with the scientific spirit; and in his anguish he also expressed most eloquently the reasons for doubt.

In the nineteenth century, Pascal's worst fears were realized, but in ways more paradoxical than he anticipated. On the one hand, the triumphant advance of science led to much more religious doubt and disbelief, while it also made men feel less dependent on God. On the other hand, it generated tendencies that undermined its own faith in reason, and that deprived man of the dignity and stature Pascal had accorded him. From the mechanistic Newtonian universe that had enthralled men by its perfect regularity, thinkers now drew out logical implications of determinism that denied man any real freedom. He was often represented as merely a creature of heredity and environment, whose behavior was governed by the same physico-chemical laws that governed the rest of the animal world. Social analysts concentrated on the impersonal, non-rational processes that determined his history. With Freud came much more awareness of the power of the positively irrational, which has been manifested all too plainly in recent history. In this century behaviorists and social scientists have concentrated still more on mechanical, involuntary, or conditioned behavior, if only to look more like pure scientists, on a par with physicists. For all such reasons modern literature has notoriously been given over to pessimism. Many writers have dwelt on the insignificance of man and the ultimate meaninglessness of his life in a universe utterly indifferent to him; many

MILDRED DUNNOCK AND LEE J. COBB IN "DEATH OF A SALESMAN"
*On the tragic stage, Oedipus Rex and Hamlet have dwindled
into little Willy Loman, a salesman*

others have belittled him by dwelling chiefly on his own meanness as a slave to banal convention, vulgar desire, or neurotic fear. On the tragic stage Oedipus Rex and Hamlet have dwindled into Willy Loman, a salesman. Needless to add, no sophisticate today speaks of "progress" except as a theme of derision.

And all this in an era when man has been literally surpassing his dreams, when science fiction has become fact! Jaded as we all tend to be, I think that the first and last word is properly one of awe over the conquest of space. At least we might try to realize how wonderful this feat is by the standards of even our boastful fathers. At the beginning of our century men were proud that they could circumnavigate the earth in two or three months, a voyage that had once taken years, and that no society before ours had ever accomplished. Now they can rocket around their earth in little more than an hour, and can count on flying to the moon and back in a day or so—an idea that once would have seemed as fantastic as cows jumping over the moon. This might remind us, too, that science has long stirred the imagination of men because it is itself a highly imaginative enterprise, a spiritual adventure—not the cold, impious, materialistic business that many literary men of today make it out to be. I propose to venture some speculation on the awesome possibilities of the future, first risking a word on behalf of the unfashionable idea of progress.

Yet in awe—which properly includes fear as well as wonder—one has immediately to face up to the worst possibilities. Respect for the stature that man has achieved calls for stress chiefly on the growing menaces to his dignity, now even to his survival. It would seem unnecessary to point out the plainest menace, the terrible destructive power he has acquired through science; but the fact remains that men have not really taken this to heart in their political behavior, and none of us can be sure that we will escape the catastrophe of nuclear war. We are no safer when America devotes fifty billion dollars a year to its Defense Department, but only six million—or about a hundredth of one per cent—to its Arms Control and Disarmament Agency. One is unfortunately obliged to spell out other obvious reasons for alarm, which never seem obvious enough.

To begin with, the driving motives in the conquest of space are of course not scientific. The American program for landing a man on the moon as soon as possible is primarily a feverish effort to keep up with the Russians. The problems it poses are chiefly matters of engineering, scientifically much less important than the researches going on in genetics, biochemistry, theoretical physics, etc. It may cost, I gather, from twenty to thirty billions over the next few years; and one can scarcely imagine Congress authorizing anything like such an expenditure for basic scientific research. Or for medical research, or any program to improve the nation's health; or for education itself. The conquest of space might do more to increase man's stature were it not a plain distraction from much more pressing needs, a reminder of how far we are from mastering life on our own earth. The rest of the world is unlikely to rejoice in the high estate of man while the overwhelming majority of men remain in a primitive state, often on a wretchedly low standard of living, with countless millions simply not getting enough to eat; but Congress would dismiss as reckless extravagance any proposal to spend a few billions on efforts to combat the menace of over-population. Overfed Americans may feel more vicarious pride in their man on the moon (saving the millions of neurotics and alcoholics, the millions more of worried old folk and unemployed); only there is no telling where those Russians will be by then.

Or where *we* are right now. The crucial decisions about the space program—as about the whole military program—are perforce made by a very few men, in America no less than in Russia, on the basis of secret information not available to the rest of us. "Man" may be getting greater, but men may feel smaller, more helpless, because ever more dependent on decisions in which they have ever less say. Moreover, the essential technical information would not be comprehensible to most of us anyway. I for one know almost nothing of the workings of rockets, have only a dim idea of how the conquest of space was managed, and I cannot judge the program in terms either of scientific value or of possible military necessity; I must depend on the judgment of scientists I respect. And though such dependence on authority is nothing new in history, it points to a cost of civilization that has grown much heavier in our massive technological civilization, and that may intensify the individual's feeling of insignificance or impotence. Knowing so much more than the prehistoric villagers, we may forget how much better they knew their little world than we can ever hope to know ours: knew their fellows, their tools, their status, their traditions, their gods, their magic—just who they were, where they stood, what they were up against, how they had to behave, when and why they had to submit. In the immense complexity and confusion of our society we have to trust to our experts, while we know that they are fallible mortals, that about economic, social, and political problems they never can agree, and that finally we are all in the same boat, in uncharted seas, under perpetually stormy skies.

In particular the conquest of space points to the terrific, irreversible, irresistible drive of modern technology. Even apart from the compulsions of the Cold War, there is no calling a halt to it; the momentum that technological development has gained makes it almost automatic, at once ultra-dynamic and oddly rigid. It dictates space programs just as it dictates the mechanization of everything possible. Likewise it requires our immense social machinery, the giant organizations in both business and government, and keeps on impelling the tendency for everything to grow bigger—except all the little men in or under the organizations. Technology remains the plainest source of the power and the pride of modern man, the growing stature of the race collectively, and needless to add, it is now absolutely indispensable to the maintenance of our civilization, with its enormously increased population; but for this reason it threatens to become ever more an end than a means, more the master than the servant of men, reducing human beings to mere functions in a regimented process, interchangeable cogs suitably identified by punch cards. The whole drive is perfectly symbolized by the latest development, automation—itself a rather dreadful word, emphasizing the mechanical, automatic aspects of the process. It is said that the complicated machinery being designed for space research should in time prove useful for other purposes, introduce a new era of automation. Some Americans may be dismayed by the news that most likely we will not send men to Mars after all; machines will be able to do all the necessary exploration, while computing machines will digest their reports. Other Americans are beginning to worry over the millions of men at home who will be

BOATMEN ON THE YANGTZE RIVER
*The rest of the world is unlikely to rejoice in the high estate of man
while the overwhelming majority of men live in a primitive state*

deprived of their jobs, left with useless skills, or without functions. In
any case, we must expect automation. Efficiency demands it.

The billions spent on the space program, in a country still full of
slums and short on schoolrooms, exemplify the compulsive tendency
to sacrifice basic human needs for the sake of material power and mechanical efficiency. They call attention to an apparent emptiness of life
on this earth, a kind of purposelessness beneath the tremendous effort
to achieve practical purposes in a society in which know-how passes for
wisdom. As Robert Hutchins observed, it appears that Americans cannot tell where they are going or how well they are doing until they have
been assured that they are keeping up with the Russians, or at least not

falling too far behind. So one may wonder again about what they thought and felt after the initial excitement over the feats of their astronauts. How much capacity do they have for reflection, wonder, awe? For appreciation of the old-fashioned values of civility and enlightenment, the spiritual ends to which science was at first hailed as a means? They cannot be expected to understand modern science, but do they cherish the scientific spirit, the pursuit of truth for its own sake? Or the joys of creativity apart from all thought of whether it "pays"? In short, one comes back to the old question about our brave new world: What kind of people in it?[2]

The plainest evidence is not heartening. The many millions who were thrilled as they followed the astronauts on their TV sets spend many more hours a week staring at trivial or tawdry programs. Their favorite pastimes suggest a dependence on mechanical aids for passing the time, or for escaping boredom, escaping as well the effort of thought, the source of man's dignity. But most depressing is the judgment of those who are supposed to know Americans best—the advertisers, the controllers of the mass media. Their sales methods scarcely imply that the ordinary American is a mature, rational, responsible person. Often they treat him as a simple dope, who will be impressed by the patently insincere testimonials of beauty queens, ballplayers, and other such persons of distinction. Otherwise they exploit chiefly his fear of not keeping up with the Joneses, or not being well adjusted to other unthinking Americans. And when they boast of him (if only because he is a faithful consumer), they are likely to betray their own low standards of human dignity or stature. Thus one New York executive, in the course of a defense of Madison Avenue, proudly reported that Americans spend three billion dollars a year on culture. In other words, they spend less than one per cent of the national income on a primary means to self-enlargement, or simply to the possession of a real self, a mind of one's own. Now they are spending more on their space program, while their Congress refused to appropriate a few millions for the maintenance of a cultural center in the nation's capital. The exploration of outer space is more important than the enrichment of inner lives.

All such problems, one must add, cannot be met by the kind of crash program that may do for technological purposes. Since eminent scientists have called for the creation of a "science of survival," I assume that the rest of us ought to know that strictly there can be no such science. Together with all possible wisdom and good will, we should of course try to bring all available knowledge to bear on our problems; but in wisdom we should never hope to come up with scientific solutions. To

2 "O brave new world,
  That has such people in 't" (Shakespeare, *The Tempest*, Vol. 27, p. 547a).

PHILHARMONIC HALL AT LINCOLN CENTER, NEW YORK CITY
*Americans . . . spend less than one per cent of the national income on a primary means
to self-enlargement, or simply to the possession of a real self, a mind of one's own*

call such a pooling of knowledge a "science" may well be good policy,
as a means of impressing both government and public. It might also
confirm the popular misunderstanding of science as a form of guaranteed
magic, the popular ignorance of the limits of science, and the confusions
that have marked its whole history and that now generate much pseudo-
science.

Nevertheless, I should emphasize chiefly the high seriousness of these
scientists. Since the unleashing of nuclear power, no profession has displayed a more urgent sense of social responsibility. Scientists are co-
operating with their fellows all over the world, in the name of duty to
"mankind"—a concept that spread in the Age of Enlightenment, and
that has become more meaningful than it ever could be when men knew
nothing about most of the globe or the history of the human race. Their
international conferences may issue statements about what men must
do in which the "must" glides too easily into "will," but even so they
recall us to the exceptionally live sense of possibility that still distinguishes our society. It is symbolized by the characteristic word "challenge"—a word that we have reason to be weary of, as every day we are
called upon to rise to some challenge, but that is none the less significant;
for no past society in crisis, to my knowledge, kept ringing with such a
word. This in turn brings up the novel idea of progress, the source of

our feeling of greater potentiality. It brings me back to the positive achievements from which our problems have arisen, and which I think too many writers now disparage or ignore.

In general, criticism of American life has itself become pretty mechanical. It is too easy, or at least much easier than doing anything like exact justice, perhaps even simple justice. As we perforce deal in very broad generalities, we may forget that the "ordinary American" is a pure abstraction, like the sociological monster known as the "average man" (the one who has two and one-half children). It conceals the innumerable different kinds of Americans, with their innumerable varieties and degrees of interest, aptitude, and aspiration, which incidentally nourish enough independence of spirit to keep advertisers worried. Likewise the standard complaints of our "standardized mass society" obscure its unparalleled heterogeneity and mobility, the remarkable range of choice and opportunity it offers, including ample provision for its many critics. In this pluralistic society intellectuals may still fairly complain of the popular disposition to measure stature chiefly by success in business (even a man's "worth" by how many dollars he possesses), and of the common hostility to them as highbrows, eggheads, pinkoes; but they might be flattered even by this hostility, which implies that they have some real influence. As a class they in fact have a considerably larger audience than their fellows had in past societies, and nowhere do they get more financial support than they get in America. Voices crying in the modern wilderness may be subsidized by foundations, broadcast in paperbacks. They may cry clichés if only because they have so substantial and ready an audience.

In particular, it is necessary to keep an eye on the basic ambiguities of our history. We are dealing with the inescapable costs of real goods, beginning with a material well-being that we too easily take for granted. Few of us would change places with the illiterate, poverty-stricken peasants who throughout history, as in "spiritual" India today, have made up the great bulk of mankind. We should now add that much of their more intimate knowledge of their world was illusion or fearful superstition, and that their magic was less effective than our technology, which today all the rest of the world is eager to adopt. We have then to pay a price as well for all our scientific knowledge of man and his world, as I indicated at the outset, and especially for our fuller, more acute self-consciousness, which can be as painful as it is fruitful. Our pains are in part growing pains, due to a real growth in stature; for in the long view, man's history has in some fundamental respects unquestionably involved a progress, intellectual as well as material—even religious, if we have any respect for the so-called higher religions that emerged late in his history. Since the rise of modern science and the attendant growth of free societies, we tend to regard as intolerable many evils that once were taken as a matter of course, and in general to judge our society in the light of higher expectations than men ever entertained before. Among other things, we are demanding more of that "ordinary" man, who in the past was expected only to toil and to obey. The ordinary, conventional, routine life—the kind of life that almost all men have lived at all times and that can be decent enough—now strikes many writers as simply dreary, indecent, almost inhuman.

As for the specific problems I have touched on, I do not for a moment wish to minimize their gravity, especially because there is no sure-fire solution for them; but again I see some need of discounting fashionable attitudes. *Angst* has become a rage, almost a cult. At literary gatherings I have heard other writers and thinkers dismissed with a single sentence —"He doesn't suffer from anxiety"; so I gather that anxiety is the badge of intellectual responsibility, if not of spiritual health. At the same time, I get an impression of a good deal of self-pity. The plight of the sensitive man in the dreadful modern world is commonly made more grievous by sentimentality over simplified, idealized views of the past. It seems necessary to remark that one can find plenty of signs of anxiety in the "golden ages," such as Periclean Athens, the Renaissance, the Elizabethan Age, and the Age of Louis XIV, and above all in the Middle Ages, the "Age of Faith." From Dante on, Europe has never lacked for writers who believed that their society was damned or doomed.

As one who is not confident of the future and has not the faintest desire to fly to the moon, but is still proud to be a member of the human race, even pleased to have lived in this era, I venture the commonplace that we perforce keep living on the assumption that our world may not end, and we might better go on thinking of the menaces as "challenges." There remains the possibility that we are living in the dawn of a new era, in which man might measure up to his scientific and technological achievements, master the One World created by these achievements. The extraordinary problems we face have called out as extraordinary creative responses. Aware of the grave shortcomings of the United Nations, we may forget that much more surprising in a historical perspective is the degree of its success, as for the first time men are attempting to realize what had been only a dream of some visionaries. The many international congresses of intellectuals are likewise as novel in their common concern for human rights, the once revolutionary principle of the Rights of Man. However futile they may seem immediately, they accentuate the fact that to every problem we bring intellectual as well as material resources beyond the ken of men in the past, and first of all a clearer, fuller awareness of both problem and possibility, a habit of efforts at rational control. Hence every reason for alarm stirs widespread alarm, which may or may not be effective, but in any case gives some reason for hope. The growing concern over the massive pressures to conformity, for example, might remind us that no previous society ever worried so much over such pressures; for until recent centuries thinkers were generally unconcerned about threats to individuality, if aware of them at all, and were as generally disposed to prize conformity in all ordinary men.

In this dual view, finally, I indulge in some speculation about the long-range possibilities of the exploration of space. Although not qualified to speak of the scientific prospects, I could appreciate the excitement I have heard expressed by biologists over the possible discovery on another planet of unimaginably different forms of life—and their resentment of science fiction writers who keep imagining creatures superficially fantastic but basically like ourselves. More remote, I should think, are the possibilities of communicating by radio signal with other beings in outer space; yet nuclear physicists are taking such possibilities quite seriously, even going so far as to design a formula for sending out pictures of our life. (Professor Philip Morrison, author of the formula, thinks it "very probable" that some community in our galaxy is communicating over vast distances and waiting to add our earth to its mailing list.) At least we know that there may well be other beings all over the universe, conceivably more intelligent than we. Given the enormous number of stars, the mathematical chances are that the combination of physical conditions that made possible the emergence of life on our planet has occurred on some millions of planets, and ours is a relatively young one. Such probabilities are strong enough to force a question of some immediate pertinence for the stature of man—a question that is already being pondered by religious thinkers, such as Paul Tillich, and that recalls the ambiguous consequences of the rise of science.

Briefly, what comes of the Christian view that the key to the meaning of life was the appearance on earth of Christ, "the Lord of the universe"? Did he perhaps appear on other planets millions of years before man evolved? Or is he only a local religious symbol of a divinity better apprehended by beings elsewhere, possibly beings who were not cursed by original sin? Hindus might suggest that their concept of an immanent God or World Soul is better suited than a personal God for such multifarious cosmic purposes, and might remind Christians that they are still a small minority on this earth. A skeptic might add that more advanced beings may well have outgrown the need of religion, if they ever knew it at all.

Presumably, simple believers will be dismayed by such questions, which their Bible hardly prepares them for. Thoughtful men may feel more keenly the insignificance of man's relatively brief history, on an undistinguished planet hardly worthy of special divine attention; or they may recall Carlyle's remark as he gazed at the stars: "A sad spectacle!

If they be inhabited, what a scope for folly and evil; if they be not inhabited, what a waste of space!" Paul Tillich, however, considers the scientific conquest of time and space a healthy challenge to religion, and concludes that Christianity cannot afford to withdraw into its old answers: it too must dare to ask new questions, to transcend our earth and our history, "even our Christianity." I should think that believers might feel at once exalted and humbled by the thought that God has suitably populated some other of the billions of planets, since otherwise the immensity of the universe might seem pointless. Unbelievers might rejoice in the thought that man is not so lonely after all in a cosmos made richer, grander, by other forms of life throughout vast reaches once thought cold and dead. All might be edified by the old story of the poet who was told that astronomically speaking, man was insignificant. He replied: "Astronomically speaking, man is the astronomer."

Returning to this earth, we have always to face the all-too-real possibility that man may end his history. Few will rejoice at the thought that this is crowning evidence of his Godlike power and stature—he is now able to do on his own what it once took God to do with a flood. Religion, let us add, can tell us nothing for certain about his immediate prospects on earth. Nor can science; it can only give us warnings about the wonderful, awful powers it continues to increase. Even the leaders of Russia —seemingly the most confident men today, the proudest of modern man's stature—acknowledge that a nuclear war might prevent the happy ending guaranteed by their Marxist gospel. Yet such uncertainty always involves the real possibility that men may avert catastrophe. They may avert it directly out of simple fear, a sign of their littleness, but in part too because of their qualities of greatness—intellectual, moral, spiritual. Or just because of the simplest paradox of the human spirit: that all men know they are going to die and yet go on living as if they weren't, or go on planting, making, creating things to outlive them, maybe daring or dying in order to win a mortal fame, and now maybe thrilling at the thought of conquering New Worlds instead of merely a new continent; though whatever their stature, they will end in a plot of earth as small as that which covered the bones of their nameless, prehistoric, magic-haunted ancestors.

ALDOUS HUXLEY, world-famous novelist, essayist and critic, was born in Surrey, England, in 1894, the grandson of the great biologist T. H. Huxley. Educated at Eton College and Oxford University, he began his literary career as a poet, but soon turned to writing novels. He has written more than a dozen novels, including *Antic Hay, Point Counter Point* (probably his most widely read early work), and *Brave New World,* a frightening picture of a scientific "utopia." He emigrated to the United States in the 1930's, and is now living in southern California. For many years he has been deeply interested in Eastern philosophy and mysticism, and their influence upon him is evident in several of his later novels and essays. More recently, he has participated in experiments with "mind-changing" drugs. He has discussed these experiences and their implications in *The Doors of Perception* and *Heaven and Hell.* Among his latest works are *Brave New World Revisited* and *Island,* a study in "positive utopianism."

Has man's conquest of space increased or diminished his stature?" These ten simple words are pregnant with almost as many major problems in semantics. First of all, who or what is the "man" whose conquest of space is under discussion? The word "man" stands, in different contexts, for at least three distinct entities. Sometimes it stands for the species as a whole—for all the three thousand million specimens of *Homo sapiens* at present inhabiting our planet, and confidently expected (unless something extraordinarily bad or miraculously good should happen in the interval) to double their numbers in less than forty years. In other contexts "man" denotes the product of acculturation—the symbol-manipulating, tradition-following, tool-using *Homo faber* and *Homo loquax* of anthropology and history. Western Man, Oriental Man, Modern Man, Primitive Man, Christian Man, Post-Historic Man—for some years now such phrases have come trippingly off innumerable tongues. And finally the word "man" may stand for the human individual, male or female, black, white, or yellow, the psycho-physical organism that actually does the living, the procreating, and the dying. "Man"—and what we are now talking about is the unique, unrepeatable person, who may behave like Hitler or Gautama Buddha, like Newton or the *homme moyen sensuel* or the village idiot. "Man"—and now we have entered the subjective world and are naming the locus (one of the three billion loci) of unshareably private experiences. "Man"—and we are back again in a relatively public universe, recommending virtue to an inheritor of anti-social instincts, and preaching sweet reason to a compound of id, ego, and superego, which is at once the beneficiary and the victim of the particular culture into which it happens to have been born.

Many of the choicest, the most powerfully persuasive effects of theological, ethico-prophetic, and historico-philosophical literature are obtained by enunciating huge generalizations about "man," arguing from these propositions as though they were self-evident major premises, and triumphantly reaching foregone conclusions—all without informing the reader (for that would spoil everything) in which sense, at any given stage of the argument, the word "man" is being used. By this systematic use of double talk, any skillful writer can easily arrive at whatever metaphysical or ethical destination he may wish to reach. People who sprinkle their prose with the monosyllables of Anglo-Saxon scatology or pornography are prosecuted. But, as a matter of plain historical fact, unambiguous four-letter smut has done incomparably less harm in the world than the studied ambiguous use of such three-letter multi-purpose words as "man" and "god," or that grand five-letter heretic-burner and crusade-starter, "Truth"—with the largest possible capital T.

In which of its meanings, we now inquire, is the word "man" being used in our question about the effects on "man's stature" of "man's conquest of space"? There is nothing in the question itself to indicate which kind of "man" is being talked about. But we may assume, I think, that all three principal meanings of the word are involved. If space has in fact been "conquered," the conquest is clearly the work of acculturated man. What in fact has happened is that a very small number of Western scientists and technologists, using all the enormous resources of a modern urban-industrial society, has achieved certain results, which we choose to call the "conquest of space." Up to the present these achievements have been of practical significance only to a tiny handful of human beings. Neither "man," the species, nor "man," the beneficiary and victim of culture, nor yet "man," the psycho-physical organism, unique person, and locus of unshareable experiences, has as yet been discernibly affected by the exploits of Gagarin and Glenn, the collective triumphs of rocketry, guidance systems, and space medicine. These by-products of the armament race have neither increased nor diminished the probability of nuclear war. Nor have they, as yet, contributed to human well-being or to human ill-being in other contexts than that of war. But perhaps at some future date the achievements of the engineers and scientists may be of real consequence to "man," in all the senses of that ambiguous word. It will be our task, in a later paragraph, to consider some of the ways in which the generic, cultural, and personal statures of "man" may be increased or diminished by tomorrow's more far-reaching "conquest of space." Meanwhile, let us look a little more closely into the meaning of this suspiciously picturesque phrase.

Inter- and intra-specific conflict in the service of the instincts is as old as life itself. But exclusively intra-specific conflict, socially organized as war, justified as economic policy, and sanctified as patriotism or a crusade—this is a strictly human invention, coeval with civilization, and a by-product of acculturated man's capacity to create and worship symbols, to hypnotize himself with his own verbiage, to rationalize his ugliest passions, and then to objectify his rationalizations as gods, goals, or ideals. Metaphors drawn from war turn up in the most unexpected contexts and bear witness to the fact that, precisely because he is *sapiens*, *faber*, and *loquax*, acculturated man is also (and up to the present inescapably) *Homo bellicosus*. Thus, a religion professedly of love and spiritual inwardness gets embodied in a *Church Militant*. This Church Militant prays collectively to a *God of Battles*, recruits *Christian Soldiers* and organizes them in *Salvation Armies* and *Companies of Jesus* under the command of *Generals*. Turning from the religious to the intellectual

94

*Socially organized war is a strictly human invention, coeval with civilization
and a by-product of acculturated man's capacity to create and worship symbols,
to hypnotize himself with his own verbiage*

field, we find historians talking of the *march of ideas*, the *overthrow* of
some system of philosophy, say, or medicine or astronomy, and the *victory* of some other system. And within another scientific and technological frame of reference we are treated to loud boasts about man's
conquest of nature, a special case of which is that *conquest of space*
with which we are presently concerned.

In the ethical system of the Greeks, *hubris*—the overweening bumptiousness of individuals or groups in their dealings with other human
beings or with the natural order—was regarded as a very grave and,
since it invited condign punishment, an extremely dangerous form of
delinquency. Monotheism de-sanctified Nature, with the result that,
while *hubris* in relation to one's fellow man was still condemned, *hubris*
in relation to the non-human environment ceased, under the new dispensation, to be regarded as a sacrilege or a breach of the moral code.
And even today, when the consequences of our destructive bumptiousness are threatening, through erosion, through deforestation and soil
exhaustion, through the progressive pollution and depletion of water resources, to render further human progress ever more difficult, perhaps
in a relatively short time impossible—even today the essential wickedness of man's inhumanity to Nature remains unrecognized by the official
spokesmen of morality and religion, by practically everyone, indeed,

*Man, the species, is now living as a parasite upon an earth
which acculturated man is in the process of conquering to the limit*

except a few conservationists and ecologists. Acculturated man's "conquest of nature" goes forward at an accelerating pace—a conquest, unfortunately, analogous to that of the most ruthless imperialist exploiters of the colonial period. Man, the species, is now living as a parasite upon an earth which acculturated man is in the process of conquering to the limit—and the limit is total destruction. Intelligent parasites take care not to kill their hosts; unintelligent parasites push their greed to the point of murder and, destroying their own food supply, commit suicide. Boasting all the while of his prowess as a conqueror, but behaving, while he boasts, less intelligently than the flea or even the hookworm, man, the acculturated parasite, is now busily engaged in murdering his host. It is still possible for him to give up his suicidal vampirism and to establish a symbiotic relationship with his natural environment—still possible, but admittedly (with human numbers threatening to double in less than forty years) very difficult. If this very difficult choice is not made, made soon, and made successfully, acculturated man's misdirected cleverness may conquer nature too thoroughly for the survival of his own high culture, perhaps even for the survival of man, the species.

The picturesque, but wholly inappropriate, military metaphor in terms of which acculturated man has chosen to speak of his parasitic relationship to our planet is now being used in relation to Russian and American successes in launching artificial satellites and putting astronauts into orbit. Space may well be infinite; and, even if finite, the universe is unimaginably vast. In a world where there are galaxies separated from our own by a distance of six billion light-years, any talk by rocket enthusiasts about "man's conquest of space" seems a trifle silly. Men will land on the moon within the next few years, and within a generation, no doubt, will land on Mars. If there is life on Mars, every round trip by an astronaut will involve grave biological dangers for all concerned. Micro-organisms, to which living things on earth possess no inherited or acquired immunity, may be brought back from our sister planet. Conversely, living things on Mars may succumb to the viruses and bacteria introduced by visitors from Earth. The fruits of this first and, in relation to the whole universe, insignificant "conquest of space" might easily prove to be sudden and irreparable disaster for two biological systems, developed through three or four thousand million years of evolution. And of course the same sort of risks would be run by earthlings visiting any life-supporting globe in any part of the universe.

Acculturated man is immensely clever, and his representatives will soon be able to land an astronaut on another planet and bring him back alive. By journalists and political propagandists, this future ability has been nicknamed "the conquest of space." In what way will this "conquest of space" affect "man's stature"?

Obviously, if the coming and going between planets should result in a biological disaster to human beings or their principal sources of nourishment, the stature of man, the species, would be diminished—conceivably to zero. But the worst may never happen. Let us assume, for the sake of argument, that round trips to other planets can be made under completely aseptic conditions or, alternatively, that terrestrial organisms will turn out to be immune to extra-terrestrial bacteria and viruses. In this event, how will the "conquest of space" affect the stature of man, the species, man, the product and producer of culture, and man, the unique individual and locus of unshareable experiences?

Preoccupied as they are with new worlds to conquer, the rocket enthusiasts are apt to forget that their much-touted Space Age is also the Age of Exploding Populations. Like unintelligent parasites draining the lifeblood of their host, three thousand millions of human beings now live, most of them very poorly, on the surface of our planet. By the end of the twentieth century there will be, in all probability, six thousand millions, desperately trying to extract twice as much food and, if industrialization becomes general, four times as much water and at least ten times as much fossil fuel and metallic ore as are being extracted from

The rocket enthusiasts are apt to forget that their much-touted Space Age is also the Age of Exploding Populations

the earth today. When the attention of our high-flying rocket enthusiasts is called down to these simple, grisly facts of terrestrial arithmetic, they airily insist that the demographic problem of man, the species, together with all the social, political, and economic problems stemming from the enormous and accelerating increase in human members, can be solved very simply. How? By shooting two or three billion people into space and telling them to go and colonize some other planet.

This method of increasing the stature of man, the species, by peopling other worlds with the overplus of this world's numbers was proposed many years ago by Professor J. B. S. Haldane in his *Possible Worlds* and again in the *Last and First Men* of Olaf Stapledon. Inasmuch as their authors thought in terms of startling genetic changes and enormous lapses of time, these books may be described as Evolutionary Utopias. Given enough time, evolution can accomplish practically anything. In the course of the last three or four billion years it has performed the almost infinitely improbable feat of developing a human being out of a giant molecule. In the future, directed by human intelligence, it might perform hardly less improbable feats in considerably shorter periods of time. But by the standards of human history, even these shorter periods will be extremely long. In the Evolutionary Utopias of Haldane and Stapledon many thousands, even millions, of years were required for the development, by controlled breeding, of new sub-races of human beings capable of surviving and reproducing themselves in the forbidding en-

98

vironments of other planets. The rocket enthusiasts seem to imagine that migration to some wholly alien world could be undertaken, within the next hundred years or so, by men and women in no way different, genetically speaking, from ourselves. Being engineers and not life scientists, they are pretty certainly mistaken in this matter. In the present context it is the Utopian dreamers of biological dreams, not the so-called "practical men," who make sense. And even in relation to such an easily calculable factor as expense, the rocket enthusiasts are wildly unrealistic. To land as few as five thousand adequately equipped colonists on another planet would cost several times the combined budgets of the U.S.A. and the U.S.S.R. Morever, even if it were physically, financially, and politically feasible to fire off whole boatloads of emigrants into outer space, would the forcible displacement of, say, five hundred million uprooted men and women solve the primary demographic problem, or any of the related social, political, and economic problems, now confronting us? During the nineteenth century millions of Europeans emigrated to the New World; but Europe's political and economic problems were not thereby eliminated, and Europe's population went on steadily increasing, as though nothing out of the ordinary had happened. There seems to be no good reason for supposing that emigration to Mars will do more for Earth as a whole than emigration to the Americas and the Antipodes did for nineteenth-century Europe.

We see, then, that our "conquest of space" is a conquest only in some picturesquely Pickwickian sense. It seems very unlikely, at least in the near future, that man, the species, will increase his stature by becoming a cosmic imperialist. Moreover, even if cosmic imperialism should ever be within our power, the colonization of other planets will bring no automatic solution to this planet's demographic, political, and economic problems. Man, the species, might add a few cubits to his stature; but the stature of acculturated man, of the creature who, for all these centuries, has been trying to make a go of collective living, will probably remain as low as it has been in the past and is today.

In the preceding paragraphs, the word "stature" has been treated as a word with a meaning expressible in concrete terms. Thus, if man, the species, should ever become a cosmic imperialist, his stature will increase in proportion to the number and size of his extra-terrestrial colonies. And if, in spite of the extra-terrestrial colonies, the stature of acculturated man should fail to increase, it will be because of some observable and even measurable failure to solve the age-old problems of collective living here on earth. But the meaning of the phrase "man's stature" is not always expressible in concrete and measurable terms. It may, and in fact often does, refer to a merely notional entity—the image which acculturated man forms of himself, when he starts to philosophize.

*In a totemistic, magic-practicing and fertility-worshiping society,
"man" has the same stature as all the other denizens of a world
in which everything is simultaneously natural and supernatural*

Used in this way, the phrase "man's stature" stands for the fancies and
beliefs about human nature current at any given time and place. Thus,
in a totemistic, magic-practicing, and fertility-worshiping society, "man"
(in all the senses of that word) has the same stature as all the other
denizens of a world in which everything is simultaneously natural and
supernatural. With the emergence of self-consciousness comes a change
in metaphysical perspective. Acculturated man separates himself from
the rest of nature, and the stature he now assigns himself is radically
different from the stature assigned to every other kind of creature. He
sees himself as a member of a species unlike all other species, the final
masterpiece of a Creator who has framed the inferior world of nature
for man's benefit and with an eye to man's moral and spiritual education. In medieval Christendom "man's stature"—the current notions, in
other words, about human nature and its place in the universe—was at
once gigantic and dwarfish. Man, the species, man, the beneficiary and
victim of culture, man, the unique individual and locus of unshareable

experiences, was the central figure in a tiny spherical cosmos, constructed expressly for the education of human beings and administered by a supernatural dyarchy, with one seat of government in heaven and another, underground, in hell. In this stuffy little all-too-human universe, words did not stand for given things; on the contrary, things stood for given words—words in the Bible or in one of the treatises of Aristotle. Nothing was studied for its own sake, but only for the sake of what it was supposed symbolically to signify. Projected into the external world, reminiscences of Roman law, Greek metaphysics, Pauline theology, Arabian astronomy, and old wives' tales of magic were rediscovered "out there" and triumphantly recognized as cosmic facts. Inasmuch as medieval man had created a world in the image of his own culturally conditioned mind, his "stature" seemed heroic. But this self-image was heroic only in relation to the windowless, artificially lighted echo-chamber which busy metaphysicians had scooped out of the totally mysterious datum of a cosmos probably infinitely extended and perhaps indefinitely self-renewing. In relation to this other universe—the universe that has gradually revealed itself to later observers—the "stature" of medieval man shrinks from the heroic to the bumptiously absurd. But, like the acculturated man of every other period and place, Europe's medieval man was something more and other than the victim-beneficiary of the locally current thought patterns. Medieval man was also man, the psychophysical organism, the unique person and locus of unshareable experiences. As such, he could always break out of the haunted echo-chamber that he had been taught to regard as the universe—could always escape from his notional prison into the wordless freedom of instinct and animality on the one hand, of mystical spirituality on the other. For the many there were sex, strong drink, and the recurrent orgies of a paganism that obstinately refused to die; and for the few there was the way of contemplation, the flight of the alone to the Alone. What passed for the universe might be no more than a grotesque projection of organized ignorance bumptiously proclaiming that it was in possession of absolute Truth; but above and parallel with his notional world stretched the boundless, unverbalized realities of unshareable subjective experience. The victim-beneficiaries of medieval culture retained their sanity by periodically de-conditioning themselves and becoming, for a little while, centers of pure receptivity, open to the dark gods, or the gods of light, or to both sets of deities alternately or even simultaneously. What was done by the prisoners of medieval European culture has been done, and is still being done, by the victim-beneficiaries of every other culture. A totally acculturated man would be a monster. Sanity and humanity can be maintained only by regular escapes from culture into the unconsciousness of sleep, and by occasional conscious escapes into "peak experiences" on the animal, aesthetic, or mystical levels. Measured

HEAVEN AND HELL: THIRTEENTH-CENTURY ILLUMINATION
*In medieval Christendom ... man ... was the central figure in a tiny spherical cosmos,
constructed expressly for the education of human beings
and administered by a supernatural dyarchy with one seat
of government in heaven and another underground in hell*

in terms of the number and quality of his unshareable peak experiences,
the "stature" of a victim of socially organized ignorance and insanity may
be much higher than that of the too-docile beneficiary of even the most
admirable culture.

I t seems hardly necessary to point out that the transformation of the
haunted echo-chamber of medieval culture into the universe of
modern science had been going on for several hundred years before anyone began talking about the "conquest of space." The Copernican revolution of the sixteenth century was followed by a succession of scientific
revolutions no less prodigious—revolutions in astronomy, in physics, in
chemistry, in geology, in biology and paleontology; revolutions, at the
same time, in technology, so that we are now equipped with fantastically
powerful instruments for the exploration of the external world and the

analysis of its fine structure. Observations from the surface of the airless moon, or from an artificial satellite outside the earth's obscuring atmosphere, will undoubtedly provide new information about the stars in our own galaxy and about the other galaxies within the range of our instruments. But, in the present context, the significant fact is that, long before space was "conquered," it was thoroughly observed. The probably infinite, perhaps everlasting and self-renewing universe, which has replaced the haunted echo-chamber of earlier centuries, was gradually constructed by logical thought working upon the raw materials provided by earth-based observers.

In relation to the fathomless mystery of a cosmos which future observations from somewhere "out there" will doubtless render even more mysterious, what has happened to "man's stature"? In other words, what kinds of self-image have been current among acculturated people since the replacement of the haunted echo-chamber by the ever vaster and ever more enigmatic universes described by successive generations of cosmologists? The combination of Cartesian dualism with post-Copernican astronomy, post-Lyellian geology, post-Maxwellian physics, and post-Darwinian evolutionary theory resulted, for a time, in a considerable diminution of "man's stature." In a cosmos of infinite extensions and durations, in which matter (in the pejorative, Platonic sense of that word) was regarded as the only genuinely real reality, and where mind, in consequence, could be nothing but an irrelevant epiphenomenon, acculturated man could hardly fail to think poorly of human nature—could hardly fail to hanker nostalgically for the coziness of the home-made medieval cosmos, the soul-satisfying indubitabilities of the scholastic world view. Each in his own way, Lyell, Herschel, Maxwell, and Darwin were mighty conquerors of space, time, and matter. But for many of their more sensitive contemporaries, these scientific conquests were cultural and psychological defeats. The realization that they were living at the heart of a four-dimensional infinity was somehow appalling to the victim-beneficiaries of a tradition which had so recently proclaimed that the world was created in 4004 B.C. and was destined, within some few centuries, to be uncreated, judged, and definitely disposed of for all eternity. Confronted by boundless space and endless time, many Europeans lost their faith. And it was not only in Adam and Eve, in Noah's ark and Joshua's trumpet, that they had ceased to believe. What had been undermined was their faith in themselves, in the human mind as a discoverer of reality and maintainer of values.

It is interesting to note that the beneficiaries and victims of Indic culture have never had the slightest difficulty in reconciling the idea of infinite time and infinite space with the idea of the potentially infinite value of the human spirit. A ninth-century Mahayana Buddhist, for example, would have felt completely at home in the universe of twentieth-century astronomy, with its observed distances of billions of light-years, its island galaxies, its innumerable stars and, presumably, habitable planets. The silent gulfs of space which Pascal found so terrifying, the endless vistas of that "mere matter" so much despised and hated by the Platonists would have left him completely undisturbed. Brought up to accept as self-evident the philosophy of the Greater Vehicle, he knew that Mind, Suchness, the Buddha Nature, the Void, is totally present at every instant of time and at every point in space. He knew too that to be conscious of the primordial fact is enlightenment and that, as a human being, he was capable of such awareness and so might become the Buddha that, in essence, he had always been.

In the West, as we have seen, scientific progress seemed, for a time, to entail a grave diminution of "man's stature." Everything human, it seemed, had been reduced to something less than human, every positive value was merely a negative value in fancy dress. In recent decades the dualistic and reductionist philosophy, which once transformed successive scientific conquests into human defeats, has been replaced, in the minds of many thinkers, by a world view a good deal more like that of the Mahayanists or of those fourteenth-century Chinese thinkers, whose philosophy, with its blending of Confucian, Taoist, and Buddhist elements, exercised an influence, by way of the missionaries, on Leibniz and (as Joseph Needham has pointed out in his great *History of Chinese Science*) anticipated, six hundred years too soon, many of the fundamental ideas of modern organicism. Modern organicism had its proximate roots in the speculations of Driesch and J. S. Haldane. In Lloyd Morgan's hands it became a doctrine of Emergent Evolution, according to which, with every increase in the complexity of organization, new and unpredictable characteristics emerge into manifest existence. Thus, molecular characteristics emerge from a higher organization of atoms; colloidal characteristics from a higher organization of molecules, and so on, up through cells, tissues, organs, organisms of greater and greater complexity, societies of organisms. Organicist ideas are fundamental in Whitehead's world view. In another form they reappear in the work of an eminent philosophical biologist, Ludwig von Bertalanffy. And here, in translation, is a notable paragraph from the work of that evolutionary scientist who was also a mystic, Father Teilhard de Chardin. There is, says Teilhard, "a third perspective, neither mechanistic nor vitalistic, towards which the new Physics and the new Philosophy seem to be converging—the conception that Mind is neither something superimposed, nor a mere accessory within the cosmos, but that it simply represents the state of higher organization assumed within ourselves and around us by that indefinable something which we may call, for lack of a better phrase, 'the stuff of the universe.' Nothing more, but also nothing less. Mind is neither a meta-, nor yet an epi-phenomenon: it is THE phenomenon."

We are now, it seems to me, in a position to answer our final question—the question about "man's stature," or (if we prefer to speak a little less portentously and more accurately) "modern Western man's self-image." The "conquest of space," whether by rocket or by radio telescope and two hundred-inch reflector, is not something which, of itself, can either increase or decrease our "stature." Its effects upon a man's view of himself depend entirely upon the nature of the philosophical frame of reference within which the results of the "conquest" are thought about. To those whose world view is dualistic and reductionist, the "conquest" of an infinity of blank space and mindless matter will bring an ever more oppressive sense of human loneliness, insignificance, and futility. By those, on the contrary, who believe (and feel that they have good reason to believe) that even atoms are organisms and possess psychoid aspects which, at progressively higher levels of organization, will emerge into life and consciousness, by those for whom, in Teilhard's words, mind is not a meta- nor an epi-phenomenon, but simply THE phenomenon, the "conquests" of science will be thought about in a very different way. These people will see themselves not as isolated and irrelevant centers of consciousness at the heart of universal mindlessness but as integral parts of an organic world, in which the potentialities of mind have always been present. They will see themselves as the emerged and still emergent products of a vast evolutionary process that has already actualized some of these potentialities and can, as individual and social organization rises to higher levels, actualize many more. Let us hope, too, that they may come to see themselves not as the murderous and suicidal "conquerors" of Nature and one another but as purposeful and responsible collaborators with the evolutionary process that is perpetually creating, transforming, and transfiguring the world.

HANNAH ARENDT, political scientist and philosopher, was born in
Hanover, Germany, in 1906. She was educated in Königsberg and at Heidel-
berg University where she studied under the existentialist philosopher Karl
Jaspers, receiving her Doctor of Philosophy degree in 1928. With the advent
of the Nazi regime in 1933, she fled from Germany to Paris, remaining there
until the fall of France in 1940. She emigrated to the United States in 1941.
With the publication of *The Origins of Totalitarianism* in 1951, her reputation
as a profound and original thinker was firmly established. Since then, she has
published three other important works (*The Human Condition, Between Past
and Future,* and *On Revolution*), and has written a series of articles on the trial
of Adolf Eichmann for *The New Yorker,* published in 1963 in a book entitled
Eichmann in Jerusalem. She has taught at several major universities, including
Princeton, Columbia, and California. Recently, she has been in residence at the
Center for Advanced Studies, Wesleyan University; she is now associated with
the Committee on Social Thought at the University of Chicago.

The question raised here is addressed to the layman, not the scientist, and it is inspired by the humanist's concern with man, as distinguished from the physicist's concern with the reality of the physical world. To understand physical reality seems to demand not only the renunciation of an anthropocentric or geocentric world view, but also a radical elimination of all anthropomorphic elements and principles, as they arise either from the world given to the five human senses or from the categories inherent in the human mind. The question assumes that man is the highest being we know of, an assumption which we have inherited from the Romans, whose *humanitas* was so alien to the Greek frame of mind that they had not even a word for it.[1] This view of man is even more alien to the scientist, to whom man is no more than a special case of organic life, and to whom man's habitat—the earth, together with earthbound laws—is no more than a special borderline case of absolute, universal laws, that is, laws which rule the immensity of the universe. Surely, the scientist cannot permit himself to ask: What consequences will the result of my investigations have for the stature (or, for that matter, for the future) of man? It has been the glory of modern science that it has been able to emancipate itself completely from all such truly humanistic concerns.

The question propounded here, insofar as it is addressed to the layman, must be answered in terms of common sense and in everyday language (if it can be answered at all). The answer is not likely to convince the scientist, because he has been forced, under the compulsion of facts and experiments, to renounce sense perception and hence common sense, by which we co-ordinate the perception of our five senses into the total awareness of reality. He has also been forced to renounce normal language, which even in its most sophisticated conceptual refinements remains inextricably bound to the world of the senses and to our common sense. For the scientist, man is no more than an observer of the universe in its manifold manifestations. The progress of modern science has demonstrated very forcefully to what an extent this observed universe, the infinitely small no less than the infinitely large, escapes not only the coarseness of human sense perception but even the enormously

---

1 The reason for the absence of the word *humanitas* in Greek language and thought was that the Greeks, in contrast to the Romans, never thought that man is the highest being there is. Aristotle calls this belief *atopos*, "absurd." See *Nicomachean Ethics*, Book VI, Ch. 7, 1141a, 20 ff. (Vol. 9, p. 390a-c).

ingenious instruments which have been built for its refinement. The phenomena with which modern physical research is concerned turn up like "mysterious messenger[s] from the real world,"[2] and we know no more about them than that they affect our measuring instruments in a certain way, suspecting all the while that "the former have as much resemblance to the latter as a telephone number has to a subscriber."[3]

The goal of modern science, which eventually and quite literally has led us to the moon, is no longer "to augment and order" human experiences (as Niels Bohr, still tied to a vocabulary which his own work has helped to make obsolete, described it[4]); it is much rather to discover what lies *behind* natural phenomena as they reveal themselves to the senses and the mind of man. Had the scientist reflected upon the nature of the human sensory and mental apparatus, had he raised questions such as *What is the nature of man and what should be his stature? What is the goal of science and why does man pursue knowledge?* or even *What is life and what distinguishes human from animal life?*, he would never have arrived where modern science stands today. The answers to these questions would have acted as definitions and hence as limitations of his efforts. In the words of Niels Bohr, "Only by renouncing an explanation of life in the ordinary sense do we gain a possibility of taking into account its characteristics."[5]

That the question proposed here makes no sense to the scientist *qua* scientist is no argument against it. The question challenges the layman and the humanist to sit in judgment over what the scientist is doing, and this debate must of course be joined by the scientists themselves insofar as they are fellow citizens. But all answers given in this debate, whether they come from laymen or philosophers or scientists, are non-scientific (though not anti-scientific); they can never be demonstrably true or false. Their truth resembles rather the validity of agreements than the compelling validity of scientific statements. Even when the answers are given by philosophers whose way of life is solitude, they are arrived at by an exchange of opinions among many men, most of whom may no longer be among the living. Such truth can never command general agreement, but it frequently outlasts the compellingly and demonstrably true statements of the sciences which, especially in recent times, have the uncomfortable inclination never to stay put, although at any given

2 Max Planck, *The Universe in the Light of Modern Physics* (1929) in *The Great Ideas Today 1962*, p. 494.
3 Arthur Eddington, quoted by J. W. N. Sullivan, *Limitations of Science* (New York: The New American Library of World Literature, Inc., Mentor Books), p. 141.
4 In *Atomic Physics and Human Knowledge* (New York: John Wiley & Sons, Inc., 1958), p. 88.
5 *Ibid.*, p. 76.

moment they are, and must be, valid for all. In other words, notions such as life, or man, or science, or knowledge are pre-scientific by definition, and the question is whether or not the actual development of science which has led to the conquest of terrestrial space and to the invasion of the space of the universe has changed these notions to such an extent that they no longer make sense. For the point of the matter is, of course, that modern science—no matter what its origins and original goals—has changed and reconstructed the world we live in so radically that it could be argued that the layman and the humanist, still trusting their common sense and communicating in everyday language, are out of touch with reality, and that their questions and anxieties have become irrelevant. Who cares about the stature of man when he can go to the moon? This sort of bypassing the question would be very tempting indeed if it were true that we have come to live in a world which only the scientists "understand." They would then be in the position of the "few" whose superior knowledge entitles them to rule the "many," namely, the laymen and the humanists and the philosophers, or all those who raise pre-scientific questions because of ignorance.

This division between the scientist and the layman, however, is very far from the truth. The fact is not merely, that the scientist spends more than half of his life in the same world of sense perception, of common sense, and of everyday language as his fellow citizens, but that he has come in his own privileged field of activity to a point where the naïve questions and anxieties of the layman have made themselves felt very forcefully, albeit in a different manner. The scientist has not only left behind the layman with his limited understanding, he has left behind himself and his own power of understanding, which is still human understanding, when he goes to work in the laboratory and begins to communicate in mathematical language. The miracle of modern science is indeed that this science could be purged "of all anthropomorphic elements," because the purging itself was done by men.[6] The theoretical perplexities which have confronted the new non-anthropocentric and non-geocentric (or heliocentric) science because its data refuse to be ordered by any of the natural mental categories of the human brain are well enough known. In the words of Erwin Schrödinger, the new universe which we try to "conquer" is not only "practically inaccessible, but not even thinkable," for "however we think it, it is wrong; not perhaps quite as meaningless as a 'triangular circle,' but much more so than a 'winged lion.' "[7]

Even these perplexities, since they are of a theoretical nature and perhaps concern only the few, are nothing compared to such paradoxes

6 Planck, *op. cit.*, p. 503.
7 In *Science and Humanism* (London: Cambridge University Press, 1951), pp. 25-26.

In our everyday world, electronic "brains" devised and constructed by men
cannot only do man's brain work incomparably better and more swiftly,
but can do "what a human brain cannot comprehend"

existing in our everyday world as electronic "brains," devised and constructed by men, which cannot only do man's brain work incomparably
better and more swiftly (this, after all, is the outstanding characteristic
of all machines), but can do "what a human brain cannot *comprehend.*"[8]
The often-mentioned "lag" of the social sciences with respect to the
natural sciences or of man's political development with respect to his
technical and scientific know-how is no more than a red herring drawn
into this debate, and can only divert attention from the main problem,
which is that man can *do*, and successfully do, what he cannot comprehend and cannot express in everyday human language.

It may be noteworthy that, among the scientists, it was primarily the
older generation, men like Einstein and Planck, Niels Bohr and Schrödinger, who were most acutely worried about this state of affairs which
their own work had chiefly brought about. They were still firmly rooted
in a tradition which demanded that scientific theories fulfill certain
definitely humanistic requirements such as simplicity, beauty, and
harmony. A theory was still supposed to be "satisfactory," namely, satisfactory to human reason in that it served to "save the phenomena," to
explain all observed facts. Even today, we still hear that "modern
physicists are inclined to believe in the validity of general relativity for
esthetic reasons, because it is mathematically so elegant and philosophic-

8 George Gamow, "Physical Sciences and Technology," in *The Great Ideas Today
1962*, p. 207 (italics added).

ally so satisfying."[9] Einstein's extreme reluctance to sacrifice the principle of causality as Planck's Quantum Theory demanded is well known; his main objection was of course that with it all lawfulness was about to depart from the universe, that it was as though God ruled the world by "playing dice." And since his own discoveries had come about through a "remoulding and generalizing [of] the whole edifice of classical physics . . . lending to our world picture a unity surpassing all previous expectations," it seems only natural that Einstein tried to come to terms with the new theories of his colleagues and his successors through "the search for a more complete conception," through a new and surpassing generalization.[10] But Planck himself, though fully aware that the Quantum Theory, in contrast to the Theory of Relativity, signified a complete break with classical physical theory, held it to be "essential for the healthy development of physics that among the postulates of this science we reckon, not merely the existence of law in general, but also the strictly causal character of this law."[11]

It may be noteworthy that, among scientists, it was primarily the older generation, men like Einstein, who were most acutely worried about the main problem in this debate

Niels Bohr, however, went one step further. For him, causality, determinism, and necessity of laws belonged to the categories of "our necessarily prejudiced conceptual frame," and he was no longer frightened when he met "in atomic phenomena regularities of quite a new kind, defying deterministic pictorial description."[12] The trouble is that what defies description in terms of the "prejudices" of the human mind defies description in every conceivable way of human language; it can no longer be described at all, and it is being expressed, but not described, in mathematical processes. Bohr still hoped that, since "no experience is definable without a logical frame," these new experiences would in due time fall into place through "an appropriate widening of the conceptual framework" which would also

---

9 Sergio de Benedetti, quoted by Walter Sullivan, "Physical Sciences and Technology," in *The Great Ideas Today 1961*, p. 198.
10 Niels Bohr, *op. cit.*, pp. 70 and 61 respectively. See also Planck, *op. cit.*, who called the Theory of Relativity "the completion and culmination of the structure of classical physics" (p. 493), its very "crowning point" (p. 517).
11 *Ibid*, p. 514.
12 Bohr, *op. cit.*, pp. 31 and 71 respectively.

remove all present paradoxes and "apparent disharmonies."[13] But this hope, I am afraid, will be disappointed. The categories and ideas of human reason have their ultimate source in the human senses, and all conceptual or metaphysical language is actually and strictly metaphorical. Moreover, the human brain which supposedly does our thinking is as terrestrial, earthbound, as any other part of the human body. It was precisely by abstracting from these terrestrial conditions, by appealing to a power of imagination and abstraction which would, as it were, lift the human mind out of the gravitational field of the earth and look down upon her from some point in the universe, that modern science reached its most glorious and, at the same time, most baffling achievements.

In 1929, shortly before the arrival of the Atomic Revolution, marked by the splitting of the atom and the conquest of universal space, Planck demanded that the results obtained by mathematical processes "must be translated back into the language of the world of our senses if they are to be of any use to us." The three decades which have passed since these words were written have proved not only that such translation seems less and less possible, and that the loss of contact between the physical world view and the sense world has become even more conspicuous, but also—and in our context this is even more alarming—that this has by no means meant that results of this new science are of no practical use, or that the new world view "would be no better than a bubble ready to burst at the first puff of wind."[14] On the contrary, one is tempted to say that it is much more likely that the planet we inhabit will go up in smoke as a consequence of theories which are entirely unrelated to the world of the senses, and defy all description in human language, than that even a *hurricane* will cause the theories to burst like a bubble.

It is, I think, safe to say that nothing was more alien to the minds of the scientists, who brought about the most radical and the most rapid revolutionary process the world has ever seen, than any will to power. Nothing was more remote than any wish to "conquer space" and to go to the moon. Nor were they prompted by an unseemly curiosity in the sense of a *temptatio oculorum*. It was indeed their search for "true reality" which led them to lose confidence in appearances, in the phenomena as they reveal themselves of their own accord to human sense and reason. They were inspired by an extraordinary love of harmony and lawfulness which taught them that they would have to step outside any merely given sequence or series of occurrences if they wanted to discover the over-all beauty and order of the whole, that is, the universe. (This may explain why they have been much less distressed

13 *Ibid.*, p. 82.
14 Planck, *op. cit.*, pp. 509 and 505 respectively.

by the fact that their discoveries served the invention of the most murderous gadgets than they have been disturbed by the shattering of all their most cherished ideals of necessity and lawfulness. These ideals were lost when the scientists discovered that there is nothing indivisible in matter, no *a-tomos*, that we live in an expanding, non-limited universe, and that chance seems to rule supreme wherever this "true reality," the physical world, has receded entirely from the range of human senses and from the range of all instruments by which their coarseness was refined.)

The modern scientific enterprise began with thoughts never thought before (Copernicus imagined he was "standing in the sun . . . overlooking the planets")[15] and with things never seen before (Galileo's telescope pierced the distance between earth and sky and delivered the secrets of the stars to human cognition "with all the certainty of sense evidence").[16] It reached its classic expression with Newton's law of gravitation, in which the same equation covers the movements of the heavenly bodies and the motion of terrestrial things on earth. Einstein indeed only generalized this science of the modern age when he introduced an "observer who is poised freely in space," and not just at one definite point like the sun, and he proved that not only Copernicus but also Newton still required "that the universe should have a kind of center" although this center of course was no longer the earth.[17] It is in fact quite obvious that the scientists' strongest intellectual motivation was Einstein's "striving after generalization," and that if they appealed to power at all, it was the interconnected formidable power of abstraction and imagination. Even today, when billions of dollars are spent year in and year out for highly "useful" projects which are the immediate results of the development of pure, theoretical science, and when the actual power of countries and governments depends upon the performance of many thousands of researchers, the physicist is still likely to look down upon all these space scientists as mere "plumbers."[18]

However, the sad truth of the matter is that the lost contact between the world of the senses and appearances and the physical world view has been re-established not by the pure scientist but by the "plumber." The technicians, who account today for the overwhelming majority of all "researchers," have brought the results of the scientists down to earth.

15 See J. Bronowski, *Science and Human Values* (New York: Julian Messner, Inc., 1956), p. 22.
16 *The Starry Messenger* in *Discoveries and Opinions of Galileo* (Garden City, N.Y.: Doubleday & Company, Inc., Doubleday Anchor Books, 1957) p. 28.
17 Albert Einstein, *Relativity, The Special and General Theory* (1905 and 1916) in *The Great Ideas Today 1961*, pp. 452 and 465 respectively.
18 See Walter Sullivan, *op. cit.*, p. 189.

GALILEO DEMONSTRATING HIS TELESCOPE
*Galileo's telescope . . . delivered the secrets of the stars to human cognition
"with all the certainty of sense evidence"*

And even though the scientist is still beset by paradoxes and the most bewildering perplexities, the very fact that a whole technology could develop out of his results demonstrates the "soundness" of his theories and hypotheses more convincingly than any merely scientific observation or experiment ever could. It is perfectly true that the scientist himself does not want to go to the moon; he knows that for his purposes unmanned spaceships carrying the best instruments human ingenuity can invent will do the job of exploring the moon's surface much better than dozens of astronauts. And yet, an actual change of the human world, the conquest of space or whatever we may wish to call it, is achieved only when manned space carriers are shot into the universe, so that man himself can go where up to now only human imagination and its power of abstraction, or human ingenuity and its power of fabrication, could reach. To be sure, all we plan to do now is to explore our own immediate surroundings in the universe, the infinitely small place which the human race could reach even if it were to travel with the velocity of light. In view of man's life span—the only absolute limitation left at the present moment—it is quite unlikely that he will ever go much farther. But even for this limited job, we have to leave the world of our senses and of our bodies, not only in imagination but in reality.

It is as though Einstein's imagined "observer poised in free space" —surely the creation of the human mind and its power of abstraction—is being followed by a bodily observer who must behave as though he were a mere child of abstraction and imagination. It is at this point that all the theoretical perplexities of the new physical world view intrude as realities upon man's everyday world and throw out of gear his "natural," that is, earthbound, common sense. He would, for instance, be confronted in reality with Einstein's famous "twin paradox," which hypothetically assumes that "a twin brother who takes off on a space journey in which he travels at a sizeable fraction of the speed of light would return to find his earthbound twin either older than he or little more than a dim recollection in the memory of his descendants."[19] For though many physicists had found this paradox difficult to swallow, the "clock paradox," on which it is based, seems to have been verified experimentally, so that the only alternative to it would be the assumption that earthbom life under all circumstances remains bound to a time concept that demonstrably does not belong among "true realities," but among "mere appearances." We have reached the stage where the Cartesian radical doubt of reality as such, the first philosophical answer to the discoveries of science in the modern age, may become subject to physical experiments which would make short shrift of Descartes's famous consolation, *I doubt therefore I am*, and of his conviction that, whatever the state of reality and of truth as they are given to the senses and to reason, you cannot "doubt of your doubt and remain uncertain whether you doubt or not."[20]

T he magnitude of the space enterprise seems to me beyond dispute, and all objections raised against it on the purely utilitarian level— that it is too expensive, that the money were better spent on education and the improvement of the citizens, on the fight against poverty and disease, or whatever other worthy purposes may come to mind—sound to me slightly absurd, out of tune with the things that are at stake and whose consequences today appear still quite unpredictable. There is, moreover, another reason why I think these arguments are beside the point. They are singularly inapplicable because the enterprise itself

---

19 *Ibid.*, p. 202.
20 I quote from Descartes's dialogue *The Search after Truth by the Light of Nature*, where his central position in this matter of doubting is even more in evidence than in the *Principles*. (*Philosophical Works of Descartes*, ed. by E. S. Haldane and G. R. T. Ross, London: Cambridge University Press, 1931; Vol. I, pp. 324, 315.)

could come about only through an amazing development of man's scientific capabilities. The very integrity of science demands that not only utilitarian considerations but even the reflection upon the stature of man be left in abeyance. Has not each of the advances of science, since the time of Copernicus, almost automatically resulted in a decrease in his stature? Man, insofar as he is a scientist, does not care about his own stature in the universe or about his position on the evolutionary ladder of animal life; this "carelessness" is his pride and his glory. The simple fact that physicists split the atom without any hesitations the very moment they knew how to do it, although they realized full well the enormous destructive potentialities of their operation, demonstrates that the scientist *qua* scientist does not even care about the survival of the human race on earth or, for that matter, about the survival of the planet itself. All associations for "Atoms for Peace," all warnings not to use the new power unwisely, and even the pangs of conscience many scientists felt when the first bombs fell on Hiroshima and Nagasaki cannot obscure this simple, elementary fact. For in all these efforts the scientists acted not as scientists but as citizens, and if their voices have more authority than the voices of laymen, they do so only because the scientists are in possession of more precise information. Valid and plausible arguments against the "conquest of space" could be raised only if they were to show that the whole enterprise might be self-defeating in its own terms.

There are a few indications that such might indeed be the case. If we leave out of account the human life span, which under no circumstances (even if biology should succeed in extending it significantly and man were able to travel with the speed of light) will permit man to explore more than his immediate surroundings in the immensity of the universe, the most significant indication that it might be self-defeating consists in Heisenberg's discovery of the uncertainty principle. Heisenberg showed conclusively that there is a definite and final limit to the accuracy of all measurements obtainable by man-devised instruments. In his own words, "We decide, by our selection of the type of observation employed, which aspects of nature are to be determined and which are to be blurred."[21] He holds that "the most important new result of nuclear physics was the recognition of the possibility of applying quite different types of natural laws, without contradiction, to one and the same physical event. This is due to the fact that within a system of laws which are based on certain fundamental ideas only certain quite definite ways of asking questions make sense, and thus, that such a system is separated

---

21 Werner Heisenberg, *Philosophic Problems of Nuclear Science* (New York: Pantheon Books, 1952), p. 73.

*The astronaut, shot into outer space and imprisoned
in his instrument-ridden capsule, might well be taken
as the symbolic incarnation of Heisenberg's man*

from others which allow different questions to be put."[22] From this he
concludes that the modern search for "true reality" behind mere appearances, which has brought about the world we live in and resulted in the
Atomic Revolution, has led into a situation in the sciences themselves
in which man has lost the very objectivity of the natural world, so that
man in his hunt for "objective reality" suddenly discovers that he always
"confronts himself alone."[23]

The truth of Heisenberg's observation seems to me to transcend by
far the field of strictly scientific endeavor and to gain in poignancy if it
is applied to the technology that has grown out of modern science. Every
progress in science in the last decades, from the moment it was absorbed
into technology and thus introduced into the factual world where we live
our everyday lives, has brought with it a veritable avalanche of fabulous
instruments and ever more ingenious machinery. All of this makes it
more unlikely every day that man will encounter anything in the world
around him that is not man-made and hence is not, in the last analysis,
he himself in a different disguise. The astronaut, shot into outer space

22 *Ibid.,* p. 24.
23 Heisenberg, *The Physicist's Conception of Nature* (New York: Harcourt, Brace
& Co., 1958), p. 24.

and imprisoned in his instrument-ridden capsule where each actual physical encounter with his surroundings would spell immediate death might well be taken as the symbolic incarnation of Heisenberg's man—the man who will be the less likely ever to meet anything but himself the more ardently he wishes to eliminate all anthropocentric considerations from his encounter with the non-human world around him.

It is at this point, it seems to me, that the humanist's concern with man and the stature of man has caught up with the scientist. It is as though the sciences had done what the humanities never could have achieved, namely, to prove demonstrably the validity of this concern. The situation, as it presents itself today, oddly resembles an elaborate verification of a remark by Franz Kafka, written at the very beginning of this development: Man he said, "found the Archimedean point, but he used it against himself; it seems that he was permitted to find it only under this condition." For the conquest of space, the search for a point outside the earth from which it would be possible to unhinge, as it were, the planet itself, is no accidental result of the modern age's science. This was from its very beginnings not a "natural" but a universal science, it was not a physics but an astrophysics which looked upon the earth from a point in the universe. In terms of this development, the attempt to conquer space means that man hopes he will be able to journey to the Archimedean point which he anticipated by sheer force of abstraction and imagination. However, in doing so, he will necessarily lose his advantage. All he can find is the Archimedean point with respect to the earth, but once arrived there and having acquired this absolute power over his earthly habitat, he would need a new Archimedean point, and so *ad infinitum.* In other words, man can only get lost in the immensity of the universe, for the only true Archimedean point would be the absolute void behind the universe.

Yet even if man recognizes that there might be absolute limits to his search for truth and that it might be wise to suspect such limitations whenever it turns out that the scientist can do more than he is capable of comprehending, and even if he realizes that he cannot "conquer space," but at best make a few discoveries in our solar system, the journey into space and to the Archimedean point with respect to the earth is far from being a harmless or unequivocally triumphant enterprise. It could add to the stature of man inasmuch as man, in distinction from other living things, desires to be at home in a "territory" as large as possible. In that case, he would only take possession of what is his own, although it took him a long time to discover it. These new possessions, like all property, would have to be limited, and once the limit is reached and the limitations established, the new world view which may conceivably grow out of it is likely to be once more geocentric and anthropomorphic, though not in the old sense of the earth being the center of the universe and of man being the highest being there is. It would be geocentric in the sense that the earth, and not the universe, is the center and the home of mortal men, and it would be anthropomorphic in the sense that man would count his own factual mortality among the elementary conditions under which his scientific efforts are possible at all.

At this moment, the prospects for such an entirely beneficial development and solution of the present predicaments of modern science and technology do not look particularly good. We have come to our present capacity to "conquer space" through our new ability to handle nature from a point in the universe outside the earth. For this is what we actually do when we release energy processes that ordinarily go on only in the sun, or attempt to initiate in a test tube the processes of cosmic evolution, or build machines for the production and control of energies unknown in the household of earthly nature. Without as yet actually occupying the point where Archimedes had wished to stand, we have found a way to act on the earth as though we disposed of terrestrial nature from outside, from the point of Einstein's "observer freely poised in space." If we look down from this point upon what is going on on earth and upon the various activities of men, that is, if we apply the Archimedean point to ourselves, then these activities will indeed appear to ourselves as no more than "overt behavior," which we can study with the same methods we use to study the behavior of rats. Seen from a sufficient distance, the cars in which we travel and which we know we built ourselves will look as though they were "as inescapable a part of ourselves as the snail's shell is to its occupant." All our pride in what we can do will disappear into some kind of mutation of the human race; the whole of technology, seen from this point, in fact no longer appears "as the result of a conscious human effort to extend man's material powers, but rather as a large-scale biological process."[24] Under these circumstances, speech and everyday language would indeed be no longer a meaningful utterance that transcends behavior even if it only expresses it, and it would much better be replaced by the extreme and in itself meaningless formalism of mathematical signs.

The conquest of space and the science which made it possible have come perilously close to this point. If they ever should reach it in earnest, the stature of man would not simply be lowered by all standards we know of, it would have been destroyed.

24 *Ibid.*, pp. 18-19.

PAUL TILLICH, considered by many to be the most important Protestant theologian of our time, was born in Starzeddel, Prussia, in 1886. He studied at several European universities, and received his Doctor of Philosophy degree from the University of Breslau in 1911. During the period following World War I, he taught at several of the leading universities in Germany. In 1933 he was dismissed from his position at the University of Frankfurt am Main because of his outspoken opposition to the Nazi regime. (He was the first non-Jewish professor to be so dismissed.) He accepted an invitation to join the faculty of the Union Theological Seminary in New York City, where he remained until 1954. Since then, he has taught at Harvard and the University of Chicago. He is the recipient of more than a dozen honorary degrees, as well as other important honors. His best-known works are *The Religious Situation, The Protestant Era,* and *The Courage to Be.* At present, he is completing the third volume of his major life work, *Systematic Theology.*

The subject to be discussed here has two sides; one is the effect of space exploration on man as such, and the other is its effect on man's view of himself. The first seems to call for a report about man's condition; the second, for an evaluation of man's stature as a consequence of space exploration. But this distinction cannot be maintained when one goes into the concrete problems which have arisen as an effect of space research and space travel. A decisive part of man's condition, as it is affected by his penetration into the space beyond the gravitational field of the earth, is his self-evaluation on the basis of this achievement. On the other hand, conflicting self-evaluations are brought about by the contrast of the negative and positive effects of space exploration on man's condition. Therefore, I intend to deal with the problems of our subject without any sharp demarcation between the effects of space exploration on the situation of man as such and on his view of himself.

The present situation is the result of many steps made by Western man since the Renaissance. It would be unrealistic, and would prevent an adequate answer to our question, if the last step, however important and unique it may be, were considered in isolation from the previous steps. It leads to a distortion of facts and valuations if contemporary writers overemphasize the uniqueness of the present achievement in comparison with what has been done and thought before.

The Renaissance was not the rebirth of the ancient traditions, as the term is often misunderstood, but it was the rebirth of Western society in all respects—religious, cultural, and political—with the help of the ancient sources of the Mediterranean civilization. In this process the traditions were transformed in many respects because of the Christian background of the Renaissance. One of the most important transformations was the turn from the Greek contemplative and the medieval self-transcending ideals of life to the active, world-controlling, and world-shaping ideal. This implied a high evaluation of the technical sciences and the beginning of that fertile interaction between the pure and the applied sciences which immensely contributed—and is still doing so—to the rapid development of both of them. There was little such interaction in Greece, the late ancient world, and the middle ages; it was something new—not a repetition, but a rebirth. One may express the situation in three geometrical symbols: the circle, for the fulfillment of life and its potentialities within the cosmos in classic Greece; the vertical, for the driving of life toward what transcends the cosmos, namely, the transcendent One, the ultimate in being and meaning, in late antiquity and in the middle ages; and the horizontal, for the trend toward the control and transformation of the cosmos in the service of God or man since the Renaissance, Reformation, and Enlightenment. The "discovery of the horizontal" is the first step of a development of which space exploration is the preliminary last step. Both are victories of the horizontal over the circular and the vertical line.

One of the most important transformations was the turn from the Greek contemplative and the medieval self-transcending ideals of life to the active, world-controlling, and world-shaping ideal

The transition from the vertical to the horizontal line in the determination of the *télos*, the inner aim of human existence, was greatly helped by the astronomy of the Renaissance and related "utopian" literature. The Copernican astronomy had thrown the earth out of the center of the universe—the least divine of all places—and elevated it to the dignity of a star among other stars. About the same time, a highly influential philosopher, Cardinal Nicholas of Cusa, taught the immanence of the infinite within the finite, *e.g.*, in earth and man. This raised the significance of everything in the world by making it an expression of the divine life, and it gave impetus to the expectations of a fulfillment of history on this planet. The "utopian" literature showed visions of a future in which religious, political, economic, and technical elements were united. This also increased the importance of technology in relation to the pure sciences far above what it had been in Greece and the intermediary periods. Typical of this situation is Leonardo da Vinci, who combined the anticipation of fulfillment in his paintings with empirical studies of natural phenomena and with technical experiments in which, just as today, war techniques played a great role.

In the seventeenth century, the realization of the problems implied in these beginnings of the modern period of Western history increased and found a characteristic expression in Pascal's confrontation of man's smallness with his greatness. Pascal experienced with many of his contemporaries the shock of man's smallness in the universe of Copernican astronomy. At the same time, he experienced in his own work as mathematician and physicist the power of the human mind to penetrate into the calculable structures of nature—man's greatness even in the face of the quantitative vastness of the universe. In Pascal many problems of man's present self-interpretation are anticipated and the human predicament in its contradictory character is shown just as we see it today. He asked the question which is most relevant to our problem: What has become, under the control of the horizontal line, of the vertical one— the line toward that which transcends the cosmos? He answered with his famous words which contrast the "God of Abraham, Isaac and Jacob" with the "god of the philosophers." (See *Pensées*, Sect. VII-VIII, Vol. 33, pp. 243b-277b.)

Pascal was struggling to save the dimension of the ultimate, which transcends the greatness as well as the smallness of man. He did it successfully for himself, but the general historical development followed the horizontal line. The horizontal was expressed in the eighteenth-century belief in human progress, in the nineteenth-century belief in universal evolution, and in the ideologies supporting the industrial, social, and political revolutions of the last three centuries. There were always theological, mystical, romanticist, and classicist attempts to recover the vertical line or to return to the circular world view of classical Greece. But the drive toward that which lies ahead proved to be stronger than the longing to return to a world in which it was more important to look at the eternal essences of the cosmos than to anticipate a future to be created by man.

BLAISE PASCAL
In Pascal many problems of man's present self-interpretation are anticipated, and the human predicament in its contradictory character is shown just as we see it today

One of the shocks connected with the removal of man and his earth from the cosmic center was basically theological. Since the biblical literature, as well as its interpretation during fifteen hundred years of church history, was based on a world view in which the earth was at the center of the universe, human history was the ultimate aim of the creation of the earth, and the Christ was the center of human history, an urgent question arose: What is the position of man in the providential acting of God? What is the cosmic significance of the Christ in the universe as a whole? Does not the moving of the earth out of the center undercut both the central significance of man and the cosmic significance of the Christ? Is not the whole drama of salvation reduced to a series of events happening on a small planet at a particular time without universal significance?

With these problems already alive in the Western world, the age of space exploration started . . .

When men broke through the gravitational field of the earth, the first reaction was naturally astonishment, admiration, and pride. The pride was increased by the national pride of those who achieved the breakthrough, and diminished but not annihilated by the feeling of national humiliation of those who could have achieved it but did not. Yet there was almost no exception to a feeling of astonishment about men's potentialities, hidden until then, but now revealed: Man is not only able to explore the transterrestrial space, he is also able to change the astronomical picture by adding something to what was given to him by nature.

Admiration was particularly directed to the theoretical and technical intelligence of those who were responsible for the successful penetration into the trans-earthly sphere, and to the moral courage of those who risked their lives in actualizing what was a human potentiality and had now become real. A consequence of this admiration was the status of heroic pioneers given to the astronauts (even to those in the enemy camp) and that of bearers of esoteric wisdom unattainable by most human beings given to the atomic scientists. The emotional power of these reactions is very strong, and not without important sociological effects. These men became symbols which were decisive for the formation of a new ideal of human existence. The image of the man who looks down at the earth, not from heaven but from a cosmic sphere above the earth, became an object of identification and psychological elevation to innumerable people.

The same image unlocked streams of imagination about encounters inside and outside the gravitational field of the earth with non-earthly, though not heavenly (or hellish), beings. The literature of science fiction, often written as a sideline by scientists themselves, preceded as well as followed the actual progress of space exploration. But it reached its full development only after actual achievements in this direction had been attained. Its real importance is not the occasional anticipation of scientific or technical discoveries, but the fulfillment of the desire of man to transcend the realm of earthbound experiences, at least in imagination. The so-called "Gothic" novel did this with the help of supranatural, divine, and demonic interferences in the natural process of life, and the spiritualistic novel did it through the use of psychic phenomena which appeared as neither unambiguously natural nor unambiguously supranatural. Science fiction, especially if connected with space exploration, transcends the bondage to earth by imagining encounters with natural but transterrestrial beings. Mythological as well as psychic supranaturalism are replaced by a transterrestrial naturalism. The earth is transcended not through something qualitatively other, but through a strange part of something qualitatively the same: the natural universe.

"THE TRIUMPH OF PROVIDENCE" BY PIETRO DA CORTONA
*The imagined worlds are constructed with elements
of earthly experiences, even if these experiences are religious or artistic*

At this point an observation can be made which should have some restraining effect on the drive toward earth-transcending imaginings (whether they are called experiences or mere fantasy). The content of these imaginings is always a combination of elements taken from earthly experience. The "beings" imagined are either glorified or vilified duplications of the human figure (angels and heavenly saints or demons and inmates of hell), or they are combinations of elements by which the human figure is disfigured, as in science fiction. This shows a definite limit to man's capacity for escaping the bondage to the earth, even in imagination. The imagined worlds are constructed with parts or elements of earthly experiences, even if these experiences are religious or artistic.

The last remark leads to another, basically negative, group of emotional reactions to space exploration. It has somehow concretely raised man's awareness of the immensity of the universe and the spatial distances in it. Just the experience of bridging some of these distances and the consequent imagination of bridging more of them has increased man's sensitivity to the actual remoteness of even the nearest solar system beyond our own. The dizziness felt by people in Pascal's time, when contemplating the empty spaces between the stars, has been increased in a period in which man has pushed not only cognitively but also bodily into these spaces. His anxiety of lostness in a small corner of the universe, which has balanced his pride about his controlling power since the time of the Eighth Psalm,[1] has grown with the growth of the controlling power. One of the reasons is the loss of the ultimate-transcendent above the greatness and the smallness of man, the answer to the question of man's predicament provided by the psalmist as well as by Pascal. The other, more particular reason, unknown to both the psalmist and Pascal, is the fact that man can use his controlling power for self-destruction, not only of parts of mankind but of all of it. The intimate relation of space exploration to war preparation has thrown a deep shadow over the emotionally positive reactions to space exploration. This shadow will not recede as long as production of weapons and space exploration are tied up with each other.

In describing the emotional effects of space exploration and its scientific precedents, we have avoided value judgments except in an implicit way. It is, however, necessary to make them explicit and to discuss some ethical problems connected with our subject.

One of the effects of the flight into space and the resulting possibility of looking down at the earth is a kind of estrangement between man and earth, an "objectification" of the earth for man. The earth is deprived of her "motherly" character, her power of giving birth, of nourishing, of embracing, of keeping with herself. She becomes a large material body to be looked at and considered as totally calculable. The process of demythologizing the earth, which started with the early philosophers and has continued ever since in the Western world, has been radicalized as never before. It is too early to realize fully the spiritual consequences of this step.

The same is true of another radicalization: the flight into the transterrestrial space is the greatest triumph of the horizontal line over the vertical. Man has gone forward in directions which are practically limitless. However, this triumph of the horizontal raises serious spiritual problems, all of which come down to the basic question: "For what?" Long before the break through the gravitational field of the earth, the

---

1   When I look at thy heavens, the work of thy fingers, the moon and the stars which thou hast established;
       What is man that thou art mindful of him, and the son of man that thou dost care for him?
       Yet thou hast made him little less than God, and dost crown him with glory and honor.
       Thou hast given him dominion over the works of thy hands; thou has put all things under his feet.

                                                                                (Psalm 8:3-6)

*The symptoms of this emptiness are already conspicuously present amongst us
in the forms of indifference, cynicism, and despair*

question "For what?" had been asked with increasing seriousness and
concern. It had been asked in connection with the endless production
of means: machines, tools, gadgets. It had been asked in connection
with the question of the meaning of life. It had been asked when the
ways of modern civilization were subject to prophetic criticism, be it
in religious, be it in secular terms. If the question is now asked in connection with space exploration, it becomes more abstract and more urgent than before. For here the horizontal line is almost completely
formalized. The task is: to go forward for the sake of going forward,
endlessly, without a concrete focus. Of course, one could call the desire
to learn more about the cosmic space and about the astronomical bodies
in it a concrete aim, but this is only an accidental stop. The desire to go
ahead whatever may be encountered gives the real impetus. But as the
exclusive surrender to the vertical line in mysticism leads to the impossibility of expressing anything and acting in any direction, so the
exclusive surrender to the horizontal line (in what one could call "for-
wardism") leads to the loss of any meaningful content and to complete
emptiness. The symptoms of this emptiness are already conspicuously
present among us in the forms of indifference, cynicism, and despair.
Space exploration is not the means of healing it, though it may become
a factor in deepening it after the first enthusiasm has evaporated and
the pride about man's almost divine power has receded. These spiritual
dangers, however, should never lead to a decision to give up either the

production of technical tools or the attempt to penetrate into the outer-terrestrial space (as the danger of radical mysticism should not lead to a rejection of the mystical element in every religious experience). For danger is not a reason to prevent life from actualizing its potentialities.

This leads to another problem, connected indirectly with our subject—the problem of the responsibility of the scientist for dangerous possibilities implied in his discoveries. The problem is as old as scholarly thought and was for millennia a source of conflict between the priestly guardians of the holy and the philosophical critics of the traditional beliefs. Even if the sociological, political, and economic causes of such conflicts are taken into account, a genuine tragic element remains. The priest is aware of the catastrophic consequences which criticism of holy traditions can have on the spirit of many people. But the philosopher cannot resign from his vocation to fight for truth, even if sacred beliefs must be destroyed. (This is probably the earliest example of the conflict between the safety of the given and the risk of the new.)

The dangers connected with present scientific discoveries refer not to the "salvation of souls," but to the very existence of mankind. But the problem itself and the tragic implications of any possible solution are the same. And the answers should be the same: Tragic consequences of the discovery and expression of truth are no reason for giving up the attempts to discover and the obligation to express truth. The danger for the soul of the believer should not stop the prophet or the reformer from pronouncing truth in the vertical dimension; and the danger of destructive consequences of scientific discoveries (including those in the social sciences and psychology) should not stop the scientists from searching for and expressing truth in the horizontal dimension. It is bad to try to avoid tragedy if the price is avoidance of truth. Therefore, even if space exploration, through its military implications, increased the chances of tragedy, this would not be a reason for stopping it. But such danger would be a powerful motive to balance the horizontal by the vertical line, in order to receive from there weapons against ultimate tragedy. In other words: The answer to the tragic implications of the pursuit of the horizontal line is not to break off this pursuit but to continue it under the criteria coming from the vertical line. But, one asks, is this still a possibility? Has not the power of the horizontal drive, especially in its scientific expressions, almost cut off the relation to what transcends the universe and its scientific exploration? Has not man's image of himself in all Western religions been made obsolete by the horizontal dynamics of the last five hundred years? And does not space exploration say the last word in this respect?

There is no doubt that science has undercut the cosmic frame within which man has seen himself in biblical literature and ecclesiastical teaching, namely, as the bearer of the history of salvation for the universe, as the *only* creature in whose nature God could become fully manifest, and as he who will experience his own historical end as the end of the universe. Today's astronomy considers the possibility of other religiously meaningful histories in other parts of the universe with other beings in whom God could have become fully manifest, though with another beginning and another end. If space exploration is seen in this context, as the preliminary last step in a long development, one can say that it has changed tremendously the cosmic frame of man's religious self-evaluation. But one must add that it has not changed the divine-human relationship which had been experienced and symbolically expressed within this frame. Therefore, one can answer the question, whether the dynamics of the horizontal line have cut off the vertical, with a definite No! It is still possible for man to break through the horizontal movement and its tragic implications to the vertical and its power to restrict and transcend tragedy. This "stature and condition" of man has not changed, although the way of its actualization must be different from that of periods in which the horizontal line had not yet shown its driving power.

While the question of the right of scientific inquiry to go ahead without considering possibly dangerous consequences was answered affirmatively, another question arises to which an answer must be given. It is the economic question: How much of the income of a nation (or of all nations) should be given to space exploration? A main argument against space exploration is the immense amount of money needed for it, which according to the critics should be used for more important projects, e.g., cancer research or study of the best ways of restricting the increase of the world population. In both cases it is the conquest of bodily evils, disease, and hunger to which priority is given. This seems to be natural from the point of view of justice and *agape* (the Greek word for the Christian idea of love). But actually it is neither natural nor was it ever real. *Agape* demands that the individual be always ready to help the sick and the poor in personal encounters as well as in social projects. And justice demands of society and its political representatives the continuous fight against the structures of social evil in all its forms. But neither justice nor *agape* prohibits the use of economic power for cultural production. Otherwise no human potentiality, neither scientific nor technical, neither artistic nor ritual, neither educational nor societal, could ever have been actualized. But they *have* been actualized at a tremendous cost, and in their development they have produced powerful weapons against the structures of evil (mostly without intending to do so). "Priority of needs" cannot mean that the whole cultural process should not have been started before the most immediate needs, e.g., conquering hunger and disease, had been satisfied. The term "priority" in

*Space exploration . . . contributes greatly to . . . the growth
of esoteric groups who by their knowledge and their inventiveness
far surpass what can be reached even by highly learned and productive people*

the context of our problem is meaningful only in a particular situation. The question is: Which demand on the economic reserves of any social group has priority at this moment? And if a definite preference is established, the next question is: In which proportion shall economic aid be given to the preferred project in relation to other important projects? Finally it must be considered whether the rejection of one project, e.g., the next phase of space exploration, implies the certainty, or at least a real chance, that one of the alternative projects will be accepted by the responsible authorities. It is, for example, highly improbable that the money saved by the stopping of space exploration would become available for cancer research or a restriction of the population explosion. Beyond this, all these considerations would become academic the moment it is manifest that space exploration has important military consequences and belongs to the realm of competition with a potential enemy. Then it has priority over against all projects without direct military importance. The decision lies in the hands of those who have knowledge of the relevant factors and the power to balance the different points of view in terms of priorities, on the basis of the actual situation. They cannot be bound by a static hierarchy of priorities. Their only criterion should be the human aim of all political decisions, which certainly transcends national power as well as scientific progress. In this they are subject to the judgment of their consciences, the criticism of their contemporaries, and the later judgment of history.

But here a conflict arises, which is intensified by one of the sociological implications of space exploration: it contributes greatly to a general trend in our period, i.e., the growth of esoteric groups who by their knowledge and their inventiveness far surpass what can be reached even by highly learned and productive people, not to speak of the vast majority of human beings. Such elites are esoteric and exclusive, partly by natural selection, partly by public prestige, partly by skillful exercise of their power. An aristocracy of intelligence and will to power has developed in the democratic West as well as in the totalitarian East, and has equalized to a considerable degree the two originally opposite social and political systems. Space exploration in the democratic world strengthens the anti-democratic elements, which are present in every democratic structure. There is a tendency in the average citizen, even if he has a high standing in his profession, to take the decisions about the life of the society to which he belongs as a matter of fate over which he has no influence. This creates a mood which is favorable for the resurgence of religion, but unfavorable for the preservation of a living democracy.

It may seem remote from our problem to raise the question of the consequences of space exploration for the ideal of education. But it is required by the actual situation. If only those having the most extraordinary mathematical and technical intelligence can reach the top of the hierarchy of theoretical space explorers, and if only those having the most extraordinary bodily and psychological fitness can reach the top of the hierarchy of practical space explorers, it is understandable that these two types of man are elevated to the place of ideal types in accordance with which every individual should be formed, though in many degrees of approximation. Such a demand has been made in the United States, most urgently after the success of the first Russian Sputnik. There was, however, a strong reaction from the side of the humanistically minded educators and also from many students who did not want, or were not able, to undergo the rigors of an education that would bring them to the top of the new hierarchy. But the question is not solved by a transitory balance between the two ways of education or by serious attempts to combine them. The preponderance of the non-humanistic way can hardly be overcome because of the actual structure of modern society and the impact it has on the life of every individual. It drives (often unconsciously) the most gifted and ambitious members of the younger generation into an educational system which guarantees them participation in the higher echelons of the social pyramid. Education cannot resist the solid structure of a social system and its demands on every individual in it. But again: There is no reason for cutting off space exploration or the developments on which it is based. Human nature in its full potentialities is not expressed by the horizontal line. Sooner or later there will be revolt against its predominance, and space exploration will be judged in the light of the meaning of life in all its dimensions.

HARRISON BROWN, one of America's leading physical scientists, was born in Sheridan, Wyoming, in 1917. He was educated at the University of California and Johns Hopkins University, receiving his Doctor of Philosophy degree in 1941. In 1942 he joined the group of scientists working on the atomic bomb project at the University of Chicago, and from 1943 to 1946, he was one of the directors of the atomic research center at Oak Ridge, Tennessee. Since then, he has taught at the Institute for Nuclear Studies in Chicago and at the California Institute of Technology. In 1947 he received the annual award of the American Association for the Advancement of Science for his work on the composition of meteorites. He was the youngest man ever to receive this award. He has written several books, including *The Challenge of Man's Future* and *The Next Hundred Years,* and has contributed numerous articles to such periodicals as *Saturday Review, The Nation,* and *The American Scholar.*

M an appeared on the earth about a million years ago. Though his technological competence has grown steadily, he has been restricted to the earth during all of that time. Now, in our generation, he has developed the competence to fly to the moon and the planets, to observe and study them at first hand. Immense new vistas have been opened to him. He can now learn things which before seemed destined to remain permanently beyond his grasp. This is a prospect which should excite everyone. Those who are not stirred by the thought of man's traveling to the planets are either devoid of curiosity or lack a sense of human destiny. The realization that we may now have it in our power to answer the question of extra-terrestrial life should in itself be sufficient to spur us on.

Throughout his history, man has pursued knowledge in large part because of its utilitarian value: it helps him to master nature. When we examine the research which is being done today, we find that the greater part of it is aimed at the achievement of practical goals: to win wars, to prolong life, to make money. It is understandable that such research is undertaken, and it is often enormously sophisticated. Yet, in a moral sense, such research is scarcely above the animal level. It is simply an attempt to extend our ancient predatory capabilities and to create protective devices of increased efficiency against predators.

However, there have always been some men who have held that the pursuit of knowledge for its own sake is one of man's most noble characteristics and the one which most distinguishes him from the lower animals. Not to pursue the exploration of space, when it is possible, would therefore be a denial by man of one of his most important attributes. Not to venture to the planets would be a negation of one of life's most noble purposes—understanding ourselves and our origins.

B efore we can rationally discuss the value of programs aimed at sending men and instruments into outer space, it is essential that we understand the kinds of problems which such programs might help solve. One of the most important of these problems is that of the origin and evolution of our solar system.

Although man, until very recently, has been earthbound, he has nevertheless succeeded in learning a great deal about our solar system. Using telescopes and other instruments, he has measured the sizes of planets and their satellites. He has learned something about the chemical compositions and temperatures of planetary atmospheres. By sub-

RELATIVE SIZES OF PLANETS SHOWN IN RELATION TO THE SUN
Using telescopes and other instruments, man has measured the sizes of planets and their satellites

jecting fragments of interplanetary matter which fall upon the earth (meteorites) to intensive chemical and physical examination, he has learned something about the distribution of elements in cosmic matter. He has even been able to determine quite accurately the time at which the earth and meteorites were formed. Naturally, he possesses considerably more information about the earth than he does about other planets, for he has been able to observe it at much closer range.

The major facts which have been accumulated, and which any general theory of the origin of the solar system must explain, fall into a most interesting pattern. It has become evident that there are two distinct groups of planets. The four planets close to the sun are *small:* Mercury, Venus, Earth, and Mars. Those farther away from the sun are very *large:* Jupiter, Saturn, Uranus, and Neptune. The small inner planets are characterized by high average densities and must therefore be composed primarily of heavy substances such as metal and rock. The large outer planets, by contrast, are characterized by very low densities and must

134

therefore be composed primarily of very light, indeed gaseous, substances. Saturn, for example, could float in water. The predominant materials in Jupiter appear to be hydrogen, helium, methane, ammonia, and water.

The atmospheres of the two groups of planets differ dramatically from each other. Mercury is too small and too warm to retain an atmosphere, but the atmospheres of Venus, Earth, and Mars contain substantial, although differing, quantities of carbon dioxide. By contrast, the carbon which exists in the atmospheres of the large outer planets appears to be primarily in the form of methane. There is a similar difference between the forms in which nitrogen is found in the two groups. The nitrogen in the earth's atmosphere is in the form of nitrogen gas, while the nitrogen in the atmosphere of Jupiter is primarily in the form of ammonia. In other words, the atmospheres of the inner planets are chemically oxidized; those of the outer planets are chemically reduced.

Traveling around the sun, then, we see different kinds of bodies. Why are some large and others small? Why are some dense and others "fluffy"? Why are some chemically oxidized and others reduced? At present, we do not have definite answers to these questions, but we have been able to fit the observed facts into a broad picture which seems clear in outline, if not in detail.

The elements which constitute our solar system appear to have been formed about five thousand million years ago as the result of a sequence of nuclear reactions which as yet are not clearly understood. About 4,500 million years ago the newly formed elements and their compounds began to condense, and the processes of planet formation were started. Many chemical compounds were present in this primordial matter, but those which predominated were hydrogen and helium. To a lesser extent, quantities of methane, ammonia, and water were present. Considerably less abundant were the substances which make up the greater part of the earth—silicates and metals.

Condensation processes took place in a gaseous cloud surrounding the primitive sun. Within the asteroid belt, which lies between Mars and Jupiter, the temperatures were sufficiently high to permit the condensation only of the less volatile materials, which were present in but small quantity. Beyond the asteroid belt, however, the more abundant substances such as water, ammonia, and methane condensed. The condensed solids amalgamated by accretion processes and gave rise to planets which, inside the asteroid belt, were composed almost entirely of rocklike material and metals. Outside the asteroid belt, the accretion processes led to the formation of planets composed in large part of methane, ammonia, and water. In the special cases of Jupiter and Saturn, which were particularly favorably situated, large quantities of hydrogen and helium were also retained as the result of gravitational pull.

We know that inside the asteroid belt no substance which was present as a gas at the time of planet formation could have been retained by a planet in appreciable quantity. In other words, none of the inner planets originally possessed atmospheres or oceans. Those which we observe today must be almost entirely of secondary origin. Yet, on the earth we observe huge oceans. If water could not have been retained in free form originally, from where did it come?

The answer appears to be that water was retained originally on the earth chemically bound within the rock-forming silicates. As the earth heated, as the result of gravitational contraction coupled with the liberation of energy stored in radioactive substances, water was liberated from the depths, and oceans were formed. Other gaseous substances were also released by this heating process, in particular methane and other hydrocarbons and ammonia.

The stage was thus set on the earth for a sequence of chemical steps leading to the buildup of carbon compounds of increasing complexity, and eventually to the evolution of molecules which could reproduce themselves. Life emerged, and the resultant living substances began to traverse the long and complicated path which we call evolution.

In the meantime, the flux of radiant energy which fell continually upon the earth gave rise to other chemical processes. In particular, it decomposed atmospheric water vapor into hydrogen and oxygen gases. Because of its lightness, a great deal of the hydrogen escaped from the earth's gravitational pull. The oxygen, which was left behind, combined with carbon compounds to form carbon dioxide and with nitrogen compounds to form free nitrogen. Over a period of time, the greater part of the carbon was converted by these processes into carbon dioxide, which combined with calcium in the ocean and was eventually deposited as limestone. A delicate balance was established among the carbon dioxide in the atmosphere, that in the ocean, and that tied up in sedimentary rocks.

Eventually, the primitive living substances learned to "feed" upon the carbon dioxide of the oceans and the atmosphere, making use of the steady flow of radiation from the sun. Photosynthesis was "invented" and made possible the continuation of life processes for an indefinitely long period of time on a stable basis.

Within the thin film of life which covered the earth, there was ceaseless pulsation. New species of living matter arose and old ones disappeared. Organisms of increasing complexity emerged: single-celled animals, multi-celled animals, animals with supporting structures (bones), vertebrates, fish with lungs, amphibians, reptiles, mammals. Eventually, and recently, man emerged—a creature possessing the power of conceptual thought, a creature which, for the first time in evolutionary history, could wonder about its past, its origins, and its place in the universe.

What about the other planets? Could life have emerged upon them as well? The emergence of life would seem to call for conditions of "chemical flexibility"—conditions in which a multiplicity of chemical reactions can take place and in which very complicated compounds are stable over long periods of time. It is difficult to imagine life on Neptune, for example, because the surface temperature is so low that rates of chemical reactions are extremely slow. It is equally difficult to imagine life on Mercury, where there is no atmosphere and where the temperature of the hot side is so high that complex organic substances would be unstable. Between these two extremes, however, there should be a broad spectrum of conditions in which life might have emerged and flourished.

One might expect *a priori* that Venus, which is about the same size as the earth, would provide conditions suitable for the nourishment of life processes. Study of the planet indicates, however, that although carbon dioxide is extremely abundant in the atmosphere, little if any water is present. Further, the temperature of the planet appears to be so high that any oceans would be vaporized. Under the circumstances, it seems dubious that life exists there today, although it might well have existed at some time in the distant past.

Why should Venus have an oxidized atmosphere and at the same time possess little if any water? It is possible that, since Venus was formed closer to the sun than was the earth, its chemical combinations of water with silicates were less stable, with the result that Venus started its life with a paucity of water. Further, the radiation intensity in the neighborhood of Venus would decompose water at a greater rate than terrestrial water was decomposed, with the result that virtually all water on the planet disappeared.

The situation with respect to Mars is quite different. Although the planet possesses no oceans, water appears to be present. The polar caps show seasonal changes in size, and, on occasion, deposits of hoarfrost can be seen during the Martian dawn. Also, there are color changes on the surface of the planet which appear to be seasonal and which might well be indicative of the presence of some form of plant life. If such life exists, however, it must be able to survive under extremely rugged circumstances. Winter and nighttime temperatures appear to fall far below those of our own Arctic regions, and Martian midday summer heat might be the equivalent of a cold fall day in New England.

It is interesting to speculate as to why Mars possesses so little water. By contrast with Venus, the planet was formed so far from the sun that hydrated rock substances should have been quite stable. It may be that, because of the smallness of the planet, the water was never liberated from the interior. It may also be that water was liberated, but because of the low gravitational pull of the planet, the water has escaped over the ages until it has by now virtually disappeared. If the latter is true, Mars at one time may have had much more water than we see today—

indeed the planet may even have had oceans. Under such circumstances, climatic conditions would have been quite different (more moderate) from those we now observe.

With this background of information and speculation, we can state one of the great unsolved problems concerning our universe as follows: Given a planet that possesses "chemical flexibility," what is the probability that life will emerge as the natural end product of a sequence of chemical events? Given a planet that is not too small (like the moon), not too hot (like Mercury), not too cold (like Neptune), not too large (like Jupiter), what is the likelihood that a sequence of chemical steps will result in the emergence, over a period of time, of living substance? Looking at the earth alone, we cannot tell. For all we know, life might be a miracle, and indeed there are many who believe that it is. But if, through space exploration, we were to find life on Venus or Mars or both, it would then appear likely that the probability of life emerging naturally, given adequate conditions, would be as high.

Such a discovery would have profound philosophical importance. We have good reason to believe that planetary systems are fairly abundant in our visible universe—indeed, perhaps as many as a billion billion stars which can be seen through our largest telescopes may have planets traveling about them in orbit. Even if only a small fraction of these were situated in such a way that they were not too close to their stars, not too far away, not too hot, not too cold, not too large, not too small, life could still be a very abundant commodity in our universe. Indeed, were we to find that life of some sort exists on Mars, the likelihood would be high that life also exists on perhaps as many as a thousand billion planets in our visible universe.

This, then, is the broad picture as it appears at the present time. Much of it is fact. A great deal is theory. Much is speculation. The picture is based upon facts gained through intensive study of the earth by men who have been confined to its surface, and by intensive study of the moon and planets from a great distance, using telescopes.

Although there is a great deal which can yet be learned about the planets using terrestrially based equipment, we can see the beginning of the end. Telescopes have limited usefulness. There are certain kinds of important planetary measurements which simply cannot be made from the earth. Indeed, were it not possible to journey to the planets, there would be many questions which would remain unanswered for all time. And of these questions, perhaps the most important is that of extraterrestrial life. Is the earth unique? Or is life abundant elsewhere?

Our newly developed capabilities of sending spacecraft out of the earth's gravitational field will make it possible for us greatly to increase our understanding of the solar system and its origins. Already

MARINER II: SPACE VEHICLE USED FOR OBSERVING VENUS
Already vehicles have struck the moon and have come close to Venus and Mars

vehicles have struck the moon and have come close to Venus and Mars. Given enough effort, it should be possible to land men on the moon and to bring them back safely. With still more effort, it should be possible to send men to Mars and Venus and to bring them back.

Much of what we wish to know about the moon and planets can be learned with instruments. It is not necessary to send men to the moon or to Mars in order to obtain most of the important information which we need concerning these bodies. Indeed, for most purposes instruments are actually more effective than man, and coupled with this, they need not be returned to the earth. The information obtained by instruments can be telemetered back.

Because the moon is so much closer to the earth than are the planets, it will, of course, be our first object of study. Using television cameras, we can obtain, even with a "crash landing," highly detailed pictures of the lunar surface. At present, our very best pictures of the moon have a resolution of about one-half mile. Using a television camera mounted on a lunar probe, a resolution of a few feet should be possible. By using television cameras placed in a spacecraft in orbit about the moon, it should be possible to obtain detailed maps of the entire lunar surface.

139

Other exciting experiments could be undertaken from such a spacecraft. The temperatures of specific areas could be measured accurately. The radioactivity of the lunar surface could be determined, and this would tell us a great deal about its chemical composition. The mass and mass distribution within the moon could be determined accurately.

With improved techniques of rocketry, it should be possible to land a probe upon the moon "softly." This would make possible a variety of important measurements. Truly detailed pictures could be obtained of the region in the vicinity of the landing. The chemical composition of the lunar crust could be determined precisely. One could determine whether or not there are "moonquakes." A variety of other important chemical and physical parameters could be measured which, taken together, would tell us much more than we now know concerning the moon's origin and history—particularly if measurements were made at a number of lunar locations. With further improvement in rocketry techniques, it should be possible to obtain samples of the lunar surface by remote control and to return them to the earth for still more detailed study.

Present techniques of rocketry permit us to launch spacecraft which can come very close to our nearest planetary neighbors—Mars and Venus. The great distances involved restrict the kinds of measurements which can be made, in part because of the increased difficulty of communication. Nevertheless, important measurements can be made, even at present. Television observations can be made, the chemical compositions of the atmospheres can be determined, and other important parameters such as magnetic fields and temperature can be measured.

We will be able to land instrument packages "softly" on Mars and Venus long before we are able to send men there and bring them back. This will mean that prior to the first human visits to these planets we should have a fairly clear picture of the conditions the visitors will encounter. Detailed television pictures can be transmitted back to the earth. The compositions of the atmospheres can be determined in detail. General climatic conditions can be followed over long periods of time. The surfaces of the planets can be observed through both microscopes and telescopes.

Lower forms of life, corresponding to terrestrial bacteria, can be searched for on Mars and Venus by culturing the material on the surface and examining the cultures with microscopes which are remotely controlled. Higher life forms can be searched for by using television and listening for sounds. Long before the first human visitors reach Mars and Venus, we should have a clear picture as to whether or not life in some form exists on these planets.

If so much can be learned about planets by using instruments, why then do we place so much effort on the manned-space-flight program?

H. M. S. "BEAGLE"
*What would the scientific productivity of the voyage of the "Beagle" have been
if a series of measurements had been substituted for Charles Darwin?*

The U. S. budget for fiscal year 1963 calls for two-thirds of the total space
effort to be placed on the manned-space-flight program while less than
one-sixth of the total budget is for scientific research in space. Is this a
reasonable distribution?

The fact is that there are few situations involving scientific measurements in which machines are not more effective than men. What, for example, in an orbiting earth satellite, could a man learn that could not
be learned with proper instrumentation? The answer is: very little. To
this must be added the fact that when we place human beings in orbit,
enormous and expensive safety precautions are necessary. We can take
a much greater risk with the life of an instrument.

The situation with respect to space is similar to that with respect to
the oceans. Most of our knowledge concerning the ocean depths has
been obtained using instruments and measuring and sampling devices of
various sorts which have been lowered into the sea from surface ships.
Recently, a lively debate took place within the government concerning
the effort, if any, which should be taken to send men to the greatest
depths of the ocean—some 35,000 feet. The arguments pro and con were
similar to those now being used in connection with the man-in-space
program. On the one hand, devices which will permit men to descend
to great depths are very expensive. Perhaps the same amount of money
invested in surface ships and in high-quality instrumentation would, in

141

the long run, yield more information about the ocean's depths than could possibly be obtained by sending men down in a thick steel sphere. On the other hand, man himself is an instrument far more complicated, and from certain points of view more effective, than those built in factories.

No matter what parameter one might be interested in, it is vitally certain that an instrument can be made which is more accurate than a human being. A man can estimate temperature, but not as accurately as a thermometer. He can look at a rock and estimate its chemical and mineralogical composition, but instruments are available which will do the job much more accurately. However, the human brain can integrate observations in terms of a broad over-all pattern. A man-built machine which could do this as well as a human being would be both unbelievably complex and expensive.

Let us imagine the geology of North America being determined entirely by remote control. It seems clear that we would know far less than we actually now know as the result of detailed human participation, and particularly as the result of human competence with respect to the integration of observations. Or, to take another example, what would the scientific productivity of the voyage of the "Beagle" have been if a series of measurements had been substituted for Charles Darwin?

The importance of man as an integrator and sifter of information should not be underestimated. Yet, we should recognize that we are as yet far from the point where such capability can be utilized effectively in the space program. For each dollar of expenditure, far more useful information can be obtained at the present time from instruments than from men. But we would be cold, indeed, were we to take the point of view that our every action must be justified by practical results or by the gleaning of specific scientific information. In particular, we should not ignore the man-in-space program as a great human adventure.

We spend very large amounts of money on games and, closely related to them, adventure. Last year about twenty million persons attended major league baseball games, and gross receipts at motion picture theaters exceeded one billion dollars. Is two or three billion dollars a year too much to pay for space adventure? One may argue about the magnitude of the space effort in the United States, and one may well argue about the proper distribution of that effort. But no matter how we look at the program, it seems clear that the adventure component must be recognized. The first non-stop flight over the Atlantic gleaned little information of scientific value. Yet, that first flight was important from several points of view, not the least of which was the adventure aspect.

The budget for the American space effort has risen from about ninety million dollars in 1958 to about 3.7 billion dollars for the National Aeronautics and Space Administration alone in 1963. NASA projects that expenditure will take place at a rate of about thirteen billion dollars annually by 1970. Today the space program consumes over twenty per cent of the total governmental research and development effort. By 1970, it is estimated, space projects will take up nearly forty per cent of the research and development budget. Considering the technical difficulties, even these large numbers may prove to be underestimates, particularly if past military experience can be taken as a guide.

The greater part of the current space allocations is for the man-in-space program. With a current budget of 2.2 billion dollars, this program is already receiving about two-thirds of the total space agency allotment, and even now there are signs that the manned space program is running short of money. According to present estimates, the Apollo project (the first manned lunar landing) will be at least 200 million dollars short of its needs with its current budget. Without a supplemental appropriation, the only way to make up the deficit will be to take money away from other programs, such as the space sciences. Yet, there is already evidence that the space sciences are not providing information sufficiently rapidly to fill the needs of the manned space program.

Thus far, and in spite of the large sums of money involved, the pursuit of space technology has received overwhelming support from American political leaders. The basis for this support is complex, but it is clear that it was triggered by the national humiliation received on October 4, 1957, when Sputnik I was launched successfully. Subsequent Soviet space successes, particularly in the manned-space-flight area, have served to strengthen American resolve to achieve leadership in this field. In addition to the Cold War aspects of space, there is undoubtedly a feeling for the drama and adventure of conquering the unknown, and a desire to achieve practical applications. But were the Cold War element suddenly removed, it is dubious that space projects would receive the enthusiastic support which they enjoy today.

The general public does not appear to be as enthusiastic about space as its leaders are. Indeed, a number of professional people, including some prominent scientists, have expressed their doubts about the wisdom of pursuing such a program. There are numerous signs of a latent uneasiness. There are even some signs of direct hostility.

A large part of the uneasiness concerning the space program probably stems from the fact that so much money is being spent on an effort which has little obvious bearing upon the major problems which confront our nation and the world today. People who are rightfully concerned about hunger in the world cannot help thinking of how much economic development could be stimulated with 3.7 billion dollars this year, growing rapidly to thirteen billion dollars by 1970. People who are rightfully worried about the alarming rate of population growth in the world cannot help thinking of what 3.7 billion dollars might do if directed toward the solution of that problem. Educators think of how much education could be purchased, and worry about the effect of the influx of space-designated funds upon the intellectual values of their staffs and students. Others argue that large expenditures on space hinder the allocation of funds to other branches of science, to social science, and to the humanities. It seems possible that this uneasiness, which has been expressed in many different ways, will permeate American political leadership in the not-far-distant future.

The political fact of the matter, however, is that if space programs were completely eliminated, allocation of the funds for other worthy public purposes would not by any means be certain. In other words, the question of the emphasis we place on space projects should be decided on the intrinsic merits of the projects and not by comparison with other projects which might, in actual fact, be more useful.

The first question which we must answer is from many points of view the most difficult. Do we really want to venture into space? My own answer is an enthusiastic "Yes," but I would like us to go into space for the right reasons and not for the wrong ones. We should venture into space simply because it is an enormously exciting thing to do. What is human destiny if it is not to learn about the universe in which we live? Americans should not engage in space projects simply because the Russians are engaging in them. I believe that the question of space in relation to "national prestige" is greatly overemphasized.

Can we afford to venture into space? At present, space expenditures do not appear to be alarmingly high. Even at the rate of expenditure projected for 1970, the cost would come to less than two per cent of the American gross national product. This represents something like three to five per cent of the activity of the industrial sector of the economy. Indeed, it may well be that the funding of space activities represents an appreciable contribution to economic growth.

Given the desirability of venturing into space and given further the estimate that we can afford it, are we going about it in the right way? My personal feeling is that the Americans and Russians have been looking at space exploration primarily as a race, and in doing so have permitted themselves to become stampeded. In their push to place men on the moon as quickly as possible, they have inflated the man-in-space project to the point where it already dominates the space effort and threatens to envelop it.

Before we attempt to place men on the moon and planets and return them to the earth, we should study the objects as carefully as we can with instruments. By all means, we should aim at eventually sending men to the moon and planets, but we should take care of first things first. Should a Russian land on the moon first, it would not be a catastrophe for America. Indeed, we should recognize that no matter how much effort is placed on the manned-space-flight program, the probability is substantial that this will happen anyway. Also, the first man will probably not learn a great deal. The moon and the planets are large, and adequate exploration will require many lengthy visits. The establishment of the goal to place a man on the moon by the end of this decade makes a certain amount of sense, for it gives a definite time for a definite limited objective. But we should not permit our program to get out of balance, nor should we permit it to become a circus just because such a goal exists.

Space experiments are, by their very nature, terribly expensive, with the result that they should be selected with the greatest possible care. It is often pointed out that the cost of a unit of information obtained in the space program is unreasonably high compared with costs of other areas of scientific inquiry. Here we must recognize that some bits of scientific information are by their very nature difficult to obtain. Nuclear physics has always been expensive relative, let us say, to the study of butterfly ecology, largely because of the high cost of the equipment involved. Yet, we are willing to spend money on accelerators because we recognize that we cannot obtain the desired information unless we do so. Just as the jump from butterfly ecology to nuclear physics was expensive, so is the jump into space. We are confronted by the fact that we can obtain valuable information only if we are willing to spend the money. Unless we are willing to make a substantial (and expensive) effort, the information simply will not be forthcoming.

What are the conditions on other plants? Has life existed there in the past? Does it exist there today? To what extent does living intelligence permeate the universe? Can we contact it? Can we understand it? What is our past? Where lies our future? These are some of the questions which can be answered over the next decades and centuries through man's exploration of space. We are indeed on the threshold of the greatest of mankind's intellectual experiences.

A COMMENTARY BY THE EDITORS

I

If "space exploration" or "the conquest of space" is understood as something that began on October 4, 1957 (with the launching of *Sputnik I*), then the Great Books would have nothing to say on this subject. But there is no reason to conceive space exploration in that narrow fashion. Long before artificial satellites were sent up, man explored space and, to a certain extent, conquered it.

Indeed, the very idea of artificial earth satellites precedes their actual existence by more than 250 years. Since all descriptions of launchings of satellites make much of the need to overcome gravity, and since a satellite is considered successful only if it is "in orbit," it is appropriate that Newton, to whom we owe the theory of universal gravitation as well as the successful explanation of planetary orbits, should himself have anticipated the existence of artificial earth satellites:

> A projectile, if it was not for the force of gravity, would not deviate towards the earth, but would go off from it in a right line, and that with an uniform motion, if the resistance of the air was taken away. It is by its gravity that it is drawn aside continually from its rectilinear course, and made to deviate towards the earth, more or less, according to the force of its gravity, and the velocity of its motion. The less its gravity is, or the quantity of its matter, or the greater the velocity with which it is projected, the less will it deviate from a rectilinear course, and the farther it will go. If a leaden ball, projected from the top of a mountain by the force of gunpowder, with a given velocity, and in a direction parallel to the horizon, is carried in a curved line to the distance of two miles before it falls to the ground; the same, if the resistance of the air were taken away, with a double or decuple velocity, would fly twice or ten times as far. And by increasing the velocity, we may at pleasure increase the distance to which it might be projected, and diminish the curvature of the line which it might describe, till at last it should fall at the distance of 10, 30, or 90 degrees, or even might go quite round the whole earth before it falls; or lastly, so that it might never fall to the earth, but go forwards into the celestial spaces, and proceed in its motion *in infinitum*. And after the same manner that a projectile, by the force of gravity, may be made to revolve in an orbit, and go round the whole earth, the moon also, either by the force of gravity, if it is endued with gravity, or by any other force, that impels it towards the earth, may be continually drawn aside towards the earth, out of the rectilinear way which by its innate force it would pursue; and would be made to revolve in the orbit which it now describes; nor could the moon without some such force be retained in its orbit (*Mathematical Principles of Natural Philosophy*, Vol. 34, pp. 6b-7a).

Notice the comparison between the moon, a natural earth satellite, and projectiles that are thrown up rapidly enough to become artificial satellites!

Undoubtedly, this is the first mention of actual penetration into space by man or man-made objects in a serious scientific book. There were, of course, earlier mythological accounts, such as that of Icarus' ill-fated attempt to fly with wings made by his marvelously skillful father, Daedalus. Icarus did not heed the warnings of his father and flew too close to the sun; the wax which held together his wings melted, and Icarus crashed to his death.

But serious concern with space far antedates even Newton. Space, as that which surrounds the earth and that in which the heavenly bodies are contained, has been a subject of interest ever since men began to think scientifically about themselves and the world in which they live. Plato, in the *Timaeus*, gives us his view of how the heavenly bodies are arranged:

> The sun and moon and five other stars, which are called the planets were created by . . . [God] in order to distinguish and preserve the numbers of time; and when he had made their several bodies, he placed them in the orbits in which the circle of the other was revolving—in seven orbits seven stars. First, there was the moon in the orbit nearest the earth, and next the sun, in the second orbit above the earth; then came the morning star and the star sacred to Hermes, moving in orbits which have an equal swiftness with the sun, but in an opposite direction; and this is the reason why the sun and Hermes and Lucifer overtake and are overtaken by each other. To enumerate the places which he assigned to the other stars, and to give all the reasons why he assigned them, although a secondary matter, would give more trouble than the primary (Vol. 7, p. 451a-b).

This is a fairly accurate account of the way in which the planets are arranged; except that, of course, Plato's system is geocentric. Interesting, too, is the purpose for which, according to Plato, the planets were made: "to distinguish and preserve the numbers of time." A similar notion is expressed by Aristotle, who calls time "the number of movement." In Aristotle's view, the various heavenly bodies each have their own sphere, with the earth at the center of all these spheres. Thus, there is first the sphere of the moon, then that of Mercury, then that of Venus, and so on for each of the planets. Beyond the last planetary sphere there is a sphere of the fixed stars, and finally there is a last sphere beyond this one.

"The heaven" includes everything within this last sphere and the sphere itself. Beyond this, there is nothing. Aristotle says:

> It is therefore evident that there is also no place or void or time outside the heaven. For in every place body can be present; and void is said to be that in which the presence of body, though not actual, is possible; and time is the number of movement. But in the absence of

natural body there is no movement, and outside the heaven, as we have shown, body neither exists nor can come to exist. It is clear then that there is neither place, nor void, nor time, outside the heaven (*On the Heavens,* Vol. 8, p. 370b-c).

Both Plato's and Aristotle's worlds seem quite small and finite. And in Aristotle's theory, it is clear that there is nothing outside the heavens. Outside the heavens there is not even any "empty space" or "void." This is quite different from the theory put forth by Lucretius. There are just two kinds of things in the world, according to this Roman poet who was a follower of Epicurus and Democritus, namely, atoms and void (or vacuum). These two things are mutually exclusive: where there are atoms, there is no void; and where there is void, there are no atoms. Void is what makes motion possible; unless it existed, the whole universe would be filled with bodies (made up of atoms), and none of them would have any place to move.

Lucretius' void is, therefore, a sort of "pure" space—pure because it is space without anything in it. His universe, consisting of bodies and pure space or void, is quite naturally conceived to be infinite. There can be nothing outside it. Lucretius proves this by reduction to the absurd:

> Again if for the moment all existing space be held to be bounded, sup-posing a man runs forward to its outside borders, and stands on the ut-most verge and then throws a winged javelin, do you choose that when hurled with vigorous force it shall advance to the point to which it has been sent and fly to a distance, or do you decide that something can get in its way and stop it? for you must admit and adopt one of the two sup-positions; either of which shuts you out from all escape and compels you to grant that the universe stretches without end. For whether there is something to get in its way and prevent its coming whither it was sent and placing itself in the point intended, or whether it is carried forward, in either case it has not started from the end. In this way I will go on and, wherever you have placed the outside borders, I will ask what then becomes of the javelin. The result will be that an end can nowhere be fixed, and that the room given for flight will still prolong the power of flight (*On the Nature of Things,* Vol. 12, pp. 12d-13a).

Interestingly enough, the idea of a "pure" space, *i.e.,* space without body in it, was criticized 1,800 years later by the philosopher George Berkeley. Berkeley's arguments were, of course, mainly directed against Newton's views, but they apply just as well to Lucretius:

> "We shall find we cannot even frame an idea of *pure Space* exclusive of all body . . . When I speak of pure or empty space, it is not to be supposed that the word "space" stands for an idea distinct from or con-ceivable without body and motion. . . . When, therefore, supposing all the world to be annihilated besides my own body, I say there still remains *pure Space,* thereby nothing else is meant but only that I conceive it possible for the limbs of my body to be moved on all sides without the

least resistance, but if that, too, were annihilated then there could be no motion, and consequently no Space" (*The Principles of Human Knowledge*, Vol. 35, pp. 435d-436a).

Although Lucretius, in the first century B.C., had already conceived of an infinitely extended universe, there is no intimation of it in the astronomical theory of Ptolemy, in the second century A.D. In the *Almagest*, Ptolemy gives a picture of a universe which, though large, need not be infinite. Nor, for that matter, need it be *very* large, at least compared to the distances which are commonplace in modern astronomy. It merely is required that the distance from the earth to the fixed stars is large enough so that the diameter of the earth is, relative to this distance, as small as a point. No matter where we are on the earth, the universe above us always seems to be exactly a hemisphere. Thus the sphere of the fixed stars and the earth are in the same relation to one another as the surface of a sphere and its center.

Copernicus' overthrow of the Ptolemaic system was a strictly intellectual conquest of space. One hypothesis—the heliocentric one—replaced an earlier hypothesis—the geocentric one. In the course of thirteen centuries, the Ptolemaic system had grown cumbersome with additions, details, and *ad hoc* solutions to problems that arose from additional observations. What had once been a beautiful and beautifully simple system was now a complex and veritably incomprehensible system of circles, circles upon circles, and imaginary points. Copernicus' revolution restored simplicity to the astronomical picture. One price to be paid for this renewed simple picture of the world was that the universe had to be conceived as vastly larger than it had been in the Ptolemaic view.

Whereas in the Ptolemaic universe, the size of the earth was unappreciable in relation to the sphere of the fixed stars, in the Copernican universe the size of the earth's *orbit* around the sun is unappreciable in relation to the sphere of the fixed stars. For, no matter where the earth is in its circuit around the sun, the universe seems to be exactly hemispherical. Thus, the earth in its entire orbit never appears to move out of the center of the universe: "Although [the earth] is not at the centre of the world, nevertheless the distance [between the earth and the center of the universe] is as nothing, particularly in comparison with the sphere of the fixed stars" (*On the Revolutions of the Heavenly Spheres*, Vol. 16, p. 517b). And again, Copernicus writes: "I also say . . . that the magnitude of the world is such that, although the distance from the sun to the Earth in relation to whatsoever planetary sphere you please possesses magnitude which is sufficiently manifest in proportion to these dimensions, this distance, as compared with the sphere of the fixed stars, is imperceptible" (*Ibid.*, pp. 525a-526a). Thus the Copernican intellectual revolution took man, as the inhabitant of the earth, out of the center of the universe; and the universe in which he now has a side seat is tremendously larger than Ptolemy or any of the ancients ever imagined it to be.

II

D oes this change in the physical location of man affect his stature? Does it affect the way in which man looks at himself? In the opinion of Sigmund Freud, the Copernican revolution deeply affected man's self-love. Finding himself no longer at the center and apex of creation, man felt deeply wounded and has felt so ever since. And this damage to his pride has been magnified by two subsequent scientific revolutions which were even more devastating than Copernicus':

> Humanity has in the course of time had to endure from the hands of science two great outrages upon its naïve self-love. The first was when it realized that our earth was not the centre of the universe, but only a tiny speck in a world-system of a magnitude hardly conceivable; this is associated in our minds with the name of Copernicus, although Alexandrian doctrines taught something very similar. The second was when biological research robbed man of his peculiar privilege of having been specially created, and relegated him to a descent from the animal world, implying an ineradicable animal nature in him: this transvaluation has been accomplished in our own time upon the instigation of Charles Darwin, Wallace, and their predecessors, and not without the most violent opposition from their contemporaries. But man's craving for grandiosity is now suffering the third and most bitter blow from present-day psychological research which is endeavouring to prove to the *ego* of each one of us that he is not even master in his own house, but that he must remain content with the veriest scraps of information about what is going on unconsciously in his own mind (*A General Introduction to Psycho-Analysis*, Vol. 54, p. 562c-d).

It is probably fair to extend Freud's statement and to say that *all* the great scientific discoveries of the twentieth century have tended to make man more and more insignificant in his own eyes. Compared to the infinitesimal particles of which matter is composed, man and his sensory apparatus seem gross and inadequate; compared to the energy released by nuclear explosions, man's physical power seems insignificant and ludicrous; compared to the size of the universe as revealed by modern optical and radio telescopes, the world that is visible to man seems to be a mere speck. At the very beginning of the modern scientific era, Pascal spoke of the "frightful spaces of the universe which surround me" and added that "the eternal silence of these infinite spaces frightens me" (*Pensées*, Vol. 33, pp. 207b, 211a).

In this view, therefore, man looks down upon himself as the result of his own discoveries and inventions; for example, automation—the result of superb technological skills combined with basic knowledge—has degraded man more than any tyrant or dictator could, in making him less useful and skillful than his own creation. Similarly, in this view, the exploration of space by means of manned and unmanned vehicles, the prospective conquest of the moon and the planets by men and their instruments, will not only be a triumph of human daring and skill, it will also be another step in a series in which each human success lowers the stature of man. Quite obviously, the "conquest of space" not only emphasizes the great achievements of which humans are now capable, it also calls attention to the frailty of human beings (through their need to be protected from a hostile environment), to the vastness of the universe (through the realization that an entire human lifetime would not be sufficient to explore more than a minute layer of space next to the earth), to the possible non-uniqueness of man (through the anticipation that living and rational beings may be found on other celestial bodies).

Yet this result seems almost too paradoxical; for, in this view of things, we infer that man is small and despicable on the basis of discoveries made by man himself. Why should not these discoveries—and their consequent technological applications—be considered a sign of man's greatness and grandeur? Is it not a sign of man's impressive stature that he is able to find out the constitution of matter down to its most minute and evanescent particles, that he is able to explore the celestial universe with telescopes for distances of millions of light-years, that he has discovered the secrets of heredity, that he is in the process of almost eliminating disease from the surface of the earth? In fact, the more complex the world is discovered to be, the more admirable is man, who is able to understand all these things. If, in Bacon's words, "Knowledge and human power are synonymous" (*Novum Organum*, Vol. 30, p. 107b), then as man acquires more and more knowledge, practical as well as theoretical, he necessarily becomes more and more powerful. And this would seem to imply an *increase* in stature.

The word "stature" has physical connotations. In its literal sense, a man's stature is his height and other dimensions. As a physical entity, man has shrunk, relative to the universe, as a result of scientific discoveries. But "stature" also refers, metaphorically, to man's dignity and worth in other respects. In these ways, man's "stature" has increased over the years. For man has used his powers of thought and reasoning to increase his knowledge and to apply this knowledge in order to conquer nature. Indeed, man's stature considered simply as physical being was never very great. Even before there was any inkling of how vast the universe might be, men realized that in size and strength they were the inferiors of many brute animals. But men have always felt that their worth was higher than that of other beings, because of their intellectual and spiritual powers. And from this point of view, man's stature is unaffected by technological progress or any discoveries about nature and the universe, either in the past or in the future.

Thus Sophocles in the fifth century B.C. wrote of man and his greatness:

> Wonders are many, and none is more wonderful than man. . . . Speech, and wind-swift thought, and all the moods that mould a state, hath he taught himself; and how to flee the arrows of the frost, when 'tis hard lodging under the clear sky, and the arrows of the rushing rain; yea, he hath resource for all; without resource he meets nothing that must come: only against Death shall he call for aid in vain; but from baffling maladies he hath devised escapes. Cunning beyond fancy's dream is the fertile skill which brings him, now to evil, now to good (*Antigone*, Vol. 5, p. 134a-b).

And similarly the psalmist, while praising the Lord and all his works, also remarks on the privileged position of man:

> . . . Thou hast made . . . [man] little less than God, and dost crown him with glory and honor.
> Thou hast given him dominion over the works of thy hands; thou hast put all things under his feet (Ps. 8:5-6).

And finally we may recall the passage in which Hamlet expresses his admiration of man:

> What a piece of work is a man! how noble in reason! how infinite in faculty! in form and moving how express and admirable! in action how like an angel! in apprehension how like a god! the beauty of the world! the paragon of animals! (*Hamlet*, Vol. 27, p. 43d).

But none of these expressions of the grandeur of man is made by a scientist; they are all made by poets. We may well wonder, then, whether perhaps scientific and technological progress has lowered man, so that scientists can no longer agree—if ever they did—with this high evaluation of him. The long passage from Freud which we quoted earlier might lead us to think so.

It is interesting to note, therefore, that some of the Renaissance thinkers who initiated the new view of the universe did not feel that they were lowering the stature of man. Giordano Bruno (1548-1600) rejected the Aristotelian view of a universe finite in space and time. The universe for Bruno is infinite and contains an infinity of worlds like our own. But this does not reduce man to an unimportant speck of dust. On the contrary, man can only reach perfection in an infinite universe. Because man's will and desire for knowledge are infinite, man can achieve his end and goal only in an infinite universe.

Similarly, Kepler (1571-1630) did not have a low opinion of man. Kepler is the father of modern astronomy, perhaps more so than Copernicus. In Kepler's work, for the first time, the ancient notions concerning the earth, the heavens, and the sun are given up. Instead of heavenly bodies being constituted of a different matter from terrestrial ones (as they are in the astronomy of Aristotle, of Ptolemy, and still of Copernicus), all bodies, heavenly or terrestrial, are recognized as being of the same kind. Instead of perfect circular motion of the stars—as something that is *due* to the stars because of their very perfection—we have irregular motions such as the elliptical orbits of the planets. Kepler was one of the first astronomers to whom the telescope was available, and he could observe such phenomena as the moons of Jupiter and the phases of Venus. The complexity and apparent confusion which had entered the astronomical picture were cleared up by the work of men like Kepler, Galileo, Newton, and their successors, and led to the recognition of the scientific laws on which modern technology, including space travel, is based.

Though well aware of what he was doing, Kepler was not worried that he was lessening the stature of man. On the contrary, throughout his works there is much praise and jubilation over the intellectual powers of man (including those of Kepler himself!), and a definite feeling that these discoveries exalt rather than degrade man. The center of the universe is the most important and dignified place in it, says Kepler, and so it belongs to the sun which is a more important and primary body than the earth. Yet this does not diminish the stature of man; for in placing the sun in the center and the earth at a distance from the center, he made it clear that he was speaking of the earth "in so far as it is a part of the edifice of the world, and not of the dignity of the governing creatures which inhabit it" (*Epitome of Copernican Astronomy*, Vol. 16, p. 854b).

In Newton's view, space is absolute and "in its own nature, without relation to anything external, remains always similar and immovable" (*Mathematical Principles of Natural Philosophy*, Vol. 34, p. 8b). It is extended infinitely in all directions; and Newton finds that "God is able to create particles of matter of several sizes and figures, and in several proportions to space, and perhaps of different densities and forces, and thereby to vary the laws of Nature, and make worlds of several sorts in several parts of the Universe" (*Optics*, Vol. 34, p. 543a).

The contemplation of infinite spaces or other worlds does not distress Newton. On the contrary, anything which increases knowledge is to be encouraged. For, he tells us, "if natural philosophy in all its parts . . . shall at length be perfected, the bounds of moral philosophy will be also enlarged" (*Ibid.*, Vol. 34, p. 543b).

The scientist who has perhaps changed modern man's ideas of space more than anyone else is Albert Einstein. In *Relativity: The Special and General Theory* (see *The Great Ideas Today 1961*, pp. 427-475), he develops the theory that there is just one four-dimensional space-time continuum. In this view, the universe is non-Euclidean (*i.e.*, the laws of

Euclidean geometry do not hold true), and Einstein envisages the possibility of a universe that is finite. Is such a radical overthrow of traditional ideas derogatory to man or to man's nature? At least one commentator on Einstein writes that "the theory of relativity has simultaneously made us freer and richer by showing in the realm of physics, not merely by way of abstract advice but in concrete performance, that our intellectual capacity of knowledge reaches farther than our sensory capacity of perception."[1]

For the boldest statement of how modern scientific knowledge has benefited man, we must return to Kepler. He finds that in his view of the universe, the dignity of the earth may have been lowered, but not the dignity of man. Indeed, he goes on to say that it is entirely appropriate to put the sun in the center of the world and make the earth travel around it, because the earth has a special station as the home of man:

> From the end of movement . . . it is proved that movement belongs to the Earth as the home of the speculative creature. For it was not fitting that man, who was going to be the dweller in this world and its contemplator, should reside in one place of it as in a closed cubicle: in that way he would never have arrived at the measurement and contemplation of the so distant stars, unless he had been furnished with more than human gifts; or rather since he was furnished with the eyes which he now has and with the faculties of his mind, it was his office to move around in this very spacious edifice by means of the transportation of the Earth his home and to get to know the different stations, according as they are measurers—*i.e.*, to take a promenade—so that he could all the more correctly view and measure the single parts of his house (*Op. cit.*, Vol. 16, pp. 915b-916a).

This point of view is immediately transferable to space travel: if the movement of man with the earth contributes to his dignity and station because of the added things he can contemplate, then so does travel through space in artificial heavenly bodies—and it does so to an increased degree, because man's travel with the earth is involuntary, but travel through space is voluntary and a conscious commitment of man to the enterprise of knowledge.

1 Aloys Wenzl in *Albert Einstein: Philosopher-Scientist*, ed. by Paul A. Schilpp, Evanston, Ill.: The Library of Living Philosophers, Inc., 1949, p. 605.

Should Christianity Be Secularized?

Introduction

Why Christianity Must Be Secularized
HARVEY COX

Why Christianity
Should Not Be Secularized
E. L. MASCALL

Does Secular Theology Have a Future?
MARTIN E. MARTY

The Need for a Theology of the World
M. D. CHENU

The Idea of Religion
IN GREAT BOOKS
OF THE WESTERN WORLD

The symposium on secularization is largely concerned with the face that Christianity puts, and should put, before the world. Artists, since the beginning of Christianity, have been imagining the face of Christ. Five images are presented here, ranging from the primitive figure of the 8th-century Celtic cross (*lower right*) to the contemporary American sculpture by Doris Caesar (*far right*). Christ the Teacher is portrayed on the south portal of 13th-century Chartres Cathedral (*far left*) and Christ the Judge on the Russian icon of the 15th century (*lower left*). The Christ on the donkey (*upper right*), 13th-century Swiss, was used in Palm Sunday processions.

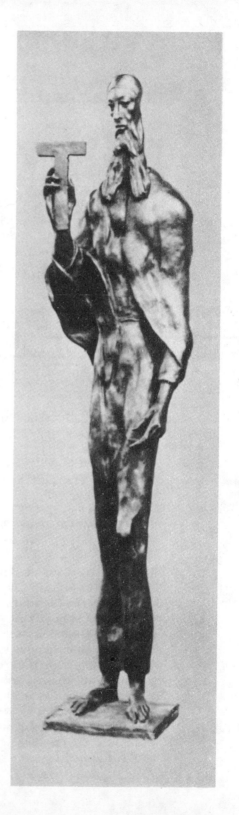

INTRODUCTION

Religion has again become a popular subject. It makes the headlines. "God is dead" appeared in large letters on the front page of *Time* announcing a long article on the latest departures in theology. The meetings of the second Vatican Council attracted a corps of reporters and frequently received more attention, for example, than the sessions of the United Nations. Thirty years ago, religion and theology had very dubious status as an intellectual subject in the university and excited no interest. Today, a "radical theologian" draws a crowd of two to three thousand students. A generation ago, theology seemed moribund even to the specialist within it. Today, there is no part of it that is not in an intellectual ferment.

Among religious leaders, the change is especially marked in the attitude that they take toward the secular world. Secularism used to be viewed as the main opponent of religion. To "go with God" meant in some basic way to turn one's back on "the world, the flesh, and the devil." Recently, however, Christians of all denominations have been reconsidering the relation between the church and the world. There are demands for an utterly new relation. Some have even called for the secularization of Christianity.

In the past, secularization has always been associated with the enemies or opponents of religion. It has been urged as a way of eliminating the influence of the church. Secularization of the schools, for example, usually consisted in transferring their control from the church to the state. Coming from churchmen, the demand for secularization seems paradoxical, if not actually contradictory. It is as striking as the declaration by a "man of God" that "God is dead."

The publication of *The Secular City* by Dr. Harvey Cox in 1964 first brought the attention of the general public to the issue. This book was originally intended as a study outline to provoke and incite the interest of theological students. But from the start it obtained a much larger hearing, and more than 200,000 copies of the book are now in print. It occasioned a many-sided discussion among theologians, which has since been published in book form as *The Secular City Debate*.

The question of secularization provides a focal point for discussion of many questions brought to the fore by the new theology. Our symposium has been organized to explore them so as to reveal the principal issues in that discussion. First, of course, is the issue of secularization itself: What is meant by secularization and why should it be recommended for Christianity? On this issue, the sides are clearly drawn. Dr. Cox represents the affirmative position in favor of secularization. The opposing and negative side is represented by the Rev. Dr. E. L. Mascall, who has written the most sustained and detailed counterargument in his book *The Secularization of Christianity*.

The question at issue involves the larger problem of the relation of the church to the modern world, and particularly how the message of Christianity can be communicated to the contemporary secularized man. It was strikingly phrased by Pastor Bonhoeffer, victim of the Nazi concentration camp: "How do we speak in secular fashion of God?" Dr. Martin E. Marty has frequently dealt with this problem in *Christian Century*, of which he is an editor, and his essay places the debate over secularization in its historical background and assesses its position and its chances for the future.

At issue in the discussion are such basic Christian doctrines as the theology of creation, of the incarnation, and of the providential course of history. Bonhoeffer has again given direction to the discussion by his paradoxical statement that the time may have arrived for a "religionless Christianity." As precedent, he refers to St. Paul's asking whether observance of the Jewish Law is necessary for justification. Since this question was satisfactorily answered in the negative by the primitive church, he asks whether today religion is at all a condition of salvation. For Bonhoeffer, as for other Christians, faith is admittedly necessary, and Bonhoeffer was in some ways a martyr to his faith. Hence his question raises the possibility of drawing a distinction between religion and faith. This possibility is explored by the Rev. M. D. Chenu, the French Catholic scholar known for his work in the history of theology.

Throughout the discussion, one of the principal questions at issue is the meaning of religion. For the most part, however, the issue rarely becomes explicit enough to be discussed in and for itself. The final part of our symposium is, therefore, devoted to the idea of religion as it is treated by the authors in *Great Books of the Western World*.

Secularization is not the only topic of discussion in the current renaissance of theological speculation. To provide a wider view of the whole discussion, we have asked Professor Langdon B. Gilkey of the Divinity School at the University of Chicago to analyze recent developments in theology. His essay appears in Part Two. *Eclipse of God*, by the eminent Jewish theologian, Martin Buber, provides still another contribution to the current debate. His book discusses many of the themes prominent among the new "radical theologians." As Dr. Cox has pointed out, there is a close line connecting the theological problems of the secular city with those involved in the "God is dead" theology.

HARVEY COX

Author of the widely discussed The Secular City, *Harvey Cox is one of the most prominent of the "New Theologians." A frequent contributor to* Christianity and Crisis, Harper's, Redbook, Motive, The Christian Scholar, The Commonweal, *and* Junge Kirche, *Dr. Cox is Associate Professor of Church and Society in the Divinity School of Harvard University. Born in Chester County, Pennsylvania, in 1929, he was educated at the University of Pennsylvania, where he earned an A.B. with honors in History in 1951, and at Yale University Divinity School, from which he received the B.D. in 1955. He was ordained in the Baptist church in 1956, and in 1963 he received his Ph.D. degree in History and Philosophy of Religion from Harvard University. From 1955 to 1958 Professor Cox was Director of Religious Activities at Oberlin College, and from 1958 to 1963 he served as Program Associate for the American Baptist Home Mission Society. From 1962 to 1963 he was a Fraternal Worker for the Gossner Mission in East Berlin. Before going to Harvard, he was Assistant Professor of Theology and Culture at Andover-Newton Theological Seminary. Active in community organizations, Dr. Cox was a member of the National Council of Churches Commission for the Mississippi Delta Ministry; the Steering Committee, Massachusetts Southern Christian Leadership Conference; and the Advisory Committee of the Christian Peace Conference. Dr. Cox was held in jail for five days after arrest in the South, while taking part in a civil rights demonstration. He lives in Roxbury, Massachusetts, with his wife and three children.*

Why Christianity
Must Be Secularized

The innocent word "secular" has been the victim of a prolonged case
of cultural deprivation. It deserves reinstatement.

The English word "secular" is derived from the Latin *saeculum* meaning either a very long time or an epoch, a "world-age." As such it is neutral
and carries no inherent sense of evil or negativity. However, early in the
Christian centuries people began to use "secular" to designate *this* world-
age or *this* world as opposed to some other or later world. Later, "secular"
was used to designate those institutions and activities that fell outside
the control of an increasingly powerful church. Still later, even priests
who served in the everyday world rather than in religious orders were
called "secular" priests, and still are in many places. This explains why,
when property was removed from ecclesiastical control or when schools
or hospitals were taken over by the state, the process was described as
"secularization."

Thus, underlying the usage of the words "secular" and "secularize" in
English, and lurking behind the unpleasant overtones these words have
for many religious people, are at least two very questionable assumptions.
The first is otherworldliness. The second is clericalism. Otherworldliness
holds that somewhere there is another world which is higher, holier, or
more sacred than the secular world in which we all live. This assumption
has little in common with Hebrew faith, if one excepts some isolated
apocalyptic passages. The Jewish scriptures teach that *this* world is the
one that God created, that he loves and is bringing to fulfillment. Otherworldliness of a sort can be found in the New Testament, but even there
the other world is seen not as a place but as a new world-age, a new *era*
which has already begun now in our era. The idea of two worlds—the
"secular" one of inferior status—stems not from biblical sources but mainly
from the Persian and hellenistic philosophies which formed the cultural
atmosphere of the Mediterranean basin in the church's first centuries of
life. There is little to commend it in our era, and it serves only to encumber
the biblical faith with a dated world view which is at once foreign to it
and also puzzling to people reared with a twentieth-century scientific
mentality.

163

The second or clericalist assumption implies the negative use of the word "secularization" to describe the divesting of ecclesiastical bodies of their properties and privileges. This criticism assumes that the church does in fact have some special inherent claim to social privileges, power, and property. It views the present earthly weakness of the church as abnormal and lamentable. It finds its ideal in those centuries when the church organized and unified the civilization of the West, a situation that can hardly be regained today.

Those who oppose "secularization" in these two standard meanings, that is, the disappearance of otherworldliness and the reduction of the temporal power of the church, thereby unwittingly defend assumptions that many thoughtful Christians would question today. Our emerging ecumenical consensus of faith is that *this* world is the world God is renewing and redeeming, that our own history is the history in which God acts, and that the final triumph of God foreseen by the Bible will be a fulfillment of this world and no other. Likewise, we are increasingly relieved to see the church divested of the pomp and pretense which have given it a costly temporal prestige. The emphasis on the Servant Church both in the ecclesiological pronouncements of the World Council and in the documents of the Second Vatican Council attests to this fact. "Triumphalism" has been laid aside. Christians now more and more see themselves as a "People of God" called to serve this world, not as a colony of privileged individuals designated for salvation in the next.

When I use the term "secularization," I intend it to mean *both* man's loss of interest in other worlds with a resulting intensification of interest in this one, *and* the newly emergent role of the church as minority and servant rather than as majority and lord. For many people, this movement away from otherworldliness and away from ecclesiastically dominated society is the occasion for hand-wringing and lamentation. I disagree. There can be no question that it poses serious problems for theology, but it also presents unprecedented new opportunities. Further, I do not believe these two movements are separable: otherworldliness was in part the sacral ideology of an ecclesiastically dominated society. Its hierarchical picture of the cosmos attributed to the church a key and powerful role in that cosmos, so the church naturally had a special interest in preserving that picture in people's minds. A new theology for a secular society will only be produced when the church accepts its diminished temporal status and discards all hankering for a rosier past.

THE POSITIVE POTENTIAL OF SECULARIZATION

When I argued in my book *The Secular City* that secularization, notwithstanding the problems it creates, has enormous positive potential for man, this assertion threatened and annoyed many traditionally religious people. I also asserted, however, that this secularization process is caused in part by the impact of biblical faith on civilization. This assertion annoyed many nonreligious people and bothered some religious folk even more than my positive evaluation of secularization itself.

It is somewhat surprising that postulating a link between biblical faith and secularization should have caused such a stir. The idea was not really new. It had been suggested several years before by Friedrich Gogarten in his book *Verhängnis und Hoffnung der Neuzeit: die Säkularisierung als theologisches Problem* ("The Fate and Hope of Our Time: Secularization as a Theological Problem"; Stuttgart, 1958). In that important work Gogarten said:

> Secularization in our day is reaching its climax, and yet our thinking about it still arises from assumptions which either know nothing about this secularization or else have a false conception of what has taken place in it and where its foundations lie. We can obviously only learn from it what must be learnt here if we understand that *secularization* regardless of what may have developed from it in modern times, *is a legitimate consequence of the Christian faith.* (Emphasis added)

Gogarten's argument is that Christianity calls man away from dependence on the cycle of nature with its demigods, sacral kings, and ecstatically revealed values. It calls him to mature and rational responsibility for this world. Thus Christianity begins a process of "secularization" including the desacralization of political structures and the disenchantment of nature. These processes in turn form the bases for our contemporary secular civilization. Without the desacralization of political structures, genuine social change would be impossible. Divine-right monarchs and holy regimes do not lend themselves to change. Without the disenchantment of nature, i.e., its transformation from a dwelling place of demons to the field of human responsibility and celebration, neither science nor art in their modern forms could have emerged. Alfred North Whitehead once argued that the combination of the Christian belief in creation and the evolution of scholastic philosophy laid the groundwork for modern science. His position merely strengthens the case for those who see the secularization of the world not as a massive defection from faith but rather as a further step in the historic relationship of Christianity to culture. Secularization is the "defatalization of history." It puts the responsibility for what happens next squarely in man's hands.

What should theology do in the face of the secularization of our world? Three types of answers have begun to arise to this question in our time. The first group of theologians might be called the pruners. They wish to pare down Christianity to fit within the assumptions of what they take to be the modern scientific world view. Paul van Buren and the so-called death-of-God theologians, Thomas Altizer and William Hamilton, typify this group. I find two difficulties with their solution. First, we can never be really clear about what "the" modern scientific world view is. Modern scientific humanism must contend with various forms of phenomenological philosophy and with a rich variety of marxist revisionisms if it wishes to supply a viable view of the world. Also, for many of the most sophisticated scientists, scientific method is understood to be operational and to utilize models of limited scope, and thus does not pretend to offer a "world view."

Second, it is theologically uncritical and nonhistorical. It assumes that the doctrines of Christianity have a given and changeless content, that their meanings are not subject to historical development, and that therefore they must either be retained or discarded. It is significant that Altizer comes to the death of God from a previous preoccupation with oriental mysticism, Hamilton from a fondness for Karl Barth, and Van Buren from an attachment to British linguistic philosophy. None of these backgrounds could be expected to prepare these men to grasp the radically historical and developmental character of Christian doctrine. These thinkers are thus guilty of a kind of reverse fundamentalism. The "God" who is "dead" is the God of a very traditional and very orthodox Christian theism.

At the opposite pole, there are those theologians who feel that Christianity must be retained in its classical philosophical housing whether it be scholastic or idealistic, or some other. They are the preservationists. An excellent and well-argued example of their work can be found in E. L. Mascall's *The Secularization of Christianity*. Oddly, theologians of this type agree with the pruners on what the "essential" components of Christianity are, but unlike the modernists they decide to defend rather than discard. They both agree on what "God" means, but the pruners say he is dead while the preservationists say he "exists." Preserving of course always entails a certain amount of pickling, and pickling prevents further growth. Hence, in order to establish their claim, the preservationists criticize not only the pruners, they also criticize those engaged in the further development of doctrine and its reinterpretation.

The third group of theologians includes all those who see Christianity from a historical or developmental perspective. They deny the idea, held by both pruners and preservers, that there is some timeless and irreducible "essence" to Christianity. They understand it rather as a movement of people, a church moving through history with a memory and a vision, entering into riotously different cultural and social forms along the way. Among Roman Catholics, it was John Henry Newman in *Essay on the Development of Christian Doctrine** who first used the concept of doc-

---

* See *The Great Ideas Today 1966*, pp. 407 ff.

trinal development successfully, but it has been used since him by Karl Adam, Hans Kung, Leslie Dewart, and Bernard Lonergan. A related category among Protestants is the idea that all texts and doctrines are located within a context of historical conditions and cannot be fully understood if this context is overlooked.

Both the idea of the development of doctrine and that of historical criticism were opposed by conservative theologians when they first appeared, and are still viewed with suspicion in many places. Nevertheless, most theologians now concede that an accurate understanding of religious truth demands a knowledge of its *Sitz im Leben*. But even those who utilize the historical critical method often balk at taking the next logical step in the process. This step sees not only the past but also the present as a field of doctrinal development. It sees the *present* form of a doctrine as a stage in its developing toward something else. Mallarmé once said that the writer's task is "to give a purer meaning to the words of the tribe." Despite hopes of positivists to find for each word one unequivocal meaning, words are alive. Their meanings are always a product both of their former usage and of their present embodiment. This is even more true of doctrines. The nuances of meaning and language in a living religious community are constantly changing, and theologians must be attentive to these changes. Hence they find themselves not only elucidating doctrines but developing them and giving a purer meaning to the symbols of the community.

I place myself within the third group in the above classification of current theological approaches. I reject as reductionistic any suggestion that we should simply abandon various classical Christian doctrines as archaic residues of the past. But I reject just as vigorously the notion that we should defend them in the form in which we have inherited them. In fact, I would argue that it is the misguided effort to defend Christianity in one or another of its classical forms (and the conservatives hotly differ with each other on which *is* "the" classical form) that unwittingly creates the very atheism it seeks to avoid. Atheism is always the shadow of some form of theism. Most atheists today, including those who still want to be Christians, disbelieve in exactly the same conventional picture of God that orthodox theologians try so vigorously to defend.

SECULARIZING THEOLOGY

How then according to this historical-development view does theology proceed in an age of secularization? *Secularization means that the world of human history now provides the horizon within which man understands his life.* Thus the task of theology is to rethink and develop the doctrines of biblical faith to engage this contemporary sensibility. Naturally, this will be a risky undertaking. But so was the valiant attempt of the early Christian apologists to cope with the thought forms of late hellenism. So was St. Thomas' splendid achievement in synthesizing biblical faith with the aristotelian tradition. Though we are now in the midst of a reaction against the way nineteenth-century German theologians worked within the ambience of philosophical idealism, I believe future generations of theological historians will also chronicle their work as a brilliant accomplishment.

It is fashionable among some theologians today to bewail Christianity's millennium-long alliance with hellenistic philosophy. Certainly it must be granted that this alliance created a theological frame of reference which produced unnumbered difficulties in subsequent years. Still, hellenism informed the *saeculum* of the early church. If Christianity was to avoid becoming just one more Jewish sect, it had to enter into the only conceptual lingua franca available to it in the early centuries of its development, and that was hellenistic. It is both cheap and unproductive to criticize the church's hellenization from the safe distance of the late twentieth century. In many ways the synthesis was a brilliant one. Our task today, however, is neither to perpetuate that synthesis nor to deride it. Rather it is to forge a new expression of the biblical faith within the cultural categories of our day. In doing so we will find a study of the apologists, of St. Thomas, of the Reformers, and of nineteenth-century theology not only rewarding but indispensable. We study these classical theological achievements, however, not to pander their particular content but to learn their method, which was always to take the spirit of their age with utmost seriousness, to enter into it with zest. Paul Tillich opens his great *Systematic Theology* by stating that theology, which is etymologically derived from *theos* (God) and *logos* (meaning), must satisfy two basic needs: It must tell the truth about God and yet also speak to the temporal situation. This is what the great classical theologians always did, and in so doing they demonstrated a confidence in the spiritual power of the Gospel and in its capacity to transform culture which seems wholly lacking in the conservative theologians today.

How do we begin to do the actual work of moving theology toward its needed "secular phase"? First we must be sure of our theological grounding. There are three major theological insights that provide the basis for a positive attitude toward our modern world and toward the process of secularization. They correspond to the three persons in the classical doctrine of the Trinity.

The first is that the God of the Bible does not operate only in and through religious or sacred institutions but through events we might call "secular." The liberation of the Israelites from Egyptian peonage, the conquest of the land of promise, the defeat and exile of the Jews and their deliverance from captivity are examples. Indeed, in this sense the career of Jesus is secular and has been assigned apocalyptic or sacred significance only because of the various prisms through which it has been appropriated. The crucifixion was a secular event. It has been a truism in recent years to say that "God acts in history." Still, if God is still alive and active, the logic of this position would lead us to try to discern his activity in our present history, and this means in secular events.

The second classical doctrine that necessitates our taking this world with full seriousness is the doctrine of the Incarnation. In Christ, God discloses himself as present for man in the grime and blood, and in the parties and festivals of earth. Nor is the Incarnation to be understood merely as an isolated episode in God's life. It signifies that God is the One who is fully and irretrievably present in the life of men, that God takes our *saeculum* with life-and-death seriousness. A church which does not identify with the world, with the same thorough solidarity that God does, betrays its mission.

The third theological base of secular theology has to do with the traditional doctrine of the Holy Spirit and points more toward the interpretation of doctrines than toward the discernment of the action of God in the secular world. It suggests that our various inherited doctrines arose in the church's effort to speak to differing ages in the history of the world. Thus a proper understanding of these doctrines will be gained only as we involve ourselves in the continuation of this mission in changed circumstances. Traditional theology teaches that the Holy Spirit reveals to believers the true meaning of the Bible. But different generations of Christians have interpreted the same texts in contrasting ways. We can see that the meaning of any text or doctrine is not fixed or closed. Meaning arises as we try in the light of altered conditions to make sense of positions held in the past. To those faithfully involved in God's action in the world, what theologians once called the "Missio Dei," the Holy Spirit reveals ever new meanings and nuances in the classical doctrines. As the famous Pastor Robinson told the Pilgrim fathers when they set sail for New England, "God has yet new truth to break forth from his Holy Word."

If God works in the world of secular events, and if it is the responsibility of his people to discern his action, this requires a theology *of the secular*. If the Incarnation suggests a worldly focus for theological work, then we need to think *in secular terms*. If the significance of the classical doctrines is not eternally fixed but open to interpretations that illuminate new concerns in history, this requires *a secular theology*.

This does *not* mean that the church should accept just any new interpretation of its doctrines. Continuity is also an element in historical development. But any theology which confuses a particular sacralized world view—be it Neoplatonic, thomistic-aristotelian, or idealist—with the essential biblical message is marked for extinction. But merely to stop defending antiquated conceptualizations of the faith is hardly sufficient.

Theologians must also venture upon new conceptualizations, expressions of the faith which utilize the sensibility and the *manière d'être* of the age. Before showing how such a reconceptualization might proceed in one area of doctrine, ecclesiology, I wish to make two further remarks.

THE OPPORTUNITY FOR CONTEMPORARY THEOLOGY

First, the contemporary theologian has a certain advantage over the apologists, since he is working in a world which has already been markedly influenced by biblical themes at the very core of its consciousness. As we have seen, theologians sometimes express this with the claim that "God works in the world and not just in the church." This same notion can also be expressed sociologically if one charts the historical sources of such modern phenomena as scientific technology, the social revolutions of exploited peoples, the modern suspicion of closed world views, and the demand of even the most common people for a share in the decision-making process in their societies. All of these movements spring in part from the influence of Christianity on the world. We have already noted the link between Christianity and modern science, a link recognized by Whitehead, even though its sad record in such cases as Galileo and Darwin shows how far the church can depart from the implications of its own message. Arend van Leeuwen in his *Christianity in World History* (London: Edinburgh House, 1964) documents the role Christianity played in sowing the seeds of the current so-called awakening in the African and Asian countries. Michael Walzer in his *The Revolution of the Saints* (Cambridge: Harvard University Press, 1965) traces the origin of radical politics and the idea of participatory democracy to the English Puritans.

The fact that so many movements in our present world derive from biblical impulses means that the modern theologian faces a very different challenge from the one presented to the church by hellenistic philosophy and by the medieval rediscovery of Aristotle. His task should be easier. But it will be made even more difficult, indeed impossible, if he insists on clinging to previous philosophical frames of reference. If those philosophical positions are either scholasticism or some other derivative of classical Greek philosophy, he will be in an even more difficult spot, since the great theological challenge of today is to make sense out of *change*, while the Greeks tended to see reality in terms of eternal being.

My second observation about the method involved in articulating a theology today relates to the pluralism and the intense historical consciousness of our time. There is no single encompassing world view today which commands anything like the universal prestige Aristotelianism or idealism did. Hence we will probably never again have a single theology. We can expect a conscious pluralism of theologies. Some theologians will work with the various contemporary forms of marxism, others with phenomenology and existentialism, still others with the systematic ways of thinking about man and society emerging from social science. But this pluralism of theological approaches should not worry us. The second hallmark of our time is its consciousness of the provisional and historically conditioned character of all thought, including theology. No theologian within the historical-development school believes he is writing the final theology, or that his is the only way to speak in the modern world. This particular form of self-delusion belongs mainly to the pruners and the preservers. There is therefore a certain freedom and willingness to take risks in theological writing today which, though it may annoy many people, contributes to the liveliness and virility of the theological conversation.

SECULARIZING THE CHRISTIAN MESSAGE

What would it mean to secularize the message of the church today? If we listen to the questions people ask most forcibly today, we discover they are not usually questions of cosmological meaning but of human significance and ethical value. Despite secularization and the loss of temporal power by the church, people do expect it to provide ethical models and guidelines, and they are dismayed when it does not. The tenor and style of a given age's criticisms of the church often suggest indirectly what people hunger for and do not get from Christianity, what sort of loaf they are asking for when the church delivers a stone. In centuries past, the church's critics hit it hard for its moral laxity, its unseemly opulence, or its intellectual obscurantism. Today, however, the most articulate critics of the church attack it for its failure to act and speak decisively on the great moral issues of the age. Marxists have flayed it for blessing war and economic injustice. Dark-skinned people have derided it for condoning racial discrimination. Rolf Hochhuth in his play *The Deputy* criticized it for not coming to the defense of the Jews during the period of Hitler's terror.

Despite the pointedness of these criticisms, what is significant in them is that people think it worthwhile to make them. They obviously *expect* a word from the church about the moral issues of the day and are outraged when it is not forthcoming. In the United States, more people have dropped out of the church because of its cautious position on racial injustice than because they found it difficult to recite the Nicene Creed.

Some theologians of course may deplore this concentration on the ethical and claim that it obscures the "truth question." I don't believe their anxiety is justified in a period which understands itself in political and ethical terms. The church's message must assume this contour. We come to the "truth question" today *through* the ethical question. In fact, it is precisely here that the whole issue of what "truth" means and what it means to "believe" comes into focus. For theologians, mired in a scholastic conception of reality, truth is a quality belonging to statements which correspond to an objective essence. For the secular mentality, truth is valency, weight, experiential significance. The Gospel is true if it is dependable. To be a Christian is not to attach credence to propositions but to be among a people whose memories and hopes illuminate human experience and provide a sense of direction. I would submit that this latter view of truth, far from being a crass betrayal of the faith, actually comes much closer to the Hebrew notion of truth, *amath*, than does some abstract correspondence view of what it means for something to be true.

A secular interpretation of the Gospel must be ethical, and in our corporately organized world this means it must be political, and worldly. When Dietrich Bonhoeffer said that the church must never be general in its preaching but must always be specific, must support *this* program, oppose *this* war, he was really asking for a secular interpretation of the Gospel. Later, when he suggested just before his death that we must search for a "nonreligious interpretation" of the Gospel, he probably had this political-secular interpretation in mind.

To say that the secular meaning of the Gospel today must be ethical-political does not mean it must be handed down in the form of moral principles. It means, rather, that the church needs to reorder its life so that Christians can come together to consult with each other about what God is doing now in the secular world, so that they may joyfully participate in this secular mission of God. The present action of God can only be discerned if people hear the recitation of what he has done in the past and celebrate their hope of what he promises for the future. Thus some kind of worship will take place in the secularized Christian church. It could well be that we will see a revival of some of the forms used by the very earliest Christians, gatherings which resembled family meals more than massive ritual performances. Thus the current liturgical revival in the church is on the right track but has a very long way to go.

When we examine forms of church life, it is important to understand that none is in itself sacral. All forms of church life are historically conditioned, fashioned by the church in response to its need to live out its mission and speak its message to succeeding generations of men. Just as traditionalist theologians make a fatal mistake when they identify "Christianity" with one or another of its previous forms of expression, we all make a similar error when we identify "the church" with a particular historical form of its life. But modernists who want to get rid of the "institutional church" are equally mistaken. The church must have some form, some institutional expression. Still, no form is eternal. Such things as parishes based on residential proximity, professional clergy, dioceses, councils, and denominations are all merely specific forms of church life, any one of which could be discarded if a more serviceable instrumentality could be found.

THE TEST OF SERVICEABILITY

B ut what is the test of a particular church institution's serviceability? Today we must ask of every particular form of church life: Does this custom, this pattern *expedite* or *inhibit* the capacity of Christians to live in critical solidarity with the secular world? Only by living in such solidarity can Christians discern and give witness to the continuing action of God for man in the world.

But what is the source of the criticism in the Christian's "critical solidarity" with the world? This raises the final and most difficult issue that a secular theology must face: the problem of what theologians have usually called "transcendence." One of the most frequently repeated criticisms of theologians such as myself who dispense with otherworldliness and Christendom ecclesiology is that we allegedly lose any dimension of transcendence and become absorbed without remainder in the natural world as such. Some critics claim we fritter away that indispensable point of leverage from which the present world may be judged and transformed, that we become "me-too" theologians. Where is the point of critical leverage in a viable theology of the secular?

Before responding to this critical question, it is important to point out that the traditional theologians who make this attack face the same problem. They believe that the "super-natural" realm or some timeless truth provides this critical perspective, but in actuality supernatural theologies have time after time deteriorated into mere sacral legitimations of particular world views. Even more frequently, churches have criticized society not from "above history" but from behind it, from the perspective of some bygone era in which the position of the church, or of the values it thought important, seems to have been more secure. Although traditional theologies have a *formal* source of critical perspective, in actuality it often displays less real transcendence than their proponents admit.

Still, the problem remains for the theologian of the *saeculum:* What is the source of the transcendence without which any theology loses its critical and renewing perspective? Amos Wilder has written,

> If we are to have any transcendence today, even Christian, it must be in and through the secular. . . . If we are to find Grace it is to be found in the world and not overhead. The sublime firmament of overhead reality that provided a spiritual home for the souls of men until the eighteenth century has collapsed. —In "Art and Theological Meaning," *The New Orpheus*, ed. Nathan Scott (New York: Sheed & Ward, 1964).

173

But what *is* a transcendence "in and through the secular"? We cannot sacralize the past. The "overhead" is gone. The "depth" language of Tillich turns out to be no more than a new spatial imagery with the same problems the "overhead" once had. What then in our existence within history does point us toward the transcendent? At what place in his life is man touched by something which accosts him, calls him to accountability, is not subject to his manipulative control?

Theologians today have begun to answer that question with the term "future." The disappearing instant where all that was and is stands before what is to be—this is the point where the transcendent touches secular man. There he senses infinite possibility, the need for choice, the reality of hope and mystery. In this respect, as in many others, modern secular man, whose horizon of intention is history itself, has more in common with biblical man than with "classical Christian man." The Jewish scriptures refer to God variously as "He That Cometh," the "God of Promise," and "the one who goes before." Early Christianity had a radically future-directed orientation: the point of leverage for the young church was not a sacral past but a *coming* Kingdom. Likewise for theologians of the secular today, history is seen as unconditionally open-ended, transcendence becomes temporal rather than spatial, and the church is viewed as that part of the world which lives already in the reality of that which is hoped for. As the writer of the *Epistle to the Hebrews* says, "Faith is the substance of things hoped for."

In political terms, this means the church's critique of society becomes radical rather than conservative. Its vision is informed not by what has been lost but by what can yet be. It summons man not to return to a lost religiosity but to move forward toward an authentic secularity. In calling for genuine secularity as opposed to spurious types of secularity, the church questions the endowment of any particular secular society with ultimacy or finality. Secularity which is closed to the future has already become sacral, and this may be why theologians of the secular, from Gogarten on, have made a sharp distinction between secularity and secular*ism*. Whenever the process of secularization is arrested or fixed at a particular point, this becomes secular*ism*, a closed world view which must in turn be broken open.

Thus the question of whether we can develop a viable secular theology today depends on whether theologians can reappropriate eschatology and make it once again as central to the life of the church as it was in the beginning of that life. Eschatology has to do with "the last things" or with the future. It is usually dealt with by theologians in a peripheral way. But Roman Catholic theologian Karl Rahner now calls Christianity "the religion of the absolute future," and Protestant theologian Gerhard Sauter argues that the "ontological priority of the future" is the unique component of biblical faith. My conviction, too, is that eschatology must

be utterly central to theology, that all doctrines must be seen in the light
of faith's awareness of an unconditionally open secular future for which
man is unreservedly accountable. When all the dogmas and institutions
of the church are seen in this light, our task as theologians becomes
clearer. It is neither to prune nor preserve the faith but to interpret and
reinterpret it for succeeding epochs of men. In our time, it means we
must take the risk the martyred German theologian Dietrich Bonhoeffer
called for, "to speak in a secular fashion of God."

A NEW THEOLOGY WILL BE PRODUCED WHEN THE CHURCH DISCARDS ALL HANKER-
ING FOR A ROSIER PAST

E. L. MASCALL

Dr. E. L. Mascall, **the distinguished Anglican theologian,** *was born in England in 1905. He received the B.A. degree from Cambridge and the B.Sc. from London, with First Class Honors in Mathematics, and also holds the D.D. degree from Cambridge and Oxford. Ordained in the Church of England in 1932, Dr. Mascall holds the unusual honor of twice being selected Bampton Lecturer, first in Oxford and then in Columbia University. He has also been Boyle Lecturer in 1965–66. Dr. Mascall's principal publications include:* He Who Is *(1943),* Christian Theology and Natural Science *(1956),* The Importance of Being Human *(1958),* Existence and Analogy *(1966),* The Christian Universe *(1966), and* The Secularisation of Christianity *(1965). Long associated with Oxford University, since 1962 he has been Professor of Historical Theology in the University of London. Dr. Mascall works at King's College in London.*

Why Christianity Should Not Be Secularized

"G od is no more," "religionless Christianity," "God without God." When phrases such as these are heard, as they are on all sides today, from the lips not of avowed atheists or skeptics but of Christian ministers and theologians, it is not surprising that people sit up and take notice. What, they find themselves asking, can Christians possibly be meaning when they use such paradoxical expressions as these? Before discussing the movement of thought that lies behind them, it may be well to devote a little space to these phrases themselves.

First, then, "God is no more." These words in fact form the title of a tempestuous book by Werner and Lotte Pelz which was published in 1963. Now when we say, for example, "Mussolini is no more," we normally mean that Mussolini was once alive but is dead at the moment of speaking. We should not say "Lemuel Gulliver is no more," because Lemuel Gulliver, as an actual person, never existed; the most we could say would be "If Lemuel Gulliver had ever existed, he would be no more by now." So when the Pelzes say "God is no more," they cannot be meaning "If God had ever existed as a real person, he would not be existing today." Nevertheless, it is difficult to suppose that they intend their sentence to have the normal meaning, "God used to exist at one time, but he does not exist today." What in fact they seem to be meaning is that, in a metaphorical sense, the *idea* of God is "no more," that is to say that it is practically impossible for the idea of God to be formed in a human mind today, or, at any rate, that if it is so formed it will carry with it no feeling of relevance to human life. The statement thus becomes an assertion about contemporary human psychology; it will not imply that *God himself* (as distinct from our idea of him) does not exist, unless we make the further assumption that no being can exist unless contemporary people can form the idea of it or, having formed that idea, feel that it is relevant to their lives. Now it does seem to be true that, as I shall go on to emphasize, people at the present day find it difficult to form the idea of God or, having formed it, to feel that it is relevant; but this will not imply that God himself does not exist unless we assume that beings and our ideas of them are practically equivalent. And this assumption is, I think, made by the Pelzes, whether they are conscious that they are making it or not. Like many other people today they are making their minds, and the minds of people like them, the criterion by which they judge the existence and importance of all other beings, even of God himself. If this discussion has seemed somewhat technical, it is none the less germane, for the assumption which I have exposed underlies most of the writing of the thinkers with whom we are here concerned.

"Religionless Christianity." This phrase is derived from the German theologian Dietrich Bonhoeffer. As Alan Richardson has pointed out,[1] the word translated by "religious" simply means individualistic, subjective, or pietistic. "Religionless Christianity" thus merely means Christianity that is objective, outward-looking, and concerned with the life of man as a whole. It certainly does not mean Christianity that is religionless in the normal English sense of the word, and those who use it in this way have little right to claim Bonhoeffer in their support.

"God without God." *Dieu sans Dieu* is the title of the French edition of the Bishop of Woolwich's book *Honest to God*, but, whatever criticisms may be made of that work, it hardly deserves such a self-contradictory title as this. It may perhaps have been suggested by the phrase "Religion without God," which was originally applied to the system of the French positivist Auguste Comte in the early nineteenth century and which provoked the famous comment *"Religion sans Dieu? Mon Dieu, quelle religion!,"* but one need only read Dr. Robinson's book to see that he certainly talks a great deal about God, whatever may be the precise meaning that he attaches to the term.

What, we may inquire, is the conception of Christianity that lies behind such phrases as these just mentioned, and what is the significance of their use? Why is it that many people today defend what they describe as "secularized Christianity," and sometimes, as with Thomas Altizer, even as "Christian atheism"? And why is it that such descriptions, which would have been repudiated indignantly by Christians in the past, are now offered as containing the key to the church's message to men and women?

THE "GODLESSNESS" OF THE WORLD

Our starting point must be the fact that since the rise of the scientific movement in the seventeenth century it has become more and more taken for granted that "this world" is the whole of reality and that

---

1 *History, Sacred and Profane* (London, 1964), p. 81.

"this life" is the total concern of man. Whether God and a future life are explicitly denied or not, it is certainly assumed that neither need be taken into account in the ordering of either individual lives or the life of the community as a whole. The tremendous transformation of civilization that has taken place as a result of the growth of scientific technology, with all that it has brought in the way of new comforts and new anxieties, has conditioned our minds in such a way that it is no longer natural for people when they contemplate the world around them to see it as the creation of a transcendent God, in whom their ultimate end and their true bliss are to be found; rather it appears to them simply as material for ever increasing exploitation by man.

Now it would be quite unjust to blame science and scientists for this, as if they were essentially Godless. From the seventeenth century to the present day there have been multitudes of scientists who were devout believers and for whom the discoveries of science provided ever fresh material for humble and marveling adoration of the Creator. In spite of what we can now see to have been stupid and unnecessary conflicts, in which church leaders were to blame not so much for opposing scientists as such but rather for allying themselves with the older and more conservative scientists against the younger and progressive ones, it is not from science that the main opposition to religion comes at the present day. What is true, however, is that the impact of scientific technology upon the lives of both individuals and communities has conditioned them to view the world simply as material for manipulation by technologists for the satisfaction of their this-worldly needs and not to see beyond this to the God who creates and conserves it.

Much could be said about this from both the historical and the philosophical point of view, but this is not the place for it. What we are concerned with is the reaction of many present-day Christians to this situation. In the past the more farsighted and sensitive Christian spokesmen have conceived their task as twofold. First, they have labored to convince their contemporaries that the discoveries of science, so far from undermining the church's agelong beliefs, are fully compatible with them and provide widening realms for their application. Second, they have tried to work out and commend principles for directing the technological developments and organizing human society in such a way that human beings, as Christianity views them, shall be able to live in this world as God's children destined for eternal life with him. This task has been difficult, not only because technological development, on the scale and the rapidity with which it has gone on, has dazzled our minds by its achievements and overwhelmed them by its sheer size but also because the modern techniques of communication—newspapers, books, radio, television, and the whole industry of advertising and propaganda—have subjected us to an incessant process of psychological conditioning through

179

which it has become second nature to us to judge all human questions by standards of value which, whether they are sordid or idealistic, are purely this-worldly in their assumptions.

Intelligent Christians in the past—and many, too, at the present day—have done all in their power to resist this process of conditioning, not because they looked upon "this world" as evil or unimportant but for precisely the opposite reason: that they believed it to be God's creation to be used for God's glory and transformed by his grace. It was this conviction, for example, that produced the great sequence of papal social encyclicals and the Anglican movement of social thinking that has extended from Frederick D. Maurice in the early nineteenth century through Charles Gore and William Temple down to the present day. For this body of thought, the world is neither irrelevant nor self-sufficient; it is material for transformation by the power of God acting in the lives of men and women. For this tradition, therefore, there is a very clear theology of the secular, that is to say, a branch of theology which is concerned with the things of "this world" and with man as a member of it; it sees nature as avid for transformation by grace, and the secular as organically related to the eternal. It assesses all man's activities in "this world" and in "this life" by its belief that he is created and sustained by God and has been redeemed by Christ for life in God. This is, as I have said, *a theology of the secular*, that is to say, a theology which has much to say about the secular order, but it is not *a secularized theology*.

On the other hand, a theology which expresses itself in phrases such as those which I quoted at the beginning of this article—and of which typical exponents are the Bishop of Woolwich, Paul van Buren, Harvey Cox, and R. Gregor Smith[2]—is quite definitely *a secularized theology*, that is to say, a theology which accepts the secularized world's estimate of itself, which forces into line with that estimate such parts of the Christian tradition as it can, without regard to the violence which may be done to the latter in the process, and jettisons such parts of the Christian tradition as it cannot. In pursuit of this program, it is willing to redefine God in secular terms (Robinson), to give up talking about him (Cox), or even to give up belief in God altogether (Van Buren). What it clearly cannot do is to abandon all belief in Jesus of Nazareth if it is to retain the name "Christian" at all, though it is ready to go very far in that direction. Thus Van Buren, while accepting the historical existence of Jesus and the fact of his crucifixion, discards almost the whole of the Gospel narrative as fictitious. He explains the church's belief in the Resurrection

---

2 John A. T. Robinson, *Honest to God* (London, 1963), *The New Reformation* (London, 1965); Paul van Buren, *The Secular Meaning of the Gospel* (London, 1963); Harvey Cox, *The Secular City* (London, 1964); R. Gregor Smith, *Secular Christianity* (London, 1966). Cf. also William Hamilton, *The New Essence of Christianity* (New York, 1961); Thomas Altizer, *The Gospel of Christian Atheism* (Philadelphia, 1966).

as having simply resulted from some mysterious and unparalleled "Easter experience" of the primitive church just after the Crucifixion, which expressed itself in an outburst of myth-making, leading ultimately to the Gospels as we have them, and which was communicated from one generation to another by a process analogous to infection by a contagious disease, although, on Van Buren's view, neither Jesus nor anyone else has ever survived the event of bodily death.

Van Buren's is, of course, an extreme position, and it would be wrong to attribute all the elements of it to all the exponents of secularized Christianity. Nevertheless, they agree in holding that in order to be relevant to modern man Christian belief must be reinterpreted so that it is concerned entirely with "this world" and "this life." Whether there are or are not a transcendent God and a future life, they are quite irrelevant to an updated Christian theology; this will be concerned entirely with the things of this world.

The lengths to which this process of "reinterpretation" has to go in order to retain anything of the language of the Christian tradition are very remarkable indeed;[3] the changes in meaning that words are forced to undergo would be described by most people not as "reinterpretation" but as rejection. This whole process has been analyzed and criticized very radically by Hugo Meynell in his book *Sense, Nonsense and Christianity*.[4] To an independent judgment it will, I think, appear as the most extraordinary failure of nerve in the realm of belief that the Christian church has ever experienced. Its exponents have become so deeply convinced of the impossibility of preaching a supernatural Gospel to the contemporary world that they are ready to refashion the Gospel to any extent if only they are allowed to go on calling it Christianity. It is therefore not surprising that they find themselves drawn toward a philosophical position for which in any case historical factuality is of no importance. Such a position is found in the existentialism of Martin Heidegger.

They are not the first theologians who have found Heidegger's existentialism congenial to them. The well-known Biblical scholar Rudolf Bultmann had already convinced himself, by a ruthless application to the Gospels of the critical method known as form criticism, that nothing was really known about Jesus except that he had existed and had been crucified; everything else, he persuaded himself, was due to the myth-making propensities of the primitive church. He was, on the other hand, convinced, as a good Protestant, that the church's essential activity was preaching, and that the object of preaching was to bring one's hearers into a vital relationship of faith, a reorientating of the personality, which

---

3 Cf. the discussion of Van Buren's "reinterpretations" in E. L. Mascall, *The Secularisation of Christianity* (London, 1965), pp. 85 ff.

4 London, 1964.

had really nothing to do with the truth of intellectual propositions or the actual occurrence of historical events. To Bultmann, therefore, the philosophy of Heidegger, for which the whole of reality was to be found in moment-to-moment existential decisions made by individual human subjects, came as a most welcome ally. If the Gospel stories could be taken not as narratives of historical events but as mythological material with which, by the technique of preaching, people could be confronted in such a way as to bring them to existential decisions, the Christian religion could be made completely immune to attacks from historians, philosophers, and scientists alike. Thus it is that the secularizers and the extreme form critics have found themselves drawn together in a holy alliance on the basis of existentialist philosophy; for both of them it is important to reconstruct Christianity in such a way that the Gospel narratives, and especially the supernatural elements in them, need not be taken as accounts of actual events.

SECULARISM AND THE BIBLE

There is, however, one consideration which is really fatal to the position of the Christian secularizers. In order to cling on to the name of Christian at all, they must believe something more about Jesus than that there was once a man with this name who was put to death by crucifixion, for if we know nothing more about him than this it is not even possible to identify him as a definite person. Many Jews were called Jesus, and not a few Jews were crucified; there may, for all we know, have been several who were both. To which of them are we to give our allegiance? In fact, both Bultmann and the secularizers do go a good way further than their professed principles should allow them. They are ready, on the whole, to accept the Gospel narrative as factual, provided the supernatural elements have been eliminated. This is in itself a highly suspicious circumstance, for it implies that the myth-making propensity of the primitive church led it to invent supernatural events right and left, but hardly ever to invent purely natural ones. However, there is something more damaging than this. When the demythologizing has been brought to its conclusion and the last shred of supernatural events has been removed, what is the figure, the human figure, of Jesus that remains? The dreadful truth is that it is the figure of a Jesus who himself believed in the supernatural. In spite of all that we are told, and told perfectly correctly, about Jesus as "the man for others," the fact is that Jesus himself believed that there was a Father in heaven and that it was his supreme duty to do the Father's will. The religion of the secularizers may be unsupernatural, but, on their own showing, the religion of Jesus was not. Have they any really valid claim to call themselves Christian, when, in the sense which they give to the word, Christ himself was not?

Furthermore, it is extremely difficult to understand what grounds they can have, consistent with their own position, for the unique status which they agree with more orthodox Christians in assigning to Jesus. For these latter, believing as they do that Jesus is both God and man, that in him human nature is united to the preexistent and transcendent Second Person of the triune Godhead, it is not difficult to see that he is unique among all the men who have ever been born and have lived on this earth. But if the whole notion of the supernatural is repudiated, Jesus must be in every respect like all other men. It is perhaps conceivable that he is in fact the best of them all, because presumably, however many men there have been, one of them must have been the best (unless several were precisely equal in goodness), in the same sort of way that among all the elephants who have ever lived on the earth, one of them must have been the heaviest (unless several were precisely equal in weight). But this would not imply that Jesus was different from us in any essential way. It would certainly not imply that we ought to have a relationship to him that was different in kind from that which we have to all other men. It would not make him, as the man for others, essentially different from any other man who had given himself to the service of his fellowmen. Nor would it rule out the possibility that somewhere there would appear on earth another man who was as self-sacrificing as, or even more self-sacrificing than, he.

If appeal is made to the Gospels in support of the uniqueness of Jesus, it must be replied that the Gospels come to us from people who held precisely that supernatural view of Jesus which the secularizers repudiate. If it is said that we know by our personal experience of him that he is unique, it must be replied that if, after demythologizing the Gospel record, we are left with nothing about Jesus except the fact that he existed and was crucified (and perhaps, not to press Bultmann too far, with a few further unidentifiable reminiscences as well), it is very difficult to see how we can identify the person of whom we have personal experience with the Jesus of the Gospel; how do we know that it is not Buddha or Krishna of whom we have this experience? And if, as thoroughly consistent secularizers, we hold with Van Buren that neither Jesus nor anyone else survives his bodily death, it is even more difficult to see how we can have any personal experience of someone who is not alive in bodily form on the earth today. The most that we could say would be that we are able to feel *as if* the Jesus of the Gospels was still alive and with us, but this would be nothing more than an interesting psychological fact about ourselves, namely the fact that we were able after reading the Gospels to construct for ourselves the image of a man, to whom we gave the name "Jesus," which we found uniquely inspiring. Now I am absolutely sure that the secularizing Christians have an experience of Jesus which is other than this; the way in which they speak and write about him shows it. But I am equally certain that they cannot account for this experience on the grounds which they themselves allege; it can be accounted for only by that supernatural view of Jesus which they professedly reject.

Surprising as such a claim may be, many secularizers of Christianity have claimed to find the basis of their position in the Bible. Thus Cox, in his very interesting book *The Secular City*, has applied to the account of creation in Genesis the description "the Disenchantment of Nature," to the account of the Exodus the description "the Desacralization of Politics," and to the Covenant at Sinai the description "the Deconsecration of Values."[5] He points out that for "pre-secular" man all natural objects are divine and magical, all social officers and organs are also divine, and all the valuations which he has inherited are absolute and immutable. "Just as nature is perceived by tribal man both as a part of his family and as the locus of religious energy, so the political power structure is accepted as an extension of familial authority and as the unequivocal will of the gods. . . . Both tribal man and secular man see the world from a particular, socially and historically conditioned point of view. But modern secular man knows it, and tribal man did not; therein lies the crucial difference."[6] I am somewhat doubtful whether the ordinary inhabitant of our secular cities—the girl behind the counter at Woolworth's or the average baseball fan—is very conscious of the relativity of the scale of values of the society of which he is a member; I think rather that he accepts them unreflectingly as part of the natural order of things and has a somewhat contemptuous attitude to those of lesser breeds outside his law. I fully agree that the Christian doctrine of the Creator-God makes it impossible to view any natural object or any human authority as intrinsically divine. But I cannot agree that the biblical view of creation is the first step in the movement toward complete secularization.

I think we may see here one of those not uncommon instances in which apparently academic theological nuances have extremely practical implications. Cox's conception of creation is a very common Protestant one. It sees the world as owing its existence to a sheer *utterance* by God, who, as it were, commands it into existence as something of a totally different nature from his and having no real relation to him. On this view it might well seem that creatures could have no knowledge of God whatever and would therefore have to order their affairs as if he did not exist. It is possible to stress God's utter supremacy and "otherness" in such a way that, for all practical purposes, he might just as well not exist. Karl Barth's rejection of all forms of natural theology would lead to this result if it were not supplemented by his further assertion that God can, when he wishes, reveal himself in arbitrary and unconditioned acts. This may

---

5 *Op. cit.*, pp. 21, 25, 30.
6 *Op. cit.*, pp. 25, 30.

possibly—though I am not sure—underlie the famous sentence of Bonhoeffer, so dear to the secularizers, "God is teaching us that we must live as men who can get on very well without him."

There is, however, another view of creation, which is common to Western Catholicism and to Eastern Orthodoxy, which sees the difference between God and his creatures as consisting precisely in the fact that there *is* a relation between them. It is quite emphatic that God and the creature are of radically different status: God is entirely self-existent and self-sustaining, and the creature is entirely dependent and finite. But it is entirely dependent *on God*, without whose incessant creative activity it could not exist for one moment. Therefore it is in perpetual communication with God, and the very genuine, but relative and finite, autonomy which it enjoys is the consequence of, and is not contradicted by, its utter dependence on God. And it is, I would hold, this view that is assumed by the Bible and not an incipient secularism. When Cox describes the Genesis account of creation as "really a form of 'atheistic propaganda',"[7] I can accept this only if the word "atheistic" is meant to imply that the world is not divine, but not if it means that God does not exist or that he is irrelevant to the world's concerns. I believe that we touch here the basic difference between Protestant and Catholic Christianity, which underlies all their more obvious disagreements; it is a difference about the relation between God and the world, about the fundamental status of the creature. I would not myself have ventured to say, especially in these ecumenical days, that the ultimate outcome of Protestantism is practical, if not theoretical, atheism. But, since such an intelligent Protestant as Cox says so, I feel that this is one of the points at which dialogue is urgently necessary. It is paradoxical, but not unintelligible, that an unbalanced emphasis upon the absolute supremacy of God can end up in a virtual denial of his existence.

THE SECULARIST CAPITULATION

I must now return to my central theme, that in their proposal to offer to a secularized world a secularized version of Christianity, the thinkers whom I am criticizing have radically misunderstood the nature both of the Christian Gospel and of the present-day world. It is not surprising that a certain initial success should attend a presentation of the Christian religion that is cut precisely to the present-day world's own measurements. I cannot think, however, that this success will be long-lived, and there are already signs that intelligent secularists have seen through it. There are also signs that some of its most vocal exponents have come to see that if you are going to secularize Christianity to this extent you had

---

7 *Op. cit.*, p. 23.

better keep the secularism and drop the Christianity. Right from the beginning, the Christian church has been conscious that it was bound to challenge the assumptions of its environment, for it knew that the world was deficient in its understanding of its own predicament. Lacking the clear recognition that man is the creature of God and yet a fallen creature, and ignorant of the fact that in Christ God himself had come to redeem him, the pagan world oscillated between cynical hedonism and frank despair. The astonishing multiplicity and diversity of the religious systems which offered recipes for human salvation testifies to the desperation and impotence to which men and women were reduced. There was little in them to appeal to intelligent people; we may recall the famous remark of Edward Gibbon that "the various modes of worship, which prevailed in the Roman world, were all considered by the people, as equally true; by the philosopher, as equally false; and by the magistrate, as equally useful."[8] It was the achievement of the Christian church to rescue men from this bondage, and to show them that the partial truths which the various cults contained were to be found in their fullness in the Christian Gospel. Christianity was both the destroyer and the residuary legatee of the pagan religions.

Our situation is very different, for the church today is confronted not by a conflicting and competing multitude of rival religions but by a miasma of sheer Godlessness, which has disintegrated the Christian civilization of the Western world and has gone far toward swallowing up the ancient religious civilizations of Asia and the tribal religious cultures of Africa as well. But different as our situation is, the task of the church is fundamentally the same. It is that of bringing men and women from darkness and the shadow of death into the glorious liberty of the children of God. The Christian attitude toward the contemporary world must be one neither of hostility nor of acquiescence but of discrimination and understanding. The total capitulation of the Christian secularizers to the climate of the time is no doubt governed by the best motives; they are so anxious to win people to a verbal acceptance of the Christian religion that they are ready to place the label "Christian" on everything that they see. But, objectively considered, this is a loss of nerve that is near to apostasy. It is, of course, true that we need to discover new ways of presenting the Christian faith in a new situation, and a situation in which we are confronted not by rival religions but by no religion is undoubtedly a new one in the church's experience. But for this very reason the utmost care and consideration are needed if we are not to defeat the very purpose for which the church is here.

I have not attempted here to disprove the arguments which are directed against the truth of orthodox Christianity, though I believe

---

8 *The Decline and Fall of the Roman Empire,* chap. ii; *GBWW,* Vol. 40, p. 12b.

HUMAN BEINGS SHALL BE ABLE TO LIVE IN THIS WORLD AS GOD'S CHILDREN
DESTINED FOR ETERNAL LIFE WITH HIM

they are in fact invalid. My reason is that the Christian secularizers themselves go in very little for argument of this kind. Anyone who has tried to argue with them will have been exasperated by their unwillingness to face straight issues of truth and falsehood. Hardly ever is one told that such-and-such a belief is false; it is always "modern man (or twentieth-century man, or secular man, or man-come-of-age) is no longer able (or willing, or prepared) to think in that way." There are, of course, newly discovered facts and truths about man and the world which need to be assimilated by Christian thinkers. There are new ethical problems, arising specially in fields as diverse as genetic studies, population planning, and methods of war, whose solutions cannot be found in the existing manuals of moral theology and which need the most frank and respectful cooperation of experts in many fields. Much work has already been done along these lines. In such a situation it is inevitable, right, and salutary that Christian theologians will sometimes feel inadequately equipped and baffled; this is true about other experts as well. But the worst thing a Christian can do in such a situation is to abandon his distinctive position and insights; that will not only be unfaithfulness to the Christian gospel, it will also deprive his non-Christian fellows of the special help that he might have been able to give them. In a situation as novel as that of the present day, the thing that is necessary above all others is that we shall keep our heads and not panic. And it is panic that is the most evident note of secularized theology.

It is natural that in the modern world Christians should be tempted to despair by the church's apparent lack of success, and that they should look back with a certain nostalgia to the days when Christianity was the avowed faith of whole nations and when as a matter of course all but the most courageous unbelievers took part in the worship of the church. But it may well be doubted whether there was in fact more deliberate, intelligent, and courageous religious practice in such times than there is today. Religious practice was often just as much a matter of social conformity then as the lack of it is now. And I am often filled with admiration for the way in which many Christian layfolk order their lives (and not merely say their prayers and come to church), in spite of the psychological and other forms of pressure to which they are constantly subjected from the circumambient secular environment. It may very well be, as Fr. Karl Rahner has suggested, that the present diaspora-situation of the church—a condition in which Christians are a minority scattered throughout a secularized community—is only temporary and may yield to a new Christendom. Whether that will be so, and if so when, we are not in a position to tell; history almost always proceeds as a succession of surprises. What we can be sure about is that a new Christendom will be very different from the old ones.

The great Christian civilizations of the past—those of medieval West-

ern Europe and Byzantium—were the outcome of the conversion (sometimes from very mixed motives) of rulers, who brought their subjects into
the church with them as a matter of course. The consequence was that,
while the social organism as a whole bore quite genuine marks of its
Christian character, the religion of individual men and women could
run all the way from cynical or superficial conformism at the one extreme
to blazing sanctity at the other. And even so, the basically insufficient
character of the structure was shown by the endemic conflict between
church and state in the West and by the Byzantine Caesaropapism in
the East. These particular forms of Christendom are most unlikely to be
repeated, for they went with a particular stage of social and political
development which was the correlate of a preindustrial and pretech-
nological economy.

Whether, and in what respects, twentieth-century man can be described as more "mature" than his ancestors is not an easy question to
answer, nor is it easy to say whether there is any intelligible sense in
which he can be said to have now "come of age." On matters such as
this, it is well to be prudently agnostic. Of one thing, however, I feel
sure: When in future ages men look back upon our present century, they
will see the movement to secularize Christian theology as an odd and
transient phenomenon, only to be explained by a loss of nerve on the
part of a group of well-meaning Christians, whose fear that the church
had altogether lost touch with the contemporary world had led them into
frantic capitulation in a desperate attempt for survival.

THE SECULARIZATION OF THE WORLD IS NOT A MASSIVE DEFECTION FROM FAITH
BUT RATHER A FURTHER STEP IN THE HISTORIC RELATIONSHIP OF CHRISTIANITY
TO CULTURE

MARTIN E. MARTY

*Martin E. Marty, Chairman of the Church History field at the
University of Chicago, was born in 1928 in West Point, Nebraska.
Dr. Marty, an ordained minister, was educated at Concordia
Seminary, Chicago Lutheran Theological Seminary, and the
University of Chicago, where he took a Ph.D. in American reli-
gious and intellectual history.* Co-editor of Church History, *the
professional journal of the American Society of Church History,
the annual* New Theology, *and Associate Editor of* Christian
Century, *Dr. Marty's voice is influential in shaping contemporary
theology. Dr. Marty has written, among many titles,* Varieties of
Unbelief *(1964),* Religion and Social Conflict *(1964),* The Infidel:
Freethought and American Religion *(1961), and* The New Shape
of American Religion *(1959). Dr. Marty lives in Riverside, Illinois,
with his wife and children.*

Does Secular Theology
Have a Future?

G od-killing philosophers in nineteenth-century Germany claimed that
they had succeeded in transforming religion into atheism. The
French critic Ernest Renan, after he had surveyed their attempts, advised people: Never believe a German when he tells you that he is an
atheist. The German's religious impulse was always too profound, his
atheism too qualified to be convincing. Today's religious thinkers often
claim to represent the advance guard of secularization. Now it is time to
advise their readers: Never trust a theologian when he tells you that he
has succeeded in secularizing religion. His religious roots remain too
complex, his definitions of the secular too specialized to convey conventional meanings. In other words, Christian secularism is by no means all
that it sometimes claims to be. That this is so becomes clear once we
consider how it has developed. To understand it, we need to know the
needs that it is attempting to satisfy.

The beginning of the Secular Theology Episode can be traced to
the end of World War II with the publication in Germany of Dietrich
Bonhoeffer's prison letters. These letters appealed for a "religionless
Christianity" in a world come of age. They summarized a generation
of German thought on religionlessness (by Karl Barth) and secularization
(by Friedrich Gogarten and others). The movement to secularize religion
crested with the publication in the early 1960's of Bishop John Robinson's
Honest to God, Paul van Buren's *The Secular Meaning of the Gospel*, and
Harvey Cox's *The Secular City*. It took a dramatic turn in William Hamilton's radical godlessness and lives a less dramatic afterlife in recent works
like R. G. Smith's *Secular Christianity*, Colin Williams' *Faith in a Secular
Age*, and Lesslie Newbigin's *Honest Religion for Secular Man*. Frontier
theologians have begun to move to other concerns, but the issues presented during this episode will remain as public disturbances.

The very idea of secularizing anything religious seems startling. *New
Yorker* writer Ved Mehta, after he had visited representative radicals,
summarized their efforts from what we may take to be a characteristic
public point of view: "The New Theologian set himself the old task of
equating faith and theology with reason and secularism, and doing so

without any sacrifice on either side—a task, in its way, no less tantalizing than squaring the circle."[1] Tantalizing, indeed. For half a millennium religious leaders had fought a rear-guard action against secularization, tending to bless anything religious. Then, for half a century, Christian theologians attacked "religion" because it represented human striving, which kept man from hearing the message of the Christian faith. It is only within the past five years that church people have been urged by theologians to bless the secular and told that this new attitude to secularity is not only no threat to faith but can enhance it. Secular theology claims that it has developed out of the logic of prophetic religion and lived off its biblical momentum.

The effort to bring together the world of religion and the secular had become urgent. While eventually and inevitably the debate centered on "the problem of God," it was demonstrably a debate over the human future, based on analysis of the present. "We are not talking about the absence of the experience of God, but about the experience of the absence of God," wrote Hamilton.[2] In neither version was speculative metaphysics or revelation the obsession. In either version not God but the human phenomenon was the center of debate.

That theologians do their work in an age when they must speak of God's silence or eclipse or death means only that men are experiencing his absence. Religious thinkers would fail in their duty if they did not take such an epochal change in human culture into account. Not to the accommodating spirit of traitorous theologians but to widespread public practice must be ascribed the warrant for the change in which the old cosmic backdrop, the ageless curtain of transcendence, had gradually begun to disappear from view. Theologian Rudolf Bultmann asked, in this mood: "Have you read anywhere [in the newspapers] that political or social or economic events are performed by supernatural powers such as God, angels or demons? Such events are always ascribed to natural powers, or to good or bad will on the part of men, or to human wisdom or stupidity."[3] Clerics and laymen alike read the newspapers. Their vision need not be limited by the mentality these reflect, but their language is shaped by the common experience of their time which that mentality daily nurtures.

The new theologians were not content with the newspapers' vision. They wanted to move people beyond it. They advocated a secular style but loaded the term "secular" with many different meanings and significances. In their analytic and descriptive work they used it one way; when

---

1 *The New Theologian* (New York: Harper & Row, 1966), p. 209.

2 William Hamilton and Thomas J. J. Altizer, *Radical Theology and the Death of God* (New York: Bobbs-Merrill, 1966), p. 28.

3 *Jesus Christ and Mythology* (New York: Charles Scribner's Sons, 1958), p. 37.

it turned up in their constructive and prescriptive writing it meant something else. Ved Mehta thought they were trying to square the circle. But there is another possibility: The new theologians may be providing us with clues to move both beyond religion *and* beyond secularity. To follow up these clues, I will begin by considering the relation between religion and secularity. We will then be able to see how the secularist movement answers to the need for radical religious change while it still remains deeply "religious." Finally, I will comment on some possibilities for its future development.

RELIGION AND SECULARITY

Theologians today sometimes give "religion" a dramatic definition. Ever since Barth spoke of "Religion as Unbelief," it has come to represent an obsolete and sterile individualism, an imprisoning metaphysic, a sacral sector of life, an appeal to God as problem-solver, an attempt at human self-justification. But suppose we de-escalate the usage back to the ordinary level where it incorporates faith and theology and where it deals with the whole human enterprise relating to the divine or the sacral or the ultimate. Is it possible for "religion" in this sense to be secularized?

Secularity (and not secularism, which is not at issue here) received provocative definition from Bonhoeffer when he equated it with "the world come of age." Van Buren styles the secular as empirical and pragmatic in method and mood. Harvey Cox gave it the most popular usage: Secularization is "the loosing of the world from religious and quasi-religious understandings of itself, the dispelling of all closed world-views, the breaking of all supernatural myths and sacred symbols."[4] If a world needs a religious or quasi-religious understanding of itself, it is manifestly not secular. Thus, the reintrusion of a symbol like God—including a future God of hope who is waited for—or its equivalent would be a call for at least a quasi-religious understanding of a world.

The majority of recent theologians "identify" more with the secular process and tendency than with the religious. From the public point of view, they are unsuccessful. Religious institutions employ them. They write to and speak for religious audiences; few of their books are reviewed by laymen, to say nothing of "secular man." Some are bishops; they often wear clerical garb and bear ecclesiastical titles. Jules Monnerot once observed that a religion is seen as such only by those outside it; the religionless Christians are still Christians and have not extricated themselves from the circle of religious concerns. So it is legitimate to ask, "Can and should religion be secularized?"

---

4 *The Secular City* (New York: Macmillan, 1965), p. 2.

Five possibilities can be distinguished. Religion can indeed be secularized if men play word games and change terms, giving them wholly new meanings. Anything can then become anything. Despite occasional frustrations over theological language, we can rule out this possibility, since the theologians do tell us what they have in mind in their use of the terms.

The next two choices are possibilities but are not in debate at this time. Religious thinkers could develop a humanism which remembers religion and Christianity but which is content to make absolutely no special or ultimate claims for the faith or for Jesus Christ. This human effort appears every day: Jesus is a hero in a serial of heroes, and nothing more. No theological claims are made.

Equally not at issue is an opposite extreme, in which radical religious change can occur with changed symbols. That is, men can contrive a new religion and call it a secular religion. Such contrivances were "the darling vice" of nineteenth-century French system-builders. But they, like their earlier Revolutionary counterparts, usually ended in parodies of historic faiths and found it necessary to erect new symbols like The Absolute Spirit or The Integrating Absolute or Divine Providence, any of which would embarrass the cool new theologian.[5]

The remaining two alternatives are live. Unreflective religion can be subtly transformed into unreflective secularism. People may retain symbols which have lost all cognitive import. They may see these symbols reduced to routine in service of new ideologies or practices. Much of the attempt to devise a Christian secularity is actually based on the theological judgment that this has happened in "folk religion" today. In Cox's terms, the product is a "quasi-religion," resulting not from "secularization" but from uncontrolled religious change. The new theology can then be viewed as a rescue operation from such mistaken "secularism." Social thinkers like Ernest Gellner and J. Milton Yinger have chosen to speak in those very terms.

Finally, one can foresee the development not of religion-turned-secular but of radical religious change, controlled chiefly under the symbols of non-change, though some new symbols may arise. This is what has been occurring in secular-oriented theology. In concentrating on this development I have not answered the question of whether religion can be secularized; I only say that the people who speak of secularizing theology are not bringing religion to complete secularization. They are working for dramatic religious change—an effort no less radical and potentially more productive than attempts at theological squaring of the circle would be.

---

5 For examples *see* D. G. Charlton, *Secular Religions in France, 1815–1870* (London: Oxford, 1963).

THE NEED FOR RADICAL RELIGIOUS CHANGE

The question can now be reformulated: *Should* men work for religious change under the category of secularity? Yes, for two general reasons. The theologians are moved first by concern for the Christian faith, for which they are apologists and evangelists. Those who speak of Christian secularity or Christian atheism do not abandon the religious community. Second, humanist concerns are evident. The new orientation in theology is ethically motivated. For these religious thinkers, vestigial religion from the presecular era as well as today's secular paganisms are inhibiting human freedom and love. They thus share the grand argument of the nineteenth-century God-killers who saw religion as the opium and the oppressor. In Marx's terms, they would interpret *and* change the world. They have carried theology from seminaries into the streets.

The new theologians, then, resist the attractions of straight-line humanism and make distinct (if often imprecise) theological demands. Such efforts are audacious, hardly deserving E. L. Mascall's judgment that they represent a failure of nerve. If their language is sometimes strident, it may be occasioned not only by narcissism (who can judge motives?) but also by the need to gain attention for a discipline which had been safely sequestered from life.

When they avoid straightforward humanism and make special theological claims, their work is marked by an attempt to locate properly the scandal of the faith. Believing that the Christian call to discipleship does not call people out of the world but is designed to confront them with a special demand in the middle of the world, they would strip away the extraneous "religious" dimensions of culture and help people seek a view of reality inside the circle of faith which is congruent with the views held outside: Only *then* would they come to the mandates and promises of faith.

That religious thought in our time reflects our time should not surprise us. Theologians are "born secular" in a world in which most people most of the time make decisions the same way whether or not God exists. They work in the empirical and pragmatic environment of American universities. Trained in iconoclasm and exorcism, they oppose quasi-religions. They want men of faith to inaugurate change, wearied as they are of seeing four centuries of drift and of grudging adaptations or surrenders to secular autonomies. They seek a vantage point for criticizing subliminal, unreflective, and unproductive secularism. Thus they employ Christian norms to attack the "real" religions of the modern world: nationalism, communism, The American Way of Life, etc. Most of all, they want to do what theologians of every age have tried to do: to speak meaningfully to people who inhabit mentally furnished apartments different from those they lived in when the scriptures were first written.

197

Given such a charter, it is difficult to see how recent theology could have taken a different course; if the account sounds sympathetic, it should. My criticisms after a decade of involvement are from within and in no case evidence a desire for regress to an earlier religious moment. If the new theologians are to be faulted, it should be less for failure of nerve and more for inaccuracy in stating their purpose and lack of imagination in describing the secular and settling for too little.

DEBATE OVER THE FUTURE

The new theologians are engaged in a debate about the future of man. Their mode of discourse is ordinarily prophecy under the guise of reporting. They analyze, assess, and portray the human "prophetic past," the present, and then they point to the future. Such an approach compels them to make one-dimensional generalizations about the secular tendency of history which few empirical historians or social analysts would make. Their attempt to charter a view of human historical evolution as a sequence of all-encompassing epochs, each colored by a single embracing and inclusive mode of thinking and acting, recalls, surprisingly, the hopes of Hegel and Comte. Each epoch is somehow an integral and wholistic spiritual system. One basic norm of understanding colors it. There is a single social and cultural ideal of rationality. Whatever occurs counter to this charter must be overlooked or explained away as obsolete, extraneous, or mutational.[6]

Most secular sociologists or historians would gasp at the idea that the world is, or is on the point of being, loosed "from religious and quasi-religious understandings of itself." The theologians' vision is selective. Hegel had to "rule out Siberia" from his consideration of the tendency of the world-spirit in his time. The Slavic people "remains excluded from our consideration, because hitherto it has not appeared as an independent element in the series of phases that reason has assumed in the world."[7] Secular-oriented theologians have to exile most of the world to Siberia because they extrapolate from the main line of Western academic and technological-industrial development as normative for all dimensions of human spiritual fruition. "Just as if the world and its history had existed for our sakes! For everyone regards all times as fulfilled in his own, and cannot see his own as one of many passing waves . . . If he looks for change, he hopes that he will soon see it come, and may help to bring it about."[8] Jacob Burckhardt's complaint against his system-hungry contem-

---

6 This insight is developed from Walter A. Stromseth, "A Society Without God?" in *Dialog*, V, No. 4 (Autumn, 1966), 282 ff.

7 *The Philosophy of History*; GBWW, Vol. 46, p. 319b.

8 *Force and Freedom*, ed. J. H. Nichols (New York: Meridian, 1955), p. 317.

poraries is curiously fresh today.

Given such a passion for one's own kind and stage of development, the provisional descriptions of the empirical world under the category of the secular only *appear* to be historical and reportorial. The secular man of these theological depictions rarely appears on stage, and when he does he seldom recognizes himself in the portrait. The apparent reportorial inaccuracy about the human condition may alienate some "secular" men just as it may lie near the secret of the appeal to some adherents of secular-oriented theology; it pictures the world of new theologians' desires.

THE LIMITATIONS OF SECULARISM

Christian secularity is a kind of Christian utopian thought, a picture of main themes of today's world and of the foreseeable future in the light of a longer hope projected backward into our time. In a book significantly titled *The Future as History*, Robert Heilbroner provides a clue concerning the kind of discourse with which we deal from Bonhoeffer through Cox to Hamilton. "At bottom, *a philosophy of optimism is an historic attitude toward the future*—an attitude based on the tacit premise that the future will accommodate the striving which we bring to it. Optimism is grounded in the faith that the historic environment, as it comes into being, will prove to be benign and congenial—or at least neutral to our private efforts." This phenomenon of optimism as a philosophy of life, which "we find restricted to a minute period of historic time and geographic space,"[9] seems to run counter to any careful depictions of overall human tendencies that can be gathered from the actual pluralist world and yet is not simply to be equated with Christian hope.

Secular theology, in effect, tells us: The world for four centuries has been removing the shackles of superstition, religion, and quasi-religion. In the future it will purge itself further and may complete the purge. At the end of the process is a kind of serene, carefree agnostic who cares for others. Empirical and pragmatic modes of reasoning, characteristic of industrial-scientific society, are and will be all-embracing. This process toward such a fulfillment belongs to the prophetic momentum of Christian history. It is our task to hasten the process, to fight off opposition, to engage in mopping-up operations. Here is, as Heilbroner says, an "historic attitude toward the future."

Whatever else the new theology is, it is not agnostic. The effort to evangelize for this faith seems legitimate and admirable, so long as those who are confronted with it know what is occurring so that they can count the cost. Yet the effort in itself violates the basic analytic definitions of the secular provided by the secularizing theologians. It goes beyond

---

9 *The Future as History* (New York: Harper & Brothers, 1960), p. 17.

problem-solving empiricism and is, as Karl Löwith has described philosophy of history, a "systematic interpretation of universal history in accordance with a principle by which historical events and successions are unified and directed toward an ultimate meaning."[10]

Arthur Danto calls such endeavor "substantive" philosophy of history —a description that is logically inappropriate though it may be theologically appropriate. The philosopher of history does more than give an account of the past (e.g., the record of *all* of spiritual history under the category of "secularization"). He wants to deal with the *whole* of history. He employs historical data but does violence to empirical history as he seeks "meaning" and "significance" from a vantage which he could gain only if he knew the outcome of history. Not all philosophy of history is theology of history (though Danto argues that Marx and Engels wore theological spectacles, divining a divine plan without a divine being!). Secular theology is a theology of history, since it speaks at least in veiled or hopeful terms about God and makes ultimate claims for Jesus Christ.

The proper name for this part of the enterprise is prophecy, and Danto calls it that. "A prophecy is not merely a statement about the future, . . . It is a certain *kind* of statement about the future . . . an *historical* statement about the future. The prophet is one who speaks about the future in a manner which is appropriate only to the past, or who speaks of the present in the light of a future treated as a *fait accompli*." Such activity may be legitimate, but it is hardly characteristic of the secular mode.

THE "RELIGIOUS" SIDE OF THE SECULARISTS

The new theologians are never disconcerted when the selective features and inaccurate results of their reporting are pointed out to them. It takes no journalistic acuity, for instance, to demonstrate that superstition and paganism may very well be the real religions of the modern world—both in the developing nations and in the developed secular West —and we have no guarantee that the future will take this or that specific contrary form. The theologians' history of secularization with its "hope projected backward" is not agnostic. It pays no attention to religious change in cultures where religion never has been otherworldly, and is provincial. Most of all, it wants to retain a "religious" element transformed out of Christianity along with selective liberating features of secularity. "Secular man" is often a more confining model than he turns out to be in these prophecies. He has not turned out so well and is not turning out so well. Says the theologian: He needs the Christian hope and faith.

---

10 *Meaning in History* (Chicago: University of Chicago Press, 1957), p. 1. *See also* Arthur Danto, *Analytical Philosophy of History* (London: Cambridge, 1965), chap. i.

TO BE A CHRISTIAN IS TO BE AMONG PEOPLE WHOSE
HOPES ILLUMINATE HUMAN EXPERIENCE AND PRO-
VIDE A SENSE OF DIRECTION

In every instance, after the analytic description of the secular, the theologian later "pulls rank" when he turns constructive. Bonhoeffer's "world come of age" is one in which we are later told God is telling us that we do not need God in a world where we will find Christ. This is certainly secularity with a difference. Bishop Robinson questions quasi-religion but reimports Jesus and a kind of liturgy. Cox is aware that his reporting is not mere reporting. "Of course there are events and movements which momentarily raise questions about whether secularization has really succeeded in unseating the gods of traditional religion."[11] But he lets the utopian picture of *The Secular City* stand, even though not everyone is on schedule in it. And in that secular milieu, Cox wants the church to be "God's avant garde," something which is neither merely nor utterly secular. Even Hamilton repairs to Jesus and waits for God—activities which must be characterized as at least quasi-religious.

Numbers of the secular-oriented theologians give evidence that they know what they are doing. Paul van Buren recognizes that his secular man is an autobiographical portrayal which enlarges on the author's interest in language analysis. "Are we really being descriptive when we call the world secular? If so, it is a most imprecise description."[12] And "late" Cox of 1966—as opposed to "early" Cox of 1965—has moved into a creative new stage which allows for a kind of metaphysics, a kind of myth, a God of hope as a possibility. Whether those who used *The Secular City* as a manual for unburdening themselves of myth and religion can follow him into the new and more audacious phase remains to be seen. His career seems to bear out the difficulty of secularizing religion, of bringing Christian secularity into equation with either "mere" secularity as a minimal definition or with "utter" secularity as a maximal one.[13]

The secular theology episode was clearly never an assay at Christian humanism. In every case a theological claim, usually based on covert metaphysics or overt appeal to revelation and faith-commitment, eventually appeared. The Christian tradition was appealed to as containing something regulative or normative, as holding the true impetus or momentum for "authentic" secularization, as possessing a secret which the merely secular man could not find by himself. The concept of secularization died the death of a thousand qualifications. Perhaps it would be well if we could follow David Martin's example in sociology and try to expunge the concept of "secularization" from theology. It may be too late for that. But we can use the word with more care, recognizing with Martin that it is full of ambiguity, does not refer to a unitary process, and makes sense chiefly when we imply on dogmatic lines "an analytic

---

11 *Op. cit.*, p. 2.
12 *The Secular Meaning of the Gospel* (New York: Macmillan, 1963), p. 194.
13 *The Secular City Debate*, ed. Daniel Callahan (New York: Macmillan, 1966), pp. 181 f.

criterion for differentiating the real or genuine element in religion from the bogus."[14]

Unquestionably there are many accurate features to the theologians' reporting on secularization. Who would want to argue with the futuristic logic of industrial-technological development or contest the picture of widespread agnosticism in the academy or practical godlessness in the marketplace? He would be blind who would suggest that people make religious decisions against the kind of cosmic backdrop they once knew. But the scaffold built from selective features of these changes is still frail for prophets.

THREE SCENARIOS FOR THE FUTURE

The theologians, then, at the start of their work are rather original in their attempt to "travel light" in the matters of metaphysics and revelation, in their moratoriums on "God talk" or their diffidence about transcendence. They are writing scenarios about the future of man, as they believe it will be and, in part, as they want it to be.

The secular scenario does not leave man merely or utterly secular but foresees a Christian difference. Gabriel Vahanian speaks of "secularity as a Christian obligation." Arend van Leeuwen says that secularization may be "broadly described as the creative and liberating activity of the Word of God."[15] This is prophetic, protestant language. The figures of the prophets and of Jesus as scorners of quasi-religion shadow the scenario.

The secularizing theologians less regularly portray the whole complex of secular life. One inner-city minister avers that their "utopian" picture can be accounted for only because they tend to be "white Protestant Anglo-Saxon members of an affluent society who hold academic tenure." Their vision is colored by their exclusive acquaintance with "technologists, planners, architects, civil rights leaders, academicians, folk-singers, swingers." It is not the view people derive or foresee in a world of hunger, war, hatred, misery, and hopelessness.

The alternative religious scenario is equally problematic. It derives from Paul Tillich's kind of definition of man as being somehow by nature religious and borrows from sociologists' and historians' accounts of the durability of the religious response, the mistrust of the category of secularization in the interest of "radical religious change." Since *Homo religiosus* at least will let one bring up the subject of religion, many reveal a "hope projected backward" and foresee a religious human future. Ordinarily, advocates of this future tend to draw their religious models chiefly

---

14 In *Penguin Survey of the Social Sciences, 1965*, ed. Julius Gould (Baltimore: Penguin, 1965), pp. 169–82.

15 *Christianity in World History* (London: Edinburgh House Press, 1964), p. 332.

from the past. Thus Mascall advocates the category of "the supernatural" —itself a time-bound philosophical usage—as a kind of first step toward theological cure.

The third scenario deals with the "mixed" character of man, his religio-secular past and present. Such a vision is more agnostic about the future, less *a prioristic* about future development; it is no less hopeful or open and should commend itself to secular man for its honesty both in portraying man as he is and in implying that theological claims are to be made. From this vantage which hopes for culture and man "beyond religion *and* beyond secularity" the secular theologian begins to look conservative. He, too, draws his models for man from what he knows has been.

Leslie Dewart, in his book *The Future of Belief*, goes beyond the sterility of the secular model and the obsolescence of the religious one in advising: "We should not place any *a priori* limits on the level of religious consciousness to which man may easily rise. In the future we may well learn to conceive God in a nobler way."[16] Such a scenario and program would see the recovery and development of the category of human spirituality and is open to a religio-secular development in culture and man. A new religious consciousness does not solve all theological problems or problems of faith, many of us would want to be protestants in relation to future religious constructs as we are toward present ones. But stimulation of such a consciousness is validly related to the most urgent questions in humane and theological life today.

The theologians of secularity, with Comtian passion, like to tell us that, say, three kinds of cultures or men have appeared so far. We have moved beyond the tribal-primitive and the town-religious into the city-secular. In this game of numbers and epochs, the inevitable question arises: Why stop at three? Why let our version of the latest become the ultimate?

THE CHRISTIAN TEST: JESUS CHRIST'S "OTHERNESS"

Most of the examples in this essay came from Protestant Christianity; they could as well be drawn from recent Catholicism, and there are many parallels in Judaism. It would be well to suggest only what is ahead for Protestant and Catholic Christians who have been engaged in developing secular theology. Their test will have to do with Jesus Christ, who has remained central throughout the recent theological episode. Günther Bornkamm has summarized the Jesus of this movement: "Jesus belongs to this world. Yet in the midst of it he is of unmistakable otherness. This is the secret of his influence and his rejection. Faith has given manifold expression to this secret."[17] Secularizing theologians have given

---

16 (New York: Herder & Herder, 1966), pp. 184 f.
17 *Jesus of Nazareth* (New York: Harper & Brothers, 1960), p. 56.

MEANING ARISES AS WE TRY TO
MAKE SENSE OF POSITIONS HELD
IN THE PAST IN THE LIGHT OF
ALTERED CONDITIONS

eloquent witness for twenty years to the first and last sentence of this saying. If they are to sustain their witness and consolidate their gains, they will soon have to produce more compelling descriptions of his "otherness." Call such questions revelational or philosophical; call them quasi-metaphysical: they have been bypassed or suppressed. Men have carried the secularization of theology as far as it need go: to a Jesus who "belongs to this world." Regress to "religion" is out of the question. His "otherness" is to be witnessed in the ongoing debate about the future of man, one which points beyond religion *and* beyond secularity.

M. D. CHENU

Father M. D. Chenu, scholar and a priest of the Dominican order, was born in 1895 at Soisy-sur-Seine, near Paris. He studied philosophy, theology, and history in Rome from 1914 to 1920. For twenty years he was Professor of Theology at the Dominican seminary of Le Saulchoir and was rector from 1932 to 1942. Since 1946, Father Chenu has been affiliated with the Sorbonne, where he has had charge of the courses concerned with the history of civilization in the Middle Ages and the history of theology. He has also taught at the Institute of Medieval Studies in Montreal. He served as a theological expert at the Second Vatican Council and is a member of the newly established Vatican Secretariat for Non-Believers. Among his scholarly works he is perhaps best known for his Introduction a l'étude de saint Thomas d'Aquin *(1950), translated in English under the title* Toward Understanding Saint Thomas *(1964). He has also published* La théologie est-elle une science? *(1943; Eng. trans.* Is Theology a Science?, *1959),* La théologie au douzième siècle *(1957),* Pour une théologie du travail *(1955; Eng. trans.* The Theology of Work), St. Thomas d'Aquin et la théologie *(1959), and* L'Evangile dans le temps *(1964). Father Chenu lives in Paris at the Dominican Convent of St. Jacques.*

208

The Need for a
Theology of the World

W hether we agree with it or not, it is an obvious fact that the world has become "profane" and desacralized: the city henceforth qua city is secular. The theologian has joined the sociologist and the historian in making an objective analysis of the situation. Each in his own way seeks the causes of the phenomenon, in order to understand it and gain a just estimate of its extent, its import, and its truth.

This is not the place to present even summarily such an analysis. It is sufficient to recall, with Dr. Cox, the conclusions which have been reached.

Desacralization has been most visible in the political domain, especially in the relation between churches and states. Here, in fact, secularization has been brought about as the result of a deliberate and often brutal struggle for power. The states have demanded, conquered, and proclaimed their independence from the organized religions which had sacralized power and long directed political life, for good or bad.

In the twentieth century, secularization has become more radical as well as more widespread; it has reached into the daily life of all. The whole basic domain of life and health, hospitals, the medical profession itself, were formerly more or less directly under the direction and charity of religious organizations. They now fall under the care, the laws, and the offices of the civic community. Social welfare, aid to the sick and the aged, family and child aid, recreation, were all once the scene of the presence and effectiveness of religion (and they still are in nonindustrialized regions). Today, Pope John XXIII pays tribute to the *Declaration on the Rights of the Child* (1959) and to UNESCO, while Pope Paul expresses solidarity with the work and hope of the FAO.

The basic human groups—in family life, in work, in economic management—the right of property, and the prestige of authority, all were once under the protection of religion. The oath was long the guarantee, before God or the gods, of one's loyalty to society. Today, the political order stands on its own, it has its own values, and political problems are no longer resolved by referring them to religion.

The sciences, the psychological and social disciplines, and history have purged themselves little by little during the past century of metaphysical influences in order to ensure the autonomy of their methods and the specific truth of their proper object. Scientific causality no longer has recourse to a "first cause"; existentialists and Marxists denounce a God used as a stopgap for our ignorance, inadequacies, and failures. The biological rhythms, despite their mystery, are becoming desacralized: legislation concerning the "purification of women" is totally obsolete, fertility is subjected to regulation, and sexual life itself is demystified.

The highest values of the human patrimony—justice, equality, fraternity, peace—emanate from the collective conscience of peoples. They are more and more shared in common over and beyond the beliefs, the diversity, and the conflicts of religion, which are often the causes of segregation. Humanity is coming to have a universal conscience or a "catholicity" such as religion never achieved. Although the checks to this claim, both in fact and in ideology, are lamentable and overwhelming, the prospect and hope for it are making effective appeals to the masses themselves, who have now entered into history.

Industrialization is the common denominator of all these developments and of this new "civilization." As the result of scientific and technical progress, it is increasing in both quantity and intensity. Nor is it limited to the material realm of economics. By and in its transformation of matter, it is also a transformation of man—in his life as an individual as well as in his relations with others. Industrialization provokes, develops, and feeds humanization. The painful ambiguity of its results is only the ambiguity of man himself. In discovering the laws of the universe, in controlling the forces of nature, in constructing the world, man fulfills himself; he becomes more man. *Homo artifex* and *Homo technicus* are as truly man as the aristocratic *Homo sapiens*.

The technical development of man has now reached the point where the machine has replaced the tool. As a result there is not only a greater productive capacity but also a qualitative change in the relation between man and nature. The tool is only an extension and multiplication of muscular power. The machine is an embodiment of intelligence itself, which confers upon the matter of industry a quality of human autonomy. Man has discovered how to make nature produce without any direct human intervention the effects that he wants. The machine itself can repair the damages resulting from accidents. A new nature, produced by the technical genius of man, has been superimposed upon the original nature.

This is a new fact that arouses in man a new awareness of himself. Man is and knows that he is the demiurge, the "creator" of the world; he constructs it, he directs it, for good or bad, as its master. This new civilization is correctly called a civilization of work, since it is a civilization in which work is the decisive operation by which man becomes man in humanizing nature. Work, objectified in the machine, depends less and less on the worker with his intentions and projects; it depends less on the forms and immediate norms of his body and soul. Work has become depersonalized; man, his eyes, his hands, his imagination, and, added to all that, his "craft," no longer leave their mark. The worker has become *Homo artifex* of an entirely different cast from the craftsman.

The image of the world, even for the unlearned, now has a character of mobility, plasticity, and potentiality, such as it never had before. At all levels, there is a sense of change and progress and, along with it, a feeling of power in the *rule of man* inaugurating a new era of humanity. In this wondrous and dramatic condition, man is brought to question the meaning of his action in constructing the world, to inquire about his destiny, which seems unlimited, although he himself is limited in his frailty. In this questioning, which often reaches the point of anxiety, it is history itself which becomes mysterious: Sociocosmic myths may try to express the mystery of the future, but, for the Christian, the God of nature reveals himself as the Lord of history.

WHY RELIGION IS NOT FAITH

God reveals himself as the Lord of history by the fact that he himself entered *into history* by becoming man. That is the heart of our faith, the whole of Christianity. God is a historical personage. Henceforth, history is "sacred," and humanization of any kind becomes the suitable place for divinization.

For a clearer understanding of the originality of this fact, it is useful to appeal to the classical theological distinction between faith and religion —between faith, the "theological" virtue, and religion, the "moral" virtue.

Religion, in the formal sense of the word, is the virtue by which we relate our actions and our existence to the Divine. (*Religio*, according to a rather uncertain etymology, derives from *re + ligare* = to bind.) From it, our actions and our whole existence gain a new dimension, different from our relation to terrestrial realities. The justice that I practise in the contracts I have with my partners is different from the "religious" justice according to which I am indebted to the God who created me and to whom I owe a debt of homage. So too, the love that I have for my neighbor, and for my parents, my wife, and my children, can be valued for itself, but I can also consider it as an echo and an expression of the God-Love, the source and prototype of all love—a love including a "sacred" value.

Religion as such emanates from man. Its aim is to satisfy the needs he experiences in his thought and in his actions, the full meaning of which he recognizes—although in a prereflexive way—by basing them on the lived acknowledgment of a divine Being. In referring them to God, he sacralizes these needs and hopes. For that reason, he surrounds them with "signs" and rites that withdraw these terrestrial realities from current usage, and also from the investigation of reason.

These needs proliferate in great variety and differ according to time and place, person and environment. Among their manifestations various types can be distinguished which differ greatly in object as well as in the value of their sacralization. The sociologists of religion speak of a "useful" religion, aimed at reaching mysterious forces, a religion of "fear," aimed at alleviating our fears and guaranteeing a measure of security, a religion of "homage," based on a feeling deep within that reflects a divine absolute, and a religion of "communion," which is the highest because the absolute comes to fulfill man's aspirations and raise him above himself.

The common denominator of these needs and religions is the fact that they ascend from man to the divinity. They are represented, one might say, by vertical images; one looks "up to heaven," as the supreme source of our satisfaction. The sense of what lies beyond death, with its fears and hopes, underlies our feelings, our imagination, our acts, and our cults. In brief, religion is made by man in this ascension. The unbeliever will say that the consciousness of God is a projection of consciousness of self. The Marxist systematizes this interpretation and calls it "alienation."

Whatever it is, this religion springs from the nature of man—from his instincts, whether reasonable or not, and from his aspirations, whether consistent or not. It is a natural religion, inscribed on the intelligence and heart of man. It remains so despite its subsequent expressions and the deviations, degradations, or alienations of which the history books are full and which extend from the animistic religions of the primitive peoples down to the civilized "deism" of the eighteenth century, and beyond.

Faith, as such, proceeds in exactly the opposite way. Considered phenomenologically, the act of a believer has a totally different inspiration from the religious act just described. The Gospel itself suggests this to the Christian. The New Testament rarely speaks of "religion" and then seemingly only with great caution. The early Christians were sharply aware of the difference that the Christian faith had introduced into the world of "religion."

Faith is not the action of a man ascending toward the Divine. It is the act of response to and of communion with a personal God, who on his own initiative enters into conversation with men and establishes a communion in love. In accord with the logic of love, this God enters into the life of the "other" and makes himself man in order to bring this act to its full reality. Divinization thus comes by means of a humanization. All this may seem to the unbeliever nothing but myth or illusion, but it is the very object of faith and governs its design and structure.

In faith we are dealing with an event. We are no longer in nature but in history. One day, God became man and entered into the history of men. History becomes the proper dimension for this act, and not nature with its needs. God is not conceived or called for because of his usefulness. Love is freely bestowed, on my side as well as his, through my free response. To be a Christian is to be in relation to a fact—the fact of Christ —to a history, and not to a morality, a law, a theory, or a cult.

Because of this divine immersion, divinization comes through the community of men, over and above the individuals and their good will. Humanity on the march is the subject of this plan, or "economy," as the Greek fathers called it. The Man-God sums up all values, whatever their source. He achieves the realization of a fraternal humanity in the ontological plenitude of a collective consciousness—in what Paul calls the divine "pleroma." By faith, the personal history of the believer is inserted into a "sacred history," and he becomes a collaborator in bringing the creator's design to its fulfillment. Whereas the man of *religion* gropes for the link between transcendence and immanence, the man of *faith* escapes the uncertainty of both false transcendence and false immanence.

It has been said that Christianity is not a religion. This statement is paradoxical by current standards. Yet it forcibly expresses the irreducible originality of Christianity in comparison with other religious phenomena. If I approach God through a sacralization of natural forces whose mystery troubles me and goes beyond my understanding, I will contribute to acts of worship which express a religion. But these acts as such have nothing to do with the "witness" of the Word of God, in communion with the mystery of the dead and risen Christ. It is just here, in the very midst of authentic grandeurs, that I run the risk of yielding to dehumanizing transfers, to improper lures, to magical acts, to clerical castes, and to all the forms of alienation.

This distinction between the two virtues, this disjoining faith and religion, is made today in the midst of the desacralization of the world. Under the pressure of this fact, we must undertake a new criticism of the sacred and of religion as a rite, a cult, a representation and explanation of the world, and as a belief that is socially transmitted. We must revise the sacral foundations of the faith.

Given the relation between the two, it is clear that this criticism should lead to a purification of faith. Such a result is one of the implications of the reform undertaken by the Vatican Council of the Catholic Church in proclaiming, in its statement on atheism, the primacy of mystery over institution. Still more important, the move marks a return of the primitive sense of Christianity as a radical initiative. Christianity by its nature demands the desacralization of the world in the sense of purging it of its gods and demons. In making the world an object of creation exterior to God, Christianity delivers the world over to man and makes possible both experimental science and technology. One may wonder whether the Hindu, the Buddhist, even the Islamic religions will be able to resist for long the invasion of the technical and industrial mentality. Christianity can give full consent to it, since it is the Word of God addressed to man, and not an emanation or relation (*re-ligio*) of nature to God. Faith and religion are not on the same level. Thus, within the church, we must distinguish the community of salvation in the mystery of the Man-God from the sociological institution with its conceptual, functional, and ritual apparatus.

Faith consents to the decline of the sacred insofar as it demystifies nature of its false divinization as an idolatry of its powers, rhythms, and fertility.[1] Desacralization is present in the Old Testament as one of its lines of force.[2] It is also, despite its repeated failures, a law of Christian development, since nature and the world are placed in the hands of man who was created as their sovereign.

Faith does not proceed formally by "sacralization"; if it did, it would indeed be the "opium of the people." On the contrary, it calls upon man to live fully in the world, to take charge of its construction, and to give full scope to his hopes. As has been said, religion is "nostalgic" for a return to origins, which annuls history, whereas faith is "prophetic" in its understanding of history and its economy.

Paradoxically, men speak of the absence of God and of his uselessness and claim that "the believer shares with the unbeliever a certain brotherhood of weakness before the absence of God." Of course, this formula must not be taken literally, since in that case it would imply either a complete dislocation of theology or a camouflaged atheism. We must say, however, that it is not by diminishing the world that one increases God's chances in the world; it is not by denying the autonomy and terrestrial values of man that one converts him to Jesus Christ. We must not support God with the weakness of man and with his psychological, moral, political, or even his religious shortcomings. It is true that the weakness of man, ontologically, counters the "sufficiency" of man by having recourse to the strength of God, but here it is the mystery of the Man-God, weak and suffering, that takes charge of the human situation. But

---

1 Pope Paul has said that true science has demystified and desacralized the phenomena of nature; it has helped to purify the faith of its dross, of certain superstitions, and certain complexes arising from fear and insecurity. (From an interview with Cardinal Leger, reported in *Le Monde*, July 18, 1963.)

2 "The whole concept of alienation found its first expression, in the West, in the Old Testament concept of idolatry. The essence of what the Prophets call idolatry is not the fact that man adores many gods instead of one. It is rather that the idols are the work of man; they are things, and man adores what he has himself created. By doing this, he transforms himself into a thing, he transfers to the things he has created the attributes of his own life, and instead of recognizing himself as a creative person, he is in contact with himself only indirectly according as his mission in life is fixed on idols."—E. Fromm, *Marx's Concept of Man* (Mexico and Buenos Aires, 1962).

it is also true that the powerful man is like the presence of God. God is present within the world that is coming of age, and there is no need to reduce it to a status of a minor for the sake of apologetics. "To reduce the perfection of the creature is to reduce the perfection of God," Thomas Aquinas, the master of classical theology, declared in a famous formula.

MAN, THE CO-CREATOR

The Christian is defined by his faith in the coming of God into history. But this faith implies a certain vision of history, that is to say of the construction of the world by man in evolving time. The ground underlying faith is the radical relation of man to creation and hence to God the Creator. Faith is the geometrical locus of communion between man, the being-in-the-world, and God, the being-come-into-the-world. In fact, according to dogma, the incarnate Word is identical with the Word that created the world.

We must purge our conception of creation of the infantile imagery that obscures it. Creation is not the linear prolongation of an act that God performed only at the beginning of the world and that has long since ceased. Creation is the permanent, present act by which beings are themselves in act. Man, at the summit of evolution, is the creature who, with intelligence and will, freely takes over the creative enterprise of God. God did not create a fully developed universe and then place man over it like an angelic spirit over heterogeneous matter or like an alien spectator before an alluring and overwhelming landscape. God has called man to be his co-worker in the progressive organization of the universe, in which he is the image of God, the demiurge and conscience. Man is precisely and primarily the "image of God" in this association with his Creator by which he is the master and constructor of nature.

Thus it might even be said that man is the "co-creator" of the universe, although, strictly speaking, this is theologically inaccurate. He is charged with the task of assembling and recapitulating in himself the whole series of being. The lowest beings are obviously incapable of intelligence and love and hence are incapable of returning by themselves to their creator. Man, in his freedom, with intelligence and love, is the demiurge of that return.

God is no longer sought in the inspiring and unfathomable fantasies of natural phenomena. He is no longer, as Cox says, "a cosmic policeman," sanctifying the existing distribution of power and guaranteeing a universal law. Henceforth the meaning of human existence and activity appears only at the heart of a concrete experience of the human person, and not in eternal imperatives, preestablished, unchangeable, and improperly divinized. For the Christian, the historicity of man, of which we now have become aware, corresponds to the historicity of God in Christ, the Man-

God. Christianity is not an abstract system meant to explain the world, nor the model of an "order" which we are supposed to copy or restore. Christianity is the history of salvation, a history carried out by the People of God, within the freedom of the Gospel, and as an effect of freely bestowed love. The evolution of the world is coexistent with its creation, and Christ takes it up in view of a "new creation." Existence, the community, ever-expanding human history, have become the objective expression of the communication of God with man and of man's response.

THE AMBIGUITY OF SECULARIZATION

The doctrine of creation, this vision of history, this theology of the Incarnation—each on its own and all three together—help to resolve the grave ambiguities of secularization pointed out by Dr. Mascall and clarified by Dr. Marty. In fact, the doctrinal and practical misunderstandings on these three points explain why Christians and their churches for over three centuries failed to understand or even perceive the movement and causes of the world's transformations and man's new condition in it. The churches were engaged in carrying out a countermovement; inspired by nostalgia for the bygone *corpus christianorum*, they attempted "restorations" after each "revolution." The first and basic mistake was a failure to understand the humanness and Christian truth of the industrial "revolution." As the Dutch theologian J. C. Hoekendijk has said: "When the first stone of the modern industrial cities was laid, the Church was absent from the ceremony." There is no point in giving way to a bitter indictment. It is urgent, however, that we learn from this experience a renewed understanding of the Gospel and the elements of a theology of the world in its secular dimension. Secularization is a menace, even a defiance. But it is not to be met by a frightened self-defense that is content to denounce the sinister failures of the secularized world: two world wars and a profound economic depression within a single generation. It must be met by a loving confidence in this new man, whose undertakings are a conscious expansion of creation, an advance of history, and a wealth of material for the Man-God to make into a "new creation."

Secularization has cleared the way for the search for the causes that reveal man's mastery. The ambiguity begins where humanization entails the autonomy of science and of conscience. God then disappears along with the gods. Man himself becomes man's god within a world which he has built, and this is the worst sort of idolatry.

Autonomy is right and proper in the management of social affairs, in the methods of the sciences, and in the responsible exercise of freedom. Human values have a consistency of their own, a "profane" consistency, at the heart of faith under the lordship of Christ. Human values have their own laws, drawn from nature, from society, and from history, and

216

there is no need for an ecclesiastical power to sacralize them. The basic elements of human society, which for more than a millennium have been more or less inspired and directed in the West by the church, have become the common good of humanity as such. Man is learning the laws of his nature as he discovers and exploits the laws of nature. The world exists, and Christians are recognizing and discovering it as it is, in the act of constructing it today.

The church no longer has to take in hand the conduct of civilizations and the progress of peoples. It has rather to sow in them the leaven of the Gospel. It must collectively pledge its faith, its hope, and its charity —its "political charity," as Pius XI said—in service to the construction of a fraternal humanity. The church is no longer power; it is service. Its task is not to build on its own initiative and at its own expense a "Christian world," but to Christianize the world such as it is in the process of construction. At the time Dietrich Bonhoeffer was imprisoned in Germany and writing his letters on a Christianity disengaged from "religion," the worker-priests in France were giving a new look to the church, a church stripped of her paraphernalia, and turned toward the new industrial man.

Of course, we must not yield to an over-optimistic appreciation of secularization. We then run the risk of closing secularization in upon itself and turning it into a secularism. We then lose the disinvolvement, the *contemptus mundi*, that the hope of heavenly beatitude suggests that we have for earthly affairs. We would also distort secularization which, in its power, puts the mystery of man to the test and holds itself open to what is beyond itself. At a time when God seems to have become useless for the world of scientific and technical efficiency, man may perhaps have a new chance of seeking God for himself, and not for his usefulness. It is not a question of looking for God at the end of our deepest experiences as a solution for insolvable problems. We must create within ourselves a "space for questioning," so that we may wait for God as an appeal, as an "event," or as a creative word, that awakens in us new possibilities of existence.

We have a proof of this view of secularization in the position that the churches in their current renewal have taken on the layman. In fact, save for the case of the special ministry, the believer or Christian is identified with the "layman." A layman is as such a man marked by secularity. The word is an old one, but it had lost its edge and become, at least in French, deprecatory. The word derives from the Greek *laos* = people. And it is a people that is the partner of the Word, the witness of the message, the body of Christ in history. This people comes to be structured with a ministering hierarchy, but this structural distinction does not reduce at all the irreducible, ontological dimension of the Christian. The misadventures of *laicité* within the church and in profane politics cannot do away with this primary truth, although it may be obscured for a time. God enters into history by means of a people through generations of continuous incorporation. Such is the logic of the Incarnation. It too was the part of the truth contained in the medieval ideal of a *corpus christianorum* and of a Christianity that was very worldly in its clericalism.

The role of the layman in building the Kingdom of God is, consequently, not a secondary one of serving the clergy. It is a constitutive role in a regime of true evangelical responsibility, which is not at all reduced by the need for doctrinal obedience and discipline. The layman is essential for the work of evangelization precisely because he is involved with the profane. The conditions for the universal influence of the grace of Christ are set by neither a theocratic imperialism, a premature sacralization, nor a clerical mandate.

The definition of the lay believer includes secularity as its specific quality. The relation to the world belongs to his very constitution. It is part of the constitution of every Christian, just as it is of the church which has its being in the world and in history. Nevertheless, it is important to insist that this secular relation must be a Christian relation: the Christian must not only participate in the humanization of the world but he must also collaborate in the evangelizing mission of the church. By placing this emphasis upon the statements of Dr. Cox, we can avoid an improper and wrong secularization.

Since secular values enter into his very constitution, the Christian within the church, both individually and collectively, needs the world. "The church knows how richly she has profited from the history and development of mankind." These are the opening words of one of the most significant and most debated paragraphs of the *Pastoral Constitution on the Church in the Modern World* promulgated by the Vatican Council (n. 44). Throughout its history, the church has advanced through exchange with different cultures. Today, more than ever, "when things are changing very rapidly, and ways of thinking are exceedingly various she must rely on those who live in the world, are versed in different institutions and specialties, and grasp their innermost significance in the eyes of both believers and unbelievers." Note that the last clause says "believers and unbelievers." It is the "profaneness" of the world that is in question: "to be living in the world" entitles one to intervene in the dialogue. Are not the passion for Christian liberty and the concern for religious freedom tributaries of the aspiration for freedom expressed by the modern conscience? Has not Christian universalism been advanced by the expansion of Western civilization and the march toward world unity? Do not Christian brotherhood and the feeling for the poor owe something to socialism? Is not the purification of faith indebted to the democratization of culture? Has not the deeper understanding of the mystery of the church been favored by the movement for secularization? The church notes with gratitude, the Council declares, "that in her com-

218

munity life no less than in her individual sons she has received a variety of help from men of every rank and condition."

HOW FAITH SAVES RELIGION

Faith then is not only a purified religion, a higher religion of homage and communion, freed of its alienations and the elements that weigh it down. Faith introduces a radical novelty into the universe of religion. In fact, faith would be degraded if it were reduced—as is unfortunately too often the case—to even a purified religion.

In this case, we can ask, what will happen to religion? Will not the desacralization, which we have admitted, wind up by eliminating all "sacredness" from human life and even from Christianity itself? Have not we said that the Christian sanctifies the world without having to "consecrate" it? Are we not then brought to a religionless Christianity, at least as Bonhoeffer understood it?

It is not only in the tragic pessimism of Bonhoeffer that faith is built up and exalted on the ruins of religion. Under the pretext that faith is an evangelical absolute, it is quite a common thing to deprecate all *religious* values: the feeling of relation to the transcendence of a creating God, the expression in a cult of this "dependence," the tragic sense of the condition of a creature and of man's insuperable limitations. It cannot be said that faith saves religion only by removing it as though it were "the cancer of faith."

It is true that faith saves religion, but it does so by constantly criticizing its mental, cultural, and social behavior. This occurred at the beginning of faith, in Israel and the primitive church.

> In Christianity, faith cannot be separated from religion. Christianity is as it were a way of living, within religion, the conflict between faith and religion. Let the dimension of faith disappear, and all that remains is that religion of which human science has shown the conditioning and the decline. From this point of view, Christianity itself is only a limited cultural reality, limited both geographically and sociologically. But let the pole of religion disappear, and all that remains is a vague aspiration or a personal conviction. The Christian presence in the world will not be carried out for lack of support from a confessing community.[3]

It must be said that faith does not eliminate religion. Faith takes up religion, transfers it to the mystery of Christ, and so sanctifies it. Christianity is not purely a faith as is shown by the fact that, as a humaniza-

---

3 P. Ricoeur, "*Sciences humaines et conditionnements de la foi,*" in *Semaine des intellectuels catholiques* (Paris, 1965), p. 142.

tion of God, it lives by faith under a human regime. The whole economy of the Man-God, which a moment ago led us to differentiate faith from religion, leads us now to admit the normal coherence of faith and religion. There is no question here of arbitrarily juxtaposing faith and religion by means of the sociological notion of the "sacred." Faith has a religious dimension just because it is a human action. It calls for objective values of representation and intellectual formation, for symbols, rites, and institutional realization.

The elements of worship—the sacraments—must also be included within the purview of faith. Besides their symbolic function, they are efficacious representations of the "mystery" of the original divinization; they continue in history the divinizing process. The people of faith constitute the "body of Christ." Sacraments provide it with structure. In this, faith borrows from religion its elementary Nature rites—adoration, intercession, communion, repasts, sexual initiation—but only in order to be faithful to its object, the "mystery" in history of the continuity of the people of God. As a result, these sacraments are not only "sacred" acts as part of a cult but they are also effective signs of divinization in the community of believers remembering the evangelical "events."

Faith must constantly be on the alert to keep these sacraments—these worshiping and moral "practices"—up to their intended meaning: the life of Christ in us and in communion with our brothers. Always at issue with "religion," faith is ever inventing new relationships with religion and with the world and nature. The psychological, cultural, social, and national conditions of religion provide it with ground to grow in, but they also threaten to suffocate it. Religion by itself is never clear about itself and its operations. One can without injustice ascribe to it the deviations of superstition and magic, the ritualistic clear conscience, search for the marvelous, "absenteeism" from the world, and "alienation." Therefore, in helping man to hasten his historical and ethical coming-of-age and in working toward the religious disalienation implicit in the process of desacralization, human progress is working toward a purification of religion.

In the final analysis, it is a theology of the world that faith must elaborate if it is to be a theology of God-come-into-the-world. Before all, we must uphold the unity of the divine design against that dualism which has made its way more or less consciously into the mentality and practice of Christians and which appears theologically in the disjunction of nature from grace. The building of the world is not on one side and the advent of the Kingdom of God on the other; terrestrial involvement on one side and, on the other, Christian life with its hope of heaven; nature taken in hand by humanity is not on one side and, on the other, grace superimposed upon nature from the outside; the city is not on one side and the church on the other, separated like two nations by a border where rights and powers meet in conflict; creation is not on one side and, on the other, the Incarnation.

On the other hand, the building of the world and the advance of man do not by themselves result in the coming of the Kingdom of God. Neither nature nor history is capable of revealing the mystery of God; the Word of God comes "from above" through the initiative of love freely giving itself in communion. Grace is grace, and profane history is not the source of salvation. Evangelization belongs to another order from that of civilization. To feed men is not to save them, even though my salvation imposes upon me the duty to feed them. To advance culture is not at all the same as converting one to the faith. Over and above its visible signs, the church remains an original community, with its own internal laws, in the world in which it is immersed. There is no question of the world absorbing a "secularized" church, whose historical succession it then takes over.

Yet this does not mean that the "secular city" with all its human undertakings—the control of nature, the mounting conscience of nations, the cultivation of the mind, and the education of the heart—is nothing but an occasional and extrinsic condition for the individual and collective life of grace. These terrestrial goods provide points of contact for the Gospel and develop in man positive dispositions toward an incarnation of the divine life; they have what classical theology describes as obediential potency. The Lordship of Christ and the presence of the Spirit are real in them and discernible by the eyes of faith. If Christians read the signs aright in this world that is wondrous in its transformation, they can experience the surprise—a fortunate surprise if they are secure in their faith —of finding that they are in dialogue with this world which has reached autonomy in knowledge and management. They can experience the surprise—a joyful surprise if they are moved by fraternal love—of recognizing grace at work among non-Christians. For the presence of the Gospel is realized through the questions of men.

Such is the logic of the Incarnation. "The Incarnation of the Word does not represent only the historically unique appearance of God in the world, but also, more than this, the acceptance of the world by God and its admission to him, that is, the eschatological consecration of the world, sealed and sanctioned by the Resurrection."[4]

The position presented here is admittedly an optimistic view of the world and of history. It should cause no surprise if many Catholics and Protestants have certain reservations about it. In conclusion, then, I would like to cite one of the finest expressions of Greek theology on the role of Christ, the creating Word become man so that man may become, in the

---

4 These are the words concluding the article "World" in the *Handbuch Theologischer Grundbegriffe*, ed. H. Fries (Munich, 1962).

world that he humanizes, a power for divinization. It is a text in which Clement of Alexandria evokes the myth of Orpheus; the Church Fathers were less scrupulous than we in having recourse to myths as a way of giving expression to the "mystery." Here is the text:

> The Word of God has now
> abandoned the lyre and the cythera—
> instruments without soul—
> to conciliate by means of the Holy Spirit
> the whole world gathered up in man;
> He makes use of him
> as an instrument of many voices
> and, accompanying his song
> on this instrument that is man,
> He plays to God.

M. D. Chenu

A CHURCH WHICH DOES NOT IDENTIFY WITH THE WORLD WITH THE SAME
THOROUGH SOLIDARITY GOD DOES BETRAYS ITS MISSION

THE IDEA OF RELIGION IN
GREAT BOOKS OF THE WESTERN WORLD

That the idea of religion is both difficult and complex is evident from the discussion of it by the various contributors to our symposium. The full complexity of the idea, however, has not emerged. There are two reasons for this. One is that all four writers share a common belief in Christianity, and to this extent they have more or less the same idea of religion. Then, second, the analysis of the idea has been no part of their task, except incidentally; they have touched on the idea only in relation to their arguments about secularization. The extreme complexity of the idea begins to appear only when one attempts to register the range of its meaning.

William James was one of the first to make religion an object of scientific study, in the modern sense of the term. The results of his study are set forth in *The Varieties of Religious Experience*, first given in Edinburgh in 1901–2 as the Gifford Lectures on Natural Religion. Attempting to circumscribe his subject in Lecture II, James observes that it would be simpleminded and misleading to think that all that is meant by "religion" could be caught in any "single principle or essence." It is, he claims, a conception as complex as that of government and comprises "many characters which may alternately be equally important."[1]

Yet in order to delimit and locate the subject of his investigation, he does attempt to state at least the minimal meaning of "religion." It is the concern of men, he claims, "so far as they apprehend themselves to stand in relation to whatever they may consider the divine."[2] Even this minimal interpretation at once raises the question whether religion necessarily connotes a relation to God. People do sometimes speak of atheistic communism as a "religion," although theoretically it is committed to denying the existence of God.

James himself recognizes that "there are systems of thought which the world usually calls religious, and yet which do not positively assume a God."[3] As examples, he cites "Emersonian optimism, on the one hand, and Buddhistic pessimism, on the other." Both, he claims, are "in many respects identical with the best Christian appeal and response." From this he concludes that "we must from the experiential point of view call these godless or quasi-godless creeds 'religions'; and accordingly when in our definition of religion we speak of the individual's relation to 'what he considers as divine,' we must interpret the term 'divine' very broadly, as de-

---

1 *The Varieties of Religious Experience* (New York: The New American Library of World Literature, Inc., 1958), p. 39.

2 *Ibid.*, p. 42.

3 *Ibid.*

noting any object that is godlike, whether it be a concrete deity or not."[4] He finally stipulates that "the divine shall mean for us only such a primal reality as the individual feels impelled to respond to solemnly and gravely and neither by a curse nor a jest."[5]

James is certainly right in observing that the term "religion" is sometimes used without reference to God. John Stuart Mill, for example, in his essay *The Utility of Religion*, attacks Christianity and supernatural religion in the name of what he calls the Religion of Humanity: "The sense of unity with mankind and a deep feeling for the general good may be cultivated into a sentiment and a principle capable of fulfilling every important function of religion and itself be justly entitled to the name."[6]

So characterized, religion seems to differ not at all from morality, and the religious man is indistinguishable from the morally good man. The precise relation between religion and morality is, indeed, subject to controversy. Men disagree on whether religion is possible without morality as well as on the extent to which morality is possible without religion. James takes a position widely held, at least in the Western tradition, when he declares that religion supposes some relation to morality and yet also contains "some elements which morality pure and simple does not contain." In fact, at the end of his long investigation of the manifestations of religion, when he comes to "reduce religion to its lowest admissible terms, to that minimum, free from individualistic excrescences, which all religions contain as their nucleus," he retains the notion of a "proper connection with the higher powers."[7] Thus he retains a reference to the divine understood as a being not only different from man but higher than him.

All the great and classical attacks upon religion, pagan as well as Christian, agree in supposing that religion connotes some reference to the divine. In fact, the main object of attack is what is taken to be a false belief in God or the gods and its deleterious effects upon men's actions.

Lucretius in the pre-Christian world expresses the most passionate hatred for religion: its teachings are false, and the actions it leads men to commit are horrible and evil, such as Agamemnon sacrificing his daughter Iphigenia on the altar at Aulis (*On the Nature of Things*, I, 80–101; *GBWW*, Vol. 12, p. 2a–b). For Lucretius, religion is compounded of fear based on ignorance. It can and must be overcome by rational understanding of the way things operate without any divine intervention. His attack upon religion is throughout an attack upon the belief that the divine has any power over the affairs of men. Religion, as he understands it, is permeated with belief in the gods, but it is a false and ignorant be-

---

4 *Ibid.*, p. 44.
5 *Ibid.*, p. 47.
6 Ed. George Nakhnikian (Indianapolis: Bobbs-Merrill Co., 1958), p. 72.
7 *Op. cit.*, pp. 380, 383.

lief that should be dispelled.

Gibbon is more tolerant than Lucretius but no less certain that the claims of religion are false. He belittles religion by the ironic, even sarcastic, description of the inconsistencies and improbabilities of its beliefs. Yet at the center of these beliefs, as he describes them among both pagans and Christians, there is always some reference to a belief in a god. Although religion for him may amount, in fact, to no more than a human belief and invention, it claims to be more than merely a purely human moral code.

For both Marx and Freud, religion is an illusion. They would account for the genesis of this illusion in different ways, but both agree that the illusion lies in the belief that there is a god who governs the world and judges man.

The upholders of religion, of course, frequently maintain that its characteristic note is its reference to God. Augustine is typical of these. He observes that the Latin language is poorer than Greek in that it lacks any one word to denote the piety and reverence or the worship and service (*cultus*) that is due to God alone. In his time, the word "religious," like "pious," could still be applied to the relation one ought to have toward one's parents and country. It seems clear that he would have preferred to restrict "religion" to mean "nothing else than the worship of God" (*The City of God*, X, 1; *GBWW*, Vol. 18, p. 299b). Augustine's wish, of course, has since come true. Both words in their ordinary and normal usage now refer to man's relation to God.

For both its detractors and upholders, the notion of religion within the tradition of Western thought usually connotes some reference to God. But once we pass beyond this minimum, what religion is depends upon where one stands. It is one thing to those who embrace the religion and accept its belief, and quite another thing to those who reject it or who remain uncommitted. The range or scope of the idea varies accordingly. A good example of this difference is provided by the distinction between religion and superstition.

RELIGION AND SUPERSTITION

If the claims of religion are held to be false and belief in it an illusion, the distinction between religion and superstition tends to break down and disappear. Both, as contrasted with true knowledge, are dismissed together as false, and religion thus reduces to the status of superstition. Freud's writing clearly reveals such a tendency.

Freud sums up his final position on religion in the closing pages of the *New Introductory Lectures on Psycho-Analysis*. He places totemism and animism in the same line of development as the belief in a supernatural God. All are equally manifestations of religion, it seems; religion, he claims, "is an attempt to get control over the sensory world, in which we are placed, by means of the wish-world, which we have developed inside us as a result of biological and psychological necessities. But it cannot achieve its end. Its doctrines carry with them the stamp of the times in which they originated, the ignorant childhood days of the human race. Its consolations deserve no trust. . . . it seems not so much to be a lasting acquisition, as a parallel to the neurosis which the civilized individual must pass through on his way from childhood to maturity" (*GBWW*, Vol. 54, p. 878c). In short, religion, for Freud, is an infantile illusion. There is, therefore, no basis for distinguishing religion from superstition. Nor would there be any point in doing so, although Freud notes that certain manifestations are still "called *superstitions*" and contrasted with religion (*ibid.*, p. 877b). In his view, "the truth of religion may be altogether disregarded" (*ibid.*, p. 878c).

For the religious, however, superstition, far from being indistinguishable from religion, is contrasted with it as its polar opposite. Thus, according to Aquinas, religion is the virtue by which man renders to God the honor and service that is due him (*Summa Theologica*, II–II, Q81, A4). Superstition, on the other hand, is described as a vice—the very opposite of virtue. Religion, for Aquinas, establishes a norm for what man owes to God. One may depart from this norm either by excess or defect. Irreligion is the vice opposed to religion by defect, in that through contempt and irreverence one fails to render to God what is his due (*ibid.*, II–II, Q97). Superstition is the vice opposed to religion by excess. It is not that superstition "worships God more than the true religion," Aquinas writes, since superstition is not just too much religion, but rather that "it pays divine worship to whom it is not due or in an undue way" (*ibid.*, II–II, Q97, A1). Thus to worship the creature rather than the one true God is the superstition of idolatry. So also to worship God falsely or in a way that leads neither to his glory nor to man's subordination to him is likewise superstitious (*ibid.*, II–II, Q98, A1–2).

In this account, what is common to both religion and superstition is the notion of divine worship. This by itself is not enough, according to Aquinas, to characterize religion. He demands in addition that it be directed to the true God in the proper way. If, however, we were to limit our understanding of religion to worship alone and put to one side its object and manner, then we could speak of superstition as a religion. The difference for the religious man would then involve the distinction between false and true religion.

But whichever way we make the distinction—whether between religion and superstition, as Aquinas does, or between true and false religion—it still presupposes that truth can somehow be reached in matters of religion. If this were impossible, there would be no way of distinguishing religion from superstition, since for this we must be able to distinguish worship of the true God from that of the false, or true from false religion. The distinction rests on the conviction that religious knowledge is possible; in other words, that men can know the true God and can distinguish what is true about him from what is not. For those who make the distinction, there must be something that counts as a criterion of truth in religion.

Such a criterion poses an especially difficult problem for those who base their religion on a supernatural source, that is, a religion believed to have been established by revelation from a source that is by definition beyond the reach of man's natural powers. Within Christianity, which is such a religion, one formulation of the criterion has received wide acceptance. Pascal, who, it must be remembered, was not only a devout Christian, but also a great mathematician and physicist, has a version of it in the eighteenth of his *Provincial Letters* which quotes both Augustine and Aquinas.

The rule is founded on what might be called the principle of the unity of truth: Truth forms one coherent whole and no matter how many kinds or parts of truth there may be, nor how diverse the methods of attaining these parts, they are all consistent with one another; no proposition validly established as true in one field can be inconsistent with any proposition validly established as true in another. Pascal shows how this principle can be used as a rule for determining the truth in religion.

There are "three principles of our knowledge," he writes, "the senses, reason, and faith," each with its own object and its own degree of certitude. "And as God has been pleased to employ the intervention of the senses to give entrance to faith (for 'faith cometh by hearing'), it follows, that so far from faith destroying the certainty of the senses, to call in question the faithful report of the senses would lead to the destruction of faith. . . . We conclude, therefore, from this, that whatever the proposition may be that is submitted to our examination, we must first determine its nature, to ascertain to which of those three principles it ought to be referred. If it relate to a supernatural truth, we must judge of it neither by the senses nor by reason, but by Scripture and the decisions of the Church. Should it concern an unrevealed truth and something within the reach of natural reason, reason must be its proper judge. And if it embrace a point of fact, we must yield to the testimony of the senses, to which it naturally belongs to take cognizance of such matters" (*GBWW*, Vol. 33, p. 163a–b).

As applied to religion, this rule, it should be noted, is purely negative. It does not prove the truth of any religious doctrine; it only enables one to ascertain which interpretations of it are false. Thus Pascal goes on to say: "So general is this rule that, according to St. Augustine and St. Thomas, when we meet with a passage even in the Scripture, the literal meaning of which, at first sight, appears contrary to what the senses or reason are certainly persuaded of, we must not attempt to reject their testimony in this case, and yield them up to the authority of that apparent sense of the Scripture, but we must interpret the Scripture, and seek out therein another sense agreeable to that sensible truth; because, the Word of God being infallible in the facts which it records, and the information of the senses and of reason, acting in their sphere, being certain also, it follows that there must be an agreement between these two sources of knowledge. And as Scripture may be interpreted in different ways, whereas the testimony of the senses is uniform, we must in these matters adopt as the true interpretation of Scripture that view which corresponds with the faithful report of the senses" (*ibid.*, pp. 163b–164a). In support of this position, Pascal cites Aquinas: "Two rules are to be observed, as Augustine teaches. The first is, to hold the truth of Scripture without wavering. The second is that since Holy Scripture can be explained in a multiplicity of senses, one should adhere to a particular explanation only in such measure as to be ready to abandon it if it be proved with certainty to be false" (I, Q68, A1; *GBWW*, Vol. 19, p. 354b–c).

Augustine's account in *The Confessions* of his search for the true religion tells of a dramatic appeal to this rule. In fact, by employing it, he was able to reject his belief in Manichaeism. The books of the Manichees, he tells us, contained much about astronomy and were "fraught with prolix fables, of the heaven, and stars, sun, and moon." Augustine, remembering what he had studied of the astronomers, "compared some things of theirs with those long fables of the Manichees, and found the former the more probable." His belief was considerably shaken, but he was persuaded to continue with the sect by the promise that their learned Bishop Faustus would be able to resolve all his doubts. On finally meeting him, Augustine found him eloquent, but "utterly ignorant of liberal sciences"; and he could not satisfy Augustine's desire to see that "the account given in the books of Manichaeus were preferable, or at least as good" as that given by the astronomers. The failure to meet this test blunted his "zeal for the writings of Manichaeus," and, since he "despaired yet more of their other teachers," he writes that all the efforts whereby he "had purposed to advance in that sect . . . came utterly to an end" (*Confessions*, V, iii, 3-vii, 13; *GBWW*, Vol. 18, pp. 27c–30c).

RELIGION AND KNOWLEDGE

The test just described is a cognitive test. It supposes that we have attained genuine knowledge and also that religion achieves some kind of knowledge, although it may involve more than knowledge alone. The test supplies a criterion of religious truth only if religion makes statements which can then be compared with what we know from other sources.

For a skeptic, like Montaigne, it is no test at all, since he doubts the truth of both the senses and reason. His defense of religion, in the *Apology for Raimond de Sebonde*, operates on a different principle. It aims to destroy man's trust in both the senses and reason so that he may rest secure in his faith alone. The difficulty with this approach is that it leaves us with no rational basis for adjudicating between the claims of different and opposed beliefs; religion becomes a blind option. It is not surprising, then, that Montaigne, in all his many accounts of religious beliefs, makes little, if any, attempt to distinguish religion from superstition.

The cognitive test is also no criterion for those who hold that religion cannot claim any knowledge about the way things are but can only tell us what we ought to do. In this case, religion is understood as making no statements that are comparable with established scientific truth. Such a position with regard to religion differs from that taken by either Aquinas or Montaigne. Unlike Aquinas, it holds that religion makes no statement about the way things are that can be compared with scientific knowledge. Unlike Montaigne, it maintains that men can and do attain to genuine scientific knowledge.

We can distinguish two variants of this position. One takes the form that religion is not a cognitive activity at all and, hence, a fortiori, contains no knowledge comparable with scientific truth. Another form is not as radical as this. It does not deprive religion of all claim to knowledge; it holds that religion does contain knowledge, but knowledge that is practical, and not theoretical; it tells us what we ought to do, and not the way things are. Kant provides a paradigm example of this second position in his work *On Religion Within the Limits of Reason Alone*.

Kant defines religion as "the recognition of all duties as divine commands." Religion, as involving divine commands, obviously contains some relation to God. But Kant insists that there are no "special duties having reference directly to God"—no "courtly obligations over and above the ethico-civil duties of humanity (of man to man)." He also maintains that religion contains no theoretic knowledge of God: "In religion, as regards the theoretical apprehension and avowal of belief, no assertorial knowledge is required." Not even knowledge of God's existence is demanded: "This faith needs merely the idea of God, to which all morally earnest (and therefore confident) endeavor for the good must inevitably lead; it need not presume that it can certify the objective reality of this idea through theoretical apprehension." All that religion requires, according to Kant, is the minimum assertion that "it is possible that there may be a God," understood as "the object towards which our morally legislative reason bids us strive."[8]

---

8 *On Religion Within the Limits of Reason Alone* (New York: Harper & Brothers, 1960), p. 142.

In fact, the belief that anything more is required than the duties of man to man constitutes for Kant the mark of superstition: "Whatever over and above good life-conduct man fancies that he can do to become well-pleasing to God is mere religious illusion and pseudo-service of God."[9] Any departure whatsoever from this maxim is "pseudo-service of God (superstition)."[10] He goes on to say that "it is a superstitious illusion to wish to become well-pleasing to God through actions which anyone can perform without even needing to be a good man (for example, through profession of statutory articles of faith, through conformity to churchly observance and discipline, etc.)"[11] True religion requires nothing more than doing one's duty for duty's sake. For this, conscience alone is all that is needed: "Conscience needs no guide; to have a conscience suffices."[12]

Religion still involves knowledge, according to Kant. But it is a knowledge, through conscience, of moral duty, and not a knowledge of God. Indeed, Kant emphasizes morality so much that it has been claimed that the reference to God in his definition of religion is almost an afterthought. For some, however, religion consists in having a certain kind of experience that is unique, having nothing to do with any knowledge that can be communicated either of the way things are or of what we ought to do.

There is nothing in the idea of religious experience as such that requires it to be completely disjoined from any kind of knowledge. In his account of the varieties of religious experience, James is almost exclusively concerned with what he calls "faith-states"; yet he is also convinced that religion involves creeds and "a positive intellectual content,"[13] that is, it lays claim to knowledge.

RELIGIOUS EXPERIENCE

Many reports exist of what purport to be religious experiences. What is of special interest in these accounts is that some claim to be reporting an experience of the transcendent God. The experience, of course, occurs in nature, that is, it is something that happens to men in a certain time and place. Yet it carries with it the conviction that there is more in it than any purely natural event can provide.

James himself had such an experience, after he had begun work on his book on religion and while he was on a walking tour in the Adirondacks. He tells of the experience in a letter to his wife, dated July 7, 1898:

---

9 *Ibid.*, p. 158.
10 *Ibid.*, p. 160.
11 *Ibid.*, p. 162.
12 *Ibid.*, p. 173.
13 *Op. cit.*, p. 382.

. . . I have had an eventful twenty-four hours. . . . My guide had to serve for the party, and quite unexpectedly to me the night turned out one of the most memorable of all my memorable experiences. I was in a wakeful mood before starting, having been awake since three, and I may have slept a little during this night; but I was not aware of sleeping at all. . . . The guide had got a magnificent provision of firewood, the sky swept itself clear of every trace of cloud or vapor, the wind entirely ceased, so that the fire-smoke rose straight up to heaven. The temperature was perfect either inside or outside the cabin, the moon rose and hung above the scene before midnight, leaving only a few of the larger stars visible, and I got into a state of spiritual alertness of the most vital description. The influences of Nature, the wholesomeness of the people round me, especially the good Pauline, the thought of you and the children, dear Harry on the wave, the problem of the Edinburgh lectures, all fermented within me till it became a regular Walpurgis Nacht. I spent a good deal of it in the woods, where the streaming moonlight lit up things in a magical checkered play, and it seemed as if the Gods of all the nature-mythologies were holding an indescribable meeting in my breast with the moral Gods of the inner life. The two kinds of Gods have nothing in common—the Edinburgh lectures made quite a hitch ahead. The intense significance of some sort, of the whole scene, if one could only *tell* the significance; the intense inhuman remoteness of its inner life, and yet the intense *appeal* of it; its everlasting freshness and its immemorial antiquity and decay; its utter Americanism, and every sort of patriotic suggestiveness, and you, and my relation to you part and parcel of it all, and beaten up with it, so that memory and sensation all whirled inexplicably together; it was indeed worth coming for, and worth repeating year by year, if repetition could only procure what in its nature I suppose must be all unplanned for and unexpected. It was one of the happiest lonesome nights of my existence, and I understand now what a poet is. He is a person who can feel the immense complexity of influences that I felt, and make some partial tracks in them for verbal statement. In point of fact, I can't find a single word for all that significance, and don't know what it was significant of, so there it remains, a mere boulder of *impression*. Doubtless in more ways than one, though, things in the Edinburgh lectures will be traceable to it.

Dante's experience with Beatrice, as related in its beginnings in the *Vita Nuova* and carried to completion in the vision of God in *The Divine Comedy*, can also be interpreted as a transcendent experience. In terms of it, Charles Williams has elaborated what he calls "romantic theology," in his book *The Figure of Beatrice*.[14]

---

14 *The Figure of Beatrice* (New York: Farrar, Straus & Giroux, 1943).

In Augustine's account of his conversion there are at least two incidents that deserve to be counted as the same kind of experience. One is the final moment of decision when, after years of doubt and torment, he finally decides to become a Christian. It occurred at a time of particular anguish, when he felt self most divided against self; he believed the doctrines taught by the church, yet he could not bring himself to enter it; "Give me chastity," he prays, "only not yet." He withdrew from his friends to a garden in order to consider and lament his condition. There, he tells us:

> I heard from a neighbouring house a voice, as of boy or girl, I know not, chanting, and oft repeating, "Take up and read; take up and read." Instantly, my countenance altered, I began to think most intently, whether children were wont in any kind of play to sing such words; nor could I remember ever to have heard the like. So checking the torrent of my tears, I arose; interpreting it to be no other than a command from God, to open the book, and read the first chapter I should find. . . . Eagerly then I returned to the place where . . . I [had] laid the volume of the Apostle . . . I seized, opened, and in silence read that section, on which my eyes first fell: "Not in rioting and drunkenness, not in chambering and wantonness, not in strife and envying: but put ye on the Lord Jesus Christ, and make not provision for the flesh," in concupiscence. No further would I read; nor needed I: for instantly at the end of this sentence, by a light as it were of serenity infused into my heart, all the darkness of doubt vanished away.—*Confessions*, VIII, xii, 29; *GBWW*, Vol. 18, p. 61a.

The other occurs after his conversion, while he is discoursing with his mother, looking out upon the garden of their house at Ostia.

> We were discoursing then together, alone, very sweetly; and "forgetting those things which are behind, and reaching forth unto those things which are before," we were enquiring between ourselves in the presence of the Truth, which Thou art, of what sort the eternal life of the saints was to be, which eye hath not seen, nor ear heard, nor hath it entered into the heart of man. But yet we gasped with the mouth of our heart after those heavenly streams of Thy fountain, "the fountain of life," which is "with Thee"; that, being bedewed thence according to our capacity, we might in some sort meditate upon so high a mystery.
>
> And when our discourse was brought to that point, that the very highest delight of the earthly senses, in the very purest material light, was, in respect of the sweetness of that life, not only not worthy of comparison, but not even of mention; we, raising up ourselves with a more glowing affection towards the "Self-same," did by degrees pass through all things bodily, even the very heaven,

whence sun and moon and stars shine upon the earth; yea, we were soaring higher yet, by inward musing, and discourse, and admiring of Thy works; and we came to our own minds, and went beyond them, that we might arrive at that region of never-failing plenty, where Thou feedest Israel for ever with the food of truth, and where life is the Wisdom by whom all these things are made, and what have been, and what shall be, and she is not made, but is, as she hath been, and so shall she be ever; yea rather, to "have been," and "hereafter to be," are not in her, but only "to be," seeing she is eternal. For to "have been," and to "be hereafter," are not eternal. And while we were discoursing and panting after her, we slightly touched on her with the whole effort of our heart; and we sighed, and there we leave bound "the first fruits of the Spirit"; and returned to vocal expressions of our mouth, where the word spoken has beginning and end. And what is like unto Thy Word, our Lord, Who endureth in Himself without becoming old, and "maketh all things new"?—*Confessions*, IX, x, 23–24; *GBWW*, Vol. 18, p. 68a–c.

The value of such experiences, even leaving aside the question of whether or not they are necessary for religion, has been the subject of much discussion. Some argue that they constitute the very essence of religion and the only evidence for its truth. James notes that these mystical states are usually "absolutely authoritative over the individuals to whom they come." But he also points out that "no authority emanates from them which should make it a duty for those who stand outside of them to accept their revelations uncritically." The most that he allows is that they provide evidence that there is not "only one kind of consciousness" and so "break down the authority of the non-mystical or rationalistic consciousness based upon the understanding and the senses alone."[15] Religious men may disagree about whether or not religion attains knowledge comparable to scientific knowledge, but all would certainly agree that it involves more than knowledge alone.

---

15 *Op. cit.*, pp. 323–24.

Introduction

Revolution is a perennial idea. Yet there is no doubt that it has had greater currency at one time than another. We seem now to be living at a time in which the idea of revolution is again experiencing an upswing in popularity. It is therefore appropriate that we consider what we think about revolution and what we should think about it.

The West has a long tradition of thinking about the idea of revolution, which is well represented in *Great Books of the Western World*. One need only cite the authors who discuss revolution: Plato, Aristotle, Plutarch, Machiavelli, Hobbes, Shakespeare, Locke, Montesquieu, the authors of *The Federalist,* Hegel, Marx, and Engels. In organizing our symposium, was asked our contributors to continue this conversation.

Our contributors represent different approaches to the idea of revolution. None of them is as such an advocate of immediate violent political revolution. To represent that position, we reprint in Part Four Lenin's *State and Revolution,* which was written immediately before the violent overthrow of the Russian state in 1917.

Although not advocates of violent revolution, two of our authors find the idea of revolution more attractive than do the other two. Both Illich and Goodman, at least by implication, view sympathetically some of the revolutionary aspirations present in the world today, though both contend that these aspirations need redirecting. Toynbee and Buckley take a more skeptical attitude toward revolution.

The greatest difference among our four authors lies in the focus of their interest in revolution. Dr. Toynbee, as a historian, takes an admittedly long view of the subject and considers how revolutions have arisen in the history of civilization. Dr. Illich speaks as a representative of the Third World, an expression that he dislikes and criticizes, though he would not deny that the part of the world that it is used to designate is often held to be the closest to revolution, even of a violent sort. Perhaps the most remarkable feature of the current concern about revolution is the emergence of anarchism as an ideal that is considered attractive and feasible, and this is the subject on which Paul Goodman writes. The ideal of a society that can function without the use of coercion is one of the few anarchist ideals shared by Lenin; in fact, it is the essence of what he, after Engels, describes as "the withering away of the state." The impracticability, if not impossibility, of governing without the sanction, if not the actual use, of force is one of the main contentions of William Buckley's analysis of what he calls counterrevolutionary doctrine.

The last part of our symposium consists of an attempt to delineate at least the main contours of the discussion of revolution as it is found in *Great Books of the Western World*.

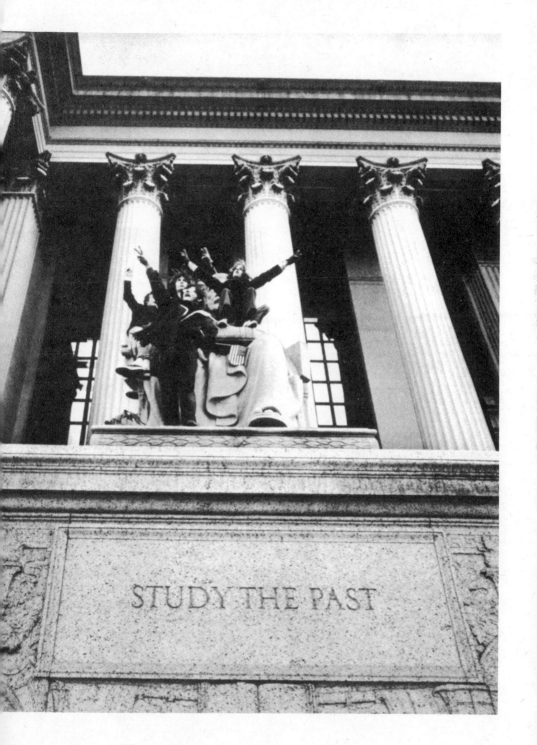

Arnold J. Toynbee

Arnold J. Toynbee is known throughout the world for his monumental work, *A Study of History* (12 volumes, 1934–61). In the eighty-one years since he was born in London (April 14, 1889), he has been indefatigable not only as a writer and traveler, but also as a man of affairs. He worked for his government during both world wars, served at the Paris peace

conferences in 1919 and 1946, and was director of studies for the Royal Institute of International Affairs from 1925 to 1955. His books run to over twenty-five titles and deal mainly with history, international affairs, religion, and travel. After preparatory school at Winchester, he followed the traditional classical curriculum at Balliol College, Oxford, where he remained as a tutor from 1912 to 1915. In 1919, he began his long association with the University of London, from which he retired in 1955. He continues to write, and last year saw the appearance of his autobiographical *Experiences*.

Revolutionary Change

E very revolution is a misfortune, and it is not even always the lesser evil. In some situations there is no choice between alternative evils. Social tension has risen to a pitch at which a revolution has become unavoidable.

The reason why a revolution is a misfortune is that it is a symptom that "the times are out of joint." Its outbreak is a sign that the traditional structure of society has ceased to answer to the conditions, needs, and demands of at least a portion of the members of the society that is numerous enough, or strong enough, to have the power to change the structure of society by force, if its demands continue to be resisted by the reigning "establishment." These are the circumstances in which revolutions occur. The objective of the makers of revolutions is to change the established institutions of the society by violence in order to make them answer, more or less, to contemporary conditions, needs, and demands.

The makers of a revolution are usually a minority of a minority. They are dissident representatives of the "establishment." Few people who are not members of the ruling class have the power and the self-confidence to take the initiative in attempting to overthrow the established order. The leaders are, however, unlikely to succeed unless they have at least the passive support of the mass of the people. This truth is illustrated by the contrast between two revolutions—the first successful and the second abortive—in the history of Pharaonic Egypt, a society that was, on the whole, singularly conservative and stable during the three thousand years and more for which this ancient Egyptian civilization lasted.

The "Old Kingdom"—a stage of Egyptian history that reached its acme in the time of the pyramid-builders—was brought to an end by a revolution that was successful and violent. We have retrospective glimpses of it in some of the literature that was written after the restabilization of Egyptian society in the "Middle Kingdom." This first Egyptian revolution was violent, because the burden placed on the backs of the mass of the people had eventually become intolerable. We do not know who the revolutionary leaders were, but we do know that, whoever they were, the

Pyramids near Cairo, Egypt

"Pharaonic Egypt, a society that was, on the whole, singularly conservative and stable"

people followed them. This revolution that liquidated the "Old Kingdom" was both social and mental. The mighty were put down from their seat, and the humble and meek were exalted, and this social revolution was evidently accompanied by a loss of faith in the efficacy and the value of the previous regime, under which a pharaoh and his courtiers had sought to win immortality for themselves by requiring the mass of the people to carry out gigantic public works. Originally the workers may have been docile and may even have believed that the labor that was being exacted from them was due from them and was worthwhile. But in the end they lost both their faith and their patience, and, when they revolted, the "Old Kingdom" collapsed.

The second revolution in ancient Egyptian history—this time an abortive one—was made, nearly a thousand years after the collapse of the "Old Kingdom," by one of the rulers of the "New Kingdom," Akhenaten. As a pharaoh, Akhenaten had absolute power, and he used it to attempt to make a revolution in almost every department of Egyptian life: in art, in literature, and in religion above all. But though Akhenaten was an all-powerful individual, he remained an isolated one. He had only a handful of followers, and therefore, after his death, the "establishment" which he had temporarily deposed was able to make a counterrevolution which the people accepted passively.

Revolution, like war, is a resort to violence, and therefore, like war, it is costly, and it seldom or never attains the objectives that its makers have had in view. Sometimes its aftereffect is actually to reinstate and aggravate the *ancien régime* against which it has revolted and which its makers believe that they have swept away. In France, for instance, recognizable elements of the *ancien régime* have reasserted themselves again and again since the Revolution of 1789. In Russia, the present Communist regime has reproduced the tyranny of the czardom, though the new Communist "establishment" in Russia claims to have made a complete break with the past. This tendency of a revolution to topple into reaction is discussed further at a later point in this essay.

Revolution is a violent form of change, and, in human affairs, change is inevitable, but the process of change need not be revolutionary. Change is inevitable in the first place because all human action produces a certain amount of change, and in the second place because human manners and customs are handed on from one generation to another mainly by tradition, which is mutable, and only to a minor extent by immutable instincts "built into" the psychosomatic structure of the species and transmitted by physical procreation. It is impossible for a younger generation—or series of generations—to take over, intact, the social and cultural heritage that an older generation has handed on by a process of education in the broadest meaning of the word. Even when the younger generation is conformist-minded and not rebellious-minded, it does not succeed in taking over and handing on, in its turn, the ancestral tradition in exactly the form in which this has been presented. This inevitability of change in human affairs is illustrated by the notorious impossibility of preserving, unchanged, the syntax, grammar, and pronunciation of some phase of a language that has been consecrated as being "classical." Later generations may try their hardest to retain the classical form of their language, but invariably they fail sooner or later. In spite of all efforts, the living speech diverges farther and farther from the arbitrary classical standard until eventually the classical form of the language becomes "dead." A would-be Latin-speaking people, for instance, had sooner or later to recognize the truth that it was now speaking no longer Latin but Italian or Spanish or French.

Thus change is inevitable in human affairs, but the process can be evolutionary rather than revolutionary. The structure of society can be changed to answer to the changing conditions, needs, and demands of the members of society by adjustments that are timely and that can therefore be made peacefully, because they are being made before the new conditions have diverged so far from the old structure that the social misfit has set up an emotional tension. This evolutionary process of adjustment is the way in which changes in human affairs are deemed to be brought about according to the medieval Latin tag: "Tempora mutantur, et nos mutamur in illis" ("Times change, and we change with them"). In this line of verse the evolutionary process of change is assumed to be a matter of course. However, when we survey the span of recorded history, we see that this assumption is too optimistic. Within the period from which records survive, we have evidence that there have been many revolutions. The revolution that liquidated the "Old Kingdom" of Egypt in the second half of the third millennium B.C. had a contemporary counterpart in the lower basin of the Tigris and Euphrates rivers, the present-day Iraq. Since then, revolutions have become more frequent. No later civilization has been so stable as the ancient Egyptian civilization was.

However, the period of recorded history, in the literal sense of the age from which we have some surviving written records, is infinitesimally short compared to the age of the human race. The earliest systems of writing were invented barely five thousand years ago, whereas the preliterate period of human history may have been a million years long. Fortunately we do have some information about this major part of human history. We are informed about it, not by surviving contemporary writings, but by surviving contemporary tools, and tools are coeval with Man himself. Indeed, it is possible that our ancestors were already making tools before they became human, and that the invention of the art of toolmaking was one (though only one) of the innovations in their way of life that enabled them to achieve this portentous advance.

Tools are our only surviving evidence for the history of human affairs during by far the greater part of human history, and they are good evidence as far as they go. It would, however, be a mistake to assume, on

243

this account, that tools were ever the sole agents of change in the conditions of life and therefore the sole sources of the new needs and demands that were generated by new conditions. If we consider the history of the latest twenty-five hundred years, we shall recognize that the founders of new religions, philosophies, and ideologies have had at least as potent an effect on the course of human affairs as the inventors of new tools (not excluding the inventors of tools for use as weapons); and, as far back into the past as our written records reach, we have evidence that religion was as important a factor in human life as technology was. This is also true today of the way of life of the still relatively primitive portions of the human race. We may infer that it has been true, likewise, ever since our ancestors first became human, although, during most of the intervening time, Man's spiritual life and the changes in his spiritual outlook have left no memorials. Even the cave paintings dating from the comparatively recent Upper Paleolithic Age enable us only to make unverifiable guesses at the character of the religious and magical beliefs to which these paintings may, or may not, bear witness.

By our time the advance in technology has shot far ahead of the advance in religion and morals, but our surviving records show that this is a recent phenomenon in human affairs. In the sixth century B.C., Man's spirit shot ahead of his technology. We may guess (though this guess is hazardous) that in the times before the beginning of recorded history, when rates of change in all dimensions of life were slow, Man's technology and his spiritual and social life kept pace with each other, more or less, and that therefore the changes in Man's tools, during the period from which nothing but his tools survives, give a fair measure of the rate of change in all sides of human life. If we now survey the total span of human history, taking tools as our evidence for the period before written records begin, we shall find that the medieval tag was not so far from the truth after all. In human history viewed as a whole, evolution has been the rule, and revolution has been the exception. In fact, it is safe to say that during the major part of human history, there was no possibility of revolutions, because during this period the pace of change in the conditions of life, and therefore also in needs and in demands, was so slow that the necessary corresponding changes in institutions were bound to be brought about by the evolutionary process of gradual adjustment.

The possibility of revolution

It is no accident that the medieval Latin tag was written at a time in the recent period of West European history at which the conditions of life were changing slowly, by comparison with the rate of change in the times that immediately preceded and immediately followed the Western Middle Ages. Of course, even in the darkest patch of the so-called Dark Ages, the pace was precipitate compared to the pace in the time of the Lower Paleolithic Age in the same region. Still, the medieval pace was just slow enough to make it plausible, in the Middle Ages, to assume that evolution, not revolution, is the normal way in which changes are made. In the present-day Western world this assumption would be unconvincing; it would be too much at variance with present-day facts; for in our day we are living in the state of "permanent revolution" that is written, both as a fact and as an ideal, into the present Mexican constitution.

The measuring rod for gauging the pace of change in human affairs is the average length of a human being's life from the dawn of consciousness till dotage or death. In the Lower Paleolithic Age, the expectation of life was considerably shorter than it is today among the minority of the world's population that already enjoys the benefits of modern medicine. But even this slightly protracted expectation of life is minimal compared to the age of the human race and also compared to that major portion of this time during which mankind has lived under Lower Paleolithic conditions of life.

If we visit an archaeological museum in which there is a display of successive types of Lower Paleolithic tools coming from all parts of the habitable surface of the globe, we find a remarkable worldwide uniformity in the representatives of each type of tool. This uniformity of Lower Paleolithic tools is reminiscent of the uniformity of present-day tools, but the reason for the uniformity is, of course, not the same.

We know why there is a worldwide uniformity in the types of present-day tools. Today, we have so efficient a network of worldwide means of communication that a tool that has been invented in one place will almost instantly be carried to all other parts of the world and will be copied and adopted there. The speed of the worldwide adoption of each successive type is so great that it exceeds the speed of innovation. Each type in its turn comes into worldwide use before it is superseded by a new type—and this though the speed of innovation, like the speed of communications, is accelerating.

In the Lower Paleolithic Age, Man's only means of communication were his feet, and his means of transport were limited to the maximum load that he could carry as he walked. Human communities were small and were widely scattered, because, in that age, Man's means of gathering his livelihood were so inefficient that a large area of territory per individual was required in order to enable a community to earn its living. In these circumstances, any type of tool must have taken hundreds and thousands of years to be disseminated from its place of origin. There must have been few opportunities for passing it on from one community to another, and, even when a community did acquire a tool of a new

245

type from its distant nearest neighbor, we may guess that it will have been slow to copy and adopt the new type, since small isolated communities are apt to be conservative-minded. The reason why, nevertheless, each Lower Paleolithic type of tool did eventually come into world-wide use was that the pace of technological progress was almost inconceivably slow, judged by present-day standards, and therefore there was time for each type of tool to spread all over the world before it was superseded by a new type. This is surely evidence that, throughout the Lower Paleolithic Age, people were unconscious of technological change or any other kind of change within the span of a single lifetime, and we may guess that, insofar as changes did occur, Lower Paleolithic Man adapted his institutions to these changes unconsciously, easily, and in fact in an evolutionary, not a revolutionary, way.

When, in the archaeological museum, we pass from the Lower to the Upper Paleolithic room, we have the impression of witnessing a revolution. The improvement in technology, as between the Upper and the Lower Paleolithic ages, looks abrupt when compared with the virtual stagnation of technology throughout the Lower Paleolithic Age. Yet this impression of a revolutionary change can be seen to be illusory when we measure the rate of the invention of Upper Paleolithic tools by our measuring rod of a human lifetime. Relatively swift though the technological advance came to be at last at this stage, it was still so slow that no one in any generation in the probably long series of generations of the inventors of Upper Paleolithic tools will have been aware that the technological conditions of life were changing within his lifetime.

The first people to become aware of a revolutionary technological change must have been the users of Lower Paleolithic tools who encountered users of Upper Paleolithic tools. The mutual isolation of communities had now resulted in one group of communities forging ahead in technology while the rest of mankind remained stationary. Technological progress confers mobility on those who achieve it, and the inventors of Upper Paleolithic tools would therefore have impinged on the Lower Paleolithic majority of the human race. This experience must have confronted its Lower Paleolithic victims with a choice between making a revolution and going under. They had now to copy and to learn to use the more efficient tools of their Upper Paleolithic tool-using contemporaries if they were not to be exterminated; if they succeeded in adopting the new technology, they would develop new needs and would make new demands; and these sudden new conditions, needs, and demands would require a rapid adjustment of traditional institutions.

The Yerba Buena section of San Francisco: an original city house against a new office building

"in our day we are living in the state of 'permanent revolution' "

Villagers of Ecuador

"Here we have put a finger on one of the causes of revolutions. This cause is the difference . . . in the rates of technological and spiritual change as between different sections of the human race."

Causes of revolution

Here we have put a finger on one of the causes of revolutions. This cause is the difference, since the beginning of the Upper Paleolithic Age, in the rates of technological and spiritual change as between different sections of the human race. When a more backward community is impinged upon by a more advanced community, the situation in the more backward community becomes potentially revolutionary.

There are many examples of this phenomenon in quite recent history. Within the modern Western society, for instance, the French political Revolution of 1789 was not inspired solely by dissatisfaction with the failure of the *ancien régime* to adapt itself to contemporary conditions of French life. It was also inspired by a knowledge and emulation, among the leaders of the Revolution, of previous events in Britain and in the United States. The development of constitutional government in Britain in the seventeenth century had been studied by the eighteenth-century French philosophes, and, even if it is true that they partly misinterpreted the seventeenth-century British facts, their presentation of these was nonetheless influential in France. The liberation of the United States from British rule had been assisted by a French army, and one of the officers who had served in this campaign was Lafayette.

The revolutionary situation is more acute when the two parties that encounter each other are not sister communities within the same society but are different societies whose characters differ more widely. A classic example of the revolutionary effect of the impact of a more potent civilization on weaker alien societies is the impact of the modern West on Russia, Egypt, Turkey, Japan, and China. In each of these confrontations with the West, the society that has suffered the impact has found itself forced to revolutionize its traditional institutions sooner or later. Whether or not these traditional institutions would have continued to be adequate for the non-Western society if it had been able to continue to live in isolation, they proved totally inadequate for enabling the threatened society to make the adjustments in its institutions that were required if it was to hold its own against Western economic or military conquest and if it was to cope successfully with the changes in its domestic conditions of life, and the consequent changes in its needs and its demands, that were set in motion by the infiltration of Western technology, ideas, and ideals.

The history of the non-Western civilizations since they first experienced the West's impact shows that the more prompt and more thorough the Westernizing revolution that the threatened society makes in response to this challenge from outside, the less violent the revolutionary recasting of its institutions needs to be. The saving virtue of promptness has been all the more important because, during the period in which the West has been making its impact on the rest of the world, the Western way of life itself has been changing all the time at an ever-accelerating pace. Peter the Great, for instance, was prompt in adapting Russian institutions to the contemporary Western way of life in the late sixteen and early seventeen hundreds. In 1825, however, Czar Nicholas I crushed the Dekabrists' attempt to bring up to date Russia's adjustment to the continuing changes in the Western civilization. The penalty for the Dekabrists' failure in 1825 was the belated, and therefore far more extreme and violent, Bolshevik Revolution of 1917. Similarly, the halfheartedness and dilatoriness of the Westernizing reforms that were started in Turkey in the late seventeen and early eighteen hundreds had to be paid for by the radicalism of the revolution that was carried out by Mustafa Kemal Atatürk in the 1920s. By the time that Turkey had been defeated in the First World War, nothing less drastic could have saved the Turkish people from being subjugated and perhaps even extinguished.

Again, the rejection of the Western civilization by China and Japan in the seventeenth century did not solve "the Western Question" for the peoples of Eastern Asia. Though the West's first assault on Eastern Asia had been repulsed, the West continued to develop at an accelerating pace. During the period for which China and Japan succeeded in virtually insulating themselves from the West, the West itself went through the British Industrial Revolution, the French Political Revolution, and a general Western scientific revolution, which had not merely intellectual but also religious effects. The transformation of the Western peoples' picture of the universe, through the discoveries made by Western geologists and biologists, undermined the belief in the West's ancestral religion, Christianity, and thereby potentially undermined the belief in all the rest of the world's traditional religions. Thus, when, in the nineteenth century, the West made its second assault on Eastern Asia, it was equipped this time with new and far more powerful weapons, and the most potent of these new weapons were not material armaments; they were ideologies: first democracy, and later communism.

This new challenge from the West evoked very different responses in China and in Japan. The Japanese decided in 1868 that their only chance of coping successfully with the West lay in deliberately putting Japan through a Westernizing revolution. The intention of the makers of the Meiji Revolution was to transform not the whole of Japanese life but only so much as would make it possible for Japan to hold her own in a world in which the West had become dominant. Their immediate objective was to equip Japan with Western-style armaments that would make her a match for any of the Western powers. They realized that Western-style armaments would require a Western style of technology, science, education, and government; but it was not till the eventual defeat and military occupation of Japan by the United States at the end of the Second

World War that the Westernization of Japan was carried virtually to completion.

All the same, Japan's revolutionary response to Western pressure was far more prompt than China's was. Japan made the Meiji Revolution of 1868 without having been goaded into this by any humiliating defeat at the hands of a Western power. The sight of Commodore Perry's guns had been enough; Japan had not waited to receive a broadside. On the other hand, China's humiliation—thirty years before Japan's Meiji Revolution—in the Opium War had not aroused the Chinese to take any similar revolutionary action. In China the inevitable Westernizing revolution hung fire for more than a century, while China suffered one further humiliation after another. It was not till the 1940s that the Chinese people prevailed upon themselves to make a genuine Westernizing revolution, and, coming so late in the day as it came, this took the radical form of communism. In fact, China paid as high a price for having failed to make her first Westernizing revolution in the 1840s as Russia paid for the miscarriage of her abortive second Westernizing revolution in 1825.

The acceleration in the rate of change that has aggravated the effect of the West's impact on the rest of the world is not a new phenomenon in human history, though it is a recent one in terms of the age of the human race. It is the most intense phase arrived at so far, in a process of acceleration that started, so far as we know, when, perhaps thirty thousand years ago, the Upper Paleolithic way of life broke in upon the perhaps one-million-year-old torpor of the Lower Paleolithic Age. Ever since then, the process of change in the conditions of human life has been gathering speed.

The innovators who have driven the rest of mankind to make revolutionary changes in order to keep pace with them have not always been the same section of mankind. The torch—an inflammatory torch—has been handed from one society to another. Most of our evidence for Upper Paleolithic Man's way of life comes from tools of his that have been discovered in Europe. Most of the evidence for the next spurt of acceleration at the dawn of the Neolithic Age, perhaps eight thousand years ago, comes from the outer rim of the "Fertile Crescent" in southwest Asia. This next spurt brought with it not only the art of grinding stone tools, which has given the Neolithic Age its label, but the equally important arts of agriculture and animal husbandry, spinning and weaving, pottery-making and navigation.

The third spurt was the dawn of civilization about five thousand years ago. This was signaled by an innovation that was social rather than technological. The jungle swamps of the lower Tigris-Euphrates basin and the lower Nile basin were now drained and irrigated, and these great feats of civil engineering must have been achieved by the organization of the labor of large numbers of human beings who had been persuaded or coerced into working for long-term objectives. The unknown leaders who wielded this "man-power" must have had both great administrative ability and great personal magnetism. The fruit of their leadership was that, when the former jungle swamps had been transformed into unprecedentedly fertile fields, societies were created that, for the first time in human history, were able to produce a surplus beyond the minimum requirements of food and shelter. During these last five thousand years the greater part of this surplus has been spent on the destructive game of war. The margin of the surplus that has been spent on fostering the arts of peace has been the source of all improvements in the conditions of human life that have been achieved since then.

The most recent of the successive spurts is the Industrial Revolution that started in Britain about two centuries ago and that has spread meanwhile, first to the rest of the modern Western society, and then to almost all the rest of the world. This is the spurt in which we, in our time, are still being swept along at a pace and with a momentum that are ever increasing.

It is evident that, with every increase in the pace of change in the conditions of life, it becomes increasingly difficult to make timely and therefore peaceful adjustments of traditional institutions. It is therefore not surprising that, when we survey the last thirty thousand, eight thousand, five thousand, and two hundred years of mankind's history, we find revolutions becoming ever more frequent and more violent. Technology, systematized and reinforced by science, has now obliterated the natural environment in which the human race came into existence and has overlaid it with an artificial man-made environment. This man-made new world of ours is both material and mental. We have conjured up for ourselves a new technological apparatus and a new outlook on the universe, and, in performing this double conjuring trick, we have set ourselves the problem of creating new social and religious institutions that will make life possible in these entirely novel circumstances.

It has been suggested already that, perhaps not more than about thirty thousand years ago, on the eve of the advent of the Upper Paleolithic Age, our Lower Paleolithic ancestors were still unconscious of any change in the conditions of life within a single lifetime, or indeed within a span of many lifetimes on end. In our time, a human being, between the dawn of his consciousness and his dotage or death, may find himself challenged to make as many and as momentous changes in his personal way of life as his ancestors made gradually in the course of many aeons. Learning to use an ever-changing output of new material apparatus is the least of contemporary man's difficulties. He may also find that his ancestral religion has given way under his feet, and that he has to make his arduous and painful journey through life in a state of spiritual nakedness. It is no wonder that these extreme demands, on contemporary society and on its

253

U.S. soldier and watchdog guard nose cones for Matador guided missiles in West Germany, 1958

"A second of our glaring misfits is that we have not yet discarded the five-thousand-year-old habit of going to war"

members, for revolutionary readjustments of the traditional regime in matters that touch human life to the quick should have produced a malaise that rankles into an unrest which finally boils over into violence.

The situation today

Nor is it surprising that in our time the misfit between traditional institutions and actual conditions, needs, and demands should have become almost intolerable. Try as we may to recast our institutions and our beliefs to keep pace with the accelerating changes in our way of life, we are failing, at present, to win this desperate race. A full catalog of present misfits would be endless. We must illustrate them by picking out a few of the most flagrant of them.

There is, for instance, a glaring misfit between our inherited institutions and the present facts on the political plane. Today the surface of our planet is still partitioned politically among 147 sovereign independent states; yet we are living in an age in which the progress of technology has unified the whole habitable and traversable part of the surface of this planet and in which we are reaching out to the moon and, far further afield than this, to some of the other planets that travel, as our own planet travels, in elliptical orbits round our sun.

A second of our glaring misfits is that we have not yet discarded the five-thousand-year-old habit of going to war, though the accelerating advance of technology has now equipped us with annihilating weapons. Technology may prove to have knit together the whole surface of this planet in order to make it a potential arena for atomic or bacteriological warfare; and, so long as local sovereignty survives, wars, waged with the most deadly weapons at our command, continue to be possible, since going to war is the principal prerogative of sovereignty.

The third of the particularly glaring misfits has been touched upon already. Our new scientific knowledge has discredited our traditional religions and the traditional codes of morals that are so closely bound up with traditional religion, and we have not yet found even a stopgap to plug this devastating and demoralizing spiritual vacuum.

These misfits explain why the rising generation is today in a recalcitrant and rebellious mood—particularly the university students, whose education makes them aware that the times are out of joint and whose assemblage on university campuses gives them opportunities for debate that is apt to find vent in action. The rising generation sees that the disparity between existing institutions and the actual conditions of life has now become so extreme that the whole fabric of society may collapse and may bury youth under its ruins. Naturally the young resent having been born and brought up to be threatened with becoming the victims of some appalling catastrophe, and, like Hamlet, they indict their parents' genera-

255

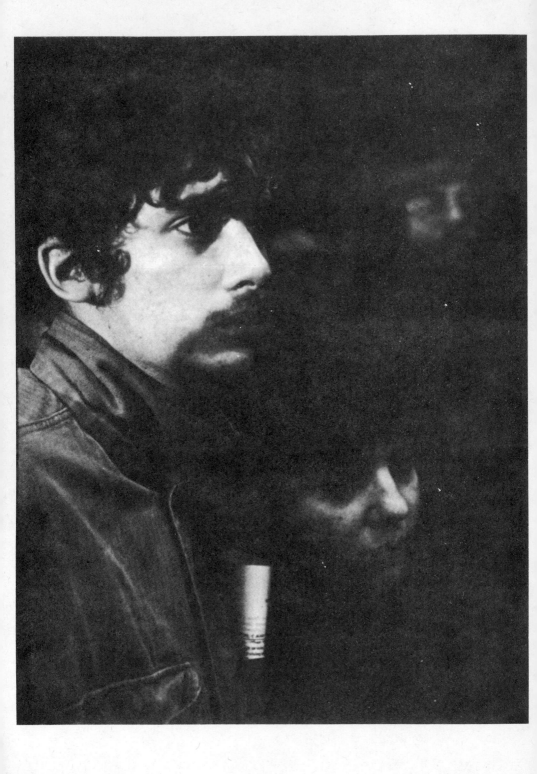

tion. This generation is now in power, and therefore, in the younger generation's eyes, it is responsible for having allowed human affairs to come to this pass and is criminal in its failure to put things right.

It is true that the middle-aged generation is responsible in the sense that it is momentarily in power. Yet in a few years the power, and, with it, the responsibility, will be transferred to the shoulders of the present "establishment's" youthful critics. Moreover, the present holders of power have only recently taken over the burden from their predecessors, and they have had to take it as it was unloaded on them and to do the best that they can, in their time, to reshape this heritage, which was not of their making, into greater conformity with the present situation. The young perhaps do not realize—and may not realize till they have to shoulder the burden in their turn—that, though the temporary holders of power do have some freedom of action and are therefore to blame for not using this freedom better, their room for maneuver is restricted. The institutions that are so perilously at variance with the present facts of life have not been created by the present holders of power *de novo*. They have been inherited from the past, and the habits, customs, and traditions with which the present holders have to wrestle are the cumulative product of human history since the origin of our species. This is the defense that each successive generation of the "establishment" can fairly make for the inadequacy of its response to the challenge of the times. The generation now in power has the same right as any other to offer this plea for a partial mitigation of the severity of the rising generation's judgment, but this does not make the present situation any the less menacing.

Total revolution

The young today are in a mood for demanding something like a total revolution. Some of them contemplate scrapping the whole set of inherited institutions and replacing these by a new man-made heaven and earth. This current mood among the younger generation raises two questions: first, what is human nature's reaction to a demand for total revolution; and, second, is total revolution a practical possibility?

When human nature is confronted with the prospect of revolution, it finds itself pulled in two opposite directions, and, on each such occasion, there is no telling in advance which of the two opposing psychological forces is going to win. Discontent contends with resignation; a hankering after innovation contends with a yearning for stability. It has been observed that there is no exact correspondence between an intolerable situation and a revolutionary mood. A population that has been ground

SDS rally outside the Conrad Hilton Hotel, Chicago, on election eve, 1968

"like Hamlet, they indict their parents' generation"

down may have no spirit left in it for revolting. It may accept the situation as being its fate, however monstrous this situation may be. On the other hand, a population whose condition has improved may not be appeased by the betterment of its conditions; so far from that, it may be stimulated by this to ask for more. The masses who make a revolution succeed by giving the leaders their support are, as often as not, already moving on the upgrade, not lying prone in the bottom of the trough.

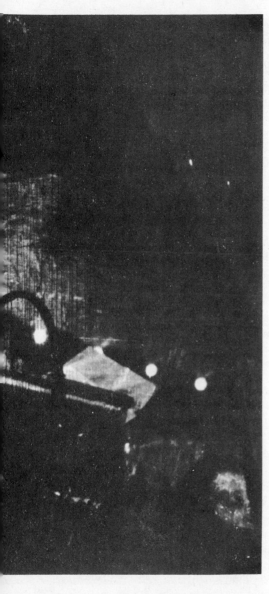

Leon Trotski speaking in Copenhagen in 1931

"Their founders have undertaken to right all wrongs, solve all problems, and answer all questions."

This conflict of contrary reactions to revolution in human nature attracts people to revolutionary programs that purport to reconcile the two reactions by giving satisfaction to each; and this can be offered by proposing "a revolution to end revolutions." This has, in fact, been the program of all the missionary religions, philosophies, and ideologies that have captivated large portions of the human race within the last twenty-five hundred years. Their founders have undertaken to right all wrongs, solve all problems, and answer all questions. A revolution that carried out this program would be definitive. Life would be restored to the static condition of mankind's first million Lower Paleolithic years, though the promised new stability would be at a far higher level of well-being, virtue, and happiness.

This undertaking cannot be fulfilled, and there are at least two decisive reasons for this. One reason is that, at least since the beginning of the Upper Paleolithic Age, the conditions of human life—and, with them, Man's needs and desires—have been changing at an ever accelerating pace. There is no ground for expecting that this process of change can be arrested; and, if it cannot be, a regime that might be perfectly satisfying at the moment of its inauguration would immediately begin to fall out of step with the continuing march of events. A classic illustration of the impossibility of "freezing" any post-Upper Paleolithic society is the ultimate failure of the Tokugawa regime in Japan. Though its fall was actually brought about by its inability to cope with the situation when the West knocked for the second time at Japan's door, it is certain that the regime would have fallen before long in any case. This is certain because the regime had already proved unable, on its domestic front, to prevent a fargoing transfer of wealth, and therefore of power too, *de facto,* from the samurai to a new class of bourgeois businessmen.

A deeper reason why the promise of a "revolution to end revolution" is bound to be illusory is that it is impossible to give genuine answers to the fundamental questions that the human spirit asks. The human race and every individual representative of it has been born into a universe that is mysterious to us, and, in the light of past experience, it seems unlikely that the riddle of the universe will ever be solved by human insight. In our day, mankind has made sensational advances in its understanding of physical nature and of psychic nature too. Yet, if both these realms of nature were one day to be fully explored and charted, we may guess that our descendants would still find themselves left facing something unknown, and that they would recognize that this unknown residue of reality was the key to the rest. There are indeed more things in heaven and earth than are dreamed of in any philosophy.

However, even if we conclude that the promise of a "revolution to end revolution" is illusory, it does not follow that a religion or philosophy or ideology that makes this promise will fail to win allegiance. So far from that, history testifies that it may captivate a large portion of the human race for many centuries on end, even though it may be destined inevitably to lose its hold sooner or later. A professedly total revolution may have a long-enduring success, because the consequence of its triumph is the imposition of a totalitarian orthodoxy, and this answers to the human longing for stability and certainty. This longing is always competing with the itch for change, and there is a premium on it in a time of troubles of the kind in which we find ourselves today. Under this ordeal, people become weary and frightened, and their fear and fatigue may reach a pitch at which they become willing to sacrifice freedom to the prospect of security.

Here lies the potential tragedy of the present revolt of youth. The rebels may bring on themselves the very opposite of what they intend, and they themselves may be the agents of this ironic result. The libertarian rebel of yesterday is often the authoritarian tyrant of tomorrow. We have already noticed the tendency of the aftermath of a revolution to revert to a reproduction of the *ancien régime*. A would-be total revolution is virtually doomed to recoil into an ultraorthodoxy which may be an avatar of the *ancien régime* under a thin disguise. This is why a truly revolutionary total revolution is an impossibility.

If we assume that the outcome of a revolution is likely to be at least a temporary authoritarian regime, a practical question presents itself. How much freedom are we prepared to sacrifice in our day for the sake of averting the catastrophe with which we are threatened? The catastrophe might take any one of a number of forms. Besides the risk of atomic or bacteriological warfare, there is, for instance, the risk of mass psychosis, when the planet's rapidly increasing population is herded into cities in which the conditions of life are becoming more and more unnatural. Undoubtedly we need a breathing space in order to give statesmanship and expertise a chance of averting these terrible dangers. Does the only opening for this lie in a revolution that will contradict itself by ushering in an authoritarian regime? Any human being who is in his senses will prefer an evolutionary to a revolutionary solution of human problems. But evolution is a process that requires time. Is the necessary time for this going to be denied to us by the acceleration in the pace of change in human affairs?

Dr. Ivan Illich has been described as "the unwilling hero of the reformers of the Catholic left," and CIDOC, the educational organization that he founded and directs in Cuernavaca, Mexico, is viewed by some as a center for revolutionary activity. CIDOC —Centro Intercultural de Documentacion —is an educational center devoted to improving the cultural and social envi-

ronment of the Latin American peoples. Founded in 1961, it grew out of Dr. Illich's experience as vice-chancellor of the Catholic University of Puerto Rico and as a priest assigned to a parish of Puerto Ricans in New York City, to which he had come fresh from his ordination in Rome. He was born in Vienna in 1926 of a Croatian Catholic father and a Sephardic Jewish mother. Before going to Rome, he took his doctorate at Salzburg, writing a dissertation on the work of Arnold Toynbee. Convinced that the church should not be identified with any kind of political activity, he requested and was granted by his religious superiors a suspension from his priestly functions.

The Need for Cultural
Revolution

During the decade just past, we have gotten used to seeing the world divided into two parts: the developed and the underdeveloped. People in the development business may prefer to speak of the developed nations and the less developed or developing nations. This terminology suggests that development is both good and inevitable. Others, especially protagonists of revolutionary change, speak of the "Third World" and wait for the day when the wretched of the earth will rise in armed revolt against the imperialist powers and shift control over existing institutions from North to South, from White to Black, from Metropolis to Colony.

A vulgar example of the first assumption is the Rockefeller Report on the Americas. Its doctrine is aptly summed up by President Nixon: "This I pledge to you tonight: the nation that went to the moon in peace for all mankind is ready to share its technology in peace with its nearest neighbors." The governor, in turn, proposes that keeping the pledge might require a lot of additional weaponry in South America.

The Pearson Report on partnership in development is a much more sophisticated example of the development mentality. It outlines policies that will permit a few more countries to join the charmed circle of the consumer nations but that will actually increase the poverty of the poor half in these same countries, because the strategies proposed will sell them ever more thoroughly on goods and services ever more expensive and out of their reach. The policy goals of most revolutionary movements and governments I know—and I do not know Mao's China—reflect another type of cynicism. Their leaders make futile promises that—once in power for a sufficient length of time—more of everything that the masses have learned to know and to envy as privileges of the rich will be produced and distributed. Both the purveyors of development and the preachers of revolution advocate more of the same. They define more education as more schooling, better health as more doctors, higher mobility as more high-speed vehicles. The salesmen for U.S. industry, the experts for the World Bank, and ideologues of power for the poor seem to forget that

Revolutionist party leader addressing Indians near Lake Titicaca, Bolivia

"Others . . . wait for the day when the wretched of the earth will rise in armed revolt"

heart surgery and college degrees remain beyond the reach of the majority for generations.

The goals of development are always and everywhere stated in terms of consumer value packages standardized around the North Atlantic—and therefore always and everywhere imply more privileges for a few. Political reorganization cannot change this fact; it can only rationalize it. Different ideologies create different minorities of privileged consumers, but heart surgery or a university education is always priced out of range for all but a few: be they the rich, the orthodox, or the most fascinating subjects for experiments by surgeons or pedagogues.

Underdevelopment is the result of a state of mind common to both socialist and capitalist countries. Present development goals are neither desirable nor reasonable. Unfortunately, anti-imperialism is no antidote.

264

Although exploitation of poor countries is an undeniable reality, current nationalism is merely the affirmation of the right of colonial elites to repeat history and follow the road traveled by the rich toward the universal consumption of internationally marketed packages, a road that can ultimately lead only to universal pollution and universal frustration.

The central issue of our time remains the fact that the rich are getting richer and the poor, poorer. This hard fact is often obscured by another apparently contradictory fact. In the rich countries the poor expect a quantity and quality of commodities beyond the dreams of Louis XIV, while many of the so-called developing countries enjoy much higher economic growth rates than those of industrialized countries at a similar stage of their own histories. From icebox to toilet and from antibiotic to television, conveniences are found necessary in Harlem which Washington could not have imagined at Mount Vernon, just as Bolívar could not have foreseen the social polarization now inevitable in Caracas. But neither the rising levels of minimum consumption in the rich countries, nor those of urban consumption in the poor countries can close the gap

Harlem, New York City

"From icebox to toilet and from antibiotic to television, conveniences are found necessary in Harlem which Washington could not have imagined at Mount Vernon"

New York City ghetto (above); anti-pollution march, New York City (below)

"In the late sixties attention was suddenly drawn to the inability of man to survive his industry."

between rich and poor nations or between the rich and poor of any one nation. Modern poverty is a by-product of a world market catering to the ideologies of an industrial middle class. Modern poverty is built into an international community where demand is engineered through publicity to stimulate the production of standard commodities. In such a market, expectations are standardized and must always outrace marketable resources.

In the United States, for all its gargantuan prosperity, real poverty levels rise faster than the median income. In the capital-starved countries, median incomes move rapidly away from rising averages. Most goods now produced for rich and poor alike in the United States are beyond the reach of all but a few in other areas. In both rich and poor nations consumption is polarized while expectation is equalized.

New needs

During the decade now beginning, we must learn a new language, a language that speaks, not of development and underdevelopment, but of true and false ideas about man, his needs, and his potential. Development programs all over the world progressively lead to violence, either in the form of repression or of rebellion. This is due neither to the evil intentions of capitalists nor to the ideological rigidity of Communists, but to the radical inability of men to tolerate the by-products of industrial and welfare institutions developed in the early industrial age. In the late sixties attention was suddenly drawn to the inability of man to survive his industry. During the late sixties it became evident that less than 10 percent of the human race consumes more than 50 percent of the world's resources, and produces 90 percent of the physical pollution that threatens to extinguish the biosphere. But this is only one aspect of the paradox of present development. During the early seventies it will become equally clear that welfare institutions have an analogous regressive effect. The international institutionalization of social service, medicine, and education, which is generally identified with development, has equally overwhelming destructive by-products.

We need an alternative program, an alternative both to development and to merely political revolution. Let me call this alternative program either institutional or cultural revolution, because its aim is the transformation of both public and personal reality. The political revolutionary wants to improve existing institutions—their productivity and the quality and distribution of their products. His vision of what is desirable and possible is based on consumption habits developed during the last hundred years. The cultural revolutionary believes that these habits have radically distorted our view of what human beings can have and want. He questions the reality that others take for granted, a reality that, in his view, is the artificial by-product of contemporary institutions, created and re-inforced by them in pursuit of their short-term ends. The political rev-olutionary concentrates on schooling and tooling for the environment that the rich countries, socialist or capitalist, have engineered. The cul-tural revolutionary risks the future on the educability of man.

The cultural revolutionary must be distinguished not only from the political magician but also from both the neo-Luddite and the promoter of intermediary technology. The neo-Luddite behaves as if the noble savage could either be restored to the throne or have the Third World transformed into a reservation for him. He opposes the internal com-bustion engine rather than opposing its packaging into a product de-signed for exclusive use by the man who owns it. Thus the Luddite blames the producer; the institutional revolutionary tries to reshape the design and distribution of the product. The Luddite blames the machine; the cultural revolutionary heightens awareness that it produces needless de-mands. The cultural revolutionary must also be distinguished from the promoter of intermediary technology who is frequently merely a superior tactician paving the road to totally manipulated consumption.

The myth of schooling

Let me illustrate what I mean by a cultural revolution within one major international institution, by taking as an example the institution that currently produces education. I mean, of course, obligatory schooling: full-time attendance of age-specific groups at a graded curriculum.

Latin America has decided to school itself into development. This de-cision results in the production of homemade inferiority. With every school that is built, another seed of institutional corruption is planted, and this is in the name of growth.

Schools affect individuals and characterize nations. Individuals merely get a bad deal; nations are irreversibly degraded when they build schools to help their citizens play at international competition. For the individ-ual, school is always a gamble. The chances may be very slim, but every-one shoots for the same jackpot. Of course, as any professional gambler knows, it is the rich who win in the end, and the poor who get hooked. And if the poor man manages to stay in the game for a while, he will feel the pain even more sharply when he does lose, as he almost inevitably must. Primary-school dropouts in a Latin American city find it increas-ingly difficult to get an industrial job.

But no matter how high the odds, everyone plays the game, for, after all, there is only one game in town. A scholarship may be a long shot, but it is a chance to become equal to the world's best trained bureau-crats. And the student who fails can console himself with the knowledge that the cards were stacked against him from the outset.

More and more, men begin to believe that in the schooling game, the loser gets only what he deserves. The belief in the ability of schools to label people correctly is already so strong that people accept their vocational and marital fate with a gambler's resignation. In cities this faith in school-slotting is on the way to sprouting a more creditable meritocracy —a state of mind in which each citizen believes that he deserves the place assigned to him by school. A perfect meritocracy, in which there would be no excuses, is not yet upon us, and I believe it can be avoided. It must be avoided, since a perfect meritocracy would not only be hellish, it would be hell.

Educators appeal to the gambling instinct of the entire population when they raise money for schools. They advertise the jackpot without mentioning the odds. And those odds are high indeed for someone who is born brown, poor, or in the pampa. In Latin America, no country is prouder of its legally obligatory admission-free school system than Argentina. Yet only one Argentinean of five thousand born into the lower half of the population gets as far as the university.

What is only a wheel of fortune for an individual is a spinning wheel of irreversible underdevelopment for a nation. The high cost of schooling turns education into a scarce resource, as poor countries accept that a certain number of years in school makes an educated man. More money gets spent on fewer people. In poor countries, the school pyramid of the rich countries takes on the shape of an obelisk, or a rocket. School inevitably gives individuals who attend it and then drop out, as well as those who don't make it at all, a rationale for their own inferiority. But for poor nations, obligatory schooling is a monument to self-inflicted inferiority. To buy the schooling hoax is to purchase a ticket for the back seat in a bus headed nowhere.

Schooling encrusts the poorest nations at the bottom of the educational bucket. The school systems of Latin America are fossilized deposits of a dream begun a century ago. The school pyramid is a-building from top to bottom throughout Latin America. All countries spend more than 20 percent of their national budgets and nearly 5 percent of their gross national products on its construction. Teachers constitute the largest profession, and their children are frequently the largest group of students in the upper grades. Fundamental education is either redefined as the foundation for schooling and therefore placed beyond the reach of the unschooled and the early dropout, or is defined as a remedy for the unschooled, which will only frustrate him into accepting inferiority. Even the poorest countries continue to spend disproportionate sums on graduate schools—gardens that ornament the penthouses of skyscrapers built in a slum.

Bolivia is well on the way to suicide by an overdose of schooling. This impoverished, landlocked country creates papier-mâché bridges to prosperity by spending more than a third of its entire budget on public education and half as much again on private schools. A full half of this educational misspending is consumed by 1 percent of the school-age population. In Bolivia the university student's share of public funds is a thousand times greater than that of his fellow citizen of median income. Most Bolivian people live outside the city, yet only 2 percent of the rural population makes it to the fifth grade. This discrimination was legally sanctioned in 1967 by declaring grade school obligatory for all—a law that made most people criminal by fiat, and the rest immoral exploiters by decree. In 1970 the university entrance examinations were abolished with a flourish of egalitarian rhetoric. At first glance, it does seem a libertarian advance to legislate that all high-school graduates have a right to enter the university—until you realize that less than 2 percent of Bolivians finish high school.

Bolivia may be an extreme example of schooling in Latin America. But on an international scale Bolivia *is* typical. Few African or Asian countries have attained the progress now taken for granted there.

Privately owned school in Latin America that is part of a reform program for poor children. Teacher reads poetry to this rural class

"for poor nations, obligatory schooling is a monument to self-inflicted inferiority"

Cuba is perhaps an example of the other extreme. Fidel Castro has tried to create a major cultural revolution. He has reshaped the academic pyramid and promised that by 1980 the universities can be closed, since all of Cuba will be one big university, with higher learning going on at work and leisure. Yet the Cuban pyramid is still a pyramid. There is no doubt that the redistribution of privilege, the redefinition of social goals, and the popular participation in the achievement of these goals have reached spectacular heights in Cuba since the revolution. For the moment, however, Cuba is showing only that, under exceptional political conditions, the base of the present school system can be expanded exceptionally. But there are built-in limits to the elasticity of present institutions, and Cuba is at the point of reaching them. The Cuban revolution will work— within these limits. Which means only that Dr. Castro will have masterminded a faster road to a bourgeois meritocracy than those previously taken by capitalists or bolsheviks. Sometimes, when he is not promising schools for all, Fidel hints at a policy of de-schooling for all, and the Isle of Pines seems to be a laboratory for redistribution of educational functions to other social institutions. But unless Cuban educators admit that work-education that is effective in a rural economy can be even more

Free school built by small farm owner in Bahia, Brazil

Bolivian boy from the Altiplano area does his homework

"Bolivia is well on the way to suicide by an overdose of schooling."

effective in an urban one, Cuba's institutional revolution will not begin. No cultural revolution can be built on the denial of reality.

As long as Communist Cuba continues to promise obligatory high-school completion by the end of this decade, it is, in this regard, institutionally no more promising than fascist Brazil, which has made a similar promise. In both Brazil and Cuba, enough girls have already been born to double the number of potential mothers in the 1980s. Per capita resources available for education can hardly be expected to double in either country, and even if they could, no progress would have been made at all. In development-mad Brazil and in humanist Cuba, waiting for Godot is equally futile. Without a radical change in their institutional goals, both "revolutions" must make fools of themselves. Unfortunately, both seem headed for manifest foolishness, albeit by different routes. The Cubans allow work, party, and community involvement to nibble away at the school year, and they call this radical education, while the Brazilians let U.S. experts peddle teaching devices that only raise the per capita cost of classroom attendance.

The production of inferiority through schooling is more evident in poor countries and perhaps more painful in rich countries. The 10 percent in the United States with the highest incomes can provide most of the education for their children through private institutions. Yet they also succeed in obtaining ten times more of the public resources devoted to education than the poorest 10 percent of the population. In Soviet Russia a more puritanical belief in meritocracy makes the concentration of schooling privileges on the children of urban professionals even more painful.

In the shadow of each national school-pyramid, an international caste system is wedded to an international class structure. Countries are ranged like castes, whose educational dignity is determined by the average years of schooling of its citizens. Individual citizens of all countries achieve a symbolic mobility through a class system that makes each man accept the place he believes he has merited.

The political revolutionary strengthens the demand for schooling by futilely promising that under his administration more learning and increased earning will become available to all through more schooling. He contributes to the modernization of a world class structure and a modernization of poverty. It remains the task of the cultural revolutionary to overcome the delusions on which the support of school is based and to outline policies for the radical de-schooling of society.

The basic reason for all this is that schooling comes in quanta. Less than so much is no good, and the minimum quantum carries a minimum price. It is obvious that with schools of equal quality a poor child can never catch up with a rich one, nor a poor country with a rich country. It is equally obvious that poor children and poor countries never have equal schools but always poorer ones and thus fall ever farther behind, so long as they depend on schools for their education.

Another illusion is that most learning is a result of teaching. Teaching may contribute to certain kinds of learning under certain circumstances. The strongly motivated student faced with the task of learning a new code may benefit greatly from the discipline we now associate mostly with the old-fashioned schoolmaster. But most people acquire most of their insight, knowledge, and skill outside of school—and in school only insofar as school in a few rich countries becomes their place of confinement during an increasing part of their lives. The radical de-schooling

School in the Peruvian highlands has science class

"an international caste system is wedded to an international class structure"

of society begins, therefore, with the unmasking by cultural revolutionaries of the myth of schooling. It continues with the struggle to liberate other men's minds from the false ideology of schooling—an ideology that makes domestication by schooling inevitable. In its final and positive stage it is the struggle for the right to educational freedom.

A new bill of rights

A cultural revolutionary must fight for legal protection from the imposition of any obligatory graded curriculum. The first article of a bill of rights for a modern and humanist society corresponds to the first amendment to the United States Constitution. The state shall make no law with respect to an establishment of education. There shall be no graded curriculum, obligatory for all. To make this disestablishment effective, we need a law forbidding discrimination in hiring, voting, and admission

to centers of learning based on previous attendance at some curriculum. This guarantee would not exclude specific tests of competence, but it would remove the present absurd discrimination favoring the person who learns a given skill with the largest expenditure of public funds. A third legal reform would guarantee the right of each citizen to an equal share of public educational resources, the right to verify his share of these resources, and the right to sue for them if they are denied. A generalized GI bill, or an edu-credit card in the hand of every citizen, would effectively implement this third guarantee.

Abolition of obligatory schooling, abolition of job discrimination favoring persons who have acquired their learning at a higher cost, plus establishment of edu-credit, would permit the development of a free exchange for educational services. According to present political ideology, this exchange could be influenced by various devices: premiums paid to those who acquire certain needed skills, interest-bearing edu-credit to increase the privileges of those who use it later in life, advantages for industries which incorporate additional formal training into the work routine.

A fourth guarantee to protect the consumer against the monopoly of the educational market would be analogous to antitrust laws.

I have shown in the case of education that a cultural or institutional revolution depends upon the clarification of reality. Development as now conceived is just the contrary: management of the environment and the tooling of man to fit into it. Cultural revolution is a re-view of the reality

276

A return to the American spirit of sharing and understanding the land; commune in New Mexico

"a cultural and institutional revolution that reestablishes man's control over his environment"

of man and a redefinition of the world in terms that support this reality. Development is the attempt to create an environment and then educate at great cost to pay for it.

A bill of rights for modern man cannot produce cultural revolution. It is merely a manifesto. I have outlined the principles of an educational bill of rights. These principles can be generalized.

The disestablishment of schooling can be generalized to freedom from monopoly in the satisfaction of any basic need. Discrimination on the basis of prior schooling can be generalized to discrimination in any institution because of underconsumption or underprivilege in another. A guarantee of equal educational resources is a guarantee against regressive taxation. An educational antitrust law is obviously merely a special case of antitrust laws in general, which in turn are statutory implementations of constitutional guarantees against monopoly.

The social and psychological destruction inherent in obligatory schooling is merely an illustration of the destruction implicit in all international institutions that now dictate the kinds of goods, services, and welfare available to satisfy basic human needs. Only a cultural and institutional revolution that reestablishes man's control over his environment can arrest the violence by which development of institutions is now imposed by a few for their own interest. Maybe Marx said it better, criticizing Ricardo and his school: "They want production to be limited to 'useful things,' but they forget that the production of too many *useful* things results in too many *useless* people."

Paul Goodman

Paul Goodman, social critic, educator, novelist, dramatist, has described, analyzed, even articulated the anguish and aspirations of contemporary youth in several of his books, especially such works of social criticism as *Growing Up Absurd* (1960), *The Community of Scholars* (1962), *Compulsory Mis-Education* (1964), and *People or Personnel* (1965). Born in New

York City September 9, 1911, he received his bachelor's degree from City College of New York and his doctorate from the University of Chicago. He has taught at various universities, including Chicago and Wisconsin, and at Black Mountain College. When not in his country retreat in New Hampshire, he resides in New York City. His most recent book is *New Reformation: Notes of a Neolithic Conservative* (1970).

Anarchism and Revolution

In anarchist theory, the word *revolution* means the process by which the grip of authority is loosed, so that the functions of life can regulate themselves, without top-down direction or external hindrance. The idea is that, except for emergencies and a few special cases, free functioning will find its own right structures and coordination.

An anarchist description of a revolutionary period thus consists of many accounts of how localities, factories, tradesmen, schools, professional groups, and communes go about managing their own affairs, defending themselves against the central "system," and making whatever federal arrangements among themselves that are necessary to weave the fabric of society. An anarchist history of the French Revolution is not much concerned about Paris and the stormy assembly but concentrates on what went on in Lyons—how the bakers carried on the production and distribution of bread though everything seemed to be in chaos, how legal documents were burned up, and how a hastily assembled militia fought off an invader. And of course general history is concerned, not with kings, statesmen, warriors, and politics, but with molecular social conditions, cultural and technical innovation, and the long-range development of religious attitudes and social "movements."

From this point of view, Western history has had some pretty good anarchist successes; anarchy is not merely utopian dreams and a few bloody failures. Winning civil liberties, from Runnymede to the Jeffersonian Bill of Rights; the escape of the townsmen from feudal lords, establishing guild democracy; the liberation of conscience and congregations since the Reformation; the abolition of serfdom, chattel slavery, and some bonds of wage slavery; the freeing of trade and enterprise from mercantilism; the freedom of nations from dynasties and of some nations from imperialists; the development of progressive education and the freeing of sexuality—these bread-and-butter topics of European history are never called "anarchist," but they are. The anarchist victory was won by human suffering and often at the cost of blood; it has somewhat persisted; and it must be vigilantly defended and extended. Any new political revolution, even if it calls itself liberation, cannot be relied on to care for these ancient things. In fact, we see that some liberators impatiently brush them aside—civil liberties go overboard, labor unions are castrated, schooling becomes regimentation, and so forth. But even this is not so annoying as to hear defenders of a present status quo with its freedoms call those who want to extend freedom aimless anarchists.

With regard to freedoms, even "eternal vigilance" is not enough. Unless freedoms are extended, they are whittled away, for those in power always have the advantage of organization and state resources, while ordinary people become tired of battle and fragmented. We may vigilantly defend constitutional limitations and privileges that we have won, but new conditions arise that circumvent them. For instance, new technology like wiretapping and new organizations like computerized Interpol must be offset by new immunities, public defenders, etc.; otherwise the adversary system of Runnymede is nullified. Labor leaders become bureaucrats and are co-opted, and union members do not attend meetings, unless new demands revitalize the labor movements—in my opinion, the labor movement can at present only be revitalized by turning to the idea of workers' management. Triumphant science, having won the battles of Galileo and Darwin, has become the new orthodoxy. We see that ecological threats have created a brand new freedom to fight for—the right to have an environment.

On the positive side, the spirit of freedom is indivisible and quick to revive. A good fight on one issue has a tonic effect on all society. In totalitarian countries it is very difficult to control a "thaw," and we have seen how contagious populist protest has been in recent years in the United States. In Czechoslovakia an entire generation was apparently totally controlled since 1948, but—whether because of native human wildness or the spirit of Hus, Comenius, and Masaryk—the youth acted in 1968 as if there were no such thing. And in the United States, twenty-five years of affluent consumerism and Organization mentality have not seemed to dampen the youth of the present decade.

Anarchists rely on the inventiveness, courage, and drive to freedom of human nature, as opposed to the proletarian industrialized mentality of Scientific Socialism, which takes it for granted that people are essentially and totally socialized by their historical conditions. But anarchist philosophers disagree sharply on the conditions that encourage freedom. (Characteristically, disagreements among anarchists are taken by them as "aspects" of some common position, rather than as "factions" in a power struggle, leading to internecine strife.) Bakunin, for instance, relies on the unemployed, the alienated, the outcasts, the criminal, the uprooted intelligentsia—those who have nothing to lose, not even their chains. But Kropotkin, by contrast, relies on the competent and independent, the highly skilled—small farmers with their peasant community traditions, miners, artists, explorers, architects, educators. Student anarchism at pres-

Fidel Castro and soldiers in Cuba

"a new regime establishes itself and reorganizes the institutions according to its own ideas and interests"

ent tends to be Bakuninist because, in my opinion, the students are inauthentically students; they are exploited and *lumpen* in principle—kept on ice. "Students are niggers." But hopefully the Movement is now beginning to have a more Kropotkinian tendency—authentic young professionals in law, medicine, and ecology. The March 4 (1969) movement of the young scientists at M.I.T. is significant of the new trend.

Revolution and counterrevolution

In ordinary usage, of course, including both liberal and Marxist usage, the word *revolution* has meant, not that controls cease to operate and hinder function, but that a new regime establishes itself and reorganizes the institutions according to its own ideas and interests. (To anarchists this is precisely the counterrevolution, because there is again a centralizing authority to oppose. The counterrevolution occurred with Robespierre, not during Thermidor or with Napoleon.) Liberal historians describe the abuses of the tyrant that made the old regime illegitimate and unviable, and they show how the new regime instituted necessary reforms. Marxists show how in changed technological and social conditions, the class conflict between the dominant and exploited classes erupts: the old dominant group is no longer competent to maintain its power and ideology, the system of belief that gave it legitimacy. Then the new regime establishes institutions to cope with the new conditions, and from these develop a "superstructure" of belief that provides stability and legitimacy. Agitational Marxism, Leninism, works to *make* the old regime unable to cope, to make it illegitimate and to hasten its fall; it is then likely to take power as a minority vanguard party which must educate the masses to their own interests. In this stringent activity, any efforts at piecemeal improvement or protecting traditional freedoms are regarded as mere reformism or tinkering, and they are called "objectively counterrevolutionary." After the takeover by the new regime, there must be a strong and repressive administration to prevent reaction; during this period (indefinitely prolonged) anarchists fare badly.

Of the political thought of the past century, only Anarchism or, better, anarcho-pacifism—the philosophy of institutions without the State and centrally organized violence—has consistently foreseen the gross dangers of present advanced societies, their police, bureaucracy, excessive centralization of decision making, social engineering, processing schooling, and inevitable militarization—"War is the health of the State," as Randolph Bourne put it. The bourgeois State of the early nineteenth century may well have been merely the instrument of the dominant economic class, as Marx said, but in its further development its gigantic statism has become more important than its exploitation for profit. It and the socialist alternatives have not developed very differently. All have tended toward fascism—statism pure and simple. In the corporate liberal societies, the Bismarckian welfare state, immensely extended, does less and less well by its poor and outcast. In socialist societies, free communism does not come to be, labor is regimented, surplus value is mulcted and reinvested, and there is also a Power Elite. In both types, the alarming consequences of big-scale technology and massive urbanization, directed by the State or by baronial corporations, make it doubtful that central authority is a workable structure.

It could be said that most of the national states, once they had organized the excessive fragmentation of the later Middle Ages, outlived their usefulness by the seventeenth century. Their subsequent career has been largely their own aggrandizement. They have impeded rather than helped the advancing functions of civilization. And evidently in our times they cannot be allowed to go on. Perhaps we could be saved by the organization

Cityscape in California

*"the alarming consequences of big-scale technology and massive urbanization . . .
make it doubtful that central authority is a workable structure"*

of a still more powerful supranation; but the present powers being what they are, this would require the very war that would do us in. And since present central powers are dangerous and dehumanizing, why trust super-power and a central international organization? The anarchist alternative is more logical—to try to decentralize and weaken top-down authority in the nation states, and to come to international organization by piecemeal functional and regional arrangements from below, in trade, travel, development, science, communications, health, etc.

Thus, for objective reasons, it is now quite respectable to argue for anarchy, pacifism, or both, whereas even a generation ago such ideas were considered odd, absurd, utopian, or wicked. I do not mean that anarchy answers all questions. Rather, we have the dilemma: it seems that modern economies, technologies, urbanism, communications, and diplomacy demand ever tighter centralized control; yet this method of organization patently does not work. Or even worse: to cope with increasingly recurrent emergencies, we need unified information, central power, massive resources, repression, crash programs, hot lines; but just these things produce and heighten the emergencies. There is real confusion here, shared by myself.

Anarchism and the young

In any case, now hundreds of thousands of young people, perhaps millions, call themselves anarchists—more so in Europe, of course, where there has been a continuing tradition of anarchist thought. It is hard to know how to assay this. There are isolated phrases with an anarchist resonance: "Do your thing!" "Participatory democracy," "I scoff at all national flags" (Daniel Cohn-Bendit). These do not get us far, but certain attitudes and actions are more significant. The young are severely uninterested in Great Power politics and deterrence "strategy." They disregard passport regulations and obviously want to do without frontiers. Since they are willing to let the Systems fall apart, they are not moved by appeals to Law and Order. They believe in local power, community development, rural reconstruction, decentralist organization, town-meeting decision making. They prefer a simpler standard of living and try to free themselves from the complex network of present economic relations. They balk at IBM cards in the school system. Though their protests generate violence, most tend to nonviolence. But they do not trust the due processes of administrators, either, and are quick to resort to direct action and civil disobedience. All this adds up to the community anarchism of Kropotkin, the resistance anarchism of Malatesta, the agitational anarchism of Bakunin, the anarchist progressive education of France, the guild socialism of William Morris, the personalist politics of Thoreau. Yet in the United

284

States at least, except for Thoreau (required reading in Freshman English), these thinkers are virtually unknown.

The problematic character of youthful anarchism at present comes from the fact that the young are alienated, have no world for them. Among revolutionary political philosophies, anarchism and pacifism alone do not thrive on alienation—unlike, e.g., Leninism or fascism. They require a nature of things to give order, and a trust in other people not to be excessively violent; they cannot rely on imposed discipline to give the movement strength, nor on organized power to avert technological and social chaos. Thus, historically, anarchism has been the revolutionary politics of skilled artisans (watchmakers or printers) and of farmers—workers who do not need a boss; of workmen in dangerous occupations (miners and lumbermen) who learn to trust one another; of aristocrats who know the inside story and can economically afford to be idealistic; of artists and explorers who venture into the unknown and are self-reliant; among professionals, progressive educators and architects have been anarchist.

We would expect many students to be anarchist, because of their lack of ties, their commitment to the Republic of Letters and Science, and their camaraderie; and so it was, among many European students of the classical type—just as others were drawn to elitist fascism. But contemporary students, under the conditions of mass education, are in their schedule very like factory proletariat, and they are not authentically involved in their studies. Yet their camaraderie is strong, and in some respects they are like aristocrats *en masse*. The effects are contradictory. They are daring in direct action, and they resist party discipline; they form communities; but they are mesmerized by the charisma of administration and Power, and since they only know going to school, they are not ready to manage much.

In both Europe and America, the confusion of alienated youth shows up in their self-contradictory amalgam of anarchist and Leninist thoughts and tactics, often within the same group and in the same action. In my biased opinion, their frank and clear insight and their spontaneous gut feeling are anarchist. They do not lose the woods for the trees, they feel where the shoe pinches, they have a quick and naïve indignation and nausea, and they want freedom. What they really hate is not their countries, neither repressive communism nor piggish capitalism, but how Modern Times have gone awry, the ubiquitous abuse of technology and administration, and the hypocritical distortion of great ideals. But their alienation is Leninist, bent on seizing Power. Having little world for themselves, they have no patience for growth; inevitably frustrated, they get quickly angry; they want their turn on top in the Power structure, which is all they know; they think of using their youthful solidarity and fun-and-games ingenuity to make a *putsch*.

As anarchists, they should be internationalist (and regionalist) and create an international youth movement; but in the United States, at least, their alienation betrays them into the stupidity of simply fighting the Cold War in reverse, "smashing capitalism" and "building socialism." Of course, this does not ally them with the Soviet Union, which in obvious ways looks uncomfortably like their own country and worse; about Russia, they tend to say nothing at all. They say they are allied with the underdeveloped socialist countries—China, Cuba, North Korea, North Vietnam—and all anticolonial liberation movements. This is a generous impulse, and it provides them a relevant activity that they can work at, trying to thwart American imperialist intervention. But it is irrelevant to providing models or theory for their own problems in the United States. I am afraid that an advantage of the "Third World" is that it is exotic, as well as starving; one does not need to know the inner workings. Certainly their (verbal) alliance with it has given the Leninist militants some dubious bedfellows —Nkrumah, Nasser, Kim Il Sung, Sukarno, Ché Guevara in Bolivia, etc. In the more actual situation of the Vietnam war protest, where young militants might have had some influence on American public opinion, I have always found it impossible to have a serious discussion with them whether it was to the advantage of South Vietnamese farmers to have a collective Communist regime or just to get rid of the Americans and aim at a system of small landowners and cooperatives, as the radical Buddhists seemed to favor. To the Leninists it was more satisfactory to chant "Ho Ho Ho Chi Minh, the NLF is going to win"; but anarchists might prefer the Buddhist solution, since, as Marxists scornfully point out, "Anarchism is a peasant ideology," and pacifists cannot help but see the usual consequences of war, the same old story for ten thousand years.

Historically, the possibility of an anarchist revolution—decentralist, antipolice, antiparty, antibureaucracy, organized by voluntary association, and putting a premium on grass-roots spontaneity—has always been anathema to Marxist Communists and has been ruthlessly suppressed. Marx expelled the anarchist unions from the International Workingmen's Association. Having used them to consolidate their own minority power, Lenin and Trotsky slaughtered the anarchists in the Ukraine and at Kronshtadt. Stalin murdered them in Catalonia during the Spanish Civil War. Castro has jailed them in Cuba, and Gomulka in Poland. In the Western press, *anarchy* is the term for chaotic riot and aimless defiance of authority; in official Marxist statements, it appears in the stereotype "bourgeois revisionists, infantile leftists, and anarchists." They are bourgeois revisionists because they want civil liberties, a less restricted economy, and a better break for farmers. They are infantile leftists because they want workers' management, less bureaucracy, and less class distinction.

Youth and power

The American young are not really interested in political economy. Their "socialism" is a symbolic slogan, authentic in expressing disgust at the affluent standard of living and indignation at the existence of so many poor people. Historically, anarchists have been noncommittal or various about socialism, in the sense of collective ownership and management. Corporate capitalism, State capitalism, and State communism have all been unacceptable to anarchists, because they trap people and push them around; and there can easily be too much central planning. But pure communism, the pie-in-the-sky future of Marxists, connoting voluntary labor and free appropriation operating by community spirit, is an anarchist ideal. Yet Adam Smith's free enterprise, in its pure form of companies of active owner-managers competing in a free market, without monopoly, is also congenial to anarchists and was called anarchic in Smith's own time. There is an anarchist ring to Jefferson's agrarian notion that a man needs enough control of his subsistence, or tenure in his work, to be free of irresistible political pressure. Small community control—kibbutzim, workers' management in factories, producers' and consumers' cooperatives—is congenial to anarchism. Underlying all anarchist thought is a hankering for peasant independence, craft guild self-management, and the democracy of the village meeting or of medieval Free Cities. It is a question how all this can be achieved in modern technical and urban conditions, but in my opinion we could go a lot farther than we think if we set our sights on decency and freedom rather than on delusory greatness and suburban affluence.

If young Americans really consulted their economic interests, instead of their power propaganda or their generous sentiments, I think they would opt for the so-called Scandinavian or mixed economy, of big and small capitalism, producers' and consumers' cooperatives, independent farming, and State and municipal socialism, each with a strong influence. To this I would add a sector of pure communism, free appropriation adequate for decent poverty for those who do not want to make money or are too busy with nonpaying pursuits to make money (until society gets around to overwhelming them with the coin of the realm). Such a sector of pure communism would cost about 1 percent of our Gross National Product and would make our world both more livable and more productive. The advantage of a mixed system of this kind for the young is that it increases the opportunities for each one to find the milieu and style that suits him, whereas both the present American cash nexus and socialism necessarily process them and channel them. (Cf. *People or Personnel,* Vintage edition, 1968, pp. 114–22.)

Despite their slogans of "Student Power" and "Power to the People," I do not think that the young want "power," but just to be taken into account and to be able to do their thing—just as, despite the bloodthirsty rhetoric, the most militant seem to be pacifist: with meticulous planning, they blow up a huge Selective Service headquarters and meticulously see to it that nobody is injured. (The slogan "Black Power" has more substance, since it means getting absentee landlords and foreign social workers, cops, and schoolteachers off the backs of the black communities; but here again, despite the bloodthirsty rhetoric, there has been little personal violence, except that instigated by the police.)

The young indeed want a revolutionary change, but not by the route of "taking over." So except for a while, on particular occasions, they simply cannot be manipulated to be the shock troops of a Leninist coup. If a large number of young people go along with actions organized by Trotskyites or the Progressive Labor party or with some of the delusions of the various splinters of Students for a Democratic Society, it is because, in their judgment, the resulting disruption does more good than harm. And let me say that, compared with the arrogance, cold violence, and occasional insanity of our established institutions, the arrogance, hotheadedness, and all too human folly of the young are venial sins.

My real bother with the neo-Leninist wing of the New Left is that its abortive manipulation of lively energy and moral fervor for a political revolution that will not be, and ought not to be, confuses the piecemeal social and cultural change that is brightly possible. This puts me off— but of course it is their problem, and they have to do it in their own way. In my opinion, it is inauthentic to do community development in order to "politicize" people, or to use a good do-it-yourself project as a means of "bringing people into the Movement." Good things should be done for their own sake and will then generate their own appropriate momentum. The amazing courage of sticking to one's convictions in the face of the police is insulted when it is manipulated as a means of "radicalizing." The loyalty of youth to one another is extraordinary, but it can turn to disillusionment if they perceive that they are being had. Many of the best of the young went through this in the thirties, and it was a bad scene.

In an important sense, the present bandying about of the word *revolution,* in its usual connotations, as in the present symposium, is counterrevolutionary. It is too political. It seems to assume that there could be such a thing as a Good Society or Body Politic, whereas, in my judgment, the best that is to be hoped for is a tolerable society that allows the important activities of life to proceed—friends, sex, arts and sciences, faith, the growing up of children with bright eyes, and the air and water clean.

I myself have a conservative, maybe timid, disposition; yet I trust that the present regime in America will get a lot more roughing up than it has: from the young who resent being processed; from the blacks who have been left out; from housewives and others who buy real goods with hard money at inflationary prices, hiked by expense accounts and government

Police confront demonstrator in New York City

"The danger is not in the loosening of the machine but in its tightening up by panic repression."

subsidies; from professionals demanding the right to practise their professions rather than be treated as personnel of the front office; not to speak of every live person in jeopardy because of the bombs and CBW. Our system can stand, and profit by, plenty of interruption of business as usual. It is not such a delicate Swiss watch as all that. The danger is not in the loosening of the machine but in its tightening up by panic repression.

It is true that because of massive urbanization and interlocking technologies, advanced countries are vulnerable to catastrophic disruption, and this creates intense anxiety. But there is far more likelihood of breakdown from the respectable ambitions of Eastern Air Lines and Consolidated Edison than from the sabotage of revolutionaries or the moral collapse of hippies.

In a modern massive complex society, it is said, any rapid global "revolutionary" or "utopian" change can be incalculably destructive. I agree. But I wish people would remember that we have continually introduced big rapid changes that have in fact produced incalculable shock. Consider, in the past generation, the TV, mass higher schooling, the complex of cars, roads, and suburbanization, mass air travel, the complex of plantations, government subsidies to big planters, chain grocers, and forced urbanization, not to speak of the meteoric rise of the military industries. In all these there has been a big factor of willful decision; these have not been natural processes or inevitable catastrophes. And we have not yet begun to compound with the problems caused by these utopian changes. Rather, in what seems an amazingly brief time, we have come to a political, cultural, and religious crisis, and talk of "revolution." All because of a few willful fools.

A decade ago it was claimed that there was an end to ideology, for the problems of modern society have to be coped with pragmatically, functionally, piecemeal. This seems to have been a poor prediction, considering the deafening revival of Marxist-Leninist rhetoric and Law and Order rhetoric. Yet it was true, though not in the sense in which it was offered. The ideological rhetoric is pretty irrelevant; but the pragmatic, functional, and piecemeal approach has not, as was expected, consigned our problems to the expertise of administrators and engineers but has thrown them to the dissenters. Relevant new thought has not been administrative and technological, but existentialist, ethical, and tactical. Pragmatism has come to be interpreted to include the character of the agents as part of the problem to be solved; it is psychoanalytic; there is stress on engagement. (Incidentally, it is good Jamesian pragmatism.) Functionalism has come to mean criticizing the program and the function itself, asking who wants to do it and why, and is it humanly worth doing, is it ecologically sound. Piecemeal issues have gotten entangled with the political action of people affected by them. Instead of becoming more administrative as expected, every problem becomes political. The premises of expert planning are called into question. The credentials of the board of trustees are scrutinized. *Professional* and *discipline* have become dirty words. Terms like *commitment, dialogue, confrontation, community, do your thing* are indeed anti-ideological—and sometimes they do not connote much other

290

thought either—but they are surely not what *The End of Ideology* had in mind.

The crisis of authority

Our revolutionary situation is not a political one, and yet there *is* a crisis of authority. This is peculiar.

There is a System and a Power Elite. But Americans do not identify with the ruling oligarchy, which is foreign to our tradition. A major part of it—the military-industrial and the CIA, and FBI—even constitute a "hidden government" that does not thrive on public exposure. The daily scandals in the press seem to indicate that the hidden government is coming apart at the seams. Politicians carefully cajole the people's sensibilities and respect their freedom, so long as these remain private. And we have hit upon the following accommodation: in high matters of State, War, and Empire, the oligarchy presents *faits accomplis;* in more local matters, people resent being pushed around. Until 1969, budgets in the billions were not debated, but small sums are debated. From a small center of decision, it has been possible to spend a trillion dollars for arms, employ scores of millions of people, transform the universities, distort the future of science without public murmur; but where a regional plan might be useful—e.g., for depollution or better distribution of population —it fails because of a maze of jurisdictions and private complaints.

In such a case, what is the real constitution? The social compact becomes acquiescence to the social machine, and citizenship consists in playing appropriate roles as producers, functionaries, and consumers. The machine is productive; the roles, to such as have them, are rewarding. In the galloping economy, the annual tax bite, which ordinarily strikes home to citizens everywhere, has been tolerable. (Only the draft of the young hits home, but this was noticed by few until the young themselves led the protest.) Then, human nature being what it is, the Americans have accepted the void of authentic sovereignty by developing a new kind of allegiance to the rich and high-technological style itself, which provides the norm of correct behavior for workmen, inspires the supermarkets, and is used to recruit soldiers.

A typical and very important class is the new professionals. Being essential to tend the engine and steer it, they are high-salaried and prestigious. An expensive system of schooling has been devised to prepare the young for these roles. At the same time, these professionals are mere personnel. There is no place for the autonomy, ethics, and guild liberty that used to characterize professionals as persons and citizens. *Mutatis mutandis;* the same can be said of the working class. It reminds one of the development of the Roman Empire, when personal rights were ex-

291

Puerto Ricans on the East Side of New York City (left); the old and forgotten (above); ʰe deviant (below)

'large groups of the population are allowed to drop out as socially useless—farmers, racial minorities, the incompetent and deviant, the old, many of the young. . . . They are treated as objects of social engineering and are also lost as citizens.''

tended under the *jus gentium,* but the whole world became one prison.

On the other hand, large groups of the population are allowed to drop out as socially useless—farmers, racial minorities, the incompetent and deviant, the old, many of the young. When these are not altogether neglected, they are treated as objects of social engineering and are also lost as citizens. This too is like Rome.

In an unpolitical situation like this, it is hard for good observers to distinguish between riot and riotous protest, between a juvenile delinquent, a rebel without a cause, an inarticulate guerrilla, a protestant for legitimacy. Student protest may be adolescent identity crisis, alienation, or politics. On a poll, to say "I don't know" might mean one is judicious, a moron, or a cynic about the questions or the options. Conversely, good behavior may be rational assent, apathy, obsessional neurosis, or a dangerous prepsychosis about to murder father, mother, and four siblings.

With this background, we can understand the rash of "civil disobedience," "lawlessness," and the general crisis of authority. What happens politically in a country like the United States when the government steers a disastrous course? There is free speech and assembly and a strong tradition of democracy; it is false that these do not exist, and—with some grim exceptions—they have been pretty well protected. But the traditional structures of remedy have fallen into desuetude or become phony, or are terribly rusty. Critical professionals, bourgeois reformers, organizations of farmers and industrial workers, political machines of the urban poor have been largely co-opted. Then, inevitably, protest appears at a more primitive or inchoate level.

"Civil disobedients" are nostalgic patriots without available political means. The new "lawless" are the oppressed without political means. Instead of having a program or party, protesters have to try, as Mario Savio said, to "throw themselves on the gears and levers to stop the machine." Scholars think up ways to stop traffic. Professionals form groups to nullify a law. Middle-class women go by trainloads to Washington to badger senators and are hauled off to jail for disorderly conduct. The physically oppressed burn down their own neighborhoods.

The promising aspect of it is the revival of populism—sovereignty reverting to the people. One can sense it infallibly during the big rallies, the March on Washington in '63 or the peace rallies in New York and at the Pentagon in '67 and in Washington in '69. Except among a few Leninists, the mood is euphoric, the heady feeling of the sovereign people invincible—for a couple of hours. The draft-card burners are proud. The children of Birmingham attacked by dogs look just like Christians. Physicians who support Dr. Levy feel Hippocratic, and professors who protest classified research feel academic right back to Abelard. On the other hand, the government with the mightiest military power in the history of the world does not hasten to alter its course because of so much sweet determination. The police of the cities have prepared arsenals of antiriot weapons. Organized workmen beat up peace demonstrators. Judge **Hoff**-man does not allow relevant evidence to be heard in court. Tear **gas is** dropped on the Berkeley campus because some people have **planted** trees.

I do not think this conflict is much the result of evil motives, though there are some mighty stupid people around. There are few "pigs" as well as few "subversives" and plenty of patriots on both sides. And I have **not** heard of any institutional changes that would indeed solve the inherent dilemmas of Modern Times. The crisis of legitimacy is a historical **one.** Perhaps "social contract," "sovereignty," and "law" in any American sense are outmoded concepts.

The crisis of belief

Among the young especially, the crisis is a religious one, deeper than politics. The young have ceased to "believe" in something, and the disbelief occurs at progressively earlier years. What is at stake is not the legitimacy of American authority but of any authority. The professions, the disciplines, reasoning about the nature of things—and even if there is a nature of things—these are all distrusted.

Thus, for instance, the dissenting scientists and professors of M.I.T. and Harvard, who want to change the direction of research and alter the priorities of technology, do not seem to me to understand the profound change in popular feeling. (They often seem just to be griping that the budget for Basic Research has been reduced.) Put it this way: Modern societies have been operating as if religion were a minor and moribund part of the scheme of things. But this is unlikely. Men do not do without a system of meanings that everybody puts his hope in even if, or especially if, he doesn't know anything about it—what Freud called a "shared psychosis," meaningful simply because shared, and with the power that resides in dream. In advanced countries it is science and technology themselves that have gradually and finally triumphantly become the system of mass faith, not disputed by various political ideologies and nationalisms that have also been religions. Marxism called itself "scientific socialism," as against moral and utopian socialisms, and this has helped it succeed.

For three hundred years, science and scientific technology had an unblemished and justified reputation as a wonderful adventure, pouring out practical benefits and liberating the spirit from the errors of superstition and traditional faith. During the twentieth century, science and technology have been the only generally credited system of explanation and problem-solving. Yet in our generation they have come to seem to many, and to very many of the best of the young, as essentially inhuman, abstract, regimenting, hand in glove with Power, and even diabolical. Young people say that science is antilife, it is a Calvinist obsession, it has been a weapon

Berkeley, California: People's
Park before and after seizure
by sheriff's deputies, 1969

*"Tear gas is dropped on the
Berkeley campus because
some people have planted
trees."*

of white Europe to subjugate colored races, and manifestly—in view of recent scientific technology—people who think scientifically become insane.

The immediate reasons for this shattering reversal of values are fairly obvious—Hitler's ovens and his other experiments in eugenics, the first atom bombs and their frenzied subsequent developments, the deterioration of the physical environment and the destruction of the biosphere, the catastrophes impending over the cities because of technological failures and psychological stress, the prospect of a brainwashed and drugged 1984. Innovations yield diminishing returns in enhancing life. And instead of rejoicing, there is now widespread conviction that beautiful advances in genetics, surgery, computers, rocketry, or atomic energy will surely only increase human woe.

In such a crisis it is not sufficient to ban the military from the universities, and it will not even be sufficient, as liberal statesmen and many of the big corporations envisage, to beat the swords into plowshares and turn to solving problems of transportation, desalinization, urban renewal, garbage disposal, cleaning up the air and water, and perfecting a contraceptive. If the present difficulty is religious and historical, it will be necessary to alter the entire relationship of science, technology, and human needs, both in fact and in men's minds.

I do not myself think that we will turn away from science. In spite of the fantasies of hippies, we are going to continue to live in a technological world; the question is, is that viable?

The closest analogy I can think of is the Protestant Reformation, a change of moral allegiance: not giving up the faith, but liberation from the Whore of Babylon and a return to the faith purified.

Science, the chief orthodoxy of modern times, has certainly been badly corrupted, but the deepest flaw of the affluent societies that has alienated the young is not, finally, imperialism, economic injustice, or racism, bad as these are, but the nauseating phoniness, triviality, and wastefulness, the cultural and moral scandal that Luther found when he went to Rome in 1510. And precisely science, which should have been the wind of truth to clear the air, has polluted the air, helped to brainwash, and provided weapons for war. I doubt that most young people today have even heard of the ideal of the dedicated researcher, truculent and incorruptible, and not getting any grants—the "German scientist" that Sinclair Lewis described in *Arrowsmith*. Such a figure is no longer believable. I don't mean, of course, that he doesn't exist; there must be thousands of him, just as there were good priests in 1510.

The analogy to the Reformation is even more exact if we consider the school system, from educational toys and Head Start up through the universities. This system is manned by the biggest horde of monks since the time of Henry VIII. It is the biggest industry in the country. It is mostly hocus-pocus. And the abbots of this system are the chiefs of Sci-

An automobile graveyard

"the nauseating phoniness, triviality, and wastefulness"

ence—e.g., the National Science Foundation—who talk about reform but work to expand the school budgets, step up the curriculum, inspire the endless catechism of tests, and increase the requirements for mandarin credentials.

These abuses are international, as the faith is. For instance, there is no essential difference between the military-industrial systems, or the school systems, of the Soviet Union and the United States. There are important differences in way of life and standard of living, but the abuses of technology are very similar—pollution, excessive urbanization, destruction of the biosphere, weaponry, disastrous foreign aid. Our protesters naturally single out our own country, and the United States is the most powerful country, but the corruption we are speaking of is not specifically American nor capitalist; it is a disease of modern times.

But the analogy is to the Reformation; it is not to primitive Christianity or some other primitivism, the abandonment of technological civilization. There is indeed much talk about the doom of Western civilization, young people cast horoscopes, and a few Adamites actually do retire into the hills. But for the great mass of mankind, that's not where it's at. Despite all the movements for National Liberation, there is not the slightest interruption to the universalizing of Western civilization, including most of its delusions, into the so-called Third World.

Needless to say, the prospect of a new Reformation is a terrifying one. Given the intransigence and duplicity of established Power on the one hand, and the fanaticism of the protesters on the other, we may be headed for a Thirty Years' War.

William F. Buckley, Jr.

William F. Buckley, Jr., editor, writer, television personality, is well known for his articulate exposition and defense of the new conservatism. "Firing Line," the name of his weekly television show, also appropriately names the position he has taken as a commentator on public affairs. Editor since 1955 of the weekly *National Review,* a journal of conservative opinion,

he has also expounded his views in a number of books, of which the best known are *Up From Liberalism* (1959) and *The Unmaking of a Mayor* (1966). His most recent books are *Did You Ever See a Dream Walking?* (1970) and *The Governor Listeth* (1970). Buckley was born in New York City November 24, 1925, served in the army from 1944 to 1946, and received his B.A. degree from Yale in 1950.

The Sorry Condition of Counterrevolutionary Doctrine

> *What we opprobriously call stolidity, though not an enlivening quality in common society, is nature's favourite resource for preserving steadiness of conduct and consistency of opinion.*
>
> Walter Bagehot

I t is commonplace to observe that those of a rebellious spirit in our midst do not know what they want. And even that they do not know by what means to achieve the conditions they cannot specify. I consider these data rather less reassuring than otherwise. If the revolutionists were committed to a program, they could be approached, or bombarded, with demonstrations that their program, or an approximation of it, is not producing the goods (in Cuba, say, or in the Soviet Union). But precisely the de-ideologization of their movement, the disembodiment of their *eschaton,* the loose-jointedness of their approach, leaves them in a frame of mind at once romantic and diffuse, and the rest of us without the great weapon available to King Canute when he was able to contrive what would nowadays be called a confrontation between the ineluctable laws of nature and the superstitious indulgences of his subjects.

So, the idea of revolution continues to excite the political and moral imagination. But it is necessary, in making one's complaints against the society we intend to replace, to be vague and disjointed. To be specific, or to be orderly, is once again to risk confutation. General charges are not easily confuted; indeed they are not really confutable (how do you confute, e.g., "Politics is the organization of greed"?). *Misery abounds . . .* is a descriptive phrase which could accurately be used about every society that was ever organized. One can of course do better than that in describing the shortcomings of a particular society. Plato complained about the despoliation of the Attic forests and has therefore something in common with those who complain about the pollution of American rivers. The language is general, and the solutions most vaguely adumbrated, but even so the evangelist of revolution can draw a profile of the problems of a particular society that is custom-made. Misery must abound in a way that seems to be distinctively American. So the revolutionist sets out to describe conditions that our society—and other societies organized around such institutions as our own—suffers from; conditions which necessarily issue from distinctive institutional evils that only revolution will extirpate.

What ails them? Or, rather, us? I read now not from the better-known advocates of revolution, reaching instead for a stretch of prose unencumbered by sophistication of style or thought. The Volkswagen of revolutionary manifestos. Here it is, from a professor of political science in New York City, as published in Volume 1, Number 1f, of a revolutionary journal.

The established system, he complains, "comprises elements of

the archaic Judeo-Christian theocratic traditions,
elements of the dark-age autocracy,

Black janitor cleaning the Roseland ballroom in New York City during the Christmas season

"Misery must abound in a way that seems to be distinctively American."

feudalism,
militarism,
zoological [*sic*] capitalism,
corporate monopolism and plutocracy,
with an admixture of 19th century liberalism
and trade union socialism."

Concerning all this there is no doubt, and these are indeed, as the author of the manifesto complains, "but a few" of the historical, cultural, and philosophical tributaries that flow into America. But hear what they have produced.

They have produced an "anti-social orientation, based on the private profit motivation." This in turn has "produced most (but not all) of the evils of the present system. Among these evils are the following:

transformation of man into an instrument of production,
indiscriminate exploitation of natural and human resources,
promotion of vulgarity,
excessive consumption coexisting with poverty,
scarcity of housing,
pollution of air, water, and food,
unemployment,
urban decay,
reduction of woman to a sex-symbol,
crime (the highest in the world),
racial discrimination,
transformation of universities into an instrument of the military-
·industrial complex,
a total neglect of the qualitative aspects of man's social life."

Now one can either pause to argue point by point these allegations, which is time-consuming, or simply dismiss the professor as an etiological simpleton. But it is not the purpose of this essay to argue with the revolutionist the justice of his indictments or the merit of his "solutions." It is all very well to contend, as Professor Toynbee persuasively does, that revolutions historically have not brought about the ends desired, but something very like their opposite, but the success of such demonstrations presupposes a clinical attitude on the part of the observer, and such is not the temper of those in America who are talking about revolution. The point to stress is that the idea of revolution, and its importance in contemporary political and social affairs, is bound to grow, in the existing climate, precisely because every modern aggravation—as we have just seen—is subsumed into the motivation for revolution, and the ideologists of revolution are careful, as in the passage above, to tread a line enough this side of generality to describe an American situation, and far enough short of particularity to permit them constantly to nourish the revolutionary imagination, to stimulate the confidence that liberation lies just over there on the other side of the barricades, even as Nat Turner dreamed that if only he could make it to the Dismal Swamp, the world would begin anew.

Dissatisfaction

De Tocqueville made the point, echoed by Mr. Toynbee, that the draining of the causes of social dissatisfaction does not necessarily lead pro tanto to the lessening of social dissatisfaction, quite the contrary. As an outcast element of a society is gradually incorporated, its appetite more often rises sharply, demanding now what the society cannot give it (e.g., the disappearance of racial discrimination), even as a hungry man is more dangerous than a starving man. The figures, for instance, indicate that, using constant dollars, the poverty rate in America has come down from about 50 percent at the turn of the century to about 10 percent today in a fairly steady line, and there are formal legislative motions even now lying before Congress, the enactment of which would prove that we are not burdened with an asymptotic line, that we mean precisely to *eliminate* poverty, clinically described. Even so poverty and hunger fuel more revolutionary rhetoric now than they did at the turn of the century, and notwithstanding that during this interval the world experimented so disastrously with socialism.

It is perhaps this subconscious awareness of the thin case for material grievances against our society that causes so much of the revolutionary stress on the intangible dissatisfactions ("the indiscriminate exploitation of human resources"). But once again, that matters less than the undeniable meaning of the larger experience, which is that idealistic impatience is lurching about; that so long as we know what little we do know about life on earth, namely, that it is and always will be flawed, we know that the worst species of idealism is political idealism—ideology—because its designs are on all of us. The modern revolutionists do not want merely to reenact Brook Farm (a failure, by the way); they want, as the poster puts it, *you.*

In the beginning—for our revolutionists—was the American Revolution. It is as important to their rhetoric as Prohibition is to the young pot-smoker. The revolutionists insist that this country was baptized in revolution, and indeed that revolution is genetically a part of the American way. Some go so far as to say that we are in a state of permanent revolution, an unhappy formulation because it takes from the word *revolution* what is distinctive to it, the eructation of the old, in one violent upheaval.

Although historians have insisted ever since Edmund Burke that the American Revolution was not a revolution but an act of secession, it is instructive to recall that whichever of the two it was, the British were by contemporary standards entitled to resist it. *"When . . . it becomes necessary for one people to dissolve the political bands which have connected them with another,"*[1] certainly suggests *dissociation* as distinguished from *revolution*. World opinion has pretty well come around to believing that anticolonial uprisings are justified. The inertia of anticolonist rhetoric carries forward contemporary revolutionists who persuade themselves that the same considerations that legitimized the secession of the American colonies before the Supreme Judge of the world now authorize the revolution for which they currently agitate. Again, they fail to deal with the complementary point.

Indeed, I do not find anywhere in the literature of the period the suggestion that it was other than the accepted right of the British throne to resist the American secessionists. Burke, whose sympathies were plainly with America, never suggested that the king was violating any concept of sovereignty in sending an army to America to say no to the army of George Washington, and if Washington had been caught and hanged, Burke would perhaps have deplored British severity, but there was no higher law around to appeal to than was available to Vercingetorix to use on Julius Caesar.

What, then, about the abstract, as distinguished from the historical, "rights" of the American secessionists? The wording of the Declaration clearly shows the mark of the social-contract theorists, e.g., *"governments are instituted among men,"* in order *"to secure"* certain *"rights."* These governments derive *"their just powers from the consent of the governed."*[2] Here is an interesting distinction, obviously done in passing, between "just" and "unjust" powers, and a tacit acknowledgment that even governments that are licensed by the governed typically exercise both powers that are just and powers that are unjust. The contemporary revolutionist would presumably argue that those unjust powers the government exercises are not in fact intelligently sanctioned by the majority but rather are institutional mutations. The initial mistake, you see, was to permit a free economy. What happens then is history—"Politics in this country," writes our professor of revolution, "[became] long ago a superstructure of economics; that is, an instrument of organized business" (one wishes for a permanent revolution against Marxist clichés).

Mr. Jefferson's Declaration of Independence goes on to acknowledge the *"right of the people"* to *"alter or abolish"* their government, and *"to institute a new government, laying its foundation on such principles, and organizing its powers in such form, as to them shall seem most likely to effect their safety and happiness."*[3] That is surely a charter for democra-

---

[1] *GBWW*, Vol. 43, p. 1a.
[2] Ibid.
[3] Ibid.

"a hungry man is more dangerous than a starving man"

tism, and indeed a dozen years later the Constitution went on to guarantee to the several states a republican form of government, a guarantee which (as we shall see) puts into focus Jefferson's most frequently quoted declamation in favor of toleration.

The Declaration goes on to enumerate the grievances of the colonies. It is a stirring catalog, but it finally reduces to the matter of the source of power, i.e., who should decide? *"He [King George] has refused his assent to laws the most wholesome and necessary for the public good."*[4] Who is to decide what are the laws most wholesome and necessary for the public good? Why, the people—the people who are affected. But Mr. Jefferson, perhaps from a sense of tact—perhaps even from a sense of cunning—introduces into the peroration of the document a subtle distinction. *"We, therefore, the representatives of the United States of America, in general Congress assembled, appealing to the Supreme Judge of the world for the rectitude of our intentions, do, in the name, and by the authority of the good people of these colonies, solemnly publish and declare. . . ."*[5] The *good* people of these colonies? A ritual obeisance? Or a punctilious recognition that there are plenty of colonials around who oppose secession? Bad people.

Mr. Jefferson always acknowledged the existence of bad people, but his rationalist's faith in the inherent power of good ideas to defeat bad ideas in the marketplace (a faith he preached more often than he practised it) was triumphantly embodied in his ringing declaration, "those who wish to dissolve the union or to change its republican form should stand undisturbed as monuments of the safety with which error of opinion may be tolerated where reason is left free to combat it." It isn't of course suggested in this passage what is the indicated course of action if reason should fail in the performance of its duty, but we know from Jefferson's own autocratic habits that he often gave reason a helping hand; and we know from the Declaration of Independence that he dubbed some truths as self-evident; and, derivatively, that he judged those people who acknowledged these truths as good, and those who did not as something other. It was also Jefferson, presumably in a crosser frame of mind, who said, "let no more be heard of confidence in man, but bind him down from mischief by the chains of the Constitution." From all of which one infers that in Jefferson's America, (a) there is a right and a wrong position; (b) the probability is that the people will opt for the right position, prodded by reason to do so; but (c) it sometimes becomes necessary to resist the bad people, whether they are numerous, or whether they are, simply, the King

---

4 Ibid., p. 1b.
5 Ibid., p. 3a.

of England.

Concerning the problem of indigenous threats to the Republic, Alexander Hamilton (along with Madison and Jay) wrote most directly. This plea for a constitution was an appeal not merely against the anarchy that every schoolboy knows he abhorred but also against revolution: against anyone else's succeeding in such a venture as the Founding Fathers had most recently succeeded in. "It is impossible to read the history of the petty republics of Greece and Italy without feeling sensations of horror and disgust at the distractions with which they were continually agitated, and at the rapid succession of revolutions by which they were kept in a state of perpetual vibration between the extremes of tyranny and anarchy." [6] He went on to argue that a historical advance in the science of government now permitted on the one hand a granting of powers sufficient to avoid anarchy, but insufficient to promote tyranny.

But he insisted that the government must have the power necessary to make its laws obeyed—such power, it might be argued, as the contemporary revolutionists are quick to criticize, pleading the absolutism of the Bill of Rights. "The United States, as now composed [i.e., under the Articles of Confederation], have no powers to exact obedience, or punish disobedience to their resolutions, either by pecuniary mulcts, by a suspension or divestiture of privileges, or by any other constitutional mode." Unless that situation changed, he warned, the United States would "afford the extraordinary spectacle of a government destitute even of the shadow of constitutional power to enforce the execution of its own laws." In pleading for a guarantee by the federal government of republican government in the individual states, he argued that "without [such] a guaranty the assistance to be derived from the Union in repelling those domestic dangers which may sometimes threaten the existence of the State constitutions" might just as well be renounced. "Usurpation may rear its crest in each State, and trample upon the liberties of the people, while the national government could legally do nothing more than behold its encroachments with indignation and regret." [7]

But the guarantees Hamilton had in mind were (he assured the public) intended only to protect the states from revolutionary reform. "The guaranty could only operate against changes to be effected by violence. Towards the preventions of calamities of this kind, too many checks cannot be provided. The peace of society and the stability of government depend absolutely on the efficacy of the precautions adopted. . . ." At this point Hamilton makes the ritual obeisance to the notion that the majority of the people will always be on the right side of fundamental social controversies; on the side of stability. And he proceeds contentedly with the great syllogism that modern revolutionists are now precisely challenging, namely, that if the government is of the majority, there is no reason to suppose that there is latent support for revolutionary disruption. "Where the whole power of the government is in the hands of the people, there

Walls at Columbia University bear the graffiti of young militants

"one wishes for a permanent revolution against Marxist clichés"

is the less pretence for the use of violent remedies in partial or occasional distempers of the State. The natural cure for an ill-administration, in a popular or representative constitution, is a change of men."[8]

Comes now the question of how much power ought a government to have in order to protect the republic against insurrection. A very important question, which is being fought out today, in one of its modalities, in the courts, where the surrealistic language of the American Civil Liberties Union lounges about feeling utterly at home. It is being tested, for instance, whether the government may impede those who allegedly met in Chicago to conspire against the freedom of others to transact their business at the Democratic Convention. "The idea of restraining the legislative authority, in the means of providing for the national defence, is one of those refinements which owe their origin to a zeal for liberty more ardent than enlightened." He argued that, after all, "confidence must be placed somewhere"; and that "it is better to hazard the abuse of that

---

[6] *The Federalist,* No. 9; *GBWW,* Vol. 43, p. 47a.
[7] *The Federalist,* No. 21; Ibid., pp. 78c–79a.
[8] Ibid., p. 79b.

confidence than to embarrass the government and endanger the public safety by impolitic restrictions on the legislative authority."[9]

Repression? Exactly. "The hope of impunity is a strong incitement to sedition; the dread of punishment, a proportionably strong discouragement to it."[10] Over and over again Hamilton leans on the operative assumption that the general majority are after all bound to be pleased by laws which are after all of their own devising. ". . . if the general government should be found in practice conducive to the prosperity and felicity of the people, it were irrational to believe that they would be disinclined to its support." But to assume that the government will not from time to time need to use force is nevertheless naïve. ". . . the idea of governing at all times by the simple force of law (which we have been told is the only admissible principle of republican government) has no place but in the reveries of those political doctors whose sagacity disdains the admonitions of experimental instruction."[11]

Only the one concession would he make—appropriately, in the light of the fresh experience of the Republic: "If the representatives of the people betray their constituents, there is then no resource left but in the exertion of that original right of self-defence which is paramount to all positive forms of government, . . ."[12]

The modern tocsin

The political problem in America derives from the absolutization of the Bill of Rights, such that the old correlations no longer hold. It is clear (from the acceptance of the Constitution) that the founders intended the government to have sufficient power to repress revolution, and indeed these powers were grandiosely invoked in the Civil War, against even such cogent theoretical obstructionism as Calhoun's. Hamilton spoke about the developing science of government, indispensable to the avoidance of the great oscillations between tyranny and anarchy which were the history of the Greek states. It is obvious that he did not foresee the development of the arts of revolution in a free society—which have advanced at least as much as the science of free government had done when Hamilton absorbed the findings of Locke and Montesquieu. The great rationalist optimism that carried John Stuart Mill to reveries of universal franchise and ordered liberty are crisply shattered by a modern world composed of approximately 150 states, less than two dozen of which permit political liberty.

The second-string argument that democratic experience is all that is required in order for a people to learn how to exercise liberty is disconcerted by the two dominant continents of the Southern Hemisphere. Latin America had its secessionist revolutions a century and a half ago.

Africa had its during the last decade. Approximately the same percentage of the population of each continent now has parliamentary government. About 15 percent. The contemporary revolutionist has a leverage on events that issues in part from what Prof. Daniel Boorstin calls a "rise in flow technology." "It used to be that if you wanted to hurt somebody you had to hit him. But nowadays when everything is in motion, all you have to do is stop. If you are on a superhighway, all you have to do is drive slower. The result is that other people then seem to do the damage." The old distinctions between violent and nonviolent disobedience lose their significance, is Mr. Boorstin's special point.

The tradition of toleration and magnanimity, which is so strong in the American temperament, elides now toward ambiguity and self-doubt—a self-doubt that encourages revolutionists to believe that the countdown has already begun. The general acceptance of civil disobedience as an honorable alternative for an individual in pursuit of his own objectives is the principal symbol of it. It is I think true that the intellectual community has yet to make a resonant commitment to some of the principles that Hamilton considered as axiomatic, in the absence of which America cannot handle its revolutionists with any sense of self-assurance. What it comes down to, I think, is that many opinion makers prefer a highly elastic line between the law and the defiers of the law; believing, as they really do, that salients struck across that line by the defiers of it are events that require urgent democratic attention: believing as they do that if young demonstrators in Chicago are prepared to throw themselves into police lines, they are saying things to us that we ought to hear, even as, finally, Constantine heard the marginal cry of the marginal Christian who stood up against the lions. (It is their epistemology.) I suspect that that is why if Thomas A. Edison were to appear on the scene tomorrow with an antiriot weapon that would totally immobilize unlawful demonstrators without causing them an instant's pain or humiliation, Mr. Edison and his machine would be promptly run out of town, proscribed by the forces of enlightened opinion, to end in the company of that long list of anathematized riot-control weapons that have been serially denounced, from fire hoses to cattle prods to tear gas to Mace.

"What is needed now is the multiplication of the nuclei capable of spontaneous and coordinated resistance to the existing system," writes our professor. "Such a system of decentralized nuclei of confrontation is preferable to (and under existing conditions promises to be more effective than) a single centralized organization which would be open to the establishment's infiltration." There is much work to do, he concedes,

---

9 *The Federalist,* No. 26; Ibid., p. 92a–b.
10 *The Federalist,* No. 27; Ibid., p. 95b–c.
11 *The Federalist,* No. 28; Ibid., p. 96d, c.
12 Ibid., p. 97c.

before a revolutionary class is finally equipped. "Ideally, one would expect a modern revolutionary to be versed intellectually, ideologically and practically. But since this ideal cannot be attained immediately, especially in the initial stage, each nucleus should be left to what it is best equipped for, while broadening its knowledge in the deficient areas. Thus, some . . . can concentrate primarily on technical activities, for the purpose of disrupting crucial business operations; some on the development of social consciousness among the uncommitted portion of the civilian and uninformed population, by revealing the anti-social nature of the present system and drawing it away from the establishment as its potential supporters. . . ." He recommends a "revolutionary journal—a journal that would deal with the practical, ideological, and intellectual aspects of the social revolution."

Thus the tones of the modern tocsin, a little etiolated when read in contrast with, say, the verses of "La Marseillaise," or the galvanizing imperatives of the *Communist Manifesto*. But the earnestness is there, and the revolutionists have a great weapon: the de-ideologization of their revolution *pari passu* with the ideologization of our Bill of Rights. The latter threatens the Republic with that powerlessness which is so attractive to those who, perhaps rightly, understand it to issue from possibly a suspended commitment to republican practices; certainly, from a lesion of self-confidence.

The Idea of Revolution
In Great Books of the
Western World

The fact that a whole chapter in the *Syntopicon* is devoted to the idea of revolution is an indication of its importance. In the tradition represented by *Great Books of the Western World,* the discussion of the idea is long, deep, and perennially "relevant." Evidence of its range is found in the first topic of the topical analysis of the idea in Chapter 80 of the *Syntopicon:* "The nature of revolution: The issue concerning violent and peaceful means for accomplishing social, political, or economic change." On this topic the first reference is to a famous passage in Thucydides' *History of the Peloponnesian War;** the last one is to two passages in the closing pages of Freud's last work, *New Introductory Lectures on Psycho-Analysis.†*

After having narrated in detail the revolution in Corcyra, Thucydides writes: "So bloody was the march of the revolution, and the impression which it made was the greater as it was one of the first to occur. Later on, . . . the whole Hellenic world was convulsed; struggles being everywhere made by the popular chiefs to bring in the Athenians, and by the oligarchs to introduce the Lacedaemonians." Thucydides then proceeds to a justly famous, passionate, generalized analysis of the ravages of this epidemic of revolutions in small cities, precipitated by the war of the two big powers.

Freud, in the first of the passages cited, makes an anticipatory comment, as it were, upon current efforts, such as those of Marcuse and Fromm, to apply the insights of psychoanalysis to revolution. "Psychoanalytic education will be assuming an unwarranted responsibility if it sets out to make its pupils into revolutionaries," he writes. "I should go so far as to say that revolutionary children are not desirable from any point of view." In the second passage, in the course of a review of current doctrines, Freud writes: "Theoretical Marxism, as put into effect in Russian Bolshevism, has acquired the energy, the comprehensiveness, and the

---

* *GBWW,* Vol. 6, pp. 436c–438b.
† *GBWW,* Vol. 54, pp. 870d–871a, 883d–884c.

exclusiveness of a *Weltanschauung;* but at the same time it has acquired an almost uncanny resemblance to what it was opposing . . ." with its establishment of "a ban upon thought." Freud also comments skeptically on the millennial dimension of communism that appears so unqualifiedly in Lenin's *State and Revolution:* "And although practical Marxism has remorselessly swept away all idealistic systems and illusions, it has nevertheless developed illusions itself. . . . It hopes, in the course of a few generations, so to alter men that they will be able to live together in the new order of society almost without friction, and that they will do their work voluntarily. . . . But such an alteration in human nature is very improbable."

No one definitive map of the discussion of revolution has yet been made. It is possible, however, to locate some of the turning points in the long course of the discussion from antiquity to the present.

Plato and Aristotle, the founding fathers of political analysis, both discussed revolution at length. They could hardly not have done so, since, as the Thucydides text indicates, the Greek city-states had abundant experience of revolution. Plato, in Book VIII of the *Republic,* sets forth a pathology of states in which different forms of government appear as successive departures from his ideal state. His analysis, needless to say, is full of interesting points, but it was perhaps too much a product of imaginative reason—a sort of exercise in the philosophy of history—to cast much light on the idea of revolution. Aristotle's treatment of the idea, which was far more empirically grounded, became more influential in the whole tradition.

Aristotle announces the subject of Books V-VI of his *Politics* in this way: "Next in order follow the causes of revolution in states, how many, and of what nature they are; what modes of destruction apply to particular states, and out of what, and into what they mostly change; also what are the modes of preservation in states generally, or in a particular state, and by what means each state may be best preserved." * The position that he takes in this announcement seems to be that of a latter-day "value-free" political scientist. In the ensuing discussion he seems to maintain this stance; indeed, when he comes to giving tyrants advice on how to keep their power, he seems to be anticipating Machiavelli.

To be sure, Aristotle considers the cause of revolution to consist in quarrels about *justice,* precipitated by desires and discontents about existing equalities and inequalities in gain and in honors. But he makes his diagnosis again in a wholly nonnormative manner: "The universal and chief cause of this revolutionary feeling . . . [is] the desire of equality, when men think that they are equal to others who have more than themselves; or, again, the desire of inequality and superiority, when conceiving themselves to be superior they think that they have not more but the same or less than their inferiors; pretensions which may and may not be just." †

314

Nowhere in Books V and VI does Aristotle explicate his own views on what claims about equality justice would validate; no evaluative phrases enter his numerous accounts of particular revolutions.

It is instructive to note some other things that are absent from Aristotle's treatise on revolution. There is no distinction between society and the state; no discussion of the nature of law or of the nature, source, and scope of authority in government; no mention of political, civil, or personal liberty as involved in the issue of revolution. Again, because there is no theory of rights at all in Aristotle, there can be no mention of a "right to revolution."

When such things are noted, Aristotle may sound antiquated despite the acuity of his analysis of political phenomena. Things happened in the Great Conversation after Aristotle that came to be judged deeply relevant to an adequate discussion of the idea of revolution.

When we think of the last three centuries as preeminently the age of revolutions, we do not do so because ancient Greece or Renaissance Italy lacked revolutions or theorists of revolution. Nor is it a matter of change in scale. It is because long-evolving changes in the discussion of revolution have altered the character of modern revolutions.

Those changes are such that merely descriptive analyses of revolutions as quasi-natural phenomena can no longer reach the important questions. Revolution becomes something intrinsically and objectively normative or evaluative, not merely descriptive. The important questions have to be responsive to that. A theoretical framework arising from political philosophy, jurisprudence, and constitutional law made it possible, even necessary, to discuss revolution, whether in general or in particular historical situations, as something good or bad. Intelligibility was asserted for the claim of a "right to revolution" and for the analysis of the conditions for its rightful exercise.

Aristotle had made central to his analysis contentions about various sorts of equalities and inequalities among men. Cicero, the Stoics, and Christian writers affirmed an underlying fundamental equality of all men, in specific nature and in intrinsic dignity. That affirmation rendered firmly normative all further questions about the several sorts of equality and inequality in all dimensions of human life. It raised questions about the justice of equality in such intangible things as rights and liberties. Although the importance of affirming a fundamental equality of all men is now questioned by some, belief in it lasted at least long enough to become a premise of the American and French revolutionary manifestos.

Not unrelated was another change, a change in jurisprudence—in ideas about the nature of law and the source of law's binding power. Again,

---

* *GBWW*, Vol. 9, p. 502a.
† *GBWW*, Vol. 9, p. 503c.

Cicero, the Stoics, and Christian theologians affirmed the existence of natural law, discoverable by reason reflecting on what in general the very nature of man required in human association if men were to pursue personally and cooperatively the happiness they, by nature, desired. By this doctrine of natural law, the conception of positive law was transformed. Positive law could no longer be rightly understood as nothing but the expression of the will of *de facto* rulers. As Aquinas put it, law was essentially a thing of reason, not of will. Natural law was not only prior to, but the measure of, enacted positive law. To be truly a law, a law had to be in conformity with, a specification in the line of, natural law. Aquinas expressed no hesitation in calling a law lacking such conformity, and therefore a bad law, not a law at all and without binding power in conscience.

Such a doctrine clearly has implications for a theory of revolution. Although it underwent profound modification in social contract theory, yielding natural rights inviolable by government, this natural law doctrine continued long enough to provide substance for the modern English, American, and French revolutionary movements.

A closely related, even parallel, development of doctrine treated of the nature, source, and scope of the *authority* of government. Whatever the ambiguities and turmoils of its actual history, the jurisprudence of the Roman Republic was a major development in the discussion. The SPQR (*senatus populusque Romanus*) stood for something. Certainly it did so in the order of reason. As interpreted, it signified that the people, juridically a single entity, were the source of all authority, and therefore of all law; that all other authority for making law was delegated authority—its scope and the forms for its exercise being rightly subject to determination by the people. In the order of reason, this doctrine about the popular source of all authority retained such vigor that the jurisprudence of the succeeding Roman Empire resorted to the famous ignoble lie: that "what pleases the prince" is to be construed as having "the force of a law," because, as the lie went, the *populus* had somehow, somewhere, permanently transferred to the emperor its whole authority and power (*imperium et potestas*).

The juridical thought of the Middle Ages did not accept the ignoble lie. It reinforced and developed the views of the Roman Republic about the juridical role of "the people." A deservedly famous maxim from medieval jurisprudence read: "Whatever touches the life of the people should be approved by the people."

Tracing long-term lines of intellectual influence is a difficult intellectual operation. However, historians of constitutional jurisprudence have no doubts about finding the Roman and medieval ideas that flowed toward Jefferson's revolutionary idiom about governments being "instituted among men, deriving their just powers from the consent of the governed."

316

All the developments mentioned tended to coalesce in the tradition now called *constitutionalism*. This tradition had slow and precarious victories in actual history over absolutisms of various kinds. Its elaboration in the order of reason was slow, and sometimes tortuous. However, a leading historian of constitutionalism, Charles H. McIlwain, can formulate briefly its "two fundamental correlative elements" as, first, legal (constitutionally placed) limitations on the power of government, and second, political responsibility of government to the governed. This tradition, for the most part, originated with the Roman Republic. It was developed and reinforced, at least in the order of thought, in the Middle Ages, in which the kings swore to uphold the laws of the land; and Aquinas could say with ease that it is the tyrant who is seditious and that bad rulers may be resisted as one may resist robbers.* The firmest historical embodiment arose in the Middle Ages and continued as the *common law*. The second element of constitutionalism was the juridical ground of the modern English, American, and French revolutions.

Just by considering the implications of its "two fundamental correlative elements," it is possible to see how constitutionalism can frame a discussion of revolution and of the right to revolution. The constitution, written or unwritten, or the putative social contract, has declared which powers are granted to government and which are not. Any sustained action outside the powers granted is unconscionable usurpation, an intolerable violation of contract.

According to the second element of constitutionalism, government is to be held politically accountable to the governed for the quality of its exercise of the powers granted. This would seem to have implications that can reach to revolutionary queries. Any practices of government that tend to deprive the people of political control of government would be violations of fundamental intent. If a long train of abuses results from a consolidation of such practices, the governmental forms and procedures that have allowed such violation may be called into question. If governments over a long period support or permit economic and social institutions that gravely weaken the people's supreme political power, the reality of the people's sovereignty may be called into question. If, in an age of rapid historical change, governments acting constitutionally prove unable to secure the rights and purposes for which government was instituted, it is the right of the people to alter the constitution and to question the adequacy of existing constitutional means for such redesign.

The suggestion here has been that the long discussion of revolution gradually developed from tenets such as these about human equality, about the nature of law, about liberties and rights, about the source and scope of governmental authority, about the political supremacy of the people. If a full theory of revolution were to be composed from such

---

* *GBWW,* Vol. 20, p. 584d.

tenets (and, of course, Locke's *Second Essay on Civil Government** is the nearest to that), it would pivot on the *right* to revolution and the kinds of socioeconomic-political pathology that would make it proper, even obligatory, to exercise that right. It would make sense to call this traditional theory the "conservative theory of revolution," since it would be a *normative* theory, in no way precluding the conservation of whatever was rationally judged worth conserving, in no way requiring judgments that revolution was always necessary, always prudent, or always progressive.

The new theory of revolution is, of course, the Marxist-Leninist theory, its main contours indicated in the *Communist Manifesto*† and in Lenin's *State and Revolution,* published here.‡ While the traditional theory is a *normative* theory, the Marxist-Leninist one is presented as a *scientific* theory, explaining why the revolutions that have occurred, and will occur, had to and will have to occur. It may be called a "radical theory of revolution," since it holds revolution to be rooted in the historical process as the necessary means by which the contradictions of class conflicts within economic systems are resolved. It is also, of course, a progressive theory. As the theory has it, each revolution has advanced mankind; and the communist revolution to end all revolutions will eradicate class conflict and the state and eventually produce a transformation of human nature and true human freedom.

One thing the traditional and the Marxist theories have in common—they are both theories. It is permissible to wonder whether much of the traditional theory, battered by various kinds of positivist philosophy, still stands, commending itself to reason. It may be that in the age of nation-states, the traditional theory has shrunk to one tenet—the absolute sovereignty of a people's *will*. Such a voluntaristic version of the people's supremacy would be a grave departure from the traditional theory, which, while acknowledging that no practical limits can be put on a people's power, never asserted that there were no rational limits—that anything a people wills to do is *ipso facto* all right to do.

Indeed, the doctrine of the absolute sovereignty of the people does not so much ground a *theory* of revolution as issue an open and standing invitation to a sort of permanent revolution, with all having equal right at any time to agitate for an alteration of the people's will or to record a change in that will by suitably fraudulent plebiscites. If, after all, revolution is not something subject to either normative or scientific theory but is merely an especially violent struggle for power, then theories are really ideologies, and we may witness a return to a convulsive situation like that described by Thucydides and a return to the merely descriptive analyses like those of Aristotle.

---

* *GBWW,* Vol. 35, pp. 23–81.
† *GBWW,* Vol. 50, pp. 413–434.
‡ *GIT 1970,* pp. 386–453.

The Hero and
the Heroic Ideal

A Symposium

Introduction

E ach year for a number of years the editors of *The Great Ideas Today* have presented a symposium in which eminent persons undertake to discuss an idea that is of current interest. Each time this has been done, four or five such persons have been invited to contribute to the discussion. Usually they have been persons of very different backgrounds, with extremely divergent views of the subject at hand, whose comments have reflected these disparities, sometimes to good effect and sometimes not. The editors have therefore thought it proper to bring a measure of unity to the proceedings by adding a sort of coda or appendix in which they recall the ways in which the idea being considered is treated in the great books, and what the tradition with respect to it is.

This year the editors have reversed their usual procedure. In arranging a symposium on the hero and the heroic ideal, they have not begun by inviting comments on the subject, nor have they gone on to add the customary discussion of relevant material from the great books at the end. Instead, they have prepared a summary of this material at the outset, and have submitted it to the contributors for their use, as background, in preparing their comments. For this reason, the summary—or editorial essay, as perhaps it should be called—has been made considerably longer than usual. Based upon a draft submitted by our consulting editor, Otto Bird, the essay undertakes to review the great books tradition concerning the hero and the heroic ideal in an effort to suggest just what tradition it is that we are talking about when we use those terms, which we hope other readers will understand in the same way. The assumption in preparing such a review was that the contributors, having it before them, would not feel obliged to cover the same ground themselves (except where they thought that our report was inadequate or mistaken), and would thus be free to concentrate upon contemporary aspects of the subject. On that same assumption, it was felt that their comments could be shorter than the comments have been in previous years, with the result that it has been possible to include a somewhat greater number of contributors than we have had in the past: there are six this year, rather than four or five.

That there was and is some reason to consider the idea of heroism and the figure of the hero as they may appear in, or may be absent from, the contemporary world will seem obvious to some readers of *The Great Ideas Today*, perhaps not obvious at all to others. Among the latter are likely to be those who will not have thought that there is anything timely to say about human characteristics that they regard as permanent. And in deference to these readers, it may be acknowledged that there is a conventional regard for heroes and heroism nowadays—at least as they are discussed by the media or in popular literature, or in everyone's casual conversation—which is probably as strong as it ever was, and which implies that we are dealing with a fixed and familiar aspect of human affairs.

Nevertheless, it is from a sense of the opposite—a sense that the hero and the heroic ideal are no longer evident or even conceivable in the world as we know it, or are no longer evident or conceivable as they used to be—that the editors have proposed the subject for consideration. How such a sense could have developed may be easy enough to understand for anyone who regards the low estate of various roles—the military, for one—that the hero has traditionally seemed able to fill, either within society or outside it. Further recognition may come after reading the editorial summary with which the symposium begins. This summary is not organized in historical terms and does not attempt more than to suggest the current status of the idea of heroism—that is left to the contributors—but it records what may be thought of as a decline, or at any rate a profound change (perhaps several profound changes), in the force of the idea and in the extent of its acceptance since ancient times. Of course that is itself a well-worked theme. One has only to compare the *Odyssey* with James Joyce's *Ulysses* to see how great the difference is, and how well at least one modern writer has understood it. Still a further grasp of the matter may be derived from other contemporary witnesses who have remarked the fact that heroism does not fare—does not, indeed, regard itself—in the modern world as it once did. Thus Mr. Norman Mailer observed recently that the astronauts, who performed prodigies of skill and strength and even intelligence in getting to the moon, were all the same disappointing as heroes—did not seem to wish to be heroes, and if they had wished, did not seem to know how. The same thing was noted many years ago with respect to Charles A. Lindbergh, who was hopelessly incompetent in the heroic role that a frenzied public, inspired by his solitary flight across the Atlantic, attempted to force upon him. And examples of this sort could be multiplied indefinitely.

With such considerations in mind, the editors of *The Great Ideas Today* have solicited comments from a variety of contributors, asking them to regard the occasion as one on which they should "address themselves to the question whether the idea of the hero is any longer viable in the modern world, and if they think it is viable . . . to suggest what form it can credibly take." It seemed wise to allow each contributor to put this question to himself in particular terms if he liked. If he felt especially qualified to consider whether the hero can exist in the army of today, given the complex, remote, highly technical character of its mission, he was free to do that. If he were competent to suggest whether heroes can be imagined among the leaders of contemporary nation states, except as creatures of propaganda, he could do that instead. If he wished to confine himself to deciding whether there can be heroes in commercialized sports, he could also do that. Those who could sensibly discuss the lack of heroes in contemporary fiction, poetry, and drama, were not required to speak of other human enterprises. On the other hand, those who wished to consider whether heroism is possible at all in our psychoanalytical age, given what we know or think we know about subconscious motivations, were free to discuss human endeavors generally.

While not all of those who responded to our invitation accepted the assignment on quite these terms, and while, even if they had, they could not have dealt with every aspect of the subject, the symposium covers a considerable range. On the one hand is the defense of heroism offered by S. L. A. Marshall, brigadier general, USA (retired), who speaks as a dedicated soldier. At perhaps the opposite extreme is the sharp criticism of the heroic ideal provided by Ron Dorfman, editor of the *Chicago Journalism Review*, who writes as a journalist who must contend with the pretenses and deceptions of men in public life. Alternatively, we have the philosophical and even theological implications of the heroic life considered by Josef Pieper, the author of *Leisure, the Basis of Culture,* and other works; and, as distinct from that, we have a discussion of the ways in which heroes are currently portrayed in films by Joy Gould Boyum, the film critic of the *Wall Street Journal,* who specializes in the study of this form of popular art. And whereas Professor Sidney Hook undertakes to suggest the heroic possibilities of contemporary power figures on the world stage, Chaim Potok, the novelist, reflects upon the common stuff out of which all men, and thus even heroes, are made.

In the opinion of the editors, these several discussions of heroism and the heroic ideal are better differentiated than has been the case with symposiums in the past, and yet there is at the same time, if not quite a unity, at least a measure of common understanding that seems to run through them all—the result, as we like to think, of the fact that each contributor had our editorial summary before him to start with. However this may be, we hope that readers of this year's *Great Ideas Today,* who themselves should begin by reading the summary before going on to what the contributors have to say, will find their comments more than usually interesting, and that the symposium as a whole will seem both fresh and substantial in its consideration of the subject.

The Hero and the Heroic Ideal in Great Books of the Western World

For readers of *Great Books of the Western World,* the obvious place to begin in undertaking a study of the hero and of heroism is with the *Syntopicon.* As is indicated there in the "Inventory of Terms," the main consideration of this subject is to be found in the chapters on History, Honor, and Life and Death, under the following topics:

> History 4a (4)   The role of the individual in history: the great
> man, hero, or leader
> 　Honor 5.   Honor, fame, and the heroic
> 　　　5a. Honor as a motivation of heroism
> 　　　5b. Hero-worship: the exaltation of leaders
> 　　　5c. The occasions of heroism in war and peace
> 　　　5d. The estimation of the role of the hero in history
> 　Life and Death 8c.   The contemplation and fear of death: the
> attitude of the hero, the philosopher, the martyr

Subsidiary treatments of the subject can also be found under:

> Courage 5.   The motivations of courage: fame or honor, hap-
> piness, love, duty, religious faith
> 　Honor 3a.   The reaction of the community to its good or great
> men
> 　Love 3d.   The heroism of friendship and sacrifices of love
> 　Temperance 6a.   Asceticism: heroic temperance
> 　War and Peace 8.   The desirability of war: its moral and polit-
> ical benefits

This survey of the places where discussions of heroism can be located in our set of books serves at once to indicate something of the range and scope of the idea. The chapters into which the treatment of it falls identify the great ideas with which it is most closely associated, the company it keeps.

Definition

In some of these discussions, the word *hero* is practically synonymous with that of great man or leader, as in History 4*a* (4). Heroism is then considered to be identical with the greatness of men in general, and with human achievement in any course of action or kind of work. Such is the sense in which Carlyle, for example, used the term, when in 1840 he began a famous series of lectures by declaring:

> *We have undertaken to discourse here for a little on Great Men, their manner of appearance in our world's business, how they have shaped themselves in the world's history, what ideas men formed of them, what work they did;—on Heroes, namely, and on their reception and performance; what I call Hero-worship and the Heroic in human affairs.*[1]

In this sense of the term, we have to deal, as Carlyle went on to say, with "a large topic; indeed, an illimitable one; wide as Universal History itself." And in fact the hero and heroism are found associated with the idea of history not only in the discussions listed under History 4*a* (4) but also in those under Honor 3*a* and 5*b*, the last of which uses Carlyle's own expression, "hero-worship."

In other places the consideration of heroism is stricter than this. The term is used to denote a form of human greatness that is thought to be essentially distinct from other forms, though it may have something in common with them. Such a use occurs, for example, in Life 8*c*, where in connection with the attitude that one may have toward death the hero is distinguished from the philosopher and the martyr. The hero in this narrower sense of the term is commonly identified with military greatness, with valor, prowess, and extraordinary achievement in war. Some writers limit the subject still further and suggest that only a certain kind of military greatness is truly heroic. Thus La Bruyère, the seventeenth-century French moralist, says:

> *It seems that the hero has only one profession—that of arms— whereas the great man can belong to any—to that of the robe, the sword, the cabinet, or the court. . . . In war the distinction between the hero and the great man is a fine one: Both need all the military virtues. Nevertheless, it appears that the former is young, enterprising, of great valor, steadfast in perils, intrepid; whereas the latter excels in great sense, vast foresight, great capacity, and long experience. Perhaps, Alexander was only a hero, whereas Caesar was a great man.*[2]

However he is defined, the warrior-hero is not only discussed both by the authors in our set of books and by others outside it; he appears also by example, often as a figure of invention, in many works. He is most familiar, perhaps, in the stories of Homer, particularly the *Iliad.* Virgil, too, depicts him, as in much later times do Chaucer, Shakespeare, and Cervantes. Of course military heroes are also historical figures in the writings of Herodotus, Thucydides, and Plutarch, among older authors, and among more recent ones, in Tolstoy.

Few of these authors—indeed, perhaps only Homer, and to a lesser extent Plutarch and Tolstoy—concern themselves with the hero who, as one might say, is nothing *but* a warrior. The battles fought by Aeneas are important to Virgil only insofar as they are necessary to the business of founding Rome. Shakespeare in his historical plays is concerned with kingship, of which warfare is only a part. Cervantes, himself a soldier, gives us in Dox Quixote a man who cares about combat only because he is a knight, or would like to be one. Even Tolstoy's preoccupation with Napoleon in *War and Peace* is less with the warrior than with the world conquerer. And Plutarch does not confine himself to military figures any more than he does to morally good ones in rendering his *Lives* of the noble Greeks and Romans; his requirement is simply that the subjects of whom he writes be those who, as the *Syntopicon* chapter on Honor states, "were acknowledged to be great men, leaders, figures of eminent proportions, engaged in momentous exploits."[3]

Poetry, in the sense of the term that includes all imaginative literature as well as the great myths, depicts still other heroic types. Chief among them, perhaps, are the heroes of tragedy, who are discussed by the authors listed in the *Syntopicon* at Poetry 4*b.* Of such heroes the earliest is really Achilles in the *Iliad,* though by *tragic hero* is usually meant a figure of the sort that appears in the Greek dramas of a later time (not to speak of the plays of Shakespeare, the French classical drama, or a work such as *Samson Agonistes),* and who is discussed as a type by Aristotle in the *Poetics.*

There are heroes, too, of comedy, who as a kind are more difficult to define (the portion of the *Poetics* in which Aristotle presumably did so is not extant), and who, insofar as they constitute the antithesis of their tragic counterparts, are in some conventional respects not heroic at all. Homer may be said to be the original poet also of this kind of hero, who appears first as Odysseus in the *Odyssey*—which is not to say, of course, that he is a clown, or that the *Odyssey* is a funny book. A later Greek instance of a deeply comic character is the Socrates who dominates the *Dialogues* of Plato (himself originally a dramatist, according to some accounts). Still later examples of the type are the narrator (as distinct from the author) of the *Divine Comedy,* the Gargantua of Rabelais, Falstaff, Don Quixote, Lemuel Gulliver, Tom Jones, and Don Juan.

Earlier than either of these types of hero is the hero of myth, such as Hercules, Perseus, or Theseus, who achieved his status by virtue of great deeds that he performed, or who was held to have brought benefactions to mankind. On the other hand, of mostly subsequent formulation is the anti-hero (as he has come to be called) who explicitly defies either God or man—among the great examples is Faust, and likewise Melville's Ahab—though precedents for this heroic type are perhaps to be discerned in both the Prometheus of mythology and the Satan of *Paradise Lost,* as well as in the Robin Hood of legend, and may include all those tempters and cor-rupters of mankind (Fielding's *Jonathan Wild* is another example) whom Dr. Johnson once called the "splendidly wicked."[4]

Religion, like poetry and history, has also provided a fully formed con-ception of the hero and the heroic life. Particularly has this been so, as the *Syntopicon* chapter on Honor points out, since the days of medieval Christianity, when the practice of heroic virtue was regarded as a form of sanctity that was considered to be manifest in the lives of those martyrs, virgins, confessors, doctors, and others who through grace received the superhuman strength that was acknowledged in conferring sainthood upon them. It became settled Christian doctrine, as Sainte-Beuve in more recent times has pointed out, that "the soul arrives . . . at a certain fixed and invincible state, a state which is genuinely heroic, and from out of which the greatest deeds which it ever performs are executed."[5]   Less set-tled, perhaps, but not without support has been the idea that there can be something heroic not only in great deeds but in great patience. So at least we seem to hear the old, blind Milton say in the famous sonnet where, contemplating his inability to do more than he can do in the ser-vice of his God, he reminds himself that

God doth not need

Either man's work or his own gifts, who best
Bear his milde yoak, they serve him best, his State
Is Kingly. Thousands at his bidding speed
And post o're Land and Ocean without rest:
They also serve who only stand and waite.[6]

Finally, there seems to be at least one further distinct heroic type in the tradition of which we are speaking—the hero of intellectual pursuits, the man of genius, whose eminence is not in worldly affairs, nor in godly ones but in the life of the mind. The paradigm of this type is perhaps the Socrates of the Platonic dialogues, and more particularly the philosopher described in the *Republic,* who Plato seems to have hoped might replace the poetic conception of the warrior-hero that dominated the Athenian education of his time. But the tradition offers many figures in real life who have had something of the same quality. One of these is Saint Augus-tine, who in the *Confessions* tells us how he rejected the pagan learning he had taken years to master for the sake of the Christian doctrine that alone could satisfy his mind. There is Dante (the poet), who in his *Comedy* likens his genius to a little ship that sails along easily enough until it comes to the task of depicting paradise, when he notes that "the water which I take was never crossed."[7] There is Milton, expressing similar concern at the beginning of *Paradise Lost,* where he sets out to sing of "things unattempted yet in Prose or Rhime."[8] There is Gibbon, a century later, recalling the resolve with which, musing "among the ruins of the Capitol,"[9] he undertook to tell the long story of Rome's decline and fall. There is Marx, still later, struggling in exile to write *Das Kapital;* there is Freud, analyzing himself as the condition of analyzing others; there are the two Curies, unswerving in the researches that led to the discovery of radium. Not all of these figures, perhaps not any of them, would have regarded themselves as among those "men of great genius" of whom Schopenhauer speaks, who "stand in all ages like isolated heroes" against the multitude.[10] But such phrases reflect only a particular attitude, in a particular idiom, toward a kind of human greatness that nevertheless appears in essence to be rightly named.

Characteristics

The qualities that distinguish the hero from other men vary somewhat according to the kind of heroism that is being considered, but certain characteristics are constant. First among these is some form of strength or skill. The hero is typically capable of feats that are beyond the ability of ordinary men. Compared with them he can throw the spear farther, pull the stronger bow, run the faster race. Sometimes such abilities are of prodigious or fantastic extent, as with Hercules, or in American legend with Paul Bunyan, the logger, and Mike Fink, the riverboatman (of whom it was said that he could dive deeper, swim farther, and come up drier than any man alive). At other times heroic capacity is of a quite different order, belonging rather to the mind than to the body. It is then a strength of spirit, a defiance of soul. Milton's Satan seems to embody this in *Paradise Lost:*

> *What though the field be lost?*
> *All is not lost; the unconquerable Will,*
> *And study of revenge, immortal hate,*
> *And courage never to submit or yield:*
> *And what is else not to be overcome?*[11]

Whatever his moral condition, the hero cannot be himself without his power. Where that is diminished, or is seen as insufficient to support heroic reputation, the reputation withers. So Shakespeare's Cassius thinks, hearing the public shout for Caesar, and reflecting that the object of its adoration is really a fearful and short-winded fellow. To be sure, the power that is lost may be recovered:

> Samson *hath quit himself*
> *Like* Samson, *and heroicly hath finish'd*
> *A life Heroic....*[12]

327

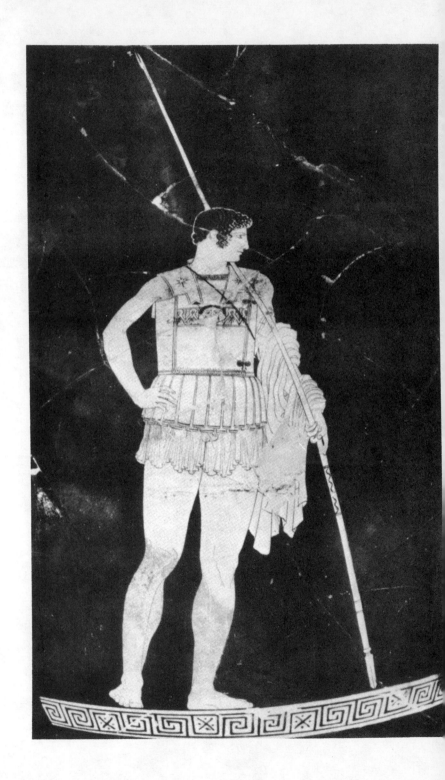

"It seems that the hero has only one profession—that of arms. . . . it appears that [he] is young, enterprising, of great valor, steadfast in perils, intrepid." (Left) Achilles; (above) American soldiers

But it is more usual that the hero is always what he is, not only at times, and certainly not just on some single, fortuitous occasion. There must be more than accident or impulse in the contest between any hero and his adversary, his task, his fate. "The characteristic of heroism is its persistency," Emerson says.[13] Tennyson's Ulysses, old though he is, is still not sated in his quest for experience as he embarks on one last voyage.

Along with strength or durability goes the characteristic heroic virtue of courage. Except in one instance, which we will discuss in a moment, some form of this is everywhere acknowledged to be indispensable to the heroic role, whatever else that role entails. As the *Syntopicon* chapter on Courage states, "The heroes of history and poetry may be cruel, violent, self-seeking, ruthless, intemperate, and unjust, but they are never cowards":

> *They do not falter or give way. They do not despair in the face of almost hopeless odds. They have the strength and stamina to achieve whatever they set their minds and wills to do. They would not be heroes if they were not men of courage.*[14]

Some writers indicate that it is courage that gives heroic stature not merely to those who accomplish great things but to all those serious and thoughtful persons who, contemplating the harsh uncertainties of human existence, are nevertheless able to endure it. "When a dreadful object is presented," William James writes,

> *or when life as a whole turns up its dark abysses to our view, then the worthless ones among us lose their hold on the situation altogether. . . . But the heroic mind does differently . . . it can face them if necessary, without for that losing its hold upon the rest of life. The world thus finds in the heroic man its worthy match and mate. . . . He can* stand *this Universe.*[15]

Other, special forms of courage have been thought in certain instances to make heroes of the scholar, the scientist, and the saint. One such special kind of courage was that which the Greeks recognized in the heroes of tragedy, and to which they gave the name *até*. By this they meant the high bravery, amounting to a sort of inspired madness, that enabled such heroes to plunge into the sea of difficulties that surrounded them and force their fate to reveal itself, though the cost of doing so was death or ruin. Some analogue to this quality, often thought to indicate the intercession of the gods, may be found in most other forms of heroism as well.

The excepted instance, mentioned earlier, in which not courage but prudence seems to be the characteristic heroic virtue is found among the heroes of comedy, who are therefore by some authors considered to be misnamed, and are disallowed as a variety of the heroic ideal. And it is true that even the great comic prototypes—Odysseus, for instance, or Socrates, or Don Quixote—appear unheroic alongside the tragic or epic or romantic heroes with whom they invite comparison. That is how they are supposed to appear. But apart from anything else that may be said about them, it may be argued that in their various destitute, impoverished, or absurd fashions, they actually possess courage of a very rich and complex kind, and it has been suggested, notably by Socrates in the *Symposium,* that other forms of heroism cannot finally be understood except by those who understand the comic form of it.

We commonly know the hero also by one further characteristic. That is his apartness, even his isolation, from other human company, if not as well from every abstract context—home, history, and laws both human and divine—in which other men move and have their being. There is something elect in the heroic role that makes each instance of it unique. The great warriors of the *Iliad* battle in what may be regarded as armies only up to a point. Beyond that, each man carries the fight, or is forced to carry it, wholly on his own. On the other hand, when a monument was erected to the Spartans who died at Thermopylae, instructing whoever came upon it to tell their countrymen that they had given their lives in obedience to their country's laws, heroic status was thereby rejected by them, or in their behalf. It is fundamental to the great tragic dramas— *Oedipus at Colonus,* for instance, or *King Lear*—that they explore the farthest implications of what it means to be naked, wretched, and alone. Even the heroes of comedy, who cannot be themselves unless they are in human company, are as a rule rejected, ridiculed, or otherwise despised, at least through some part of their careers. And in the case of the Romantic hero, the rejection is not so much endured as it is actively sought. Such a hero does not suffer isolation, he asserts it.

A question arises as to whether this isolation of the hero can or should be complete. It seems to be so among the heroes of the *Iliad,* given as they are to furthering their individual reputations, though the individuality of Achilles, say, for which all things—friends, honor, and ultimately life itself—are sacrificed, is something much greater than a mere private ego. Since the time of Virgil, however, a less extreme conception of heroic isolation has offered itself, if it has not always prevailed. It is of the essence of the hero of the *Aeneid* that he pursues an end which is not personal to himself—in the interest of which, indeed, he sublimates his own judgment and feelings. As founder of the race that in time will rule the earth, Aeneas acts in obedience to the expressed will of Jove, and while this sometimes puts him in conflict with other men and sets him always at some distance from them, it secures him against the kind of abandonment that occurs when fate itself turns hostile or seems indifferent, as it does with the heroes of epic tragedy. The result seems at first to be a loss of stature. By comparison with those heroes, Aeneas is a protected and somehow insufficient figure in whom we shall always be disappointed until we realize that it was Virgil's purpose to redefine the heroic role. From his Roman point of view the heroes of the epic tradition, especially the Achaeans of the *Iliad,* were of an obsolete type, willful and wantonly destructive, who could no longer be accepted as models in a world dedicated to peace under the rule of law.[16]

A further and related question about heroic isolation is whether it can be extended into the historical order of things without becoming either a part of that order, and thereby no longer isolated, or opposed to it, and thus something merely futile. Carlyle, for one, denied that this must happen. He insisted that throughout the course of history the dominating force in historic events had been and would continue to be the words and acts of great men. But Hegel considers such men to be great only insofar as they sense some historical process, identify themselves with the wave of the future, and conform to the irresistible march of worldly events. They are "world-historical individuals," he says, whom we may like to think of as heroic, but who are really only puppets, creatures of historical forces that come about as the result of innumerable acts by countless human beings.[17] These opposed views of Carlyle and Hegel would appear not to be reconcilable. But a compromise of sorts between them seems to be achieved by William James when he affirms that

> *the relation of the visible environment to the great man is in the main exactly what it is to the "variation" in the Darwinian philosophy. It chiefly adopts or rejects, preserves or destroys, in short selects him. And whenever it adopts and preserves the great man, it becomes modified by his influence in an entirely original and peculiar way. He acts as a ferment, and changes its constitution, just as the advent of a new zoological species changes the faunal and floral equilibrium of the region in which it appears.[18]*

Motivation

The heroes of the Trojan War are what they are, Homer indicates in the *Iliad,* by virtue of the ideal to which they hold, and which they endeavor to realize by their acts. It is an ideal of preeminence. Whatever the differences among them—and each of the important figures in the poem is rendered memorably distinct—they are all alike in that by training, aspiration, and continual exertion they strive to be the best. We are told that Achilles, who is called "chief of heroes," was brought up by his father, Peleus, "to be ever the best and to excel all others."[19] Precisely the same words are used by the Trojan, Glaukos, to describe what his own father wished of him. Such claims of supremacy can be demonstrated only by putting them to the test. Hence the great battle scenes of the poem are among other things the testings of the various heroes—the proofs, as it were, of their merit. In fact, it is customary to identify certain parts of the poem by these trials, which are known variously as the *aristeia* of Diomedes (Book 5), of Agamemnon (Book 11), of Menelaus (Book 17), and—longest of all—the *aristeia* of Achilles (Books 19–22).

This word is derived from the adjective *aristos,* which means "best," and that in turn comes from the noun *areté,* which for Homer means something like "excellence," and which has been said to embody as well as any single word can the heroic ideal of the *Iliad. Areté* was later used by Aristotle to mean excellence of a moral and intellectual kind, or virtue, and in this sense it can, as for Aristotle it does, mean virtue in general. In the *Iliad,* however, it is something that only warriors have, the virtue that is peculiar to them, the thing that *makes* them "best." We could embrace much of what it means, though not all, if we translated it as "valor."

A similar evolution seems to have overtaken the Latin word that has the same meaning. Plutarch relates that among the early Romans, who were as remote from him as Homer was from Aristotle,

"The hero is typically capable of feats that are beyond the ability of ordinary men. Compared with them he can throw the spear farther, pull the stronger bow, run the faster race." (Left) The "Discobolus" (discus thrower), Roman copy of a bronze by Myron, ca. 450 B.C.; (below) Mark Spitz after the 1972 Olympic Games

that kind of worth was most esteemed which displayed itself in military achievements; one evidence of which we find in the Latin word for virtue, which is properly equivalent to manly courage. As if valour and all virtue had been the same thing, they [the early Romans] used as the common term the name of the particular excellence.[20]

It is consistent with this, as Plutarch means to indicate, that the word *virtue* includes the Latin word *vir*, or "man," and that the root meaning of *virtue* is therefore "manliness."

What presumably underlies the old equation of manliness with military distinction is the fact that among men it is chiefly the warrior who undergoes the ultimate trial, which is the threat of death, as a matter of deliberate confrontation. We must say chiefly here, rather than only, because of course the hunter of savage beasts does the same thing, or once did (and was then regarded as heroic), as does the person who commits ritual suicide (in a different tradition), and perhaps certain others. But at any rate the acceptance of mortal danger is fundamental to the profession of arms and is the basis of claims such as Don Quixote makes when he argues that no other profession, not even that of clergy or the law, stands so high. Indeed, a readiness to die is by itself sufficient to raise a man above his fellows, in the opinion of some writers, whatever kind of man he is, and providing only that he act with some cause. "No matter what a man's frailties may otherwise be," William James has said in discussing what he called "life's supreme mystery,"

if he be willing to risk death, and still more if he suffer it heroically, in the service he has chosen, the fact consecrates him forever. Inferior to ourselves in this or that way, if yet we cling to life and he is able to "fling it away like a flower," as caring nothing for it, we account him in the deepest way our born superior.[21]

The heroes of the *Iliad*, who are depicted by Homer as facing death with grim awareness and understanding, would appear to be the signal instance of what James has in mind. Yet they are none of them careless of life in the way his statement implies they should be. As Achilles says, when death after all has overtaken him and his spirit has gone to Hades, "rather would I live on ground as the hireling of another, with a landless man who had no livelihood, than bear sway among all the dead that be departed."[22] The meanest life is better in his view that the highest place among those who have ceased to live at all.

Nor does any of the heroes forget that death as such is no distinction, is only what all men, heroic and otherwise, must suffer. Again it is Achilles who says, with bitterness,

We are all held in a single honour,
  the brave with the weaklings.

> *A man dies still if he has done nothing,*
> *as one who has done much.*[23]

What makes the heroes different from ordinary men is their determination to force the issue, to place their lives in danger which they could, if they chose, avoid. They do this in part knowing it is expected of them, because their position demands it. The honors and perquisites accorded to them in this world, withheld from lesser men, are given to them in recognition of their willingness to leave it. But the willingness itself comes from their perception of the fact that they are doomed to die in any case. As mortal men, hatefully limited by their condition, they feel that they can exist beyond their alloted time only in the sense, and to the extent, that they are remembered by those who come after them. It is in the effort to gain such remembrance, the nearest men can come to being like the deathless gods, that the heroes put their lives in the balance, striving to do great deeds. If an easier way were open to them, they would take it—so Sarpedon the Trojan at one point frankly admits:

> *Man, supposing you and I, escaping this battle, would be able to live on forever, ageless, immortal, so neither would I myself go on fighting in the foremost nor would I urge you into the fighting where men win glory. But now, seeing that the spirits of death stand close about us in their thousands, no man can turn aside nor escape them, let us go on and win glory for ourselves, or leave it to others.*[24]

There is no easier way. Unable to avoid death, the heroes can only hope to transcend it.

James's essential point seems borne out, however, by the Greek dramas of a later age. The prospect of death, or at least of destruction, enters into the lives of the heroes of all the great tragedies. It is not, perhaps, so clearly visible to them as the likely consequence of their acts as it is for the heroes of Homer. Nor do the protagonists of the tragedies see themselves as endeavoring in the same way to overcome it. Oedipus, who as portrayed by Sophocles seemed to Aristotle the best representative of the type, is not a warrior but a king, with problems that may perhaps be described as political or moral, but are at any rate not military. The same is true of Orestes in the trilogy by Aeschylus. Yet the question of life and death, of survival or annihilation, is there for both figures to confront, and it is their willingness to do so that gives them—that for the Greek audience certainly gave them—their heroic stature. It was fitting that this audience, which in other terms comprised the citizenry of Athens, should be seen subsequently as the hero of a tragedy of real life, its long struggle with Sparta, and that its fate should have been recorded with dramatic insight by one of its own number, the historian Thucydides, in *The Peloponnesian War*.

335

Death or the threat of death is faced, too, by the Virgillian hero. But whereas the Homeric warrior confronts it in hope of the glory he may win, and the protagonists of the tragedies to the end that they may, for at least one brief instant, be masters of their fate, the hero of the *Aeneid* risks his life in the furtherance of the mission he has been elected to perform. This election is security against the dangers and difficulties through which he must pass. We realize that Aeneas cannot really die, in the ordinary sense, any more than he can fail in what he undertakes to do; either result would violate Jove's plan, which for the reader of Virgil's poem has become history. At the same time, it is clear that in another sense Virgil does have a kind of death in mind, and that he depicts Aeneas as having with much pain and sense of loss to undergo it. This is the death of his former self, belonging to the heroic age that is past, which must be supressed insofar as its feelings are in conflict with the high public duty to which he has been called. Among these feelings is love for Dido, the queen of Carthage to whose land Aeneas comes in his wanderings, and with whom he would remain if he could. "Not self-impelled steer I for Italy," he tells her when the time comes for him to leave.[25] Yet leave he must, the lover in him denied, his personal wishes opposed, for the sake of the great city whose progenitor he has been chosen to be. The Latin word for Rome is *Roma,* which is *amor,* the Latin word for love, spelled backwards.

There is much in the poem to indicate that Virgil means to set forth an idea of heroism that is not only different from the Homeric one but anti-

Just as history has recorded the great deeds of heroes, so too the artist has invented figures of heroic stature. Some are the heroes of comedy and tragedy, embodying the ideal or circumstance of heroism. (Opposite) Cervantes's Don Quixote drawn by Gustave Doré and Charlie Chaplin's "Little Tramp." (Right) Shakespeare's Hamlet painted by Delacroix and (below) Arthur Miller's Willie Loman

thetical to it. Both the *Iliad* and the *Odyssey,* dissimilar as they are, deal with ways in which the hero loses or remains or recovers himself, in peace no less than in war. The *Aeneid* shows him in the same situations as *relinquishing* himself, not in the manner of one who is defeated or withdrawn from human concerns but for the sake of a higher identity that he comes to accept—the identity of a participant in a great world task. No such identity is available to the Homeric hero, in whose universe there is nothing between the individual man and the Olympian gods, and whose heroism consists precisely in his efforts to close the gap. This means, since he cannot bring the gods down to his level, that he must try and raise himself to theirs—must endeavor to enlarge himself beyond his mortal limits. In the Virgillian universe, however, the gods have descended part way, in the sense that they have revealed their purpose, and the Virgillian hero has to rise only to the intermediate level which is the realization of that purpose in human terms. To accomplish this is in its own right a heroic undertaking, since much must be risked for it, and much rejected. But at least it does not require the utter abandonment of the mortal condition, which in Homeric terms is the price of glory. And although it does not confer true immortality either, which is what glory in the root sense of the word means, what it does give is the honor of having served the living god upon the earth, so that his work, if not his worker, may survive.

It is easy to see in this Virgillian conception a prefiguration of Christianity, and particularly, in heroic terms, of the Christian knight. Even the language that Virgil uses reinforces our sense of connection between the two. Where Homer speaks of Achilles as "wrathful" or "swift-footed," and of Odysseus as "of many councils," or just "wily," the standard Virgillian epithet for Aeneas, in Latin, is *pius.* This cannot be translated properly as "pious," though it sounds much the same, since it does not for Virgil have the specifically religious connotation of that term. Nor can the Latin noun from which it comes, which is *pietas,* be translated as "piety," for the same reason. Nevertheless, and although Virgil never defines either word explicitly, it is clear from the context of his poem that by *pietas* he means the virtue Cicero had in mind when he spoke of "that through which one conscientiously renders duty and reverence to kin, country, and friends." [26] We are on firm ground, therefore, if we interpret *pius* as meaning "dutiful and reverent," or perhaps "obedient," and if we understand Aeneas to be possessed of the qualities those terms describe. And it is but a step—a very great step, to be sure, but one that Rome itself eventually took—if we add the religious, specifically Christian, meaning that *reverence* and *obedience* later acquired, and find that we have arrived at, though we have by no means altogether encompassed, the Christian, knightly, medieval idea of the hero.

Although there is an extensive literature on this kind of hero in the medieval romances, particularly the stories that deal with King Arthur and the Knights of the Round Table, and although something about his general character may be learned, for example, from Chaucer's story of the Knight in *The Canterbury Tales,* the richest and best account of him is by Cervantes, who professed not to believe in him, and who wrote *Don Quixote,* as he said, so that those foolish persons who did believe in him would realize how incredible he was. We do not know how seriously Cervantes meant this, or if he ceased to mean it as he wrote the book. All we know is that his intention, if it was real, somehow backfired, that the absurd and gallant figure of the Don turned out to be strangely convincing, so that he is the only knight that ever was, as one reader has said, in whom we *can* believe, and that his adventures, which were ostensibly set down to destroy chivalry, have preserved it in the world's imagination ever since.

The Christian pretensions (as Cervantes allows us to believe they are) of knights are described by Don Quixote early in his story, when he compares what he calls his "profession" of arms with that of priests and other churchmen. "My meaning is," he says,

> *that churchmen in peace and quiet pray to Heaven for the welfare of the world, but we soldiers and knights carry into effect what they pray for, defending it with the might of our arms and the edge of our swords, not under shelter but in the open air, a target for the intolerable rays of the sun in summer and the piercing frosts of winter. Thus are we God's ministers on earth and the arms in which his justice is done therein.*[27]

But it is part of Cervantes's own meaning that Don Quixote does not perceive all that he is saying here—does not acknowledge the conflict between the welfare of the world that churchmen pray for and what may be accomplished by force of arms, overlooks the pride in his assumption that he is the agent of divine justice. It is true, he understands very well what he says later on, when he explains to his listeners that in his knightly adventures he is limited by his Christian responsibility, which gives his acts their true significance:

> *In what we do we must not overpass the bounds which the Christian religion we profess has assigned to us. We have to slay pride in giants, envy by generosity and nobleness of heart, anger by calmness of demeanor and equanimity, gluttony and sloth by the spareness of our diet and the length of our vigils, lust and lewdness by the loyalty we preserve to those whom we have made the mistresses of our thoughts, indolence by traversing the world in all directions seeking opportunities of making ourselves, besides Christians, famous knights.*[28]

Yet it is one thing to understand this and another to be able to live up to it, and one of the things *Don Quixote* is about is the fact that being a knight, or trying to be one, can become a self-serving enterprise. The Don

339

"... the hero of intellectual pursuits, the man of genius, whose eminence is not in worldly affairs, nor in godly ones, but in the life of the mind." (Above) Marie Curie; (opposite) "The Death of Socrates" by Jacques Louis David

himself seems to take note of this when he asserts that the rewards of knightly exploits "are, were, and will be, the work of fame that mortals desire as a reward and a portion of the immortality their famous deeds deserve." He then corrects himself, as it were, by observing that Christian knights "look more to that future glory that is everlasting . . . than to the vanity of the fame that is to be acquired in this present transitory life." But this leaves him open to the question Sancho Panza asks, which is whether in that case the two of them had not better join a religious order and "set about becoming saints . . . [in order to] obtain more quickly the fair fame we are striving after." In answer, Don Quixote, trying to defend the heroic life he has chosen, can come up only with the perilous doctrine that chivalry too is "a religion, there are sainted knights in glory." [29]

What is evident in these various works, taken together, is a sort of progression or enlargement of heroic motivation. This is derived at first from a sense of the person. At a later time, it arises from an idea of country or the State. Still later it is found in religious zeal. We have seen that there is a fundamental conflict between the first and second stages of the progression, and we can infer a still greater conflict between the first and the third. For, as the glorification of the person in Homeric terms is incompatible with the glorification of the state that Virgil celebrated, so it is even more profoundly opposed to the glorification of God that is proper to Christianity. It is not surprising that such conflicts show themselves in the internal struggles of the hero, who has greater difficulty meeting the requirements of these successive allegiances as they become more abstract and otherworldly. That the Homeric warriors value women, who indeed provide their heroic occasions, is not regarded as inconsistent with their status. Aeneas, on the other hand, suffers a kind of fall, from which he must recover, in his infatuation with Dido. And the Christian knight, or at least the knight-errant, though he always serves an idealized mistress, as Don Quixote says, nevertheless can and sometimes does become the lover of a real one, with an irretrievable loss of purity. Of all the knights of the Round Table, only Gawain was worthy of the Holy Grail.

It is not surprising either that, as the third of the motivations, which is the glorification of God, is an ultimate one, the progression of which we are speaking should seem to reach an end with it. And it is true that after the decline of Christian chivalry any fresh conception of heroic purpose, as being in the service of a new doctrine or idea, is hard to find. Only with modern times, perhaps, and the idea of Revolution, does such a thing appear. Of course there have been reaffirmations at different historical periods of the idea of the national hero, who is a descendent of Aeneas, as there have been revivals of the heroic ideal in individual terms. The latter reappears notably during the romantic era of the last century, and to some extent in more recent times, when it is discerned, for example, in the figure of the artist. It may be doubted, however, whether the modern heroic ideal, if any such can be said to exist, is a person of any kind, so much as an abstraction or a collectivity. The true hero of the present seems to be a country, a people, or a movement—even history itself, as Hegel would appear to have believed. Or perhaps the person in whom we find it is the person of Everyman. Freud, who was convinced that "the secret of heroism," its psychological root, was not so much the desire to win immortality as the inability of the unconscious to recognize or admit death, argues that the heroic act arises from the conviction every man unconsciously has that he cannot really die, that he is somehow immortal. "The rational explanation for heroism," Freud writes,

> is that it consists in the decision that the personal life cannot be so precious as certain abstract general ideals. But more frequent, in my view, is that instinctive and impulsive heroism which knows no such motivation, and flouts danger in the spirit of Anzengruber's Hans the Road-Mender: "Nothing can happen to me."[30]

Criticism

While there does not seem to have been any period of history in the tradition of which we are speaking that has utterly lacked heroic ideals, neither has there been any age in which these ideals were immune to criticism or above disbelief. This has sometimes been expressed, as we have seen, by those who seek to establish a different conception of the hero from one that happens to prevail. More often it has been articulated by authors who dislike or are skeptical of heroism in any form. Such an attitude is found in Euripides, of whom Aristotle remarked that, as compared with Sophocles, he depicted men not as they ought to be but as they are, and who seldom missed an opportunity in his plays to attack heroic pretensions. Typical is a passage from *Medea*:

> Great people's tempers are terrible, always
> Having their own way, seldom checked,
> Dangerous they shift from mood to mood.
> How much better to have been accustomed
> To live on equal terms with one's neighbors.
> I would like to be safe and grow old in a
> Humble way. What is moderate sounds best,
> Also in practice is best for everyone.
> Greatness brings no profit to people.
> God indeed, when in anger, brings
> Greater ruin to great men's houses.[31]

Similar words are used later by Montaigne when he asserts that he prefers Socrates to Alexander, since he feels he "can easily conceive Socrates in the place of Alexander, but Alexander in that of Socrates, [he] cannot." All that Alexander can accomplish, he says, is contained in the command, "Subdue the world," whereas Socrates acts according to the maxim, " 'Carry on human life comformably with its natural condition'; a much more general, weighty, and legitimate science than the other."[32] On the other hand, Cervantes is more severe (or seems to be; again, we never know just how serious he is) with his own hero, Don Quixote, whose goings-on are characterized as not only futile and destructive but insane, the result of reading too many chivalric romances. And Pope simply takes it for granted, in the *Essay on Man,* that heroism is in general the product of derangement or perversity:

> Heroes are much the same, the point's agreed,
> From Macedonia's madman to the Swede;
> The whole strange purpose of their lives, to find
> Or make, an enemy of all mankind.[33]

Some authors—Cervantes, of course, is one—provide their own commentary on the heroic ideal they present. The greatest critic of the Homeric warrior, notwithstanding Virgil, is Homer himself—if we can assume, as tradition has it, that the man who wrote the *Iliad* also wrote the *Odyssey.* For the latter tells us how it is that, in making his way home, one of those who fought at Troy, Odysseus, unlearns his warrior role, and of how this is in a profound moral sense the price of his safe return. Just

what sort of figure he becomes in the process is something that only his complete story is sufficient, perhaps, to explain. The heroic ideal that emerges from the *Odyssey,* if ideal it can be said to be, is much more difficult to define than its counterpart in the *Iliad.* This is partly because it reflects the distinction Aristotle made between tragedy and comedy when he said that the former was simple and disastrous, while the latter was complicated and moral. It is also because we perceive the *Odyssey*'s heroic type only in its embodiment, which is Odysseus himself, of whom the single conclusive thing there is to say is that—wanderer, pretender, and liar that he is—there is nothing fixed or final to be said. It is clear, however, that he is something different from the Achaean warriors, his former comrades, of whom he hears along the way of his return, since they have already become the stuff of which songs are sung and stories are told before he reaches home. Infinitely artful, he uses all his skills on that long journey to preserve his life and extend his experience—as distinct from Achilles, who had been intensely alive, and who elected by the manner of his dying to turn himself into a work of art. The course Odysseus takes leads him, too, toward immortality—not, however, through a death that is gloriously met but by a resourcefulness that keeps off any death at all.

344

"We have undertaken to discourse here for a little on Great Men, . . . how they have shaped themselves in the world's history, what ideas men formed of them, what work they did." (Opposite-left) Moses by Michelangelo; (opposite-right) Joan of Arc by Ingres; (above-left) Winston Churchill, 1940; (above-right) a painting of young Mao

Achilles is the prince of the fallen, but Odysseus is the king of survivors.

To say that Homer, in depicting such a figure, is a critic of the tale he —or someone—told in the *Iliad* is not to imply that he had come to disapprove of that earlier production (as we must assume it was), or of its central hero, but only that he understood the different nature of his later task. For the point of view that makes the *Odyssey* possible is inherently critical of the passion that creates the *Iliad,* which it has time to see around, and which in its wide perspective looks rash and ruinous. Odysseus may and does love the memory of those with whom he fought at Troy, as he is proud of the glory they achieved, but he knows he can no longer afford to be what they were, that he must reconstitute himself if he is to recover his place in the common world of men, in the normal order of things. The heroism of the *Odyssey* excludes the heroism of the *Iliad,* as peace displaces war.

A similar kind of understanding produces another hero with some of the same qualities in the Socrates of the Platonic dialogues. There is general agreement that this figure is in part Plato's invention, though a real Socrates did exist, did teach in the manner Plato describes, and was tried and executed for the crimes that are discussed with such devastating irony in the *Apology*. What Plato brought to the account of him, among other things, was a purpose that in the nature of the case his career could not have acquired on its own, though the real Socrates may have intended that it should. For his death more or less coincided with the final defeat of Athens in its decisive war with Sparta. He was thus unable to complete or perhaps even consciously to begin the project that Plato, his most brilliant student, undertook on his behalf, which was an inquiry into the causes of that catastrophe. The *Dialogues* can be read as steps in such an inquiry. Plato seems to have decided to write them because he saw, as perhaps the real Socrates also saw, that what had happened to their city was not so much that it had lost a war as that in the process it had somehow lost its soul. The *Dialogues* explore the implications of this tragedy, which raise questions about the nature of men and things and the origin of the world, but which lead at the end to the task of reconstituting the laws. Plato, the guiding spirit of the inquiry, having, so to say, taken the city on a lengthy speculative journey, at last brings it home to contemplate its civil condition.

It is appropriate not only to his ultimate situation but to the special nature of his heroic role that in the last discussion he has with his followers, just before he dies, Socrates is concerned with life and death and the immortality of the soul. The followers, despairing in the fact that they are about to lose him, seek reassurance that in doing so they will not lose the life of the mind as well. "I would ask you to be thinking of the truth and not of Socrates," he tells them. In thus addressing himself to their doubt and grief he is likened to "a general rallying his defeated and broken army," determined to restore their faith in the power of rational discourse to survive his impending death.[34] It was his last accomplishment to make this event seem less important than the speculative enterprise that had brought it about, and that seemed finally to require it.

Christian writers, at least until the time in the tenth and eleventh centuries when chivalry brings about an uneasy union of Christian and heroic ideals, are also critical of the heroic tradition, which they perceive only as a pagan thing. Augustine even regarded it as vicious, since it seemed to him grounded in the sin of pride. If great Rome, the seat of Christian faith, had been built by men who nevertheless adhered to such a tradition, what could be discerned in the fact but the providence of God, who had chosen that method of building his empire upon earth? Heroic ambition, though sinful in Augustine's eyes, was yet capable of great undertakings, for which reason, he wrote, God could be supposed to have instilled it in

> *such men as, for the sake of honour and praise, and glory, consulted*
> *well for their country, in whose glory they sought their own, and*
> *whose safety they did not hesitate to prefer to their own, sup-*
> *pressing the desire of wealth and many other vices for this one vice,*
> *namely, the love of praise.*[35]

Of course Augustine could not accept the higher mission of Aeneas that
Virgil had conceived to justify the founding of Rome and assert her
destiny. Though cast in verse that Augustine never ceased to love, that
conception was in his view merely an expression of civic vanity accorded
the false sanction of a pagan god.

Dante seems more tolerant than Augustine does of some of the ancient
heroes, to whom in the *Divine Comedy* he grants a place in limbo. Yet he
cites others, such as Capaneus the blasphemer, who defied the gods before the gates of Thebes, in illustration of grave sins. Odysseus, in particular, who was known only by tradition in medieval times, occupies a
place far down in Hell among the evil counselors. He is there as the symbol he had become for Dante's age (a very different age of course from
Tennyson's, which took a very different view) of those who look not
heavenward for their salvation but to the world and worldly things for
the satisfaction of their vain and idle curiosity, and who persuade other
men, their followers, to do the same thing.

It is rather the analogue of heroism which consists of martyrdom that
is honored by Dante, as it is by Christian tradition generally. And what
we might otherwise think of as heroic courage in Dante himself, the voy-
ager who makes his way through the terror of Hell, the trial of Purgatory,
and the vision of Paradise—what would seem to be courage, too, later on
in the story of *The Pilgrim's Progress*—is really not that in Christian
terms but something very much greater. It is the work of the specifically
Christian virtues of faith, hope, and charity, which are required of those
who take salvation's path. Nor can those who follow that path be regarded as heroic in this tradition. For they are thought of as distinguished
less by the effort they have made than by the grace they have received,
without which the effort would come to nought.

Even where among later authors an idea of heroism survives the restraints, amounting almost to suppression, that Christianity places upon
it, there is apt to be criticism of what are considered its extremes. Shakespeare's plays imply as much in some of their characterizations. Hotspur
in *Henry IV, Part I* is clearly an instance of a distempered heroic spirit,
as is Falstaff, though his distemper is of the opposite kind. On the other
hand, Prince Hal, who in the same play appears worse than either of these
figures, shows himself to be their better upon his father's death—

> *The breath no sooner left his father's body,*
> *But that his wildness, mortified in him,*
> *Seem'd to die too; yea, at that very moment*

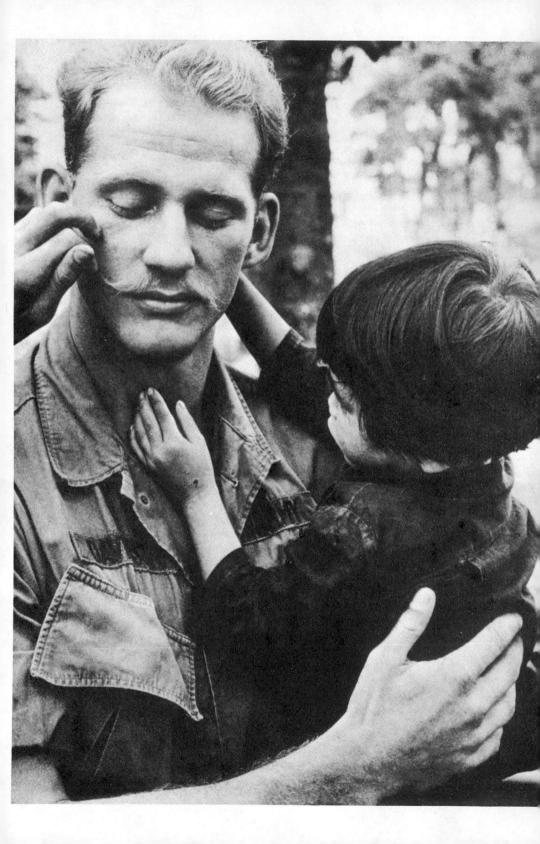

Whatever form the idea of the hero takes and however the idea may change, people reach out to touch their heroes. They will have their heroes

> *Consideration, like an angel, came*
> *And whipp'd the offending Adam out of him,*
> *Leaving his body as a paradise,*
> *To envelope and contain celestial spirits.*[36]

—when he proceeds to become, as Henry V, what we are given to understand is the ideal hero-king. But Shakespeare seems to have recognized the poetic limitations of this type, if not the political ones, in his later plays. When in those plays he drew imperfect men, he did not pretend that they were heroes—as, at the same time, in contemplating perfect ones, he ceased to pretend that they were real:

> CLEOPATRA: *I dream'd there was an Emperor Antony.*
> *O, such another sleep, that I might see*
> *But such another man!*
> DOLABELLA: *If it might please ye—*
> CLEOPATRA: *His face was as the heavens; and therein stuck*
> *A sun and moon, which kept their course, and lighted*
> *The little O, the earth.*
> DOLABELLA: *Most sovereign creature—*
> CLEOPATRA: *His legs bestrid the ocean; his rear'd arm*
> *Crested the world; his voice was propertied*
> *As all the tuned spheres, and that to friends;*
> *But when he meant to quail and shake the orb,*
> *He was as rattling thunder. For his bounty,*
> *There was no winter in't; an autumn 'twas*
> *That grew the more by reaping. His delights*
> *Were dolphin-like; they show'd his back above*
> *The element they lived in. In his livery*
> *Walk'd crowns and crownets; realms and islands were*
> *As plates dropp'd from his pocket.*
> DOLABELLA: *Cleopatra!*
> CLEOPATRA: *Think you there was, or might be, such a man*
> *As this I dream'd of?*
> DOLABELLA: *Gentle madam, no.*[37]

The idea that heroism is larger than life, and that it is therefore contrary to nature, is what Dr. Johnson also seems to have had in mind when he said that "Shakespeare has no heroes; his scenes are occupied only by men who act and speak as the reader thinks that he should himself have spoken or acted on the same occasion: Even where the agency is supernatural the dialogue is level with life." In this Shakespeare is superior to other dramatists, Johnson wrote, who "can only gain attention by hyperbolical or aggravated characters, by fabulous and unexampled excellence or depravity, as the writers of barbaric romances invigorated the reader by a giant and a dwarf."[38]

For Hegel, however, as for other writers of the romantic age, the hero, far from being contrary to nature, can exist only *in* "a state of nature." But of course by *nature* Hegel does not mean what Dr. Johnson meant, which was more or less what we would mean by the term *human nature;* Hegel means what might be called the primal order of things, or in Hegelian terminology, "a state of affairs where mere force prevails and against which the Idea establishes a right of Heroes." It was Hegel's theory that the hero serves the evolution of ethics—the Idea of Right—in the world, where he is of use to the Idea, at a time when brute strength would otherwise prevail, in organizing human life. But such a use lasts only until the Idea has brought about the creation of the State, which for Hegel is not civil society but rather its constitutional form and sanction. When this occurs, Hegel says, "there can no longer be any heroes," since the "uncivilized conditions" that make it right for such figures to found cities, establish institutions, and maintain order, no longer exist.[39]

This assertion of a kind of subordinate moral right in heroic action recalls Hegel's belief that heroes, or at least great men, are the creatures of something larger than themselves—specifically, of "historical forces" that it is their heroic distinction to perceive and seem to lead. Hegel's views on that subject are discussed in the *Syntopicon* chapter on History. Such a belief leaves little to the hero, of course, except an extraordinary capacity for insight. And even that is denied by Tolstoy, whose favorite figure in *War and Peace,* General Kutúzov, does not pretend to know what will happen, still less how to make it happen, in Russia's struggle with Napoleon, and whose strength derives precisely from his lack of any illusion that he does. No other attitude, Tolstoy feels, is really consistent with history. "We need only penetrate," he writes,

> to the essence of any historic event—which lies in the activity of the general mass of men who take part in it—to be convinced that the will of the historic hero does not control the actions of the mass but is itself continually controlled.[40]

It follows from this, Tolstoy adds, that once we have disabused ourselves of false notions of historical causality, "not only shall we have no need to see exceptional ability and genius in Napoleon and Alexander, but we shall be unable to consider them to be anything but like other men."[41] Tolstoy is thus in sharp disagreement, as Hegel is also, with ancient historians such as Thucydides, who regarded Pericles as the controlling figure in the fate of Athens, or Plutarch, for whom the history of civilization could be told in terms of the *Lives* of the noble Greeks and Romans.

The idea that the hero is at bottom like other men is exhaustively explored, too, in the plays of Bernard Shaw, who as a comic artist made it his business to puncture heroic pretensions. "There's no such thing as a real hero," says the character of Napoleon in *The Man of Destiny.*[42] Raina, in *Arms and the Man,* implies the same thing when she remembers that at her last meeting with her heroic lover, Sergius, "it came into my head just as he was holding me in his arms and looking into my eyes, that perhaps we only had our heroic ideas because we are so fond of reading Byron and Pushkin."[43] And in their various ways Shaw's greatest people —Caesar, John Tanner, Andrew Undershaft, Saint Joan, and so forth—all stand corrective of the heroic ideal in its romantic form.

Corrective, it is important to note, rather than destructive. For Shaw develops a heroic conception of his own in the man—or woman— of reason and good sense who reveals the vanities and vital lies by which most men attempt to live. This is the figure that dominates so many of his plays—that is to be found, perhaps, in all of them. Sometimes the figure is merely a critic, uninvolved, content to point out what other men do not see. At other times he seems to foreshadow the Superman, capable of changing the world, of whom Shaw liked to talk. Always he is possessed of supreme self-confidence. "What is the secret of your power?" the Lady of *The Man of Destiny* asks Napoleon:

> Only that you believe in yourself. You can fight and conquer for yourself and for nobody else. You are not afraid of your own destiny.[44]

Even Shaw's Joan, of whom it must rather be said that she does nothing for herself, least of all fight and conquer, and who believes not in any destiny of her own but only in what her voices direct her to do, has this confidence, this high courage, this immense personal force. As she has something also of the wit, the brilliance, and the intellectual passion of her creator, whose dramatic projection she partly is.

In more recent times a far more radical challenge to the traditional idea of the hero, or at least to some of its familiar forms, has of course appeared in the conception of the antihero, who takes many forms of his own. An interesting account of this peculiarly modern figure is offered by Maurice Merleau-Ponty, who maintains that he is distinct from such prototypes as Lucifer or Prometheus in being marked by an experience of confusion and failure that is an inescapable part of the modern condition. A more extended philosophical justification of him is to be found in the writings of Jean-Paul Sartre, who sees him, at least in the form of the intellectual, which is the form Sartre cares about, as doomed to failure from his very lucidity. By this Sartre means that because such a hero is necessarily conscious of himself, he is unable to lose himself in any commitment he makes to action. That is his tragedy, Sartre argues. Forced nevertheless to act by his moral sense, in doing so he merely reinforces his private ego. The more intensely he gives himself to others, the more completely he is alone. Fulfilled at last by his very inability to fulfill himself, he is finally made aware of his "impossible condition" when he suffers the realization that he cannot even suffer, that he must endure the ultimate anguish of not being able to feel pain.[45]

But these recent discussions of the heroic role, implying as they do a critique and a rejection of previous formulations, are as yet imperfectly absorbed—are perhaps not possible to absorb at all—into the long tradition that we have been considering. And whatever may ultimately be made of them, they have not so far been as influential, nor are they as widely known, as certain personifications of the type they undertake to define that appear in the work of still other contemporary writers—Samuel Beckett, for instance, and Albert Camus. Particularly has Camus, with his celebrated essay *The Myth of Sisyphus* and still more with his brief novel *The Stranger,* seemed to create the hero of his time. It is a long way from Achilles to Meursault or Sisyphus—too long, it may be argued, for any connecting line to stretch. But it may also say something about the strength of the heroic tradition we have discussed that at least in Camus's own view the doomed and lonely figures he conceived, unheroic as they may seem, represent no denial of heroic possibility but its contemporary affirmation.[46]

---

1 *On Heroes, Hero-Worship, and the Heroic in History* (London: Oxford University Press [World's Classics], 1946), p. 1.

2 *Les Caractères,* "Du mérite personnel."

3 *GBWW,* Vol. 2, p. 731.

4 *The Rambler,* no. 4.

5 Quoted in William James, *The Varieties of Religious Experience* (London: Longmans, Green & Co., 1908), p. 260.

6 Sonnet XVI; *GBWW,* Vol. 32, pp. 66–67.

7 *GBWW,* Vol. 21, p. 107.

8 *GBWW,* Vol. 32, p. 93.

9 *The Decline and Fall of the Roman Empire; GBWW,* Vol. 41, p. 598.

10 "On Reputation," from *The Art of Literature,* in *Complete Essays of Schopenhauer* (New York: Willey Book Co., 1942), bk. 4, p. 87.

11 Bk. 1, lines 105–9; *GBWW,* Vol. 32, p. 95.

12 Milton, *Samson Agonistes,* lines 1709–11; *GBWW,* Vol. 32, p. 377.

13 "Heroism," in *Essays, First Series.*

14 *GBWW,* Vol. 2, p. 252.

15 *The Principles of Psychology; GBWW,* Vol. 53, p. 826.

16 Virgil seems to have felt, however, that a world without heroes, though better in that respect than any previous world, would in every other way be a diminished thing. For if the heroic age, which he thought of as the age of the Greeks, had been self-destructive, it had also been brilliant. That Rome would have no such brilliance in its own right, but would be distinguished only for the stern arts of war and peace, is the melancholy purport of a famous passage of the *Aeneid* (6. 847–53; *GBWW,* Vol. 13, pp. 233–34) in which the Greek and Roman achievements are looked forward to prophetically and compared:

> *Others the breathing brass shall softlier mould,*
> *I doubt not, draw the lineaments of life*
> *From marble, at the bar plead better, trace*
> *With rod the courses of the sky, or tell*
> *The rise of stars: remember, Roman, thou,*
> *To rule the nations as their master: these*
> *Thine arts shall be, to engraft the law of peace,*
> *Forbear the conquered, and war down the proud.*

[17] See the discussion in the *Syntopicon* chapter on HISTORY, *GBWW*, Vol. 2, p. 717.

[18] "Great Men and Their Environment"; *GGB*, Vol. 7, p. 177.

[19] *Iliad* 11. 784. Cf. *GBWW*, Vol. 4, p. 80.

[20] *Lives*, "Coriolanus"; *GBWW*, Vol. 14, p. 175.

[21] *The Varieties of Religious Experience*, p. 364.

[22] *Odyssey* 11. 488–91. Cf. *GBWW*, Vol. 4, p. 247.

[23] *Iliad* 9. 318–19; trans. Richmond Lattimore (Chicago: University of Chicago Press, Phoenix Books, 1961), p. 206. Cf. *GBWW*, Vol. 4, p. 60.

[24] Ibid., 12. 322–28; Lattimore, pp. 266–67. Cf. *GBWW*, Vol. 4, p. 85.

[25] *Aeneid* 4. 364; *GBWW*, Vol. 13, p. 177.

[26] *Rhetoricae Libri Duo, sine de Inventione Rhetorica* 2. 53. There is a discussion of the same term in Aquinas, *Summa* 2–2, Q. 101.

[27] *Don Quixote*, pt. 1, chap. 13; *GBWW*, Vol. 29, p. 33.

[28] Ibid., pt. 2, chap. 8; *GBWW*, Vol. 29, p. 227.

[29] Ibid., pt. 2, chap. 8; *GBWW*, Vol. 29, p. 228.

[30] *Thoughts on War and Death; GBWW*, Vol. 54, pp. 761d, 765.

[31] Lines 119–30. Cf. *GBWW*, Vol. 5, p. 213.

[32] *Essays*, bk. 3, chap. 3; *GBWW*, Vol. 25, p. 391.

[33] Epistle IV, lines 219–22. Cf. Henry Fielding, *Jonathan Wild* (London: J. M. Dent & Sons, 1964), p. 176, "Greatness consists in power, pride, insolence, and doing mischief to mankind."

[34] *Phaedo; GBWW*, Vol. 7, p. 236.

[35] *The City of God*, bk. 5, chap. 13; *GBWW*, Vol. 18, p. 219.

[36] *King Henry V*, act 1, sc. 1; *GBWW*, Vol. 26, p. 533.

[37] *Antony and Cleopatra*, act. 5, sc. 2; *GBWW*, Vol. 27, p. 347.

[38] *Preface to Shakespeare; GGB*, Vol. 5, p. 319.

[39] *The Philosophy of Right*, "Additions" 58, Par. 93; *GBWW*, Vol. 46, p. 125.

[40] *GBWW*, Vol. 51, p. 563.

[41] Ibid., p. 647.

[42] *GGB*, Vol. 4, p. 317.

[43] Act 1; *Selected Plays of Bernard Shaw* (New York: Dodd, Mead & Co., 1948), 3:127.

[44] *GGB*, Vol. 4, p. 318.

[45] Cf. Victor Brombert, "Sartre: The Intellectual as 'Impossible' Hero," in Victor Brombert, ed., *The Hero in Literature* (Greenwich, Conn.: Fawcett Publications, 1969), pp. 239–65.

[46] Cf. Conor Cruise O'Brien, *Albert Camus of Europe and Africa*, in Modern Masters, ed. Frank Kermode (New York: Viking Press, 1970), pp. 31–34.

We Must Have Heroes

S. L. A. Marshall

Born in Catskill, New York, in 1900, Brigadier General S. L. A. Marshall began his military career early, becoming at eighteen the youngest American officer in World War I, when he fought with the AEF in France. After the war he became a newspaperman, working for various papers, notably the *Detroit News,* for which he was a military critic and editorial writer from 1927 to 1961, and which he served also as a correspondent in Latin America (1927–35) and Spain (1936–37). In 1942 he reentered military service as special consultant to Secretary of War Stimson, and was subsequently chief of orientation for the army before joining the newly formed Army Historical Division in 1943. As army historian he covered campaigns in both the Pacific and Europe, and at the end of the war was historian of the Armies of Occupation. He reentered military service in 1948 to prepare army staff studies for NATO, and later served as operations analyst for the Eighth Army in Korea. After further assignments in the Middle East and Africa he returned to the United States, where at his retirement in 1960 he was deputy chief of information for the army. Awarded numerous military and academic honors, among them a presidential citation, he is the author of some twenty-seven books and many technical articles, as well as of frequent reviews and comments on military affairs in newspapers and periodicals. General Marshall lives in Birmingham, Michigan.

An overextended, hand-to-hand experience with the making of heroes does not necessarily qualify one to dilate on the question: The Hero Image, indispensable or outmoded? But it does harden a view, and may narrow it. Having worked overlong the field where more legitimate heroes are made than any place else, I am not concerned about contemporary doubts that cause the question to be raised. The hero image will not be retired short of Utopia, which is some distance off.

I am convinced of this principally because I know there is nothing to replace that image. I see no prospect of an increase in man's humanity to man, should the time arrive when acts of supreme courage are no longer revered by society. Were life on this planet to degenerate until great risks for the good of others seemed no longer worth running, we would have a surrender to selfishness that would ultimately result in passive submission to tyranny.

So, reversing the usual order of things in a trial court, I start with my conclusion, then call to the stand my star witness, the late Justice Oliver Wendell Holmes. More and more as he aged, the Great Liberal loved to dwell upon the lessons he had learned under ordeal by fire. Some term this tendency a weakness in old soldiers.

Risking being called a militarist, Holmes spoke of war virtually as a therapy. At the Harvard commencement of 1895 he said: "Some teacher of the kind we all need. In this snug, over-safe corner of the world we need it, that we may realize that our comfortable routine is no eternal necessity of things, but merely a little space of calm in the midst of the tempestuous untamed streaming of the world, and in order that we may be ready for danger."

Then he moved to the essential point: "High and dangerous action teaches us to believe as right beyond dispute things for which our doubting minds are slow to find words of proof. Out of heroism grows faith in the worth of heroism."[1]

Other writers have gone even beyond this, of course. John Ruskin, artist and lover of peace, extolled war as the crucible for the proving of character. "The great justification of this game is that it truly, when well played, determines *who is the best man*—who is the highest bred, the most self-denying, the most fearless, the coolest of nerve, the swiftest of eye and hand. You cannot test these qualities wholly unless there is a clear possibility of the struggle's ending in death."[2]

That I call a little extreme, however. Monk Watson, a World War I hero, had been a New York gangster. The boldest flamethrower operator in the Pacific in World War II had been a derelict until battle reclaimed him. What I know from firsthand experience is that battle stress is felt less by some men, just as there are others who feel less pain from wounds. They are the fortunate, not the most heroic.

My thoughts are Holmesian. I agreed with these commencement words when I first read them. That was after my first go in battle. Many years and more battles later my beliefs are unchanged.

Unless courage is itself to be discouraged as no longer the chief virtue when coupled with honor, the need to raise up the hero image will not be less in the unforeseeable future than it was in those distant ages when mythology flowered that mortals might be inspired by examples of immortal courage.

In his will to endure, man has not measurably grown since his beginnings, though today his hunger for some little success that will lift him above the crowd must be greater than ever before. Lacking courage, he cannot make it. Denied a star to guide him, he must stumble in the dark. Were there no heroes, it would be necessary to invent some. And indeed, it is done every day by the media, as if they feel compelled to gratify some natural longing in mankind.

The Vietnam War being unpopular, its heroisms were largely ignored, though that was a phase, of passing significance only. The urge to honor the heroic did not diminish; there was merely a temporary shifting of standards. The vacuum being there, the synthetic hero, the lone adventurer, the minor nobleman, and even the small bureaucrat who purloined papers in the name of peacemaking were given more than due homage by press and public. Not to be placed in that category is the epic deed of the young British Columbian who recently married the girl he rescued when she was attacked by a grizzly. Although he might have held back from the encounter without being shamed as a coward, he fought off the bear with an eight-inch hunting knife. So doing, he lost one ear, one eye, and the whole of his scalp, besides breaking a wrist. But he won the Royal Humane Society's Stanhope Gold Medal, the Carnegie Medal for heroism, and—still more important—the girl.[3] What human does not feel pride in kinship with such a man? It would be the same heart that felt no shame on reading the mournful story of the young woman in New York who was torturously murdered while dozens of neighbors watched, making not one move to help her lest they get involved.

Finally, however, the pent-up emotions caused by public confusions over Vietnam created its own ironic aftermath. The popular hunger for military heroics did not die; it was simply dormant. The same people

357

who had stayed indifferent to the valorous acts of men in the fighting line made heroes en masse of the returned American POWs. It was a transfer of adulation without precedent in all military history.

True heroism essentially is a selfless act with a degree of ultimate risk. By definition, this excludes the athlete and the sportsman, the race driver, alpinist, poloist, and others who voluntarily risk life and limb when they participate, for thrill, fame, or fortune, taking the same gamble as the steeplejack and test pilot take to earn a living.

Risk-taking is not in itself heroic. The only way to avoid risk is to curl up and die. Moreover, we are where and what we are only because, through the centuries, some individuals have accepted nigh incalculable risk. I cannot conceive of civilization's making any advance without that spirit being present.

Paradoxically, however, the person who satisfies some urge to take risks, whether in the hope for glory or the easing of self-doubt, contributes directly to making a hero image. So does the adored professional athlete or the actor who, playing the hero role, is more likely to become lionized than is his real life prototype. Though it sounds like a contradiction, the authentic hero, the synthetic hero, and the stage hero have much in common. That is as elementary as is the fact that there would be no heroes if there were no one to sing them. An act may be intrinsically heroic yet not make a hero. He who perishes out of sight trying to save his friend has made a wasted sacrifice. By the same token, an act may be unheroic and still a hero may come of it. Recognition and acclamation are the essentials in image-making.

"Show me a hero," wrote F. Scott Fitzgerald, "and I will write you a tragedy."[4] He might more accurately and sensibly have said: "Show me a hero and I will still be from Missouri."

A few examples should illuminate these points. Start with Major Rowan. At the suggestion of his son, Elbert Hubbard elected Rowan as the no. 1 hero of the 1898 war with Spain, not for what he did but for how he set about it, a theme on which Hubbard so rhapsodized that the tale lives on to this day. What gripped Hubbard was that when President McKinley handed Rowan a message to be delivered to Garcia, Rowan went on his way without asking one question. That was not heroism. Rowan merely responded to an order in the manner prescribed for an officer, and being no fool, he did not seek to draw from his commander in chief answers that are only to be found at operating levels.[5]

In the small battle of Pork Chop Hill, Korea, April 1953, a shrunken garrison under 2d Lt. Joe Clemons beat off attacks by Chinese Communists for three days. The losses in dead and wounded were two-thirds of the defending force, whose heroism was monumental. The U.S. press missed it wholly. Being the only writer present during the battle, I wrote a book about the defense. The book was a commercial failure until Gregory Peck used two of its chapters as the scenario for a war movie still celebrated for its realism. Thus Pork Chop came to be bracketed with such famous stands by Americans as Bunker Hill, the Alamo, and Bastogne. Then who made the heroism of Pork Chop Hill legendary? Not Joe Clemons, nor this writer, but Gregory Peck.[6]

Recently, the front pages of metropolitan dailies and the voices of John Chancellor and Walter Cronkite acclaimed the heroism of Roberto Clemente. The great outfielder of the Pirates was always good sports copy. In death he was practically canonized by senior editors, and the Baseball Writers' Association set aside the rules and voted him into the Cooperstown Hall of Fame at once. Had he been killed in a car crash while on holiday or had an unknown Puerto Rican met death trying to help Nicaraguan earthquake victims, the event would have been little noted. But because Clemente was on a mercy mission when his plane failed, the diamond hero became superhero.

War has been my school and combat my major course. My experience with situations under fire spanned fifty years, extending from Soissons in July 1918 to the Delta, Vietnam, in June 1968. In that time I cited thirteen men for the Medal of Honor, of which number eleven were pinned with it. The count of soldiers I put up for the Distinguished Service Cross, the Silver Star, and lesser valor awards runs well into the hundreds.

Many of these men I came to know well. Remembering them, I am only amused when I hear it said that the hero type is thus-and-so. The novelist, the playwright, or possibly the psychiatrist might wish us to think this way. But as is said of good horses, legitimate combat heroes come in all shapes and sizes.

On the other hand, it may be said with some accuracy and fairness that individuals bent on winning regard as heroic figures have certain characteristics in common. The foremost is a drive for recognition, how this is gained being a lesser consideration. I think first of Douglas MacArthur and George S. Patton, Jr. Their early papers and much else make their aim quite clear. If there was anything the early Patton cared more about than proofs of his male fortitude, which he discussed in letters to his wife and her father, it was the decorations for which he pressed in official correspondence.[7] MacArthur at Veracruz cited himself for the Medal of Honor, narrating an action that no one else had witnessed. In Pershing's AEF, where he won several DSCs, it was invariably when he was the senior officer present.[8] To most serving officers, the winning of baubles in those circumstances is beneath dignity.

Patton had something that MacArthur lacked: an almost hypnotic sway over the military crowd. Tens of thousands of men believed they were lucky to be in his army rather than some other. Whether he was as superior as all that is irrelevant. His achievement was the quintessence of generalship. If the men believed it, they must have tried harder, and some died making the extra effort. To them he was indeed the heroic figure.

Ernest Hemingway was the literary counterpart of these men. More astonishing than his great courage and his penchant for risk-seeking was his parading of these qualities, his vainglory.[9] He wore his heart on his sleeve, or more accurately, he wore his complex. In bold company he would go out of his way to impress with his boldness, which was plain boring. Yet in spite of this, his friends loved him. To the end, he was still the adolescent, holding high for the camera a woodchuck, shot dead center.[10]

When we dwell on classical heroism, that of antiquity and mythology, the temptation is to get away from the nature of heroism itself—the exceptional readiness of the singular individual to dare greatly for the sake of someone else because no one else steps forward. Regarding that sort of man, I would have to say that since the time when our ancestors descended from the trees there has been no doing without him. He is identified in the Bible long before the birth of Christ. He had to be present during the Dark Ages, active in the Hundred Years' War and the Thirty Years' War. Things do not finally work together for good; mankind is not saved by some law in nature or because faith works miracles. So I speak of the uncommon courage of common men.

In April 1957, Walter Reed Army Institute of Research conducted a three-day symposium on preventive and social psychiatry. Present at the meeting were psychiatrists serving the armed forces. One speaker was Dr. James S. Tyhurst, the brilliant Canadian who had devoted a quarter century to studying the phenomena of natural disaster in the hemisphere —ravaging floods, holocausts, the explosion from which chain reaction shattered a community.

When Tyhurst spoke on that subject, I sat as critic on his lecture as he did later on mine, which was titled Combat Leadership. Perplexing him more than all else was the nature and motive of the faceless leader. In every great emergency he had analyzed, where constituted authority could not cope with the problem owing to its magnitude or to human frailty, there came out of the crowd four or five persons who took charge and organized the recovery amid danger. Their duty done, once the crisis had passed, these persons returned to the crowd and did not again figure in the forefront of activity. Their disappearance baffled him.[11]

Responding, I said that I saw no mystery. My experience with combat leadership ran parallel. At the breaking point in every company fight covered by my field notebooks (there are more than eight hundred), the situation was saved by the heroic action of two to five individuals previously inconspicuous and unmarked for promotion or citation. If they survived, and if the company was similarly endangered some days later, they again came to the fore. They could continue being repeaters until they died.

But they did not aspire to leadership or seek the role of hero. Out of an instinctive reflex, they moved in and took over because other men had failed, and they were equal to the task. Fear of death was not to them a deterrent, and a medal was not an esteemed prize. The very select company here described included a high count of reservation Indians, Mexicans, and European-born immigrants. They were not antisocial recluses or withdrawn individuals. They enjoyed military comradeship. None was an illiterate, most were in the middle I.Q. range, and only one could be properly described as a scholar.

What might have happened in the situations that Dr. Tyhurst and I described to the meeting had these individuals not been present is beyond speculation. The only reasonable assumption is that the stress would have been prolonged, the cost in life would probably have been higher, the social distress, disorder, and final damage would have been greater.

There is no profit in inquiring if any of these leaders who emerged was inspired by a hero image, though I learned at Pork Chop Hill that fifty-two of the seventy-three prime movers, decorated as such, felt that way about their fathers. What counts is that each in his own way became a hero to others. They were adored by the people closest to them. These people were heartened by their example and rallied around to find greater resources of strength within themselves. Such is the impact of the hero image at point-blank range.

What line of reasoning then may justify its devaluation?

I am well aware of the stentorian outcry against war. Far from being anything new in this world, it is more ancient than the Sphinx or Nineveh and Tyre. If I believed war could be exorcized by indignant noisemaking, I would join the clamor.

What may be new and in some degree different about the present round of discussion is the vehemence of the assertion that the ideals that make it possible for armed forces to hold fast when life is at stake are to be discounted herewith and hereafter. For these are the same ideals that make possible a congenial living together, which is peace. Hence when I regard some of the people who preach against war nowadays, I am reminded of a descriptive passage from Edmund Burke:

"The slightest severity of justice made their flesh creep. The very idea that war existed in the world disturbed their repose. Military glory was no more, with them, than a splendid infamy. Hardly would they hear of self-defence, which they reduced within such bounds, as to leave it no defence at all." [12]

Unthinking pacifism is no more courageous or heroic than is outright militarism. The patience to carry on, holding the head high, is the prerequisite to progress. As C. F. Smith said: "You can pursue the ideal of peace, that is, until there's nothing left but apathy—and then, on the rebound of appeasement, have nothing left but war."[13]

To say that we should have learned better may be to imply that someday we can and will learn not to fight. Fair enough. But not knowing how much time is allowed us for learning, we need heroes no less and hero images the more.

[1] *The Mind and Faith of Justice Holmes,* ed. Max Lerner (New York: Modern Library, 1954), pp. 18, 23.

[2] *The Crown of Wild Olive* in *The Works of John Ruskin,* eds. E. T. Cook and Alexander Wedderburn (London: George Allen, 1905), p. 470.

[3] The Associated Press file, Dec. 15, 1972.

[4] *The Crack-Up* (New York: New Directions, 1945).

[5] *A Message to Garcia* (East Aurora, N.Y.: The Roycrofters, 1917).

[6] *Pork Chop Hill* (New York: Wm. Morrow & Co., 1956).

[7] Martin Blumenson, *The Patton Papers, 1885–1940* (Boston: Houghton Mifflin Co., 1972).

[8] D. C. James, *The Years of MacArthur* (Boston: Houghton Mifflin Co., 1970).

[9] *Why Man Takes Chances,* ed. S. Z. Klausner (Garden City, N.Y.: Doubleday & Co., Anchor Books, 1968).

[10] M. H. Sanford, *At the Hemingways: A Family Portrait* (Boston: Little, Brown & Co., Atlantic Monthly Press, 1962).

[11] *Symposium on Preventive and Social Psychiatry* (Washington, D.C.: U.S. Government Printing Office, 1958).

[12] *A Letter to a Noble Lord,* ed. Albert H. Smyth (Boston: Ginn & Co., The Athæneum Press, 1898), p. 41.

[13] T. V. Smith, *Live without Fear* (New York: Signet Key, 1958), p. 18.

No More Heroes

Ron Dorfman

Ron Dorfman is editor of the *Chicago Journalism Review* and president of the Association of Working Press.

A native of Philadelphia, Mr. Dorfman was graduated in 1963 from the University of Chicago, where he was active in movements for civil rights and university reform, and was an editor of the quarterly *New University Thought,* a progenitor of much of the New Left political thinking of the 1960s. Upon graduation, he became editor of the *Mine-Mill Union,* the organ of the International Union of Mine, Mill and Smelter Workers, in Denver, Colorado. Returning to Chicago the following year, he became a reporter and deskman for the City News Bureau of Chicago and in 1966 joined the staff of *Chicago's American* (now *Chicago Today*). Mr. Dorfman was a professional journalism fellow at Stanford University in 1968 and again returned to Chicago to cover the Democratic National Convention, after which he participated in the founding of the *Chicago Journalism Review.* He lectures widely on journalism before professional and lay audiences and is considered a leader and spokesman of the movement for institutional democracy in news organizations. He has served as a consultant to many media organizations and groups dealing with the media.

Society requires for its internal stability—that is to say, for the preservation of its hierarchical arrangements and the myths that shore them up—a continuing supply of external menaces and the motivation to cope with them. Hence it fights wars, and in fighting wars it creates heroes—or it used to. The system thrives only as it is celebrated, and that requires minstrels willing to compose songs of glory. Without music, the myth fails. When Homer is David Halberstam, Agamemnon becomes General Westmoreland—not a hero, but a bureaucrat. Plato knew what he was doing when he excluded from the *Republic* any poet who told human truths about the gods.

I hold that a free society has neither room for nor need of heroism, because the heroic ideal is rooted in a soil of moral and ideological absolutism, and flowers in an atmosphere of xenophobic ignorance and cruelty. Of course, this is not how acts committed in its name are justified. As John of Salisbury once wrote:

> *But what is the office of the duly ordained soldiery? ... The high praises of God are in their throat, and two-edged swords are in their hands to execute punishment on the nations and rebuke upon the peoples, and to bind their kings in chains and their nobles in links of iron. But to what end? To the end that they may serve madness, vanity, avarice, or their own private self-will? By no means. Rather to the end that they may execute the judgment that is committed to them to execute; wherein each follows not his own will but the deliberate decision of God, the angels, and men, in accordance with equity and the public utility. ... For soldiers that do these things are "saints," and are the more loyal to their prince in proportion as they more zealously keep the faith of God; and they advance the more successfully the honor of their own valor as they seek the more faithfully in all things the glory of their God.*[1]

God, it may be presumed, conveys his decisions to the bishop's office (no madness, vanity, or avarice there!), which in turn relays them to the prince for implementation. It is but a short step to the Crusades.

In his novel *Grendel,* which is based upon the medieval tale of *Beowulf,* John Gardner places a character called the Shaper, who turns up one

364

night in the meadhall of King Hrothgar. The Shaper, who is blind, carries a harp, on which he begins to play:

> *As if all by itself, then, the harp made a curious run of sounds, almost words, and then a moment later, arresting as a voice from a hollow tree, the harper began to chant:*
>   Lo, we have heard the honor of the Speardanes,
>   nation-kings, in days now gone,
>   how those battle-lords brought themselves glory. . . .
> *He knew his art. He was king of the Shapers, harpstring scratchers (oakmoss-bearded, inspired by winds). . . . He would sing the glory of Hrothgar's line and gild his wisdom and stir up his men to more daring deeds, for a price.*[2]

The monster Grendel knows the history of the world, knows the Shaper's tale is a lie. But who among the thanes can resist the thought of himself being someday sung of in such a manner? And so the hero Unferth seeks out Grendel in his cave beyond the lake of the fire snakes, where at last, exhausted from his pursuit, he collapses on the floor before the creature by whose hand he expects, quite mistakenly, to die.

> *"It will be sung year on year and age on age that Unferth went down through the burning lake—" he paused to pant "—and gave his life in battle with the world-rim monster." He let his cheek fall to the floor and lay panting for a long time. . . .*
> *"Go ahead, scoff," he said, petulant. "Except in the life of a hero, the whole world's meaningless. The hero sees values beyond what's possible. That's the nature of a hero. It kills him, of course, ultimately. But it makes the whole struggle of humanity worthwhile."*
> *[Grendel] nodded in the darkness. "And breaks up the boredom," [he] said.*[3]

Unferth's speech may be read as a morbid parody of our most recent, and perhaps our last, hero. "Great crises produce great men," John Kennedy wrote as a young man—and proceeded, when he had the power, to produce the crises that would, in the management of them, lend credence to his and the nation's determination to "pay any price, bear any burden" in defending the ramparts of liberty.

The American press played the Shaper to Kennedy's Hrothgar. The president's very language rang with echoes of an epic age, great rolling periods expressing the loftiest motives and the grandest designs. Kennedy wanted to "go forward," wherever that was: the journalists, who enjoyed under Kennedy a proximity to power previously unknown in Washington, thought it would be a good direction, after the aimlessness of the Eisenhower years.

Henry Fairlie, in *The Kennedy Promise: The Politics of Expectation,* expresses bewilderment at the journalists who allowed—indeed, who encouraged—the president and his courtiers to use them as heralds and troubadours. There was Benjamin Bradlee, now executive editor of the *Washington Post,* who fell "flat on his face before this one politician, and before no other," Fairlie says,[4] and "even as careful a reporter as Hugh Sidey"

> . . . *could write of "an awesome presence in that Oval Chamber which was then quiet, cool, sunlit," just as he said of the televised press conferences that they showed "the worried face of a young man with an amusing accent trying desperately to do a job which anybody could tell you was impossible, beyond the bounds of human capacity." It will appear to be beyond the bounds of human capacity only if one expects of politics, not the modest arrangements which are their proper concern, but a superhuman achievement, an inhuman fulfilment.*[5]

Those were the heroic terms on which Kennedy—with the help of the press—defined his task. But it is one thing for a hero to go out with lance and shield and risk his own life for honor, or even the lives of a few vassal heroes who play the same game. It is quite another matter when the hero is armed with atom bombs. They are dangerous men, these heroes, for one never knows what voices they hear, or how "the deliberate decision of God" will be made known to them. It may be that in the modern world the voice of the people is the voice of God, but it is also the case that, for all practical purposes between quadrennial Novembers, the people speak only through their elected leaders.

It is important that our journalists note well and long remember the lessons of the decade that is just past. True, President Nixon clearly and explicitly desires the press to return to its previous role as celebrant of the civil order and protector of the official mythology. But the press has tasted of forbidden fruit.

It has reported from an enemy capital in wartime (Harrison Salisbury, of the *New York Times,* in Hanoi). It has revealed the government's own inner doubts and ambiguities about the war even while that same government publicly preached a bellicose patriotism and sent fifty thousand young men to their deaths (the Pentagon Papers). It has helped to force one president into retirement, and to make politically necessary the withdrawal from Vietnam that another president claims as his own inspiration.

That is heady stuff for an institution that a decade ago sang of Camelot and the new frontiers of freedom. One can only hope that our journalists will continue to live in sinful curiosity, that they will have done with the inflated rhetoric of heroes and the choplogic of the notion that because men *can* be stirred to battle for ideals, they *ought* to be so stirred at every opportunity.

As this is written, the word *hero* appears with increasing frequency in the popular press. It is used to describe the returning prisoners of war. But the term is strangely applied to these men except as it may serve to acknowledge the ordeal of their imprisonment. For almost all of them are field-grade officers who as highly trained professionals, skilled in the operation of complex technical systems, were remote from their antagonists until shot down on bombing runs, and never fought on the naked terms that heroism, as traditionally understood, would seem to require. On the other hand, those who did fight on such terms—the grunts, as they were called, who slogged their way through the jungles of Vietnam under conditions of constant danger and hardship—have returned to another sort of welcome from their countrymen, who regard them with indifference if not outright hostility. It would thus appear that the POWs are heroes not so much because of anything they did as from the fact that many people have an emotional investment in them, and because the government thinks it has a stake in preserving the myth of war's nobility.

Whatever sympathy one may feel for the POWs, was there not a disquieting contrivance in their carefully staged return, wrapped in the flag and a public relations cocoon, their "freely elected" spokesmen (always the senior officer aboard the flight) repeating a litany of thanksgiving to God, country, and commander in chief, their subsequent statements indicating their belief that the press's reporting from Hanoi prolonged their captivity by boosting the enemy's morale?

United Press International has ceased to use the word *enemy* in reference to those with whom the United States is at war. UPI Editor H. L. Stevenson has explained that "the dispatches of an international news agency go to news media in many countries that are uninvolved . . . and 'enemy' would clearly be objectionable to them." He might have added that it is also objectionable to many in this country who opposed its involvement in Vietnam. If "objective journalism" means anything, it means being able to transcend nationalistic visions, through an attitude that is not unpatriotic but nonpatriotic. The journalist's job is to provide information, not inspiration, which will come if it must from the people's own experience of their institutions and leaders.

---

1 *Policraticus*, in *Medieval Reader*, ed. James Bruce Ross and Mary Martin McLaughlin (New York: Viking Press, 1949), p. 90.
2 *Grendel* (New York: Alfred A. Knopf, 1971), pp. 41–42.
3 Ibid., pp. 87–89.
4 *The Kennedy Promise: The Politics of Expectation* (Garden City, N.Y.: Doubleday & Co., 1973), p. 218.
5 Ibid., p. 220.

Heroism and Fortitude

Josef Pieper

Josef Pieper, who is among the most respected and widely read philosophers of the present day, was born near Münster, Germany, in 1904. He studied philosophy, jurisprudence, and sociology at the University of Münster and also at Berlin. In the course of his career he has at various times worked as an assistant at a sociological research institute and has been a free-lance writer. Since 1946 he has been on the faculty of the University of Münster, where at present he is professor of philosophical anthropology. He has spent considerable time in the United States, having served as visiting professor at Notre Dame (1950) and Stanford (1956 and 1962), and has taught also in India and Japan. In 1967 he was appointed centennial professor at the University of Toronto, Canada, and in 1968 he received the Aquinas Medal of the Philosophers' Congress held in New Orleans.

   Of Professor Pieper's voluminous writings, a number are available in English, among them *The Four Cardinal Virtues: Prudence, Justice, Fortitude, Temperance* (1965); an essay on Plato's *Phaedrus* called *Enthusiasm and Divine Madness* (1964); *A Guide to Thomas Aquinas* (1962); and, what is perhaps his best-known work, *Leisure, the Basis of Culture* (1963). These and other books by Professor Pieper have to date been translated into twelve languages and have sold more than a million copies.

I

C an the "hero" be conceived as the principal figure of a great modern novel or a drama? Is "heroism" to be found in the real life of contemporary society? The first of these questions might be answered immediately with a spontaneous "no." Obviously the age of the heroic epic is a thing of the past. Yet we observe that the popular literature of our time abounds in heroes of adventure, is full of hero worship. Even in works produced under totalitarian regimes, glorification of the worker-hero is as evident as the "cult of personality" that supports the political leader. At the same time, we should recall that some of the great poetic works of the past, which we may have regarded as fundamentally simple in their portrayal of the heroic type, are actually sophisticated and multifaceted in this respect—as Schiller, for one, acknowledged when he observed, in connection with the *Iliad*, that after all it is Patroclus who lies buried and Thersites who returns. And those who in my opinion are the finest modern writers remain greatly interested in heroism, even where they appear, like Virgil, Calderón, and Cervantes before them, to reject it. Perhaps the modern difference is only that we realize a little better than past ages seem to have done how hidden, how endangered, how close to caricature true heroism is, and how easily it can be misconstrued.

II

The second question, whether heroism is to be found at the present time in real life, requires us to suppose that we know what "true" heroism is. And if we conceive of this mainly or exclusively as exceptional ability, developed through extraordinary effort in any sphere—football, boxing, scientific experimentation, or landing on the moon—or, similarly, if we demand of the "hero" exceptional success, the brilliant fortune of the general, the surgeon, and the politician that captures the popular imagination, then we are saying that the hero is nowadays as much alive as he ever was—for heroism in this sense is not less evident in the contemporary world than it was in previous epochs. But what if we conceive it otherwise? What if we recognize and accept the fact that the essence of true heroism is the virtue of fortitude—that it is through this virtue, indeed, that the "hero" differs from the average man? Because if we do this, we

369

shall have to acknowledge that fortitude cannot be described except through a multitude of ostensibly (or perhaps seemingly) contradictory characteristics. And if we concede that this is so, we shall understand better than we are otherwise likely to do how it is that the image of the hero in the great works of world literature (which is based to a large extent upon the idea of fortitude), far from being as simple as our notion of the "true" hero of real life, is instead bewilderingly ambiguous.

Fortitude is one of the four cardinal virtues; the others are prudence, justice, and temperance. For more than two thousand years these virtues have been looked upon, in the tradition of Western thought, as a kind of four-color spectrum in which the concept of the "good" person fans out. In the formulation of this spectrum, all the original forces of the Occident—the Greeks and the Romans, Judaism and Christianity—participated. This explains why the concepts of "prudence," "justice," and "temperance" are also complex for us, and even contradictory in their elements, quite as much as "fortitude" is, which came into being in the same manner.

III

The concept of fortitude will be misunderstood if the world-view that underlies it is not clearly comprehended. The German author Bertolt Brecht says: "When I hear that a ship needs heroes for sailors, I ask whether the ship is not too old or moldering away." In his opinion there is something rotten about a state that forces the average man always to be brave. "The world—an abode for heroes: where do we come in then?!" A similar idea appears (as Brecht would not have suspected) fifteen hundred years earlier in the writings of Saint Augustine. Fortitude, Augustine says in *The City of God,** is a testimony to the existence of evil —by which he means that fortitude is necessary because, in the world, evil is powerful, is even at times a superior force. In view of this, to be brave can be taken to mean that something must be risked whenever the obviously weak offers resistance to evil. And nobody who wishes to be a good human being, and who is unwilling to commit an injustice, can avoid this risk.

Christianity has always been convinced that something really is, as Brecht remarks, rotten in the world. This is not, of course, the same thing as saying that the world is absurd—an existentialist thesis which may seem even more terrible, though curiously enough it causes contemporary man few difficulties. No, here it is stated: the world, along with existence itself, has lost the primordial order; but, like existence, it still remains capable of good and is directed toward it. At the same time, the good is not realized by itself, but requires for that end the effort of an individual who is willing to struggle and if necessary to sacrifice on its behalf. It is simply a liberalistic illusion to believe that one can be consistently just, for example, without having to risk something for it. That is why fortitude is necessary. What is risked, if the occasion arises, may be something less than life itself. It may instead be a question of immediate well-being, of daily tranquillity, possessions, honor, or face-saving. On the other hand, what is required may be the surrender of life, or more exactly, the acceptance of death at another's hands. The martyr is the ultimate symbol of fortitude.

In these terms, of course, fortitude is both a virtue fundamentally required of everyone and the essence of "heroism." And if that is so, then "heroism" is viable in every age, today no less than in the time of Homer or in that of the *Song of the Nibelungs*. But it is not for this reason a quality that is easily identifiable, and it obviously cannot be represented adequately in the unproblematic, radiant figure of the "hero."

IV

Fortitude is not an absolute ideal, nor is it even foremost among the cardinal virtues. Its realization is linked to several requirements. A brief adage of Saint Ambrose states: "Fortitude must not trust itself." It matters little that we "live *dangerously*," according to Nietzsche's maxim, but rather that we lead a "good" life. For this the virtue of prudence is the first necessity. That is to say, we must be able to recognize the elements of life as they really are and to translate this recognition into resolution and action. Otherwise, because the fearful is encountered as a stark reality in the world, we may be fearless in a manner that should not be confused with true fortitude—as, for example, when we make a false evaluation of danger, or when we are reckless from an inability to love anything or anyone ("Fear is fleeing love," says Saint Augustine). Sigmund Freud's assertion that most heroism stems from an instinctive conviction that "Nothing can happen to *me*" is true in a sense that possibly he did not perceive—the deep sense in which it is seen that for one who loves good, death cannot be entirely evil (as Socrates, along with Saint Paul, realized and affirmed).

Another requirement of true fortitude is justice. The fortitude of a criminal is a misconception; there are no criminal heroes. Our generation is aware that the fruits of fortitude can be corrupted by injustice, chiefly by the injustice of political power. We have come to know firsthand the truth of the old adage: "The praise of fortitude is contingent upon justice." When I used this in the second year of National Socialist tyranny (1934) as the motto of my short book, *On the Meaning of Fortitude,* my friends immediately recognized its dangerous implications; and these were probably noticed as well by others who were less kindly disposed toward me.

---

* *GBWW*, Vol. 18, pp. 129–618.

V

It has been said that the hero is a figure whose proper element is war. And it is precisely on this point that the complexity of the relationship between heroism and fortitude comes to the fore most dramatically. On the one hand, there may be agreement that fortitude presupposes the conflict of hostile forces; it manifests itself in combat, though *combat* does not necessarily mean *war*. Even where it does mean war, it does not necessarily mean enthusiastic war. There is a statement by Thomas Aquinas, as there is one by Aristotle, to the effect that perhaps the better soldiers are those who are less brave. Here the word *perhaps* is to be underlined, for it is bravery and aggressiveness that distinguish the born soldier. But that is something different. The surrender of one's life, which can be demanded of a soldier in the just defense of the community, can scarcely be expected without the moral virtue of fortitude.

On the other hand, we are more apt to perceive and honor the hero in the figure of conqueror than in one who merely suffers. And since fortitude means precisely to endure "wounds" incurred on behalf of justice (from loss of reputation or well-being to imprisonment or bodily harm), we are really looking, when we contemplate someone who has manifested this virtue, at the antithesis of the "conqueror." Such a person does not vanquish, he sacrifices. In the ultimate test of fortitude, which is martyrdom, there is absolutely nothing of the victorious, though this characteristic is essential to our more usual conception of the hero as conqueror. Nor is there any supposition that fortitude or heroism will be spoken of in true cases of martyrdom. If such things are discussed, it is almost a sure sign that no instance of genuine fortitude has occurred. When it comes to a pornographic novel, which may be hailed as "daring" or "bold," the author in reality risks nothing. Far more courage and perhaps genuine fortitude is required to call such a product repugnant, or to say in public that purity is a fundamental element of human dignity. Talk of the "martyr" always occurs *post festum*. In the act of fortitude itself, such a person does not appear to be a martyr but is rather the accused, the prisoner, the crank, or the lone wolf, abandoned and ridiculed; above all, he proves himself to be a mute. Perhaps doubt even penetrates his own heart, so that fortitude itself may be in question, leaving him to speculate whether he is really *der Dumme* (the "dumb" one) in the end.

Thus fortitude is, according to its very nature, *not* the virtue of the stronger but instead that of the seemingly vanquished. Accordingly, it can almost be said that we are dealing with a falsehood in the prevailing notion of the "hero," which veils and perverts the essential qualities of genuine fortitude. It should be remembered that in the eyes of the ancients the decisive criterion for fortitude consisted primarily in steadfastness and not in attacking.

372

To be sure, the coin must be turned over again so that its reverse side is displayed. The reverse side is that this mortal steadfastness of the martyr has always been *understood* as a victory and celebrated as such, not only from the Christian standpoint but also from that of Plato's Socrates. "We conquer while we are being slain," wrote Tertullian. Who was ultimately the victor: the boasting commandant of Auschwitz or the Polish Franciscan father Maximilian Kolbe, who, in order to save a fellow man, went into the starvation bunker and perished miserably there? In spite of everything the martyr is truly a "hero," and so is every unimposing or unknown individual who risks his life for the sake of truth and good, whether in the pointedly dramatic act of martyrdom or in lifelong devotion—in acquiescence to the absolute will of God at the cost of one's own worldly comfort. The great Santa Teresa of Ávila writes in her autobiography that an imperfect human being needs greater fortitude to travel the path of perfection than to take martyrdom upon himself in a brief moment. Perhaps this statement, based upon life experience, renders a little more plausible the term *heroic* virtue, which is the signum of a hallowed life in the Christian tradition.

VI

From time immemorial, heroism has been looked upon as inseparable from honor and glory; the hero is, by the same token, always the celebrated, the one distinguished by universal acclaim. It is not customary to reduce this stature even if he seeks self-recognition and accomplishes his deeds for that reason. Strangely enough, the great teachers of Christianity have regarded the virtue of fortitude in much the same way, designating as one of its fundamental elements *magnanimitas,* which seeks high honor above all else and makes itself worthy of such. Is this in keeping with the conception of that virtue, the highest act of which is supposed to be martyrdom before the triumphant force of evil? It is consistent with that conception under *one* condition, namely, that one is capable of realizing the idea of *gloria,* which the ancients defined as *clara cum laude notitia* and by which they meant the state of "becoming acknowledged publicly," the attainment of recognition through God himself. This also means the infallibly true sanction by the Sovereign of the world who, in the presence of the whole of creation, at once declares and effectuates that it is "glorious" to be what one is.

I fear that whoever, for whatever reason, is incapable of accepting this dimension of reality—the life beyond death—will have to be on his guard against the danger of being fascinated by a pseudo-hero borne on the acclaim of the entire world. From the time of John at Patmos to that of Wladimir Solowjew, Christendom has held a certain idea about the end of the world. This idea implies that in the final age we must be prepared for a figure who, though the ultimate personification of evil, will be a hero of a bewitching splendor hitherto unknown to all of mankind: the Antichrist. His almost irresistible allure and universal fame will overshadow all other false heroes of history, while his global tyranny will force true fortitude into the most merciless of trials. It will further render totally unrecognizable this fortitude, the essence of all genuine heroism—the virtue of martyrs.

*   *   *   *   *

I cannot see why this conception of heroism, both the true and the false, should lose even an iota of viability in the present age or in the future.

Heroes in Black and White

Joy Gould Boyum

Joy Gould Boyum is professor of English education at New York
University. Born in New York City in 1934, she graduated from Barnard
College in 1955 (with a year at the University of Michigan and a summer at
Harvard) and took her M.A. (1957) and her Ph.D. (1962) from New York
University. Her chief professional interest is teacher education, and her
current course offerings include one intended primarily for teachers of
secondary schools in which she undertakes to contrast films and the literary
sources from which they are drawn. Besides a weekly column "On Film"
for the *Wall Street Journal,* she has published articles on film, literature, and
television for professional journals, and she contributed the article on
motion pictures for the 1973 *World Book Year Book.* She is coauthor, with
Adrienne Scott, of a text, *Film as Film: Critical Responses to Film Art* (1971).
Married in 1960 to Asmund Boyum, she has two children, David and Ingrid.

To say that it is no longer possible to believe in the great man, the man distinguished by his special excellence—in, that is, the traditional hero of literature, legend, and history—may be only to admit, somewhat regretfully, to our cultural age. Heroes, we can suppose, are the stuff that youth is made of, and the passing of youth is painful to contemplate, perhaps especially so in our time. It is not surprising that we are unhappy at the thought, if the thought is one we happen to have, that as a society we have grown up, are now skeptical of ideals, and certainly of the heroic ideal, in the manner of those who have reached their middle years.

Of course, a peculiar set of historical circumstances has hastened what seems to have been an aging process over the course of the century in which we live. Within thirty years of each other two devastating wars have occurred, producing disillusionment and a crisis in values. Particularly has this been so with respect to the heroes, statesmen as well as soldiers, whose reputations were created by those conflicts and then were forgotten or brought down. Many of the great names of the first World War had become pathetic or villainous, so far as they were remembered at all, when the second one began, and in the interval since that one ended grave doubts have been expressed as to the integrity and even the competence of many of its own leaders—doubts that have made it hard to look on any of the contemporary forms of human greatness without distrust.

On top of this has come the exponential growth in this century of science and technology. The paradox of such growth is that while it seems to affirm the largest dreams of human achievement, at the same time it has worked to reduce human stature. Earlier, the comprehensive structure of biology had brought man down from something created in the image of God to a place among the animals. Then physics and astronomy reduced him to a speck in the vastness of the universe. Still later, instructed in psychology, he came to doubt his moral being. Now, caught as he is in the great web of the electronic media, his freedom seems impossible, a distrust of himself and all his institutions almost imperative. For our technology has succeeded in democratizing *angst*, once the special privilege of artists and thinkers. Television, film, and radio, processing the cultural materials of the past and present, making palatable for mass consumption great art and great ideas, have informed the self-satisfied *homme moyen* of what the *élite* had thought it alone was able to perceive: that the human condition is absurd, that man is alienated and miserable. Popularizing contemporary philosophy and literature, the mass media have made "hope" and "meaning" seem naïve terms; domesticating war they have made "courage" and "glory" seem incredible fictions; peddling statesmen, and marketing politics, they have made "honor" and "dignity" into sick jokes. And if the greatness of man has come to seem an illusion, how can there be great men? In our time the star system seems finished, both in the movies and in real life.

It may seem frivolous to mention the movies in connection with "the great ideas today," but movies can in fact tell us a good deal about the status of ideas in our culture. For even in their economic decline, movies remain both our most popular art form and our most telling social barometer. We are, after all, the media's children, and movies depend for their life on their sensitivity to our values and attitudes. Looking for immediate returns on their very large investments, needing popularity and committed to what is topical, they will rarely risk exploring truly innovative ideas. Movies tend, instead, to adopt attitudes in the public mind that have already been put to the test of acceptability. Movies will, of course, widen the audience for whatever viewpoint they express, which they emphasize and perhaps even clarify, but it is the proven idea they are after, just as much as they seek the proven property.

Thus, in the period of the two great wars, and in the century's youth and Hollywood's own, the movies overwhelmed us with heroic men and heroic actions. And the range of the special skills dramatized for us was extraordinary. On a single Saturday afternoon, we could see one man test his valor and strength in a struggle with a crocodile while another proved his superior mettle merely through ratiocination. The following week we might encounter the mighty modern warrior, outnumbered but steadfast on his lonely Pacific isle, and featured with him the man of faith whose wisdom and patience brought straying humans back to the straight and narrow. But our most pervasive fictional heroes at that time were our American knights errant, lone and courageous creatures righting wrongs in crowded metropolises and in wide open spaces: the private eye and the gunfighter. If today the hero no longer persists in these particular guises, that is sign enough, for a good many of us, that the heroic ideal has vanished.

True, we seem unable to let go of it completely. If that had happened, films would simply ignore the traditional hero—as some of them do anyway, having gone the way of modern literature, often by borrowing from it. Such films of the late sixties and early seventies as *M*A*S*H, Carnal Knowledge,* and *A Clockwork Orange* offer us that by now familiar anti-heroic type, the victim, in his various guises: the schlemiel, the delinquent, the disaffiliate, the self-destroyer. But for the most part, and in those genres most deeply committed in the past to the portrayal of heroic action, the traditional hero has remained with us—if only to the end of being unmasked. This is indeed the chief intent of westerns in the new style, sometimes (and not insignificantly) called "adult." These films take a representative figure, quite frequently a historical hero who has often been pictured in films (Wyatt Earp, for instance, or Doc Holliday, or General Custer), and then pierce through his myth to what purports to be reality. Once in this real world, we find the formerly heroic figure's motivations to be impure, his skill ordinary, his morality ambiguous. But we do not debunk with unalloyed delight. Such realism is somehow deeply unwelcome, as John Huston, for one, has recognized with his current film, *The Life and Times of Judge Roy Bean.* "West of the Pecos, there was no law, no order," a title reads at the outset of this comic tall tale. "Maybe that isn't the way it was, but the way it should have been." In putting it that way, we are affirming our lost dreams, lamenting our lost youth, in which heroes had a place.

Our attitude reveals itself in many recent works, among them Sam Peckinpah's much revered *The Wild Bunch,* a 1969 release that can serve us well as an example of the new-style western and of its ambiguous view of the hero. From one angle of vision, we can say the film has no heroes, only protagonists—specifically, a gang of outlaws. And they are not outlaws of any familiar breed: not rebels against their fate or badmen who will either reform or give up their lives with generosity to pay for past sins. They lack moral necessity of any kind, just as they lack relevance. The time is 1913, and while these men ride on horseback, other men are driving automobiles. Most significantly, they are all middle-aged, aware of their mortality and their lack of purpose. They are weathered and weary Sisyphuses, tied to a boulder of violence. And partly because there is no moral center anywhere in their world, neither in the bounty hunters who pursue them, nor in the Mexican rebels who hire them, nor in the townspeople slaughtered by their crossfire (the film has begun with a sequence where we see a group of children take delight in watching ants devour a scorpion), our sympathies go out to them. We bemoan with them the passing of time that has drained their energy and carried away opportunities for heroic action. At one point in the film the gang's leader (a very paunchy William Holden, whom we remember in the youthful image of a very golden boy) cannot quite make it up on his horse, and our bones ache with his.

Perhaps even more direct in its exposure of the heroic ideal and its simultaneous romantic yearnings is another western released in 1969, George Roy Hill's highly successful *Butch Cassidy and the Sundance Kid.* Again, the setting is the turn of the century; again, the protagonists are outlaws of dubious morality; again, they are out-of-date; and again, they engage our sympathies largely because of their obsolescence. But this time the protagonists are younger men in fact and very much younger in fantasy. They play, and charmingly, on bicycles, in their bedrooms, and of course at the game of banditry. But it is the harmful fun of men who won't put away childish things, and because these two are no more skillful and no more brave than other men, they are bound sooner or later to be losers. And they know it, too, being self-conscious to the point where they recognize their own value as emblems of roguish youth. One day they enter a movie theater, and we watch with them a film within a film where facsimiles of themselves are shown upon the screen. *There* is the heroic myth in all its glorious danger; here in the audience is safe, mundane reality. With *Butch Cassidy and the Sundance Kid* we find ourselves in the ironic mode, where ideals and heroic actions generally have little place.

This is the mode, of course, of James Bond, who in our politicized, international age is appropriately the private eye *cum* secret agent, saving the entire Western world rather than mere damsels in distress, and who in his enormous popularity tells us all we need to know about current attitudes toward this variety of hero. A conscious ironist, Bond never really demands that we suspend our disbelief before his astounding feats and larger-than-life adversaries. Instead, he presents himself to us as a mock hero, a superhuman blend of the exquisite taste and stunning intelligence of a Sherlock Holmes with the supercharged sexiness and raw physical toughness of a Sam Spade. But Bond's creators are aware that we are unwilling skeptics and provide him with sufficient glamor so that he is never completely comic, with sufficient danger so that his actions are never totally trivial. With Bond, in other words, we enjoy the pleasures of the double vision. We can have our hero, and dismiss him, too.

Such contradictory impulses pervade our attitudes toward the hero. Still, there seem to be some among us who hold more tenaciously than others to faith in the heroic ideal: the implied audiences for that new genre, the black movie, and especially its subgenres, the black western and the black crime melodrama. Although such representative films as *The Legend of Nigger Charley* and *Shaft* are marked by a tongue-in-cheek quality, they do present us with unambiguously heroic types, men superior to other men in their physical prowess and often in their moral fiber as well. Their scales tipped on the side of belief in this figure, these films have only such irony as can be directed at the hero's environment, not the kind that points at the hero himself. His world may be undependable, his opponents may invite our laughter, he may have a sidekick for comic relief, but the hero in his superstrength is reminiscent of the heroes of our youth.

And yet the black hero is different, too, from the heroic type of which he reminds us. As a black gunfighter, Nigger Charley has a more clearly defined social identity than, say, the Lone Ranger, and a less patronizing attitude toward the people he serves. The old-style hero of a thousand westerns was a man who stood outside society, a man without class or rank. Perhaps this was American democracy's way of embodying the aristocratic spirit that lay in the European background of the heroic tradition. In any case, the hero of the old western was never one with those he served. The black hero, on the contrary, stands strongly rooted in a particular milieu, where he has been brutally victimized before rising to heroic stature. His daring deeds thus inevitably affect his own well-being and not merely (as in the case of the Lone Ranger) the fortunes of those he rescues. Nigger Charley is at the outset of his story a slave, driven to rebellion and superhuman feats by the cruel mistreatment of his white owners. Here, as in most black films, evil is situated in white society, goodness in black. In these modern morality plays, hero and villain have exchanged color imagery—and with what seems an ever growing consistency. Where private eye John Shaft in his first screen appearance fought black villains from his Greenwich Village base, in his subsequent appearance (in *Shaft's Big Score*), he was situated in Harlem and brought white hoodlums down to defeat.*

Whatever else one can say about these black films—that they are really exploitative, since they are made, by and large, by whites, or that they are therapeutic for the angry audiences who attend them—their huge box-office returns make clear that they are striking a responsive chord among the black population and that here the heroic ideal has a viability it lacks in the mainstream. Of course, to see the heroic ideal as still vivid within black films is, in a sense, to see these films as other than "adult" and to risk the offense of reviving the stereotype of the black man as child. But it is a risk one must take, since black culture is, in fact, in America much younger than white. It is only now that blacks have begun to assume mastery over their lives; it is only now that they have been able to work toward a positive self-identity; and it is only now that the media have begun to address them. In this process, blacks cannot afford the luxury (if that is what it is) of existential despair, of distrust in possibility, of a dismissal of hope. They must assert the vigorous optimism of the youthful imagination—even at the expense of realism and complexity. They need an instant imagery of inspirational powerful figures. In other words, they cannot yet relinquish the hero and the heroic ideal.

---

* This same racial antagonism emerges from those black films that would seem to be reviving still another heroic type traditional to American movies: the gangster hero. In *Super Fly*, for example, the central character is a cocaine pusher who sells his wares to whites. *The Godfather* notwithstanding, such a belief in the gangster hero does not seem to be reasserting itself elsewhere. In any case, *The Godfather*, with its painstaking recreation of the forties and its emphasis on time past, seems once again an exercise in nostalgia rather than a reaffirmation of an ideal. Moreover, the implication is that Don Vito's heirs will in the present generation be absorbed by mainstream society and will become indistinct from other organization men. They will then have lost the absolute requisite for heroism: individuality.

The Hero as a World Figure

Sidney Hook

Sidney Hook was born in 1902 in New York City. He attended the city's
public schools and took his degree at the College of the City of New York,
where he studied under Morris R. Cohen. In 1926 he received his master's
degree and in 1927 his doctorate in philosophy from Columbia University,
working chiefly with John Dewey and F. J. E. Woodbridge. Afterward he
joined the philosophy faculty at New York University, where he became a
full professor in 1939 (he is now professor emeritus) and where he was
subsequently head of the philosophy department. He was also for many
years on the faculty of the New School for Social Research in New York.
He is the author of *The Metaphysics of Pragmatism* (1927), *From Hegel to
Marx* (1936), *John Dewey: An Intellectual Portrait* (1939), *The Hero in
History* (1943), and *Education for Modern Man* (1946), among other works.
The recipient of numerous academic awards and honors, he has been
president of the American Philosophical Association (Eastern Division,
1959–60) and has been elected to the American Academy of Arts and
Sciences and the American Academy of Education. Recently appointed by
the White House to the Council of the National Endowment for the Humanities,
Professor Hook is currently a senior research fellow at the Hoover Institution
on War, Revolution and Peace, Stanford, California.

Judging by the popular mood, we are living in an age of the anti-heroic. This reflects a growing disenchantment with leading figures in the political life of the nation, past and present. It has also been fed by certain currents in the climate of intellectual opinion. Skepticism and moral relativism in judgments about the past have combined with an emerging moral absolutism regarding the present to diminish the stature of heroes.

In addition, the diffusion of psychoanalytical approaches in historical studies has led to a sophisticated debunking of the proclaimed ideals and motives of the great men of the past. It has become fashionable to disregard the "good reasons" offered in explanation of human behavior in a quest for the "real reasons" behind them. These invariably turn out to be more self-regarding and less flattering to the principals in historical actions of importance. Once reasons are dismissed as "rationalizations," scholars spend little time in seeking and weighing the *grounds* of human conduct. They focus on laying bare the *causes* or springs of human action, psychological or biological, that make all men akin. In the vocabulary of these reductive sciences there is no room for terms like *great* or *small,* some would even say for terms like *sane* or *insane.* It is not surprising, therefore, that the dimensions of the giants of the past, once the mists of legend are dissipated, dwindle in the ever lengthening historical perspective from which we survey them.

At the same time, vehement political moralists without a sense of historical perspective have also contributed to the decay not only of hero-worship but of belief in heroes. I refer here to the harsh judgment of self-righteous absolutists for whom the founding fathers and philosopher-statesmen of the American republic are primarily "racist slaveholders," and who regard the compassionate Lincoln as an opportunist and hypocrite because of his views on slavery. The heroes of the counterculture and the so-called New Left, especially on American campuses, are more likely to be drawn from third world countries than from their own. And they are invoked not because of the existence of any exemplary attributes and personality traits for which a convincing case can be made but as symbols of resistance to oppression. In the judgment of this counterculture the national temple has been emptied of its altars. Only the Hall of Fame remains—and to be famous is obviously not the same as to be heroic.

Perhaps of greater influence in bringing about the current acceptance of a "demythology" of the heroic in history is the increasing mechanization and computerization of industrial society. Despite the clamor for participatory democracy, and notwithstanding the genuine growth in forms of shared power, there is widespread testimony to a pervasive cultural and political malaise. Complaints abound on all levels of a sense of frustration in shaping the patterns of personal life, and especially of social life. As the power of man collectively to control things becomes more manifest, the more numerous seem the confessions of a mood of personal helplessness before massive anonymous forces whose presence dwarfs the individual's role. Indignant or acquiescent, he stands overwhelmed by the happenings that engulf him. Just as no individual created the Industrial Revolution and no individual, however powerful politically, could have prevented it, so seemingly no one person in our time can initiate or abort the successive technological revolutions that accelerate the dizzying pace of social change.

Nonetheless, there is an instructive paradox in the judgments of the estranged and helpless. Eloquent in their lamentations on the passing of effective human initiatives, at the same time they are aware and alarmed that in our world of baffling complexity the decisions of a few strategically situated men may destroy civilized society. Ours is the age in which the sudden death of cultures at the hands of men rather than nature is possible. The command of Richard Nixon or Leonid Brezhnev to trigger nuclear weapons could produce the holocaust of holocausts. Deplore it as one will, the fact remains that we still live in a world in which the acts or failures to act of some individuals can have more momentous consequences than was the case with any heroic figure of the past. If a nuclear Pearl Harbor were genuinely threatened by a first strike from an enemy power and averted by a response that still left the free world viable, the president responsible for the decision would be more fervently acclaimed than President Kennedy was at the time of the Cuban missile crisis or than Woodrow Wilson was when he first reached Europe at the close of the first World War with the unsullied Fourteen Points. In the absence of effective world government holding a monopoly of all weapons, the existence of hostile nuclear powers creates a condition in which no matter how executive power is curbed or shared, the decision of one person might determine the destiny of mankind. This is an unprecedented situation in human history.

There are other less awesome and dramatic contexts in which the activity or leadership of one man or woman may be responsible for profound changes. One thinks of the work of Ralph Nader, still unfinished, who has succeeded in focusing the attention of the country on the needs and rights of the consumer to a degree not hitherto achieved. Or the public lobby organized by John Gardner. Prosaic these undertakings may be, but they have a revolutionary potential. Despite the widespread complaint about the powerlessness of the individual, it is risky to discount

383

with finality what individuals can succeed in doing in advance of their effort. To be sure, in most of the situations in which individuals like Nader and Gardner have succeeded in initiating great changes, one may predict that sooner or later someone else would have appeared on the scene and played a similar role. But one cannot reasonably make such a prediction in the fateful case where a national leader is confronted by a threat that requires a quick decision between the alternatives of surrender or war. For what follows on either choice—and even if none is made—may be irreversible.

The demythologizing of the hero is facilitated by a recurrent tendency to conceive of the hero in moral terms. The result is that it appears almost a contradiction in terms to think of the hero as wicked or cruel. Yet almost every great figure in history from Alexander to Napoleon, from Pericles to Bismarck and Churchill, has been regarded by some historian or defeated opponent, or from some variant cultural perspective, as morally monstrous. At the time of the Cuban missile crisis, Bertrand Russell characterized President Kennedy as "the most wicked man in history," worse than Hitler and Stalin, for risking war with the Soviet Union. And this despite the fact that Russell himself previously had urged that atomic war be unleashed against the Soviet Union if it refused to accept the Baruch-Acheson-Lilienthal proposals to internationalize all sources of atomic power.

Moral judgments are indeed relevant to any adequate historical narrative. But whether such judgments are positive or negative has no bearing on an analysis of the actual consequences of the work and life of historical figures. Morally, one man's hero is another man's villain. It is not likely that in the eyes of the defeated Southern Confederates Lincoln had the same heroic stature as he did in the eyes of many Northern Unionists. This does not affect the assessment of the actual consequences of the Emancipation Proclamation, of dubious constitutional validity at the time, on the outcome of the war.

Since history is written by the survivors, it is safe to say that it will be their moral judgments that determine who is acclaimed as a hero and who is not. But the question "If this particular man or woman had not been on the scene or had not done such and such, would the ensuing history have been substantially different from what actually occurred?" is not one that depends for a warranted answer on how we grade the historical actor morally. If the question is answerable in principle—and sometimes we do not know enough to answer it at all—the answer is of the same order as answers to questions like these: What would have probably happened to X if his car had not been stopped by the guardrail when it skidded on the icy mountain pass? If Columbus's ships had foundered, would the New World have been discovered anyhow? If Oswald, Kennedy's assassin, had missed, would Johnson have been president of the United States?

Unless the concept of the hero is interpreted at least for historical purposes in an ethically neutral way, we shall never escape confusing ambiguities in usage. Ambiguities in the conception of the hero enrich folklore and literature, and it would make one an unimaginative pedant to insist upon precision and consistency in such contexts. For the understanding of history, however, some semantic clarification and economy are required if agreement is to be reached, especially on what is true or false in causal attributions to historical agents.

There is no one moral or even psychological trait that is uniformly present in the conceptions of historical greatness or heroism in legend, folklore, or literature, classic or popular. If the hero is conceived as possessing exemplary courage, we people the historical stage with too many characters. And we would shrink back in horror from some who would emerge into the light. No one can deny that the terrorists of the Palestinian Black September group displayed great courage and daring in performing their frightful deeds at the Munich Olympiad. But who except some fanatical Arab groups would regard them, no less refer to them, as heroes? Or shall we conceive of the hero as one who has withstood prolonged suffering or who has a vocation for martyrdom? Once more we shall find heroes multiplied beyond necessity, and some of them rejected by latter-day Nietzscheans. The hero is not necessarily a victor. Preeminence of any kind, even in defeat, may be a sufficient condition for achieving heroic status among some national or religious or ideological group. But because of the plurality and conflicts among such groups, there are no universal heroes.

Whatever moral or psychological assessment is made of the personalities of Alexander, Caesar, Paul (who brought Christianity to the Gentile world), Mohammed, Constantine, Luther, Henry VIII, Cromwell, Peter of Russia, Catherine II, Napoleon, Lincoln, Wilson (who kept the United States out of the first World War and then brought her in), Lenin, Stalin, Hitler, and Churchill, there is one clear sense in which they are among the great men and women of history. What makes them great? The fact that if they had not lived when they did or acted as they did, the history of their countries and the history of the world, to the extent that the histories are intertwined, would have been profoundly different. This does not entail an acceptance of the Carlylean view, because other large factors enter into historical outcomes. But it is incompatible with the theological determinism of Augustine and Tolstoy, with the organic determinism of Hegel and Spengler, and with most varieties of Marxism.

The basic and oft-repeated objection to this approach to the heroic in history is that it assumes it is possible to give intelligible and confirmable answers to "if" questions or to hypotheticals contrary to fact. If we bear in mind that the operative word is *possible,* the assumption is correct. It is often possible, but rarely easy. If causal relations between events were logical relations, as they are in the Hegelian world view, or if the web of

385

human affairs was of such spectacular complexity that isolable causal chains could not be discerned, then answers could not possibly be made one way or the other. But the world is not so constituted.

In an alliterative aside in one of his stories, Herman Melville warns the reader, "But the might-have-been is but a boggy ground to build on." Granted. The admission, however, is not fatal. For unless we can discourse validly about the would-have-beens and might-have-beens, we cannot rightfully claim to understand the whys or the causes of anything that happens in human life. Human behavior on the streets, in the home, in the courts, in the commercial marts would be completely unintelligible. The logical analysis both of hypotheticals which are contrary to fact, as of their speculative causes, may be difficult. Nonetheless, common sense and common practice—indeed, human survival—depend upon our awareness of such things. We stake our lives on them every moment of the day. "You might have been (or would have been) hurt if you had not stepped out of the path of the speeding car" is an expression that no sane man would disregard as meaningless or as not worth his consideration.

Does any informed person seriously believe that it makes no difference to the pattern of events who stands at the levers of power in our world? Whatever one may believe about the past, today, because of the destructive potentials of military technology, it would border on the frivolous to affirm such a proposition. Even so, if we stopped here our analysis would be incomplete. Grant that who stands where would make a great difference. By itself this would make some individuals *eventful* but not necessarily *event-making*. By recognizing the distinction between the eventful and the event-making man we can do justice to some of the elements associated with traditional conceptions of the heroic.

The eventful man is one who affects history in virtue primarily of the position he occupies. Confronted by a fateful alternative, he may reach a world-shaping decision, but the alternative that presents itself to him is not of his own making. The ideal type of the eventful man would be Harry Truman faced with the question whether to drop the atomic bomb or risk millions of casualties on both sides storming the beaches of Japan. The event-making man is one who by extraordinary traits of character or intelligence or some other facet of personality has largely shaped the alternatives between which he must choose, alternatives that but for him would probably not have emerged. The role of Lenin in the Russian October Revolution is a paradigm case. An event-making man may also be someone who by virtue of the strength of personality or preeminent talents reverses the direction of social change against great odds, and overcomes the heavy inertia of institutions and mores. Peter the Great or Mustafa Kemal would be instances in point.

Elsewhere I have elaborated this distinction (*The Hero in History: A Study in Limitation and Possibility*. New York: John Day, 1943), and have characterized the eventful man in terms of the legendary figure of

386

the little Dutch boy whose finger in the dike saved the town. He was a hero by happenstance; almost any little Dutch boy could have plugged the hole. It is in this special sense that one can say that some men have greatness thrust upon them. No man is born great. But the event-making man is one who acquires greatness. If we expand the connotation of the heroic to include the demonic, the event-making man comes closest to the more poetic and picturesque classic views of the hero.

The heroes of our time, because of the cumulative consequences of the scientific-technological revolutions, and because of the extension of the democratic political process, are more likely to be eventful men and women than event-making ones. In the days of political absolutism there were greater areas for creative maneuvers, like those available to Henry VIII, who played a major role in redetermining the religious and cultural destiny of England, than in the decade of Edward VIII. Even if the latter had possessed the forceful personality of the former, he would have been elbowed off the throne.

Those who contend that the direction of historical and social change is so completely determined by economic forces that there are no momentous alternatives of development must of necessity deny the presence of eventful men in history. On this view, any man in any place of strategic command would have acted like any other. In fact, the very significance of the notion of strategic command becomes problematic. We have seen, however, that this is incompatible with the recognition that in our historical epoch, the decision a commander in chief of a nuclear power may have to make within hours, or even less, may literally make all the difference in the world.

The moral of this analysis is that the anti-heroic mood of our age may result in mediocre leadership just at a time when we need at the helm of affairs men of great intelligence, compassion, imagination, and moral courage—individuals who will not panic in crises, who can see the human being in the enemy and therefore realize that not all things are permissible. At the same time they should know that mere survival cannot be an absolute end in itself save at the cost of all the moral goods and values that make life worth living.

The great and unsolved problem of all democracies is to develop an enlightened leadership through mechanisms of popular control which, unfortunately, lend themselves to manipulation by the unenlightened. One may argue that the character of presidential leadership in the United States since the administration of Woodrow Wilson is a not altogether unplausible argument for the wisdom of the Greek system of election by lot. But inasmuch as the latter was a disastrous failure, it is obviously not good enough. The remedy for unenlightened leadership in a democracy is not less democracy, as totalitarians from Plato to Santayana have taught, but a more enlightened citizenship, the never ending task of enlightened education.

Heroes for an Ordinary World

Chaim Potok

Chaim Potok was born in New York City in 1929. He graduated from Yeshiva
University and the Jewish Theological Seminary of America, was ordained
as a rabbi, and earned his Ph.D. in philosophy from the University of Pennsylvania. He entered the U.S. Army as a chaplain and was in Korea sixteen
months with a frontline medical battalion and a combat engineer battalion.
In 1967 he published the first of three novels he has written to date, called
The Chosen, which dealt with imagined possibilities of his orthodox background and upbringing, and which received the Edward Lewis Wallant Memorial Award. A second novel, *The Promise,* published in 1969, drew upon the
same materials, and was given the Athenaeum award. His most recent novel,
My Name Is Asher Lev, was published in 1972. The author also of various
articles and a number of short stories, he has been editor of the Jewish Publication Society since 1965. He is married, with three children, and lives in
Philadelphia.

When a system of values becomes so charged with vitality that people are willing to live by it and die for it, heroic figures are born. Heroes are the inevitable concomitant of a system of value and thought that has been embraced by an aggregate of men. An idea gone public produces heroes as dividends.

Heroes and the thought system in which they are embedded stand in a complementary relationship to one another: the former is the action aspect of the latter. Values and ideas that do not give rise to heroes remain abstract exercises of the mind; heroes not embedded in a system of values and ideas resemble the vacuous inhabitants of comic strips.

Heroes are often the result of man's need to salve his battered conscience. An adopted value system that is more mouthed than lived is fruitful in the production of heroic figures. Such figures help bridge the fetid gap between gritty reality and professed ideals. The Trojan War was probably an ugly trade war, but it has come down to us as a heroic response to an ungallant abduction.

In the childhood of human culture, heroes answered man's psychological need for security, his political and social needs for leadership, and his moral need to strive for perfection in thought and deed. Above all, they answered man's fundamental need to comprehend and come to terms with the world around him. Such heroes were mythic gods, demigods, extraordinary sacred mortals, or historic or fictive ordinary mortals caught up in extraordinary situations.

Now we have demythologized the sacred literature of the past with our new skills at reading and comprehending ancient texts; we have deromanticized the great personalities of the past with our new understanding of the dark motives underlying human behavior; we have leveled the world views of the past with our acquired knowledge of parallel and primitive societies; we have deflated distant heroes and epochs with our new historiographic methodologies. Those who have not yet lost the heroes of their youth are able to live on in the childhood era of civilization. Those who have lost their heroes to the new knowledge look back upon the wreckage and feel not a little bereaved.

Let us see which heroes are alive and which are dead.

There are three kinds of heroes, each dwelling in the different worlds of communication men have used when contemplating or talking to one another about the world around them. There are the heroes of myths, of sagas, and of folktales.

Myths are dim visions of reality—crude constructs or models—perceived by prescientific and prephilosophical man as being the true and fixed nature of things underlying the ever changing world that surrounded him. The heroes of myths are gods, demigods, and other supernatural beings. Myths are ritualized public models that claim to impart truths grounded in knowledge or intuitive awareness about the origin and nature of the universe and man. They are the precursors of science, philosophy, and theology.

Sagas are accounts of true past events—a long journey, a protracted battle, a great victory—that have fixed themselves upon the imagination of an aggregate of men. The heroes of ancient sagas are kings, warriors, and the like, figures who have lived in the arena of history. At the heart of each saga is truth, though the repeated telling almost always results in embellishment. This embellishment is often the outcome of a greater inclination on man's part for the ought than the is. A victory that was costly, a conquest that was bestial, a migration that was long and anguishing— these are distorted in the retelling as the popular imagination mutes the is with the ought. Sagas, then, are a kind of popular history—public models that purport to make objective statements regarding real people and events. They are the precursors of modern historiography.

Folktales are born of the storytelling nature of man. They make no assertions of truth. "We all tell a story with additions," wrote Aristotle, "in the belief that we are doing our hearers a pleasure." * The heroes of folktales may be anyone or anything—the gods and demigods of ancient myths, historical figures, creatures of the imagination. The teller of the tale may draw from anywhere—myth, saga, his imagination, the tales of others—to relate his own tale. Folktales are instruments of communication through the imagination. They have come down to us from prehistoric times, are prevalent in epic poetry, and are the precursors of the short story and the novel. It cannot be said of them that they are true or false, for they are not statements of fact; they belong to the "art of framing lies in the right way," as Aristotle put it in his discussion of Homer and epic poetry.† They can only be good or bad stories, dull or fascinating, credible or incredible, beautiful or ugly, passionate or cold. The criteria by which they are evaluated are subjective, emotive, aesthetic.

Over the centuries, the statements of mythology have had to yield to the testings of science. The result has been a loss of faith in mythological constructs that is in direct proportion to the increase of human knowledge and sophistication. It is fairly safe to say that as far as Western man is concerned the enterprise of mythmaking is at an end. The heroic inhabitants of the ancient myths are dead now, along with the world that gave them life.

The heroes of sagas and subsequent history have had to undergo investigation by historians whose task it has been to separate the ought from the is. Many an assumed major figure in history has suffered reduction, and many a minor figure has enjoyed elevation. As a result, some of us tend to look carefully at the leading figures of our contemporary world before we accept them as extraordinary; too many turn out to be the product of the image makers.

We adopted heroes easily once—political leaders, sports figures, actors, scientists, writers; their faces adorned the walls of the rooms in which we grew up. But we have grown older and are more cautious now; we have been disappointed too often. I am not referring to motivations but to accomplishments. We know of the ugly darknesses that motivate all men. If we were to use that against man, then all human achievement should be reduced to insignificance—and that is absurd. The darkness is a given, as is our biology. Psychoanalysts evaluate motivations; historians evaluate accomplishments. And in the realm of historical truth there can be real heroes only after the fact.

The area of the folktale is considerably more complex than that of myth and saga, for we are dealing here not with statements of fact but with forms and tastes. Nevertheless, it is impossible to deny that attitudes regarding the nature of the hero in literature have undergone radical change since Aristotle wrote the well-known thirteenth chapter of the *Poetics*.

"We assume that, for the finest form of Tragedy," wrote Aristotle, "the Plot . . . must imitate actions arousing fear and pity." The tragic hero must be "the intermediate kind of personage, a man not preeminently virtuous and just, whose misfortune, however, is brought upon him not by vice. and depravity but by some error of judgement, of the number of those in the enjoyment of great reputation and prosperity; e.g. Oedipus, Thyestes, and the men of note of similar families."‡

The nature of the hero is made even clearer in the second chapter of the *Poetics*: "Comedy . . . [makes] its personages worse, and the other [tragedy] better, than the men of the present day."§ And in chapter fifteen, during a detailed account of the nature of characters in tragedy, Aristotle wrote: "As Tragedy is an imitation of personages better than the ordinary man, we in our way should follow the example of good portrait-painters, who reproduce the distinctive features of a man, and at the same time, without losing the likeness, make him handsomer than he is. The poet in like manner, in portraying men quick or slow to anger, or with similar infirmities of character, must know how to present them as such, and at

* *On Poetics; GBWW,* Vol. 9, p. 696.
† Ibid.
‡ Ibid., p. 687.
§ Ibid., p. 682.

the same time as good men, as Agathon and Homer have represented Achilles."*

For Aristotle, the quality of courage—the most significant attribute we accord the term *hero* today—is a necessary but insufficient characteristic of the heroic. A hero is in all ways, not merely in acts of courage, in war, in conflict, but in all ways, superior to the ordinary mortal. He is of noble stature, a favorite of the gods. He walks with the gods and consorts with them. Still, despite his status as an idealized human, he shares in our basic feelings and emotions. And so we feel pity for him when we witness his fall from eminence, and we experience the fear that a similar tragedy might one day overtake us. The disaster that shatters the life of the hero is not caused by an evil act on his part but by some error or weakness, a minor or major flaw in his character. This flaw has been variously understood in Aristotle: an error of judgment resulting from haste or carelessness; an error due to unavoidable ignorance; a defect of character resulting from human frailty or moral weakness but not from purposeful malevolence.

Thus there are two fundamental aspects to the tragic hero in antiquity: eminence and flaw.

The serious novel has been at war with this notion of the hero throughout most of its history. Trimalchio's feast in the *Satyricon* is the opening shot in the war. With few exceptions, the great novels have been host to the ordinary world and the day-to-day conduct of life. Their concern has been with the gritty flatness of human existence. It is in such surroundings that their heroes, if they can be called heroes, have been placed. In its dense depiction of environmental detail, in its often merciless account of the seamy soil upon which the Aristotelian hero once stood so cleanly, the novel raised the level of importance of that soil and mocked the lofty eminence of that hero.

Further, the novel moved the flaw from its locus within the hero to a place outside him. Dublin; London; Hannibal, Missouri; German bourgeois society; the slums of New York and Chicago; the small towns of midwestern America—these are the locations of the flaws in most of the great novels in Western literature.

More than any other art form—with the possible exception of montage —the novel has served to reflect the breakup of the old order of things, often at the cost of committing the fallacy of imitation. Witnessing the onset of modernism, the novel has recorded events through the prism of private imaginations and has drawn for us a new model of reality. The result is a picture of things so utterly at variance with the world of the ancients that their sort of hero is no longer conceivable as an artistic possibility. The way we see the world today enables us to accept without much squeamishness the very ordinary position assumed by Leopold Bloom when Joyce brings him before us for the first time. It is intriguing to conjecture about the kind of reaction that brief scene of squatting would have elicited from Aristotle. The novel may and often does depict heroes of courage, stamina, brilliance, valor—as does the drama—but not one of those heroes can be an Oedipus. Bloom is the ultimate hero of today; his is a kind of nobility of the ordinary. The value system of the Greeks is gone; thus one of the action aspects of that value system—the tragic hero—is gone now too. The ordinary is king and hero today. And the ordinary, in all its mundane and splintered grittiness, gives every indication of being with us for a very long time to come.

Yet, having said that, I must add that those same tragic heroes still speak to me in the dimension of the mortal. I am unable to relate to their idealized status and nature, but their pain and passion are sharply felt by me. Pain and passion, after all, are quite ordinary human experiences.

I came to literature not through the heroes of Greek drama but through the people of the Hebrew Bible. Cain and Abel, Noah, Abraham, Isaac, Jacob, Joseph and his brothers, Moses and Aaron, Joshua, David, Solomon, and the others—those were my early heroes, all of them mortals with smoldering passions, jealousies, many of them experiencing moments of grandeur as well as pitiful lowliness and defeat. Rabbinic literature embellished the biblical accounts, but none of those embellishments yields an Oedipus. The depiction of King Saul is the closest historical or fictive approximation in the literature of the ancient Hebrews to the flawed tragic hero of the Greeks; yet Saul bears no significant resemblance to Oedipus. To the world of the Hebrew Bible and the Talmud, an Oedipus was an impossibility in form and thought; that was simply not the way the ancient Israelites and the rabbis took their stance in the world. Biblical heroes were not detached and sublime members of a ruling class; they came from the people, they interacted with the people; there was always for me a picture of a leader in relationship to the felt presence of the mass, never a leader alone, noble, a special favorite of the divine, working out his own private destiny. Even when we were told that God had chosen one man over others, there was never a sense that he was "better than ordinary men" in the way that Aristotle had understood those words. As a matter of fact, there is often a great deal of back talk in the Bible on the part of those chosen for leadership; few of them seem eager to take on the job.

Above all, there was always for me a sense of the real when I read about those people—a feeling that the Bible did not conceal from me the truth about the less pleasant side of man. Cain is a murderer, Noah is a drunk, Lot's daughters commit an act of incest, Abraham yields to the jealousies of Sarah, Jacob steals a birthright and a blessing, Moses, David, Solomon— all of them struggling, erring, groping about in attempts to come to terms

---

* Ibid., p. 689.

with their passions, their fears, their loves, their faith, and their tenuous lives. Beyond it all, and at the same time deep within it, reaching down to the very lowest levels of existence, was a presence—the only real hero, as it were, in the Hebrew Bible—which was not the brutally indifferent presence of the gods of Sumeria and Akkadia, or the barbarous orgiastic presence of the Thracian Dionysus, or the coolly charming and manipulative presence of the Homeric gods but a passionate and caring presence, a Being who was like a father with a child he deeply loves and to whom all those struggling humans were reaching out.

Those were the heroes that formed the action aspect of my early pictures of reality. Later, when Cain and Abel and Noah and others could no longer be historical figures for me, they still seemed all too human even in their fictive state; they remained vividly alive as heroes in a literature sacred to my people—sacred because it mirrored the commitment of my people to man and God and history; it was a record of a thousand years of my people's vision of the world.

I was in my early teens when I began to read the great novels of Western literature. I remember marveling at the honesty of those novels and at the same time feeling puzzled by the cynicism and rage of some of their heroes —or anti-heroes—at the world around them, at what they took to be its sham, its hypocrisy, its stagnation, its sordid games and masks. And I was even more puzzled by what I took to be the surprise of some of those heroes when they first encountered the true nature of the world. Hadn't their creators read the books of Samuel and Kings, the Prophets, the book of Job? Later, when I read the literature of ancient Greece, I wondered if the Greek heroes had somehow combined with the heroes of the Puritan ethic to produce a heightened, idealized, rigid picture of reality. Had this resulted in hurt and rage when those novelists had first come up against the hard and simple truth that the world was really ordinary, a place of sweat and odors, where people loved and hated and hurt one another and suffered and stumbled about and tried to carve for themselves moments of joy and meaning out of the darkness?

I was spared that particular kind of rage and never put it into my created heroes when I began to write about my own world—my ordinary world, where study and faith and a coming-to-terms with other cultures were the quite normal enterprises of life, had been the daily preoccupation of my people for at least two thousand years, and where a certain binocular vision of reality fused all activity into a meaningful unity. The heroes of my writing are the action aspect of that vision of things; they are the ordinary people of my own private and precious world.

That is what we all do when we choose or create heroes: we tell one another how we see the world and what we take to be the most important things in our lives. Through our heroes we announce to one another who and what we truly are.

A Symposium
on Tradition

Introduction

In 1970 *The Great Ideas Today* held a symposium on the idea of revolution, it being thought that, as this idea had at the time gained fresh currency and power in human affairs, there was reason to examine it to see how well we understood it. This year we take up the idea of tradition, not because it too has gained currency and power, but because it has not—because, on the contrary, as the idea of revolution has waxed in importance, the idea of tradition seems to have waned, to have grown dim, as if the thing it represented were enfeebled and might disappear or otherwise be lost from human life.

Of course it cannot be lost, and will not disappear. In a passage in the *Physics* that is often quoted by Aquinas, Aristotle remarks that man is begotten of both man and the sun.* We can take this to mean that, if we wish to understand what man is, we must look to his own work as well as to the work of nature. The work of nature is a matter of heredity, transmitted by our genetic endowment. The work of man is a matter of culture and comes to us in, and through, tradition. It provides us with, among other things, the language we use, the alphabet in which we write, the number system with which we count, the written record of what men have learned, unwritten customs and practices, the forms with which we exchange greetings and farewells, the food we eat and the times at which we eat it, the games we play, and the prayers and rituals with which we worship. Implicit, unstated, most of this is, like our genetic makeup, simply part of what we are. We could not do without it if we wanted to, and in most cases we do not want to.

There are, however, certain human activities, such as the arts, sciences, and learned professions, in which the role or influence of tradition, if not simply a matter of choice, yet is explicit, formalized, and subject to a measure of control beyond what is possible in daily life. In such activities, the extent to which we allow the past to be preserved indicates the degree to which we approve of it and wish it to survive. It could therefore be significant if changes of method or attitude had occurred in these activities—changes that might suggest that "tradition," or "the tradition," or "the idea of tradition" had indeed suffered a decline or was at least peculiarly vulnerable in our time. Hence the editors of *The Great Ideas Today* thought

396

it worthwhile to arrange a discussion of the ways in which the various disciplines and professions make use of their pasts, to note the differences among them in this respect, and to see if such changes were reported.

As sometimes happens on such occasions, the results are inconclusive. On the one hand, it is clear that in certain interesting and important respects these learned activities *have* changed recently, and can no longer regard themselves as they used to do or entertain the same expectations. On the other hand, it is not maintained that we are on the threshold of a dramatic (if temporary) eclipse of tradition such as occurred with the advent of the Romantic movement at the end of the eighteenth century, or a revival of the idea, suggested by the influence of such a figure as T. S. Eliot, which may be said to have occurred, more briefly and with slighter effect, in the twentieth.

The contributors to the symposium are Yves Congar, who speaks for theology, and in particular of Catholic theology; Harry Kalven, Jr., who represents the law; Frank Kermode, who was responsible for the arts; Theodosius Dobzhansky, who writes as a scientist of science; and J. H. Plumb, who was asked to say something about the special interest in tradition—that is to say, in the part of the past that somehow remains present—that any historian inevitably has.

---

* *Physics* 2. 2. 194b.

Tradition in Theology

Yves Congar

It is an indication of the stature of Yves Congar among contemporary
theologians that, closely identified as he has been with the ecumenical
movement that culminated in the Second Vatican Council, and an advocate
as he is of the "openness" of the Church in the modern world, he also
seemed the best person to whom the editors of *The Great Ideas Today*
could apply for an account of religious tradition (his account is only and
specifically of Catholic tradition) as part of this symposium. Such a choice
was dictated in part by the fact that Father Congar has written an important
book on the subject, translated into English as *Tradition and Traditions*
(1966), among numerous other works of great erudition and wide influence
that he has published. He is the author also of *A History of Theology* and
other writings intended for a larger audience.

   Born in Sedan, France, in 1904, Father Congar was educated at the
Institut Catholique in Paris from 1921 to 1924, and was ordained a priest of
the Dominican Order in 1930. From 1931 to 1954 he was professor of
fundamental theology and ecclesiology at the Dominican House of Studies,
Le Saulchoir. He lives and writes now at the Dominican Convent Monastery
of Saint Jacques, Paris.

Every science puts its questions in terms of the latest that has been achieved. For science, truth, or at least a greater truth, lies ahead, not behind. The case of Galileo provides an eloquent example of this. But scientists can make new discoveries only by starting from what they have received. To willingly ignore or suppress the past would amount to cutting off the branch on which one is seated. As the Polish philosopher Leszek Kolakowski declared at a recent "International Meeting of Geneva," to do so would destroy the very possibility of the future. In short, we are inheritors.

Among the sciences, theology occupies a special position. It is, in fact, the scientific cultivation of faith, the form that faith takes within a reason based on philosophy, philology, and history, the means by which the believer uses the resources of his culture and his reason to understand his faith, to interpret it, to organize it intellectually, and put it into dialogue with the questions that the world is facing. Faith addresses itself to that which is called Revelation, that is, to the sequence of facts and words attested by the Scriptures, in which God has taken the initiative within the history of the world to draw man to communion with him in his covenant of grace. Christianity is a historical religion, a religion that has been "instituted," in a theological sense, which is not exactly the sense given that term by Joachim Wach, author of *The Sociology of Religion* and other works. It has proposed to us a belief that certain facts once occurred that offered a definitive covenant destined for all men. There was *one* Abraham, *one* exodus from Egypt, *one* Moses, *one* covenant on Sinai, *one* history of the Jewish people with its prophets and psalms. There was *one* John the Baptist, *one* Mary of Nazareth, *one* Jesus Christ, God-with-us. There was *one* confession of Peter, *one* Last Supper, *one* Resurrection, *one* Pentecost. All this, along with other facts and words, constitutes "the faith which has been once and for all entrusted to the saints,"[1] of which *The Letter of Jude* speaks.

It can be said of every man that he is an inheritor and of every scientist that he has predecessors. But this is true in a stricter and more specific sense of the Christian, because of his faith, and hence of theology, which is the scientific state of the faith. The theologian does not have to discover his data; he receives it from tradition, that is, by transmission. He enters into a

---

Translated from the French by Otto Bird.

scries that has at its origin a moment that must be called *constituent* or *instituting*, as distinguished from the series itself, which is *constituted* or *instituted*.

Such being the statute of Christianity and of theology, one cannot subscribe purely and simply to the statement of the biologist Jean Rostand:

> *I am unable to accept a "revelation" claiming to have been made to our ancestors in the far past of our history. This kind of tradition may be respected and may have had a large role in our moral past, but I cannot agree to accept it as a certitude from which to begin. As I see it, the only valid beliefs are those that are repeatable at any time by the intelligence so that they can be formed de novo in the mind of a man today, starting afresh from materials furnished by science or by free reflection. . . . It is impossible for me to believe in a Truth that is behind us. The only truth I believe is one that is discovered slowly, gradually, painfully, and that imperceptibly grows each day.*[2]

We would agree with this text so far as it concerns scientific truths offered to the investigation and even to the discovery of reason. But not so far as it concerns truths of faith that have issued from the initiative and revelation of God. Of course, to refuse it or find it impossible to believe are attitudes that are possible. We respect them without sharing them. The believer, hence too the theologian, receives from tradition (by transmission) the faith that he professes, the Eucharist that he celebrates, the structure of the church to which he belongs.

Nevertheless, even for the theologian, there is some truth in what Rostand says. For although he receives his faith and the plan of his life from the initiative of a revelation made in the past, the theologian is seeking a truth that, in a certain sense, still remains to be found today and tomorrow. And this is so because of the very nature of tradition. This does not consist in a purely material repetition of the same thing, on the ground that it requires a reception. Transmission and reception are two moments of one and the same process. A completely mechanical transmission, a purely material repetition, would ruin the reality of the transmission; if nothing were truly received, nothing would be truly transmitted.

The history of the missions provides a striking illustration of this. When Constantine-Cyril and his brother Methodius undertook the evangelization of the Slavs of Moravia, they encountered adversaries who refused to allow the use of the Slavic tongue on the ground of the pseudoprinciple that there were only three sacred languages, Hebrew, Greek, and Latin. This incident shows how a completely material "tradition"—material in the sense of being limited to certain languages—would have been contrary to the real transmission of the Eucharist, as if this could not be suitably received in any other tongue. Fortunately, Pope John VIII approved the use of Slavic, first for preaching and then even for the celebration of the sacred mysteries (879–880). From that day to the present, the same history has been repeated in every missionary situation. Serious studies have shown that catechetical instruction imported as such from Europe to black Africa without any creative innovation runs the risk of transmitting nothing at all. So with other cultural and historical situations. The introduction of confessionals in the churches in the sixteenth century led to a renewal in the practice of the sacrament of penance; today it seems that confessionals have become an obstacle, and something different must be found.

Tradition contains as an essential note a reference to its origin: it transmits something without creating freely and de novo, as Rostand says. It is a communication. In Roman Law, *tradere, traditio* signified the intention, from one side, of transferring an object, and, from the other side, that of acquiring it. For example, one would hand over a field or a house by exchanging symbolically a clod of earth or a key. These are cases that involve material goods. But in the case of spiritual goods, the one who transmits does so by communicating his wealth without alienating or losing it. Thus a teacher transmits his knowledge by enabling the student to share in what he gives him, without thereby losing it himself. This is still more true in the case of Christianity. For Christianity is precisely a communion, and a communion with a universal vocation, in the gift made once for all that was described above. The unity, catholicity, and sanctity of the church are "apostolic." Thus the apostle John could write:

> *Something which has existed since the beginning, that we have heard, and we have seen with our own eyes; that we have watched and touched with our hands: the Word, who is life—this is our subject. That life was made visible: we saw it and we are giving our testimony, telling you of the eternal life which was with the Father and has been made visible to us. What we have seen and heard we are telling you so that you too may be in union with us, as we are in union with the Father and with his Son Jesus Christ.*[3]

That is a reality, unique and identical, of the faith that must be shared by a multitude across space and time. Hence, the importance of a faithful transmission, without alteration, and of the note of apostolicity.

But the faith must be communicated and received across space and time. There it meets a variety of men and of cultures, a perpetual renewal of questions, a succession of human creations of which the mind is so fertile. The Church of the *constituting* period could indeed fix the faith of the Church of the *constituted* period, that is, of the history of the people of God for however long it should last. But its task was not that of merely repeating a lesson. If no more than that had been done, the Scriptures would not have been translated, as they have been, until they exist today in more than three thousand languages. For that, the message had to be understood in the spoken language, where *language* designates not only a vocabulary and a syntax but also the expression of a culture, of a certain historical situation with its own questions and its own answers. Much is made today of hermeneutics, and, doubtless, there is sometimes the danger that personal problems tend to replace the message. Yet

Each church has its own unique ceremonies for "the celebration of the sacred mysteries." First Communion in a Roman Catholic church gives substance to the idea that "Christianity is precisely a communion, and a communion with a universal vocation . . . the believer . . . receives from tradition . . . the faith that he professes."

hermeneutics fulfills a necessary function: not only that of understanding the text exegetically, namely of what Paul, Luke, or John meant, but also that of rereading it personally so as to apply it to our lives and to the questions that are asked today. John did not foresee Arius, and yet he had to reply to him by the hermeneutics of Athanasius. Paul did not foresee Pelagius, and yet he had to respond to him by the intelligence of Augustine. Neither Paul nor John foresaw Marx, nor with them did Luke foresee Freud, nor did Matthew foresee the problems of war and of economic development. It remains for us to obtain from these original witnesses a word that is faithful to them at the same time that it applies to what is always being put forward, unforeseeably, by history, since that is the cloth the word (in this sense) is made of.

In brief, faith and the Church have been constituted, but they must always assure their fidelity by creating new expressions and new forms of that which makes their identity. The preservation of this identity calls for much more than its material repetition. What is required is a criticism of forms that have become obsolete and the creation of new responses.

The gift God made to his people, making them his people in the history of the world, did not cease with the gift of his word (*parole*). It includes the gift of his Spirit after the Incarnation of the Word (*Verbe*), the communication of his Spirit at Pentecost as a consequence of Easter. The Word (*Verbe*) is the precise form of the word (*parole*), which unrolls in the history (including the thought) of Israel from Abraham to Jesus. Through this history, which is significant as such, even in its most human aspects, the word (*parole*) established and disclosed the structure of the religious relation of covenant. The Word (*Verbe*) of God, become man in Jesus, renewed this relation and gave it a structure conforming to a new and definitive covenant: the revelation of the Father and of the appeal to us to become children of God, baptism, Eucharist, the mission of the Twelve. The Word is a form and a certain defined structure, although in the Gospel it is so only in a very large way. The Spirit is breath, impulsion, life. There seems to be a constant in the action of God, who first constructs according to a certain form or structure, and then gives animation and movement.[4]

The Spirit was given to the primitive institution of the Apostolate to teach, to recall, to actualize all that Jesus had said (John 14 : 26), to "lead you to the complete truth. . . and tell you of the things to come" (John 16 : 13). Thus the Spirit ceaselessly carries forward into history what the Word (*Verbe*) has revealed or posited once and for all. It is characterized as having been "spoken by the prophets." This means that it assures at once both what was delivered once for all and the identity of that which is transmitted and that lives in history. Technically, it is said to be the transcendent subject of tradition, always active in advance in the unknown of history. It is also said that the Church is constructed on an apostolic foundation that is at the same time prophetic.[5] The martyr Polycarp, bishop of Smyrna in 156, is called "the apostolic and prophetic doctor," which ex-

Above, a circumcision ceremony in Tanzania; facing page, a baptism. "*A reality, unique and identical, of the faith . . . must be shared by a multitude across space and time. Hence, the importance of a faithful transmission, without alteration, and of the note of apostolicity. . . . What we have called 'the traditions' belong . . . to the practical order: customs, local rites, devotions, particular forms of discipline and observance.*"

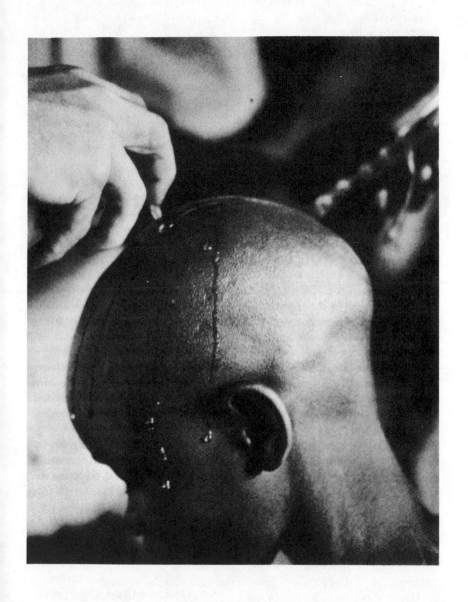

presses his character as both a faithful witness or bearer of the tradition completely posited at one time and as a summons to the mission of the time in which he lived.[6]

We have spoken of "history"; with that term, a second sense of "tradition" has begun to appear. Tradition is not simply the transmission of what has been given once and for all in the constituent moment; it is also that which develops in history through the use of new resources in response to new questions and as a result of reception in new historicocultural conditions. In theological terminology it is said that an ecclesiastical tradition is one that carries on the apostolic tradition. In fact, the two must be distinguished, as they long have been. Yet they must not be separated. For the apostolic tradition reaches us only as borne by the Church, and as read and understood in the Church, and the ecclesiastical tradition is only a deployment of that which has been received from the apostles. But whereas the apostles had the benefit of the charisms of founders and a grace of inspiration and of revelation, the Church for its historical life has only an "assistance" of the Spirit, which does not have the same guarantees.

Given the facts with which we are concerned, how have things developed? Christians at every epoch have thought and expressed their faith. Sometimes they did so simply to communicate with other Christians for edification: such are the letters of Ignatius of Antioch, about the year 110. Or the aim was to defend the Christian cause before the authorities or public opinion, as the Apologists of the second century did. But soon it was thought necessary to oppose errors, such as those of Gnosticism, as Saint Irenaeus did about 180, or to refute heresies. And, finally, the faith was proclaimed in order to instruct the people, both in schools, as Clement and Origen did at Alexandria, and by preaching, which usually consisted of a commentary on the Scriptures. When one consults a chronological tableau showing, decade by decade, the literary activity of Christian writers,[7] one is struck as by a massive fact how, after the relative scarcity of names in the second and third centuries, the columns suddenly begin to fill up between the middle of the fourth and the mid-fifth centuries. Names and works crowd the page, the greatest names and the most decisive works: Athanasius (d. 373), Basil (d. 379), Gregory of Nazianzus (d. ca. 390), Gregory of Nyssa (d. 394), Ambrose (d. 397), John Chrysostom (d. 407), Jerome (d. 420), Augustine (d. 430), Cyril of Alexandria (d. 444), Leo the Great (d. 461). Such are the principal geniuses who were also churchmen and saints and who are called "the Fathers."

They lived and worked at a time when the Church confronted a difficult but decisive situation. In an empire that had become Christian, they faced the temptation of complacency towards power and of compromises with a pagan culture whose tradition was still strong. At the same time, errors of some subtlety had begun to appear in the theology of the Trinity and of Christ. This was the moment at which the Church fixed the bases of its doctrine, of its discipline (in the canons of the councils), and the forms of

"*Tradition is the educational milieu that forms the sensibility and mind at a deeper and more vital level than that of theory.... A teacher transmits his knowledge by enabling the student to share in what he gives him, without thereby losing it himself.*"

its liturgy. The "Fathers" merit that title because they contributed powerfully to give the Church its face and its temperament. They engendered the faith for us. When we profess the divinity of Jesus, we do so thanks to Saint Athanasius; the divinity of the Holy Spirit, thanks to Saint Basil; the divine maternity of Mary, thanks to Saint Cyril. Without them, we would not be all that we are; the Church would not be all that it is.

That great epoch was for the Church a little like what a classical period is for a culture. But history did not stop with the fifth century any more than it stopped for French culture with the death of Bossuet. New questions continued to arise and new resources entered into the great current of theology. Let us cite only, in the east, Maximus the Confessor (d. 662) and John Damascene (d. 749), in the west, Saint Gregory the Great (d. 604), Saint Bernard (d. 1153), the great scholastics Thomas Aquinas and Bonaventure (both d. 1274), the Council of Trent (1545–63). Those are some of the great names, some of the peaks. There was also the life of all the Christian people, which Saint Paul describes as a letter written by the Spirit (2 Cor. 3 : 3). This life created and preserved customs that can be called traditions, particularly in their devotions. For many centuries such life remained, from lack of instruction and of knowledge, in the situation of a minority, subservient. More recently, however, worldwide social conditions have had their repercussion upon liturgical, canonical, and religious structures, and even upon doctrinal representations. On any hypothesis, today the experience of the faithful determines large sectors of Christian thought. As an example, there is the theology of liberation in South America, with its opening to socialism.

All this history has resulted in constituting a sort of treasure. Much, certainly, has been forgotten. But the Church is anything but amnesiac. Rome is a unique city: it has preserved something, often noble and beautiful, from each generation. The Church has done the same. Newman did not forget Thomas Aquinas, nor did Thomas forget Augustine, Basil, or Athanasius. Devotions have been added to the essential liturgy. The whole constitutes a treasure accumulated through the centuries. All that is called "tradition," even though many traditions are mixed in it.

The Commission on Faith and Order of the World Council of Churches established a commission in 1954, with one section in Europe and one in the United States, charged with studying "tradition and the traditions." This work reached its conclusion in the Conference of Montreal in July 1963. The two terms were not used there in exactly the sense that we have been using them. "Tradition" was taken as the transmission of the Gospel and the Apostolic Kerygma, that is, the good news of Jesus Christ and the economy of salvation of which he is the center. By "the traditions" was understood the form in which each confession or denomination has expressed and still presents that message. Our study has been located within the catholicism of east and west, so that we have been understanding by "tradition" the continuity of the great doctrinal current that issued from Apostolic Jerusalem and was enriched through centuries in which it traversed many different socio-historical-cultural conditions. What we have called "the traditions" belong rather to the practical order: customs, local rites, devotions, particular forms of discipline and observance. Tradition in the sense that we mean is a large river that has received in its course many tributaries and carries a little of all. Even the most venerated Fathers of the Church have maintained positions that we should criticize and abandon: Irenaeus professed millenarianism; Augustine hardened the affirmation of "original sin"; several Fathers taught the damnation of the nonbaptized, including even catechumens. This great river, marvelously deep and rich, indeed carries a little of all. It needs discernment, even a filter, one might say. But who will operate this, and how?

Who? The church. How? By its life. It is the Church in the unity and fullness of its communion that recognizes the faith. This Church is not a simple association established by human initiative. It is a people called together and assembled by its ministers and structured upon a sacramental basis. It is entirely animated, down to each one of its communicants, according to the condition and for the sake of its mission. That is why one recognizes in the Church an ordained ministry that exercises a public authority. For a little more than a century one has spoken of its "magisterium." This intervenes with the power corresponding to its mission to evaluate the authenticity and value of the various contributions of the tradition. But it cannot be isolated from the Christian people and their experience, nor can we attribute to it an autonomy in teaching the meaning of the deposit of Revelation. The "magisterium" witnesses, transmits, evaluates, but it does not have the creativity of a source.

Having shown what tradition is and specified its status, we must now ask what theology does with it, how it uses it.

Before theology is a product—a literary product occupying sections BJ to BX in the Library of Congress—it is the work of a man, or of a woman, but in either case it is, more precisely, the work of a believer. If a person were to take certain dogmatic propositions as principles and, without believing them, construct new conclusions and organize them into a system, the result would not be theology any more than the mimicry of a parrot is a human language. There is no theology without faith. First of all the theologian is one of the faithful. Hence his first act with regard to tradition is to be nourished by it. He meets it and practices it as, incorporated in the liturgy, in certain attitudes toward life, in practices, in art, in sensibility, it forms the Christian, and more precisely the Catholic, consensus. To the extent that it is legitimate to distinguish between instruction and education —without opposing them, however—it can be said that tradition is the educational milieu that forms the sensibility and mind at a deeper and more vital level than that of theory. How did I become a man for whom lying is a horror? Certainly not from lectures on morals, thanks be to God, but because I grew up in an environment from which lying was banned, so that love of truth came along with life, with games and festivals, with stories and concrete examples. Max Scheler has well expressed this in his analysis of the way in which models, as distinct from leaders, act upon us:

> The second vehicle for the active influence of models is called tradition. Tradition holds a place midway between heredity and the mode of reception proper to learning and education by the act of "understanding." It is communicated automatically, vitally. It consists in receiving a certain mentality and certain ways of wanting and judging things by means of contagion and mechanical imitation of the manifestations of daily life. In short, in tradition—and this is its essential note—I do not know what I receive, and I take the will of another as my own will; I make no judgment of its value before receiving it, I do not choose it. One thinks that he has himself perceived that which is transmitted, and himself has judged it. Long before education and the conscious effort to teach by influence have laid hold of the child, the broad lines of his future destiny have already been sketched in him by his actions and by all the things that he has lived through before understanding their meaning.[8]

409

Certain expressions in this text may seem to suggest the Freudian superego. In fact, in Christianity more than in any social order, we have been *preceded*. It is a question of *entering into* a communion; the Gospel speaks of "entering the kingdom." But it is a spiritual thing and must be ratified by life.

But whereas one of the faithful may do this simply by living it, the theologian must do so by making clear in a critical way the value of what he has received. Theology, as we have seen, is an effort to understand, express, and organize the content of the faith with the help of the scientific means at our disposal. The distinction between two moments in this process has become classic: "auditus fidei" (hearing the faith) and "intellectus fidei" (understanding the faith): the moment of information and the moment of elaboration, taking possession of the data, interpreting and organizing it. It is customary to speak of positive theology and speculative theology. Yet the two are certainly not separable; in any case, the second is not separable from the first, and it is the first in which we are interested.

The theologian turns to the monuments or witnesses of the tradition; he seeks out the places where it can be found. This fact has given rise to the expression "theological places" (Melchior Cano, d. 1560). The questions concerning these are rather complicated, and there is a whole "theological criteriology" that seeks to determine precisely their value and the conditions for employing them. The principal "theological places" are the following:

First, in a class by itself, are the canonical Scriptures, that is, those that the Catholic church recognizes as normative. Some fifty of the Jewish writings were left outside of the Old Testament, and fifty others were not included in the New Testament. The Bible is considered to be "inspired," and hence is for faith and theology not only an inexhaustible and invaluable source of knowledge but also an absolute and sovereign norm—*"norma normans, non normata,"*—a norm that provides a rule for everything else and is not itself ruled by anything superior to it. The "magisterium" itself is subject to it, for although the "magisterium" provides a rule for the faithful in the sense that it can judge the interpretations that individuals make of the Scriptures, that does not give it a position of superiority or of independence with respect to the written word of God; interventions of the "magisterium" in this realm have, fortunately, been very rare. Through the pains and difficulties of the complex biblical sciences (archaeology, geography, history, philology, etc.) the theologian endeavors to acquire an authentic and deep knowledge of the biblical data, a work that is for him a source of incomparable joy.

One may find it surprising that we have located the Scriptures within tradition. It has been customary to distinguish those two things and, if not to oppose them, at least to place one outside the other. Did not the Second Vatican Council, in 1962, have a debate on the "two sources"? That is true, but: first, the council explicitly put aside this way of speaking and treated

410

"It is not a matter of dogma . . . that the Church holds to tradition to the exclusion of Scripture, or to Scripture to the exclusion of tradition. . . . The Second Vatican Council, in 1962, . . . treated Scripture and tradition simply as two ways by which the Church comes to a fuller knowledge of the saving truth."

Scripture and tradition simply as two ways by which the Church comes to a fuller knowledge of the saving truth. In fact, it is not a matter of dogma either that the Church holds to tradition to the exclusion of Scripture, or to Scripture to the exclusion of tradition (beginning with the canon of the Scriptures—that is, the list of works admitted as inspired). Second, we will endeavor to make more precise how the theologian works with his "donné." The Scripture itself forms the principal part of this "donné" at the documentary level. It provides a norm, at least negative, for every other expression of tradition, both of the "donné" as well as of the "constructed." And what an inexhaustible fountain it is!

We have already mentioned the Fathers. They were assiduous commentators on the Scripture. Confronting the first heresies that attacked the basis of the faith, the Fathers centered their thought upon the essential. They introduced little by way of particular researches and arguments in their teaching; they never ceased to consider the whole of faith in the unity that it derives from its center, namely the Christian mystery, and from its end, our assimilation to God. That is why, in considering always the whole and the center, the Fathers always kept them present in considering any part. They did not speak of Christ without speaking of the Church, nor of baptism or the Eucharist without showing the totality of the mystery of our redemption and of our union with God. For them, everything is consonant, everything converges. For this reason the Fathers are privileged witnesses of the tradition. In them one breathes its very spirit and is impregnated with it. The benefit that the theologian can derive from them far surpasses anything that he can get from any other text or argument: from them one obtains an education in the *sensus catholicus,* much as one learns his native language from intimacy with the greatest writers of its history.

The same can be said of a fervent practice of the liturgy, which is "the Tradition itself at the highest degree of power and solemnity" (Guéranger), "the great teacher of the Church" (Pius XI). In its celebration the whole content of the faith is presented to us by joining together marvelously in ritual and sensible language a treasure of texts and of words. It has been said (by Pie Duployé) that "we derive greater if slower nourishment from things themselves than we do from their explanation,"[9] and, if a personal note is allowed, I would say that I owe to the practice of the sacred liturgy at least half of my understanding of the Christian mysteries.

We frequently have the illusion that the centuries of the past were calm and half empty, whereas ours is disturbed by many questions. The questions have varied according to the state of the culture, but questions there have always been. In politics, the powerful have always resorted to force. In the field that is our concern, men have always exercised their reason. That has often precipitated a crisis. In matters of doctrine, concepts are applied that betray one aspect of it; one value is privileged to the detriment of others and the balance of the whole is disturbed. Thus have

412

appeared what the Church, through the voice of its pastors and especially of its councils, has called heresies: the Gnosticism of the second century (a syncretist reconstruction of a religious universe), Arius in the theology of the Trinity in the fourth century, Eutyches in Christology in the fifth century, Pelagius on grace. Later, there were the difficult problems relating to predestination and the real presence of Christ in the Eucharist. In the sixteenth century the Reformation put in question the entire edifice of medieval Latin catholicism. Moreover, every time that new means of research emerged, there was a crisis from the side of the "traditionalists." One need mention only Abelard at the beginning of the twelfth century, with his proposal to explain everything; the invasion of theological teaching around 1220 by the dialectical method and Aristotelian philosophy; the explosion of humanism and textual criticism and printing in the sixteenth century; the introduction of comparative studies in the eighteenth century; the victorious rise in the nineteenth of history and of critical methods, not to mention the awakening of the conscience of the masses. The "magisterium" has intervened every time, first under the form of councils of bishops, then, since the sixteenth century, by the voice of the popes. As a result there is a mass of authoritative documents, rather diverse, but imposing themselves upon the consideration of the theologian and even upon his acceptance: dogmatic formulas of the councils, professions of faith, condemnations, lists of propositions, encyclicals, and so forth. All these enter also into the great river of tradition, providing the "donné" that the theologian must take into account and even with which he must begin in doing his proper work. As the river carries materials of very different value, the theologian must apply a sanely critical hermeneutic to it: he will not treat as on the same level the dogmatic definition of the Council of Chalcedon and the *Syllabus* of Pius IX, both of which are historical remains, but different in weight and import.

Such, at least, was the recognized status of theological work up until recently. It is always valid. Today, however, at least in France, theologians begin more often with a global consideration of the faith and of questions posed by the surrounding culture, questions that are philosophical, political, pastoral, and so on. Others, such as Karl Rahner, begin with the positive conclusions of the faith and proceed by a conceptual analysis to elaboration of a philosophical kind. Theology no longer presents the unity it formerly showed, but although more dispersed, it remains just as active. Its task has always been to actualize the Christian "donné" as, received from its origins, that "donné" has been developed through the centuries, in a cultural situation that changes from generation to generation. Theology is a rereading, made in a new light with the eyes of a new generation, of a life that is first of all a reality experienced by each people and each generation, and that has produced in the course of time a multitude of its own expressions that each generation takes up as its heritage and attempts to make its own, to hand on still further enriched. We would

413

willingly make our own the formula of Rabbi Safran of Geneva: "To read the past in terms of the present and the present in terms of the past." Maurice Blondel, for his part, wrote in 1904: "Tradition anticipates the future and helps to enlighten it by the very effort that it makes to remain faithful to the past." And the Orthodox theologian Paul Evdokimov wrote: "In a paradoxical way, thanks to the Witness that remains, Tradition is an agreement with the future that one finds in the past. . . . 'The Spirit has spoken by the prophets,' and it is from this prophetic dimension of the Church that it draws *from behind*, in Christ, what it announces *as ahead*."[10] That is how the theologian is nourished by tradition, in applying it to the present and carrying it forward, thereby transmitting it to a new generation that will continue the work.

---

[1] All translations from the Bible are taken from *The Jerusalem Bible* (Garden City, N.Y.: Doubleday & Co., 1966).

[2] *Ce que je crois* (Paris: Editions Bernard Grasset, 1953), pp. 15–16.

[3] 1 John 1 : 1–3.

[4] See Gen. 2 : 7 for the example of Adam; look at Ezek. 37 : 5–10, for the prophecy of the dry bones.

[5] Cf. Eph. 2 : 20 and 3 : 5 (where the article is not repeated before the word *prophets* so as to refer to the "holy apostles" themselves).

[6] *Martyrium Polycarpi* 16. 2.

[7] Cf. the *Synopsis Scriptorum Ecclesiae Antiquae* of Gervais Dumeige (Uccle, Belgium: W. Rousseau, 1956).

[8] *Vorbilder und Führer*, translated into French as *Le Saint, le Génie, le Héros* (Lyon: Editions Vitte, 1958), p. 56.

[9] In *La Maison-Dieu*, no. 10 (1947), pp. 43–46.

[10] *L'Orthodoxie* (Paris: Delachaux et Niestlé, 1959), p. 196.

Tradition in Law

Harry Kalven, Jr.

Harry Kalven, Jr., who appeared in last year's *Great Ideas Today* as coauthor with Walter Blum of an essay on taxation, is Harry A. Bigelow professor of law at the University of Chicago. He is a graduate of that university, from which he received his law degree in 1938, and where he joined the law faculty in 1945. His major fields of teaching have been torts and constitutional law, and for over a decade he was director of the Jury Project, an interdisciplinary study of a legal institution.

Among his books are: *The Uneasy Case for Progressive Taxation* (1953) with Walter Blum; *The Negro and the First Amendment* (1965); *The American Jury* (1966) with Hans Zeisel; and *Cases and Materials on Torts* (2d edition, 1969) with Charles O. Gregory. He has also published widely in legal journals.

At present he is working on a book having to do with freedom of speech and the press that will be a study of how the Supreme Court has elaborated the rule so briefly articulated in the First Amendment.

He is a member of the American Academy of Arts and Letters and was a Guggenheim fellow in 1970.

The question of the role of tradition in law poses an engaging challenge to the lawyer to look at his field freshly. Law depends much on a variety of continuities with the past; yet tradition is not a term it uses consciously in describing and understanding itself. Law does find congenial other terms that are closely, if subtly, related—role, profession, custom, institution, craft, history, practice, values, usage, precedent—but it is clear that we cannot proceed by reporting directly what the law has had to say about tradition.

We will not struggle over the troublesome problem of definition. For our modest purposes it will be a sufficient marking out of an idea to specify the passing on or handing down of a corpus of writings and practices to the next generations that is venerable, finite, respected, mulled over, and that exerts a control on the present. Tradition in this loose sense will include the unwritten as well as written and that which is unconsciously received as well as that received with full awareness.

There are then, we find, three senses in which the law responds to tradition in an important way. We shall use them to frame this essay. First, there is tradition in the sense of the unwritten complement of a legal order, the aspect the anthropologist or sociologist is most likely to call attention to; then there is the obvious sense—the use of the precedent of past decisions as a control on future decisions, the aspect the lawyer himself is most likely to be attentive to; finally, there is the difficult sense in which precedent and, in a way, practices embody values that transcend technical limits, an aspect perhaps associated most often with constitutional law.

I

Before exploring these points of legal contact with tradition, it is appropriate to note that the courts may draw on the unwritten traditions of the people as a source or clue for decision. Sometimes the court will do so in construing a statute. The formula is that since the legislature was familiar with the traditions of the society, it cannot be taken to have intended a meaning that would be inconsistent with those traditions, unless it very explicitly says so. A classic example is found in the World War I opinion of Judge Learned Hand in *Masses Publishing Co.* v. *Patten*, the first important

American free speech case. It involved editorials, poems, and cartoons in the old radical magazine *The Masses*, all of which were bitterly antiwar. The postmaster general had excluded the magazine from the mails on the ground that these materials violated the Espionage Act of 1917 because they would "cause" insubordination in the armed forces by generating disaffection and discontent in the public with the war. Judge Hand conceded that this was likely to be true, but argued that to construe "cause" so broadly would entail the suppression of all hostile criticism in time of war, and would "contradict the normal assumption of democratic government that the suppression of hostile criticism does not turn on the justice of its substance or the decency and propriety of its temper." He then made his appeal to tradition: "Assuming that the power to repress such opinion may rest in Congress in the throes of a struggle for the very existence of the state, its exercise is so contrary to the use and wont of our people that only the clearest expression of such a power justifies the conclusion that it was intended."[1]

A somewhat different example of a deep appeal to the traditions of a free people is found in an opinion some forty years ago by Justice Roberts. The case involved testing the constitutionality of an effort by a municipality to ban all distribution of leaflets in public places in order to prevent littering. Justice Roberts, infused with the customs of the people, perceived the streets and parks as constituting a public forum to which access could not be denied except for weighty reasons. He thus finds traditional practice useful in construing the Constitution itself. He states: "Wherever the title of streets and parks may rest, they have immemorially been held in trust for the use of the public and time out of mind, have been used for purposes of assembly, communicating thoughts between citizens, and discussing public questions. Such use of the streets and public places has, from ancient times, been a part of the privileges, immunities, rights, and liberties of citizens."[2]

II

Tradition as an unwritten complement of law touches it almost everywhere. We begin with the continuity stemming from law when viewed as a profession. There is the remarkable uniformity of style in the professional legal education, which pursues now a century later the so-called Langdell "case-method" of teaching law discovered and promulgated by a Harvard dean back in 1870. It is a method that has no true counterpart elsewhere in the university world—in its emphasis on concrete instances, its careful exegesis of texts, drawn largely from the opinions of appellate courts, and in its eschewing lectures for the Socratic method of discussion, even in large classes. Generations of young law teachers and law students have shown signs of rebelling against the case method, but it survives, and in most cases slowly earns begrudging admiration. This is possibly the most

"There is what might be called the tradition that the law student must literally saturate himself in legal culture once he embarks on law study so that for a period of three years his intellectual energy is fully taken up with law."

accessible instance of tradition's potency in law: law teachers tend to teach as they were taught, and the tradition is literally passed. Then, too, there is what might be called the tradition that the law student must literally saturate himself in legal culture once he embarks on law study so that for a period of three years his intellectual energy is fully taken up with law. Sociologists, who have occasionally been in residence in law schools, have observed that legal education has its features that resemble rites of passage.

There are traditions of the profession itself—aspirations to service, skill, loyalty, fiduciary trust, and courage and independence in defense of the unpopular—that warrant speaking of the practice of law as a profession and not a trade or business. These arguably have become more rhetoric than vital tradition today; the public dismay at the role and prevalence of lawyers in the Watergate affair can be read as, among other things, a measure of a departure from tradition. But lawyers would still speak of certain actions as "in the finest tradition of the bar" and would still tend to recall together Hughes's defense of the Socialist leaders in 1920, Frankfurter's public intervention on behalf of Sacco-Vanzetti, Willkie's representation of William Schneiderman in the Supreme Court when he was threatened with deportation for Communist ties, or Williams's defense of Senator Joe McCarthy in the censure proceedings in the Senate.

Then there are local practices among lawyers, particularly with respect to matters of procedure, that take on over time the status of local or regional traditions. For example, in our studies of the jury, Hans Zeisel and I discovered that the frequency of waiving jury trial for judge trial in felony cases varied greatly over the country, ranging from roughly 75 percent of all cases in states like Wisconsin and Connecticut to about 5 percent in states like Minnesota and Utah. We concluded, "The chief determinant in the decision whether or not to waive the jury in a criminal case is simply regional custom."[3] Presumably, lawyers tend to adopt the habits of older lawyers under whom they came into law practice. The example is an interesting one; it is a subtradition within the generic tradition that jury trial is a safeguard for the accused.

The jury example suggests another series of continuities predicated this time on the law viewed as an institution. Several important characteristics of the American jury, for example, depend on unwritten practices that have continued over time and may now appear almost unalterable. Among these are that the jury has twelve members, that it decides by unanimous vote, that the taking of notes by jurors during the trial is generally forbidden, that the judge's instructions to the jury on the law may come after closing argument by lawyers rather than before it, that jurors may not ask questions during the trial, that a jury elects its own foreman, that it deliberates in secrecy, and so on. Undoubtedly, all institutions acquire such marginal unwritten characteristics over time, but what may set the law apart is that on occasion it is called upon to arbitrate, as it were, the boundaries of its tradition. In recent years the United States Supreme Court has passed upon whether it is constitutionally compatible with a right to jury trial to alter the size of the jury or the unanimity requirement.

The jury instance is matched for American society by the example of the electoral college. It is an institution written into the body of the original Constitution and qualified by the Twelfth Amendment. It deals with a matter of the highest importance—the election of the president of the United States. Yet its key characteristics are defined not by the constitutional texts but rather by tradition. It was intended that the electors be an elitist group of representatives who would serve not so much to choose the president as to nominate leading candidates who, lacking a majority of electoral votes, would then be elected by the members of the House of Representatives voting by states. The electoral college became almost at once what we know today: a scheme in which the electors themselves cease to have any discretionary role and any significance as persons, but one in which the president is elected by a unit vote by states, with all the electoral votes of a state going to the candidate who receives the largest popular vote. Although nothing legally binds the elector to cast his vote as directed, there have been in the two centuries of the scheme only a handful of faithless electors. The power comes from the force of the tradition and the

419

expectations it has generated in political parties and the public as to how the role will be performed.

The most intriguing instances of unwritten tradition encrusting institutions in law are, not unexpectedly, found with the judge and his role. I single out two features for comment: first, the special etiquette accorded judges, and, second, the expectation that the judge give public reasons for his decision.

A few years ago the trial in Chicago of the so-called Chicago Seven before Judge Julius Hoffman for conspiring to violate the federal antiriot statute in connection with the 1968 Democratic National Convention made us aware that the courtroom had become a last citadel of etiquette in contemporary society. The trial lasted five months; because of the almost chemical interaction of this particular judge and these particular defendants, it supplied a national news story daily. It ended with Judge Hoffman coming down heavily on the side of etiquette, and sentencing the various defendants and their counsel to jail on 175 separate contempts of court. The example is a complex one, with undertones of civil disobedience in the defendants' behavior. A rounded account of it is not possible here, but it put to the bench and bar a genuine question as to the extent to which courtroom etiquette was functional for a rational orderly trial and the extent to which it was simply the etiquette of another day that had been passed on to an impolite, impatient age. One of the defendants, David Dellinger, had accused Judge Hoffman during the trial of being more concerned with "decorum than with justice."

The distinctive thing is again not so much the special manners in a courtroom—addressing the judge as "your honor," rising when he enters, not interrupting him, etc.—but that reflexively the law is called upon to arbitrate the limits of its tradition. The contempt citations were upset on appeal. On retrial late in 1973 before another judge, some of the defendants were found guilty of contempt, vindicating the cause of etiquette, but no sanctions other than censure were imposed, and the vast majority of the items in Judge Hoffman's inventory were discarded. A tension between justice, aggressive defense in cases with political overtones, and the unwritten tradition of high decorum in the courtroom continues.

Various practices of American appellate courts exhibit this force of unwritten traditions, such as that opinions are not delivered seriatim by each justice as in the English bench but as "a committee" opinion for the court; that there is a privilege of justices who disagree with the majority opinion to file dissenting opinions seeking to impeach it, which are published with and preserved alongside the "official" majority opinion, a remarkable example of tolerance for public dissent on serious issues. But the most important tradition is that appellate judges give reasons for their decisions and that their reasons be public reasons. The requirement goes to the heart of the judicial process as a ceremony of reason.

It should not be taken for granted that public officials always support

Some recent trials have raised "a genuine question as to the extent to which courtroom etiquette was functional for a rational orderly trial and the extent to which it was simply the etiquette of another day that had been passed on to an impolite, impatient age."

their action with reasons. The executive and the legislature often may not; trial courts rarely do; and the jury never does.

What I wish to highlight is not the giving of reasons, but that not all reasons are acceptable. The judge must give an impersonal public reason; he may not say that the defendant was Jewish or the plaintiff Republican. There are, to be sure, dangers in this tradition, as many have pointed out. It may limit the realism of the court; it may invite pieties and rationalizations; it may conceal the "real" reasons for decision; it may affect not how the court decides but simply how it talks. But the countervalues have carried the day, and the tradition is a sturdy one. The tradition in its interplay of public reason and "real" reason accounts for much of the fascination of law study.

One example, drawn from a field of special interest to me, must suffice. In 1964 the Supreme Court was faced with a libel judgment of $500,000 entered by the Alabama courts against the *New York Times* for publishing an editorial advertisement on behalf of Martin Luther King, Jr., and the civil rights movement. On a tortured technical construction, it was read to have defamed and damaged the reputation in his community of the police commissioner in Montgomery, Alabama. The case thus bristled with real-politik. The Supreme Court, however, under the tradition had to find public reasons for upsetting the judgment; the centuries-old law of libel had been thought compatible with the free speech guarantees of the First

Amendment. The Court revised substantially its interpretation of the First Amendment, finding its "central meaning" in the idea that there should be no offense of seditious libel. Writing enthusiastically a decade ago about the outcome in the case, *New York Times* v. *Sullivan*,[4] I put it this way:

> *My thesis is that the Court, compelled by the political realities of the case to decide it in favor of the* Times, *yet equally compelled to seek high ground in justifying its result, wrote an opinion that may prove to be the best and most important it has ever produced in the realm of freedom of speech.*[5]

III

The great instance of the law's relationship to tradition is the use of precedent in the common law. The predominant characteristic of legal argument is the obligation to "connect it up" with the past. The careful preservation of the written records of prior decisions and opinions of appellate courts, the careful indexing and analysis of them, and the careful arguing from them in present controversies must constitute an unparalleled dependence on a written tradition to control present action. What is especially distinctive is the degree of control. In theory, precedent does not merely inform or advise present judgment; under the principle of *stare decisis* it controls and dictates it. Professional legal education consists principally of the study of precedents; commercial legal publications consist principally of digesting, indexing, and collating precedents; scholarly commentary consists principally of analysis and criticism of precedent and the discovery of new patterns in it; lawyer's argument consists principally of citation to precedent and inferences from it; judicial opinions consist principally of justifications derived from precedent. This is equivalent to saying that in law present controversies are quite literally arbitrated by tradition.

It seems impossible to overstate the law's dependence on this written tradition. It is no accident that Karl Llewellyn's study of appellate judging, the final work of his long career as a leader of the realist school in jurisprudence, was entitled *The Common Law Tradition*[6] and was dedicated: "To the undying succession of the Great Commercial Judges whose work across the centuries has given living body, toughness and inspiration to the Grand Tradition of the Common Law."

Yet so summary a sketch of the dependence on precedent does oversimplify, if not overstate, the hold of tradition, and calls for several qualifications and corrections. The common law is itself no longer at the center of the American legal enterprise. There has in the past century been enormous growth on three fronts all outside common law tradition: the ever increasing domain and salience of constitutional adjudication; the momentum of legislation at state and federal levels so that statutes increasingly preempt what was once common law; and, finally, the growth of a vast network of administrative agencies regulating aspects of American life.

422

The school desegregation decision is a sufficient example of the first, the no-fault auto-insurance legislation of the second, and the Federal Communications Commission of the third. It is beyond the scope of this essay to attempt a summation of the relative shares of these kinds of law in the legal enterprise as a whole or to venture an account of the varying role that precedent plays in each of them. It retains, of course, some role, but that role is not so dominant nor is the hold of the past so distinctive. From this perspective, one major distinguishing characteristic of legislation is that it is lawmaking that may sever ties with tradition and break completely with the past. The legislators, however, somewhat like the scientists, may find that they have inherited ways of thought that are not so easily discarded. Lawyers are fond of quoting Maitland's epigram about older procedural rules, forms of action, which were abolished, but which "continue to rule us from the grave."

Moreover, the account thus far has advisedly concealed from view the sense of mystery about precedent at common law. There has been endless fascination with the logical puzzle of just how a decision in individual case A can control a decision in a somewhat different individual case B. There is no fire left in the old controversy over whether judges make law or find it. Edward Levi spoke of "reasoning by analogy"; Karl Llewellyn, of "leeways" and "reckonability"; H. L. A. Hart, of "open textured rules." There has also been in more recent decades the realists' curiosity as to whether, as a matter of human behavior, precedent is ever the real reason for a decision. My mature hunch is that being obedient to precedent is like riding a bicycle: it is much easier to do it than to describe it.

Viewing these matters from the standpoint of tradition brings us back to the puzzle of delimiting the term. It seems easy and appropriate to talk of precedent as the passing on of a written tradition. Yet it is widely perceived today that the common law process was but one of the ways of making law. We do not see tradition in the same sense in the other ways of making law. No one, I think, would find it profitable to talk of the continuity of a statute, which had remained in force unamended and unrepealed for, say, fifty years, as a tradition. The United States Constitution may fall somewhere in between; after almost two centuries it is more a living tradition than simply a written text passed on from generation to generation. But reference to the Constitution underscores how difficult it is to say in law where tradition leaves off and some other form of continuity begins. A constitution is an organizational blueprint for the distribution of power and function in the governance of society. It is the source of the continuity of legal institutions upon which legitimation crucially depends. It is important that law be made and enforced in the traditional ways by the traditional institutions. One source of contemporary unease about impeachment is that we have no tradition of use to appeal to. But does it foster insight to speak of the presidency, the Senate, the Supreme Court as traditions?

423

The most splendid thing about the common law as tradition is its capacity for growth, change, and self-correction. The law has a fine metaphor for the process; it speaks of the "law working itself pure." Perhaps this is a necessary characteristic of any vital tradition or any tradition subject to continuous reexamination and study. In any event, the purifying of the tradition is so recurring a phenomenon in law as in itself to be a tradition. Examples are abundant. New York for seventy-five years had an odd rule governing damage caused by the use of explosives as in blasting operations. If the damage to the plaintiff was caused by debris hurled onto his property, the blaster was held, as the law put it, strictly liable; that is, liable without the need to prove that the blasting operation was carried on in a flawed fashion. If, however, the damage was caused simply by concussion, the injured plaintiff in order to recover damages had to prove that the blasting was done negligently. The distinction was viewed as artificial and trivial, an echo of a long-abandoned conceptualization from fifteenth-century pleading in trespass and trespass on the case. It was rejected in the majority of other American states. Nevertheless, it was often applied, and survived in New York until 1969. In the case that upset the rule, Chief Justice Stanley Fuld of the New York Court of Appeal, after noting at the outset of his opinion that the rule stemmed from the 1893 decision in the *Booth*[7] case, stated explicitly: "We are now asked to reconsider that rule." He then reviewed its reception elsewhere in the United States and went on to discover that the 1893 *Booth* rule itself had been out of line with the New York cases:

> *We need not rely solely, however, upon out-of-state decisions in order to attain our result. Not only has the rationale of the* Booth *case . . . been overwhelmingly rejected elsewhere, but it appears to be fundamentally inconsistent with earlier cases in our own court which had held, long before* Booth *was decided, that a party was absolutely liable for damages to neighboring property caused by explosions.*[8]

The example is instructive in several respects. If possible, a court will alter the tradition by returning to its older, and purer, form. Thus, although a change is being made, it is done in a fashion that is highly respectful to the power of tradition. Moreover, it indicates the modest limits within which the common law struggles for consistency. Strict liability was itself out of line with the long dominant principle at common law for determining liability, the negligence principle. All Justice Fuld attempted was to iron out the small inconsistency between rules for debris and for air-wave damage. He did not trouble over the larger inconsistency between negligence liability for activity generally and strict liability for blasting. Only small inconsistencies are the hobgoblin of the law. And even then, it may take a century to iron them out.

Two other very recent instances, one involving death and the other, life, clamor for attention. A famous anomaly in the common law is the rule that

424

there was no redress for the wrongful death of another, a result attribut-able to a misplaced philosophic view that human life was beyond price and to a mistake by Lord Ellenborough in a decision in England in 1808. The rule was, in all American states and England, altered over time by the passage of statutes creating a cause of action for money damages for wrongful death. Once the statutes were on the books it was no great practi-cal matter what the common law had been. But recently, the Massachusetts court was faced with a technical problem involving the statute of limita-tions. To escape the bar of the statute it elected to reexamine the status of wrongful death at common law. Again the court found it appropriate to correct the tradition, relying largely on the total consensus for 150 years reflected in the wrongful death statutes everywhere. "We are convinced," said the court, "that the law in this Commonwealth has also evolved to the point where it may now be held that the right to recovery for wrongful death is of common law origin, and we so hold."

The final example, which seems to come straight out of news of the day, concerns that which has been called "wrongful life." May the failure to guarantee contraception be regarded as a tortious wrong when birth re-sults? The case involved a sterilization operation performed on a mother of four. It was performed imperfectly with the consequence that a fifth child was born. The lawsuit was for damages from the unwanted preg-nancy and birth. The Delaware court, with only modest hesitation, de-cided in favor of the plaintiff, even to the extent of allowing damages for the pain and suffering of the pregnancy. Here the court was filling in a gap in the tradition rather than altering the tradition. There was not, strictly speaking, a tradition on this precise point; the question had never been raised. It became possible to ask it only because of changes in the society's attitudes toward birth control. The legal tradition, although it links the society securely to the prudential judgments of the past, is capable of interstitial growth and change as the values of the society change. Moreover, the instant case fitted easily into traditional notions of medical malpractice; it stated a complaint for a negligently per-formed operation. The change, although astonishing, was handled so as to seem incremental.

The common law thus abounds in examples of a tradition that changes. The puzzle is: If tradition changes, can it still be thought of as tradition? The puzzle perplexes American legal scholars today and has been espe-cially salient in the controversy over the performance of the "Warren Court." As far as I can see, the uneasy resolution lies in the tempo of the change. If the process is speeded up and the patterns of precedent are redrawn at short intervals, then whatever the surface rhetoric, there has been a change in kind. The obligation to tradition has been dissolved. To rephrase the Chinese proverb, the wisdom of the common law was to make law slowly.

A footnote on the common law as written tradition: We have spoken only of cases and judicial opinions, not of books and commentaries. There is no doubt that the hold of books as a written tradition has changed for lawyers over the past three centuries. I have recently read a study of American lawyers and judges during the era of slavery. Their arguments over slavery reflected education in a given intellectual tradition in which the writings of Coke, Hale, Hawkins, Pufendorf, Grotius, Montesquieu, Viner, and the Bible itself loomed large, and in which Blackstone's *Commentaries* were central. To a lesser extent this could be said of the great treatises of the nineteenth century such as Kent, Cooley, and Story. But today their influence has all but evaporated, and an educated American lawyer may well never have had occasion to open Blackstone. The great treatises in particular fields of modern times, such as Wigmore in Evidence, Williston and Corbin in Contracts, or the American Law Institute *Restatements*, are respected and frequented but simply as secondary commentary, largely indistinguishable from the abundant other commentary in lesser books and innumerable journal articles. The written tradition of law, contemporary American law, is imbedded in the original authoritative data itself, the cases, statutes, and constitutions.

IV

We come then to the last sense of tradition in law. It is a difficult sense to capture; yet there are areas of law where the precedents taken as a whole, rather than in logical, precise, vertical sequences, carry a compulsion and inspiration that goes beyond literal holdings. It is here that the lawyer may find resonance in T. S. Eliot's essay *Tradition and the Individual Talent*. Eliot's advice to the poet to inform and discipline his individual talent with the tradition of English poetry is not unlike Justice Frankfurter's advice to his fellow justices on how to discipline and inform their "individual talent" in a great case. In 1951 in *Dennis* v. *United States* the Supreme Court was called upon to pass on the compatibility with the First Amendment of the conviction of leaders of the Communist party for the crime, as the law so tortuously put it, of conspiring to organize the party to teach and advocate the overthrow of any government in the United States by force or violence. In brief, did the convictions of the Communist leaders involve an abridgment of freedom of speech? Politically and legally it appeared at the moment as a great case. The appeal had followed a nine-month trial, and it exacted some 100 pages of serious opinion writing from the justices. To resolve a question of this magnitude, implicating values of this rank, required, according to Justice Frankfurter, resistance to "immediate overwhelming interest which appeals to the feelings and distorts the judgment."
He went on:

> *Unless we are to compromise judicial impartiality and subject these defendants to the risk of an* ad hoc *judgment influenced by the impregnating atmosphere*

426

of the times, the constitutionality of their conviction must be determined by principles established in cases decided in more tranquil periods. If those decisions are to be used as a guide and not as an argument, it is important to view them as a whole, and to distrust the easy generalizations to which some of them lend themselves.[9]

As the passage may make evident, Justice Frankfurter was launching an opinion that would affirm the constitutionality of the convictions. Although I think Justice Frankfurter, after taking the corpus of precedent as a whole, still reached the wrong result in the case before him, he displayed the right stance toward the tradition.

Interestingly enough, it was again Justice Frankfurter, in the same term of court in another great controversy over Communism and Communist front organizations—the case involved the so-called Attorney General's List of subversive organizations—who best articulated the sense in which legal tradition can transmit a concept or norm that transcends precedent. He is speaking in praise of the idea of "due process of law":

The requirement of "due process" is not a fair-weather or timid assurance. It must be respected in periods of calm and in times of trouble; it protects aliens as well as citizens. But "due process," unlike some legal rules, is not a technical conception with a fixed content unrelated to time, place and circumstances. Expressing as it does in its ultimate analysis respect enforced by law for that feeling of just treatment which has been evolved through centuries of Anglo-American constitutional history and civilization, "due process" cannot be imprisoned within the treacherous limits of any formula. Representing a profound attitude of fairness between man and man, and more particularly between the individual and government, "due process" is compounded of history, reason, the past course of decisions, and stout confidence in the strength of the democratic faith which we profess."[10]

There is matter for another essay in the question of why it is Justice Frankfurter, whose performance as a justice has not been uniformly admired, who proves to be the sensitive and eloquent spokesman for the role of tradition in constitutional law. Suffice it here to note that he has been the justice who most articulately struggled with the dilemmas of judicial restraint.

Another example of tradition as inspiration centers today on developments in the last fifty years of the First Amendment. Llewellyn's toast to the commercial judges who fashioned the common law tradition could well be raised to Hand, Brandeis, Holmes, Hughes, Roberts, Black, Douglas, Harlan, and Brennan, whose work over the past half-century has given "living body, toughness, and inspiration" to what is now for me the worthiest tradition in American law, the tradition of freedom of speech, press, and political action.

427

V

This has been a provincial account of tradition and law limited by the accident that my knowledge is of the Anglo-American system. Arguably, continental codes, canon law, Chinese law, primitive law, Roman law, or Soviet law would each exhibit a tradition of different strengths. But it is unlikely in the extreme that one intimately acquainted with those legal orders would be unable to trace in them the steadying, conserving, but not deadening pressures of tradition. In the end the effectiveness of law as a strategy of control lies in its combining the selective use of force with a moral tradition of obedience to law. It is respect for the past that gives law in an orderly society its crucial aura of legitimation. And it is tradition, too, that may best explain how a society can hope to have a government of laws and not of men.

---

[1] Masses Publishing Co. v. Patten, 244 Fed. 535 (S.D.N.Y. 1917).

[2] Hague v. Committee for Industrial Organization, 307 U.S. 496 (1939).

[3] *The American Jury* (Boston: Little, Brown & Co., 1966), p. 24.

[4] New York Times v. Sullivan, 376 U.S. 254 (1964).

[5] "The New York Times Case: A Note on 'The Central Meaning of the First Amendment,'" *Supreme Court Review* (1964), pp. 193–94.

[6] *The Common Law Tradition* (Boston: Little, Brown & Co., 1960).

[7] Booth v. Rome Railroad Co., 140 N.Y. 267 (1893).

[8] Spano v. Perini, 25 N.Y. 2d11 (1969).

[9] Dennis v. United States, 341 U.S. 494 (1951).

[10] Joint Anti-Fascist Refugee Committee v. McGrath, 341 U.S. 123, 162–63 (1951).

Tradition in the Arts

Frank Kermode

Photograph by Jill Krementz

Frank Kermode is a respected and influential figure in contemporary English studies. Educated at Liverpool University, from which he received his degree in 1940, he taught at Durham and Reading before going to Manchester, where he was appointed John Edward Taylor professor of English literature (1958–65). He has since been Winterstoke professor of English at the University of Bristol (1965–67) and Lord Northcliffe professor of modern English literature at University College, London (1967–74), and has just been made King Edward VII professor of English at Cambridge.

Professor Kermode is the author of *The Romantic Image* (1957), *Puzzles and Epiphanies* (1962), and *The Sense of an Ending* (1967), as well as studies of Donne, Milton, and Wallace Stevens. A book called *The Classic*, based on the T. S. Eliot memorial lectures given at Canterbury, is forthcoming.

A contributor to *Partisan Review*, the *New York Review of Books*, the *New Statesman*, and other well-known periodicals, Professor Kermode was coeditor of *Encounter* in 1966–67. He is the editor also of *The Tempest* in the Arden Shakespeare, and of the series called Modern Masters published by the Viking Press.

There is a spiritual community binding together the living and the dead; the good, the brave and the wise, of all ages. We would not be rejected from that community." So Wordsworth in his pamphlet on *The Convention of Cintra* (1809). The sentiment was earlier familiar to readers of Burke, and later to readers of W. H. Auden, who gave it equal solemnity. Wordsworth and Auden, as it happens, were both poets who had professed, but later abjured, faith in a revolutionary future, a sharp severance between the future and the past. And among the illiterate, who are less able to examine the past and its constraints, there are also millennial aspirations—blueprints of a future that shall be free of those constraints; but even in these aspirations the past continues to exercise its power, to assert the existence of old habits of thought, old psychological and cultural patterns.

"To treat the dead as entirely dead would show a lack of affection, and should not be done; to treat them as if they were entirely alive would show a lack of wisdom, and should not be done." This judicious observation was not made by a modern thinker, conscious of a need for balance between the demands of the past and those of the present; it occurs in the *Li Chi*, a Chinese work of about 200 B.C. For the Chinese the "spiritual community binding the living and the dead" was more than a matter of piety; it was a political force. The ruler assumed powers to ennoble or degrade a man's ancestors, and so lengthen or shorten their posthumous lives and dignities. But the effect of this was of course felt by the living. Confucius himself was not very interested in the supernatural; he recommended the careful observance of traditional rites, including ancestor worship, for the good of the living community, which would benefit from the civilized ritual of the cult of the dead. That is also the spirit of the *Li Chi*, which recognizes both the pastness and the presentness of the past.

Tradition is to preliterate and illiterate societies what history is to the literate. Unblemished truth was habitually ascribed to a remote original condition; it could be maintained, as a necessary component of the culture, by correct oral transmission. In time it might be written down, whereupon it would be the subject of learned commentary, and of accommodation to the needs of a society that had necessarily suffered historical change; but the word preceded the writing, and the old oral tradition is often held to be purer than the later tradition of the commentators. For this reason the

430

Jewish historian Josephus distinguished between the *paradosis pateron* (the tradition of the fathers) and the legalisms of the Pharisees.

Paradosis ($\pi\alpha\rho\acute{\alpha}\delta\sigma\sigma\iota\varsigma$) is rendered in Latin as *traditio,* which may be translated as both "handing over" and "handing down." The early fathers of the Church used the word in the first of these senses to mean the deliverance to the faithful of the divine revelation, the work of the apostles and evangelists. But what was then handed over must subsequently be handed down, and that was the work of the Church. As time went on this second sense bred difficulties; it had to be defended against protest, and given more dogmatic definition. It is not too much to say that in the ecclesiastical arguments about tradition we find the best model for the difficulties that attend its use in later and more worldly literary contexts.

The argument about the relation of Scripture and tradition anticipates, from the moment of its origin, hermeneutic problems that became apparent only much later in secular scholarship. The earliest *traditio* ("handing over") was of course oral, and preceded the documents called Scripture. These were inspired but they were also sometimes obscure, and from the time of Tertullian (late second and early third century A.D.) it was held that the Bible must be expounded by reference to a rule of faith that was continuous with the original teaching only because the Church had accurately preserved it. On the other hand, the only way to prove that tradition orthodox was by reference to the Scripture. So, as Henry Chadwick observes, "the argument is . . . circular: the tradition of Church teaching must be proved orthodox by biblical revelation; yet doubtful books are admitted to the New Testament canon because they are orthodox by the standards of Church tradition, and only the tradition can ensure that the interpretation of Scripture is sound."[1]

Tertullian came to think of tradition and Scripture as independent but complementary sources of revelation, and the Roman church has continued in this opinion, citing the words of St. Paul: "Keep the ordinances, as I delivered them to you" (1 Cor. 11 : 2), and "Hold the traditions which ye have been taught, whether by word, or our epistle" (2 Thess. 2 : 15). The tradition was appealed to whenever heresy threatened; and the responsibility for its preservation became a political matter, as for example in the dispute as to whether final authority rested with the papacy or with the general council, an issue that continually divided pope and emperor.

It was heresy that compelled the Church to stricter definitions of tradition, and these were promulgated at the Council of Trent (1545–63). Among all the issues controverted between the Protestants and Rome, this was the one that touched the authority of the Church most closely; for if Scripture was alone sufficient, the institution that preserved and derived its authority from tradition was dispensable. Consequently, the council laid down, in April 1546, that the Christian truth and discipline "are contained in written books and in unwritten traditions, which were received by the Apostles from the lips of Christ himself, or, by the same Apostles, at the

431

"The struggle between parents and children grows more obvious and intense; yet the gap between them is the gap across which the spark of tradition must leap."

dictation of the Holy Spirit, and were handed on and have come down to us . . . preserved by unbroken succession in the Catholic Church."[2] Scripture and tradition were accordingly to be reverenced alike. To believe otherwise was to allow that the first generation of Christians had no authoritative rule of faith, and also that it had taken fifteen centuries for the preeminence of Scripture to become evident, and then in such a way that this knowledge became a source not of unity but of schism.

Sociologically as well as ecclesiastically, the Tridentine ruling is of much interest. The heretical outbreaks of the Waldenses and Wycliffites in the thirteenth and fourteenth centuries had already caused theologians to deny that charity or grace was essential to the just exercise of authority; it was desirable, certainly, but not necessary; to argue the contrary would render the whole ecclesiastical hierarchy unstable and encourage charismatic heretics.[3] Now the tradition required that it be upheld by an infallible institution; and as the power of councils waned (there was none between Trent and Vatican I in 1869), infallibility came more and more to be vested in the pope himself, until Pius IX, who was responsible for the definition of papal infallibility in 1870, was capable of saying "*I* am the tradition."

We might see this as a characteristic rejection of the charismatic by the institutional, or a persistence in what Weber called "routinization of charisma," or as what some of his dissident successors think of as a diffusion through an institution of its original charismatic force; this last comes closest to the view of the Roman Catholic church, which is of course that the Holy Spirit inheres in it, and has kept the true tradition unbroken. But the forces of reform were also compelled, by the instability of charismatic succession, to institutionalize, and to do so (since there was no absolute control over scriptural interpretation) in a great variety of ways. These I cannot here describe; only two points can be made. First, the need for acceptable interpretations of Scripture was so acute that scholars such as Flacius (*Clavis scripturae*, 1567) took the first steps toward something like a modern biblical criticism; and this involved the evolution of a new attitude to history as well as to textual provenance. Secondly, Western Christendom was finally split up into sects, each claiming a different means of access to the primitive Christian truths. In short, the nature of tradition was henceforth a matter for perpetual dispute; and so there were instituted new senses of the historical past. The sixteenth-century argument about tradition may therefore be taken as a model of the modern dispute between those who speak for the past as they institutionalize it and those who charismatically ignore or attempt to abolish the past; and it also signifies the historical origin of the modern debate, which may question the validity of any tradition, or at any rate the claim of any particular group or institution to transmit, interpret, and enforce acceptance of one version.

At that time our civilization began to develop in ways unknown to others, indeed to become unique. Weber explained this development as proceeding from the Protestant ethic. "Those material and technical pre-conditions," says his expositor Herbert Luethy, "on which Europe started to build her civilisation after the late Middle Ages, existed equally or even more richly in other high cultures . . . yet in no other case did they cause a similar leap from the merely static to the irresistibly dynamic."[4] And Weber feared that what he called "rationalisation"—the substitution of rational action for compliance with inherited prerational social norms—would "disenchant" the world, perhaps had already done so. To ignore *mos maiorum* (the custom of our ancestors) is to give the society a dynamic that others, maintaining a traditional respect for tradition, must lack; but it is also to lose some or all of what they keep. The solution of the judicious Chinese—to show affection and wisdom at once—is harder to achieve in a "modern society." And the problem is complicated by the necessary restructuring of the past that comes about when there is no central tradition about which all other nongenetically transmitted information groups itself. We who lack interest in the mores of our ancestors (or even argue that they are irrelevant, because subject to different historical conditioning) must have either many pasts or no past at all, many sources of authority or none at all. This explains, in part, the flight of a Wordsworth or an Auden, or of many another, from charismatic millennialism to an institution (in both cases the Church of England) that offered a more moderate traditionalism than the Roman church; but it also explains the attractiveness, to generations of modern intellectuals, of the latter institution.

In politics it is conservatism that offers the comforts of a stable tradition. What is is right because it *is*, and because "it preserves continuity with the past and with the values of our dead forefathers. . . . The authority of existing forms of society must therefore be upheld and preserved, an authority seen as deriving, in Burke's famous words, from 'a partnership between those who are living, those who are dead, and those who are to be born.' . . . conservatism as an ideology is essentially traditionalism become conscious of itself."[5] It is founded on a quite different notion of history from any held by the parties of the Left. These may be anarchist, dedicated to the supersession or destruction of the past, to revolution for its own sake; or chiliast, expecting a millennial condition from which all history represents either a monstrous deviation or a complicated approach; or gradualist. There are, paradoxically, many *traditions* of the Left (for even anarchism has a history). But insofar as the status quo is rejected, the view of the past implied must be schismatic; and this is true of even the most gradualist of political reform movements.

Perhaps the "nuclear" political unit, the family, resisted antitraditionalist interpretation longest, though one would need to qualify that statement by reference, for example, to the history within our society of schismatic "communes" and other eschatological sects, who may hold wives and children in common. And in any case the "rationalisation" of the family is at least as old as this century; or, as it might be better put, customs once identified with nature are now seen, in the light of anthropology and psychoanalysis, as specifically cultural. Freud's insistence on oedipal conflict, and the development of the superego as the guarantee of civilization, was the cardinal lesson. He contrasts the behavior of childish people who will gratify themselves in any way provided they cannot be found out with those in whom "authority has been internalized by the development of a superego."[6] Thus authority, once externally exercised by the father (and indirectly, through him, by one's ancestral traditions), becomes a part of the personality. It is, for Freud, a sad situation, for the authority of the superego is not such that it can also offer the rewards that go with obedience to a father and with the renunciation of satisfactions forbidden by him, the rewards being love and guiltlessness.

The fact well recognized by Freud that the child's superego is likely to be based on the parents' accounts for the strength and continuity of moral systems.[7] Analysts in the Freudian tradition have developed the concept and given it a more complex relationship, both to various stages of the individual's life and to the effect upon the superego of changing cultural conditions. It now seems to many that the transmission across generations of an ancestral superego, however modified, has grown less and less a matter of course. They feel that nongenetic information is no longer transmitted as it used to be (in times when the structure of authority in the family was less controverted) and are aware of an intergenerational conflict that they often regard as untraditional. The historical uniqueness of this situation is undoubtedly exaggerated, but acuteness must in some measure be due to the "rationalizations" of what Erikson calls "the psychoanalytic enlightenment" that sought to replace "age-old repression" with "enlightened judgment."[8] It is true that the dynamic processes within our society change it ever faster, so that whereas everybody still belongs to a family, his adjustment to the culture is a different task from that of his parents, and *mos maiorum* is in general a less useful guide. The parents often know this, too, and assert the traditional sanctions more hesitatingly.

In any case, the family is changing. More frequent divorce, television, increased mobility both physical and social progressively alter it, and neither parents nor children can benefit as easily as before from the old appeal to custom. Because they are rooted in the earliest stages of life, the old unconscious struggles go on as before; and it is to those struggles that such relatively new techniques as family therapy have to address themselves. Those who speak of "the politics of the family" regard it as a miniature of the oppressive state, with the children as underprivileged citizens. If anything, familial conflicts have intensified, partly because of rehousing policies that break up neighborhoods and exile grandparents, whose role in previous generations was most important, not only because they provided a link with old forms of authority and with a lost tradition of family life but because, as everybody knows, the grandparent-child relationship is free of many of the tensions that exist between father and son, so that behind the recent and unacceptable past there was another less threatening, not requiring to be destroyed.

Thus the struggle between parents and children grows more obvious and intense; yet the gap between them is the gap across which the spark of tradition must leap. For tradition is cultural; it has to do with that which cannot be transmitted genetically from one generation to another; it is nongenetic and consists of information that can "in principle be lost, and in one generation."[9] Some of this information is secured by institutions, as, in principle, the Church of Rome preserves the original tradition; or as the law, slowly adapting itself to rapid cultural changes, hands on its qualifications of past statutes or judgments. Here are continuities, bureaucratically ensured, that will survive all but the total collapse of that more fragile institution, the family, though they are in so many ways committed to its protection.

So far I have been writing about the maintenance of tradition—and about schismatic antitraditionalism—in the contexts of religion, sociology, and analytic psychology. But this I have done as a necessary prelude to speaking of the exemplary case of the arts. It is impossible, I think, to divorce this from the other issues I have spoken of. The history of an art is the history of an institution. Heresy and revolution, as they occur in such histories, have the same typology as in the history of religion; and an art, like a church or a society or a language, would die of incommunication if it contrived to abolish its past. There are claims to the contrary, but how quickly we accommodate them into our continuities! A militant protestantism, which seeks access to original truth (a primitive church, a primitive art stripped of the sophistications laid on it by centuries during which a false authority claimed total possession of its tradition), is active also in the arts: thus the poet's proposed return to a language spoken by men, the painter's abjuration of perspective and other illusionisms, are primitivisms on the protestant model. Such heresies divide the institution into sects, and it is easy enough to argue that what Weber said of the history of our religions and our society applies also to its arts, in which a heretical dynamism produces ever more new movements, and a situation in which there is always a great need to change, to *go ahead*. Wyndham Lewis deplored this competition in *aheadofness*, and others have remarked its ill-effect on young artists, who are obliged to establish their novelties almost before they have understood what the old art was.

Yet even in this situation tradition asserts itself, as we may see by citing some familiar instances. One of the crucial dates of art history is 1907, the date of Picasso's *Demoiselles d'Avignon*. We know that this work, the first cubist painting, emerged from sketches intended to issue in a picture of quite a different kind: probably of a man entering a brothel carrying a skull. Yet the end product was the extraordinary work from which so much of the modern tradition, with its abolition of established methods of pictorial representation, is held to derive. Matisse thought it was a hoax. We can see, from our point of vantage, that behind it there is a whole history: impressionist color techniques, the powerful impulses of Cézanne, of Negro masks, of African fetishes.[10] We see the truth of Ortega y Gasset's remark, that in a culture that has chosen "futurism" rather than the hierocratic traditionalisms of Egypt, Byzantium, or the Orient, new styles grow out of antagonisms to traditional styles, which therefore have a negative influence;[11] but we see also that the increasingly complex dialogue between artist and spectator that forms part of the history of the institution of Western art could bring it to a point where traditional skills and language had to be challenged, and a whole new view of the past, and of original truth, had to be sought.

If Matisse was shocked by Picasso's painting, we need not be surprised that the Parisian audience at the first night of *Le Sacre du printemps*, doubtless adherents of conventions they identified with tradition, thought Stravinsky's music a hoax and an insult, nor that T. S. Eliot, who admired it, heard in it the sound of modern traffic, of horns and motors. Now we may watch the ballet with excitement and pleasure, observe the "period" primitivism of decor and dance, and respond to the brilliance of the orchestra without for a moment thinking the music unintelligible or for that matter confusing the sounds we hear with the noise outside the theater. What we do not feel is insult, the flouting of a cherished past. And Stravinsky later gave us cause to label him a "neoclassicist," a cultivator of that tradition, or of parts of it, that he was believed to have desecrated.

Eliot himself supplies a third familiar instance. Before and after he wrote *The Waste Land*—a poem that defies conventions of narrative sequence and traditional exposition—he was elaborating a theory of tradition that, he held, must be worked for, since its orderly transmission had been interrupted, but that placed the individual sensibility of the modern artist in a vital relationship with all past art that was not in itself heretical, which partook of an original and timeless truth.

So three crucial works of art, all of them on the face of it representing a breach with tradition, assume that tradition, in some form, as necessary to their substance; their novelty lies in a breach with the recent, rather than the remoter past; they may be said to represent to us what tradition must be in a culture that prefers change to submissiveness.

What, then, of more strident manifestations of "abolitionism"? The twentieth-century history of the arts is full of manifestos, full of avant-gardes—an expression that, even as late as Baudelaire, had a purely military sense but later was fully appropriated by the arts. On so vast a subject, an essay as brief as this one can say little. But we may again briefly consider some instances, such as futurism, Dada, the "anti-traditionalist" enterprise of Guillaume Apollinaire. All, as it happens, are associated in some way with the First World War. The futurist Marinetti proclaimed the supremacy of the machine, the death of nineteenth-century humanitarian hypoc-

Picasso's *Demoiselles d'Avignon,* 1907 (facing page), now considered the first cubist painting, encompasses many traditions, including Negro masks (above). *"Traditional skills and language had to be challenged, and a whole new view of the past, and of original truth, had to be sought."*

risy, a total break with the past and its meanings. For a time his disgust with the past and enthusiasm for a technological future unrelated to it seemed attractive, but his achievement belongs to the history of advertising rather than of art. Apollinaire, a better poet, took up futurism as he did almost all new movements; a publicist of cubism, he also produced a manifesto called *L'Antitradition futuriste,* in which he cursed traditional art and order and blessed only living artists, including himself. Because they were good artists, they demonstrated that he had a genuine sense of the tradition by becoming part of it.

Dada is perhaps a more difficult matter, more destructive and desperate, though in its way also Utopian. Its influence belongs in part to social rather than art history. Yet in urging us to be rid of false reverence, and indeed to be rid of Art, it invites us to cleanse our perceptions, to discover the truth of our activity when, because we think of it as a piece of art, we

look at an object as if it were different from others; and this is that quest
for original truth in which all heresies begin. A desperate reaction against
the previously unthinkable horrors to which our culture, its idea and its
practice of order, had brought us, gave the dadaists, as it has since given
other rebels, a specially abolitionist tone. "Is it conceivable," asked Ortega,
"that modern Western man bears a rankling grudge against his own historical essence?"[12] Dada, of all the movements of modern art, came nearest to justifying a positive answer. Yet even its direct descendant, surreal-
ism, which had a more positive stance and established strong psychoanalytical and political connections, means less to us than the artists—
Eliot, Stravinsky—who came to an understanding with tradition.

One of the largest claims for modernism as schismatic—it is founded on
Picasso, Dada, and the others—is that it depends on the abandonment of
illusion: a modern picture offers itself as a picture, a modern text as

439

Craftsmen and artisans of all countries (above and the following pages) keep alive
the artistic tradition of their culture. *"It appears that a relation to the history of art is
a precondition of being an artist, and such a relation implies an acceptance, or*

choice, of tradition. Every artist seeks to achieve something new, . . . but the best have recognized that without tradition there simply is no art, and their works are testimony to the effort they make to discover tradition in its full original purity."

necessarily opaque writing, not a fake transparency through which one sees a reassuringly settled "reality." The latest version of this claim—it amounts to a rejection of a supposedly traditional illusionism—is made in the work of the French "structuralist" avant-garde, which repeats, in its publicity as well as in its theory, the same errors. For, as Leo Steinberg has demonstrated for painting and as one could as forcefully establish for literary texts, there is no such break of continuity as the propagandists suppose. It is true that the demand of the modern arts on the interpretative cooperation of reader and spectator is more overt and more urgent, and that modern works draw attention to themselves as artifacts, incomplete without that cooperation, more insistently than the works they are held to supersede. But, as Steinberg remarks, it is "a provincialism" to suppose that there has been a schismatic change, for "What is constant is art's concern with itself, the interest that painters have in questioning their operation."[13] And this holds true for the other arts; only the questions are now asked in a new tone, and less submissively.

What we are seeing is in fact less an abolition than a multiplication of traditions as more of the past becomes available and history makes neglected parts more interesting. A young man dressed in leather wears a Marilyn Monroe button. He was only a child when Marilyn Monroe died, but she is part of a past he can accept, of a new tradition that he supposes may connect him to a primitive truth. A boy who could play Beethoven well abandons him for rock, and within months he is looking for something more than the brief excitement of the "single," seeking in rock the kind of music that will give him the pleasures of structure, of inventive play within rules inherited from the music he has, for the time, consigned to the past.

It has been argued that every artist must, in his own way, submit to the past—after a more or less bitter rebellion—for without this acknowledgment of the father, which is tradition, the child cannot renounce those satisfactions that must be renounced in order that he shall have the rewards of obedience. Whether this is true or not, it appears that a relation to the history of art is a precondition of being an artist, and such a relation implies an acceptance, or choice, of tradition. Every artist seeks to achieve something new, and we need not expect him to think much about the Burkeian community with the dead, much less to display a Chinese wisdom. His task may perhaps be expressed as that of distinguishing, from where he stands, between custom and tradition, as the old Anglicans did— custom being the dead hand of the past, imposing an authority that turns out on inspection to be spurious, merely conventional; and tradition, the conveyor of original truth. In a modern society such distinctions are hard to establish and harder to maintain, and the consequence is what Marxists, in their way highly traditionalist, call a riot of decadence. Certainly it is a situation beset with difficulties; certainly it is easy to be deceived into producing or accepting novelties of no value, to squander one's inheritance.

443

But the best have recognized that without tradition there simply is no art, and their works are testimony to the effort they make to discover tradition in its full original purity.

---

[1] Henry Chadwick, *The Pelican History of the Church*, vol. 1, *The Early Church* (Harmondsworth, Eng.: Penguin Books, 1967), p. 45.

[2] *Documents of the Christian Church*, selected and edited by Henry Bettenson (London: Oxford University Press, 1943), p. 365. Some took an even more extreme view and placed tradition above Scripture, believing that "the doctrines of faith were now so cleared that we ought no more to learn them out of Scripture" (*The Historie of the Councel of Trent*, written in Italian by Pietro Soave Polano [Fra Paolo Sarpi] and faithfully translated into English by Nathanael Brent [London, 1620], pp. 158–59). For a comparison between the Tridentine definitions and the contemporary effort to clarify the tradition of Aristotle, see my "Modern Poetry and Tradition," *Yearbook of Comparative and General Literature*, 14 (1965): 5–15.

[3] See Gerson's strictures on the heretics in John B. Morrall, *Gerson and the Great Schism* (Manchester: Manchester University Press, 1960), p. 101.

[4] Herbert Luethy, "Once Again: Calvinism and Capitalism," *Encounter* 22, no. 1 (January 1964): 26–32; reprinted in *Max Weber*, ed. Dennis Wrong (Englewood Cliffs, N.J.: Prentice-Hall, 1970), p. 126.

[5] *Max Weber*, p. 42.

[6] Sigmund Freud, *Civilisation and Its Discontents*, trans. Joan Rivière, 3d ed. (London: The Hogarth Press, 1946), p. 108; *GBWW*, Vol. 54, p. 792.

[7] See Heinz Hartmann and Rudolph M. Loewenstein, "Notes on the Superego," in *Psychological Issues* 4, no. 2, monograph 14 (New York: International Universities Press, 1964): pp. 144–81.

[8] Erik H. Erikson, *Identity, Youth, and Crisis* (New York: W. W. Norton & Co., 1968), p. 37.

[9] P. B. Medawar, *The Uniqueness of the Individual* (London: Methuen & Co., 1957), p. 141.

[10] For a brilliant study of Picasso's personal and historical situation see E. H. Gombrich, "Psycho-Analysis and the History of Art," in *Meditations on a Hobby Horse* (London: Phaidon Press, 1963), pp. 30–44.

[11] *The Dehumanization of Art* (Princeton, N.J.: Princeton University Press, 1968), p. 43.

[12] Ibid., p. 45.

[13] Leo Steinberg, *Other Criteria* (New York: Oxford University Press, 1972), p. 77.

Advancement and Obsolescence in Science

Theodosius Dobzhansky

One of the great figures in the science of genetics, known particularly for his
formulation of the role of genetics in the origin of species, Theodosius
Dobzhansky has held many academic positions and received numerous
academic and public honors and awards in a career that has lasted for more
than half a century. Born in Nemirov, Russia, in 1900, he graduated from the
University of Kiev, where he subsequently taught zoology, in 1921, and was
a lecturer in genetics at the University of Leningrad from 1924 to 1927. In
the latter year he came to the United States, of which he became a citizen
in 1937, and where he has been, in succession, professor of genetics at the
California Institute of Technology (1936–40); professor of zoology at
Columbia University, New York City (1940–62); professor at the Rockefeller
University, New York City (1962–71); and, since 1971, professor of genetics
at the University of California, Davis.

Of his books, *Mankind Evolving* (1962) was described by George Gaylord
Simpson as "the most interesting . . . the most judicious scientific treatise
that has ever been written on the nature of man." He is the author also of
Genetics and the Origin of Species (1937; 3d edition, 1951), and *Evolution,
Genetics, and Man* (1955).

A member of the National Academy of Sciences and of the American
Philosophical Society, Professor Dobzhansky has at various times been
president of the Genetics Society of America, the American Society of
Zoologists, the Teilhard de Chardin Association, and the Behavior Genetics
Association. He was awarded the 1964 National Medal of Science by the
president of the United States.

Science is cumulative knowledge. Each generation of scientists works to add to the treasury assembled by its predecessors. A discovery made today may not be significant or even comprehensible by itself, but it will make sense in conjunction with what was known before. Indeed, this will usually have been necessary to its achievement. Newton could not have done his work without Copernicus, Galileo, and Kepler. Einstein could not have done what he did without Newton. Of course, new discoveries may change the meaning of prior knowledge. Old hypotheses may be invalidated, old theories discarded. Yet many new discoveries are clearly based upon older ones even when they show these to have been inexact or incorrect. Some interpretations given by Aristotle to his observations seem naive to modern scientists. Aristotle's science is obsolete. It would be silly to set him at naught, however. The works of Aristotle were extremely powerful stimuli of intellectual life for many centuries.

Other disciplines do not show this cumulative character, at least to the same degree. In literature or music, the productions of one era are not the necessary conditions of later ones. Nor are they ever superseded. We probably enjoy Bach and Beethoven today as much as their contemporaries did. Bach and Beethoven are not obsolete. Shakespeare and Dostoevsky have at least as much appeal to us as do the works of our contemporaries. Shakespeare and Dostoevsky are in no sense obsolete. Their writings are timeless. They deal with human problems that have existed and will exist, we may suppose, forever.

Because science is cumulative, it transcends individual accomplishments. In the modern era, particularly, important advances are often based on results obtained by hundreds, even thousands, of research workers. These researchers get their salaries, but gain few prizes and honorific titles. Their names are known only within a more or less narrow circle of specialists, and are soon forgotten or at best embalmed in scientific bibliographies. Yet without the efforts of such rank-and-file scientists, the work of those with great names, winners of Nobel Prizes and such, would be impossible. We do not find this dependence in the great men of other fields. Had Dostoevsky died in his Siberian prison, or had Tolstoy perished from a stray bullet, *The Brothers Karamazov* and *War and Peace* would simply not exist. These masterpieces were contributions that only Dostoevsky or Tolstoy could have made. In contrast, had Darwin not traveled on the *Beagle* and become instead a country doctor or parson, something like *The Origin of Species** would doubtless have appeared. The data on which Darwin relied had been collected by countless other workers, without whose researches Darwin could not have propounded his theory, and with which, another than himself could have done what he did. In point of fact, one of Darwin's contemporaries, Alfred Russel Wallace, outlined a theory of evolution by natural selection independently of and simultaneously with Darwin; had Darwin not been born, we would have "Wallaceism" instead of "Darwinism." The work of Gregor Mendel, largely unnoticed in his lifetime, was repeated after his death, independently and simultaneously, by three investigators in three different countries—Correns in Germany, de Vries in Holland, Tschermak in Austria—who did not know what he had done.

The cumulative and collective aspects of the scientific enterprise make it more sensitive than other human endeavors are to historical developments. A scientific discovery may be made prematurely, or it may be inordinately delayed. Mendel's work is an example of prematurity. That it was forgotten for three and a half decades after it was written up is only partly explained by the fact that it was published in an obscure provincial journal, the last place likely to inspire further researches by a competent contemporary. After all, some competent people read Mendel, yet failed to perceive the significance of what they read. We shall forever be in doubt as to what would have happened had Mendel sent his work to Darwin. Quite possibly, not even Darwin would have understood it. On the other hand, while there have probably always been persons capable of understanding the mechanisms of sexual reproduction, these remained mysterious until the seventeenth century when the invention of the microscope made possible the discovery of the sex cells. Once a microscope became available, the Dutch pioneer biologist Leeuwenhoek and his student Hamm could examine, as they did, the seminal fluids of several animals, including man. In 1675 Leeuwenhoek and Hamm saw in these fluids the squirming spermatozoa. Leeuwenhoek sent a communication describing his discovery to the Royal Society in London, saying that its publication might be withheld if the topic were found to be offensive. Fortunately it was not so considered. A little later, egg cells were discovered by another Dutch biologist, de Graaf. Advances in the understanding of sexual reproduction became rapid thereafter, though until that time almost no progress had been made since Aristotle, who, for lack of the ability to perceive the small objects involved, had arrived at what seem to us some mighty strange ideas on the subject.

Because science is cumulative knowledge, old discoveries are as important as recent ones. In a sense they are more important, since they can be seen to have been the points of departure for all that has followed. (Of

---

* *GBWW*, Vol. 49, pp. 1–251.

course I mean old discoveries that have been validated, such as are apt to be described in the introductory chapters of textbooks and the initial lectures of science courses.) To be sure, a modern student gets his information more easily from secondary sources than from any direct report of these discoveries. Take again the topic of sexual reproduction. Must a student start with Leeuwenhoek's description of the "animalcules" in the seminal fluid? A modern textbook or manual has much better drawings and photographs of the spermatozoa of different animals, including man. Some textbooks, perhaps ill-advisedly, do not even mention the name of the original discoverer of the spermatozoa. A student is still less likely to begin his study of astronomy reading the classical work of Copernicus *On the Revolutions of the Heavenly Spheres.** In the first place, the work is rather too long; moreover, Copernicus assumed that the planetary orbits are circular rather than elliptical, and this made his computations very imprecise. It is after one becomes familiar with the fundamentals of modern astronomy that it is fascinating as well as instructive to see what Copernicus was able to accomplish with the inadequate observational data at hand.

We seem to be facing a contradiction. The discoveries of scientific classics are basic: one must know about them, but not necessarily know how and by whom they were made. Thus some as a rule mediocre but still competent scientists are callously disdainful toward the history of their own science. The history of science, they say, is mainly of interest to scientists in their dotage. Indeed, a former colleague of mine, then a young professor, proudly declared that he had no interest in reading anything written more than five years before. Fortunately, this attitude is uncommon. It is generally accepted that one does not really understand a scientific problem unless one knows at least in rough outline how it came to be formulated.

Perhaps the reason why some scientists are uninterested in the history of their field is that it does, as we have seen, imply obsolescence. This is no merely abstract concern of the scientific investigator. While every scientific advance makes previous knowledge to that extent obsolete, it also implies the eventual obsolescence of the new discovery. In that sense, the scientist is always working to make obsolete his own achievement. The more significant his discovery is, the more rapidly is the obsolescence likely to overtake him. An important idea or finding attracts the attention of many other scientists. The idea is elaborated and tested with the aid of more precise instruments and perhaps a variety of materials beyond the range of the original experiment. The results of the new tests may be more adequate and more impressive than were those of the original ones. The idea, or a theory growing out of it, may be reformulated in a more satisfactory fashion, and not only may become better known than the discovery that led to it but may be associated with a different name!

In these terms it is not hard to see why an investigator, who could be elated to see the advancement in science generated by his work, often seems moved by sentiments of the opposite kind. Scientists are human, and many of them are jealous of their colleagues. Unfortunately, they often show the fact in undignified fashion. Priority squabbles are among the saddest and most futile episodes that blacken the memories of otherwise admirable scientists. Men as great as Newton and Leibniz engaged in this folly. What does it matter now, long after their deaths, which of them was first to invent the calculus? Both of them invented it, largely independently. And nobody at present learns that branch of mathematics from the original works of either Newton or Leibniz, there being hundreds of textbooks that are better for the purpose, even though written by mathematicians of far lesser distinction. Not that this detracts anything from the glory of Newton and Leibniz. Only if mankind were to relapse into barbarism could their contributions to mathematics and science be forgotten.

The one consolation the investigator has is the fact that even the contributions of rank-and-file scientists tend to be preserved, are seldom lost, become part of the storehouse of human knowledge. They do, that is, if they are not rendered obsolete in the manner just indicated. Suppose you have measured a physical constant, determined the distance to some star, collected fossils in a geological formation, or described a new species of animal or plant. You publish an account of your work in a scientific periodical. The volume of the periodical is perused by colleagues in the same specialty and comes eventually to rest on the shelf of some library. Will anyone read it fifty or a hundred years from now? Yes, this may happen; scientists sometimes have to pore over the dusty volumes of old periodicals. More likely, your findings will make a paragraph, perhaps only a line, in some fat compendium volume. But they will survive. Of course, they sometimes remain hidden in their place of preservation. Scientists find it easier to consult summaries and compendiums than to read original papers. Even if these are looked for, they may not be found. Often enough a scientist undertakes the study of a problem unaware that it has been solved years earlier. He may eventually stumble on the forgotten work and acknowledge that what he has achieved is only the confirmation of earlier researches. That is what happened in the case of Mendel. Mendel's work could have remained undiscovered indefinitely. As scientific advances usually end in obsolescence, so the not uncommon fate of scientific investigators is oblivion. But these results are less certain in science than in other human affairs, which are not cumulative in the same way, and in which the individual achievement, not being part of any larger enterprise, will, unless it is genuinely distinguished in its own right, be quickly and utterly forgotten.

The most interesting part of the history of science and the chief reason to study it is, of course, the work of the great figures in the field. It is not only the results of their investigations that repay examination. One can

---

* *GBWW*, Vol. 16, pp. 505–838.

learn from them how to formulate problems with skill and artistry, how to plan experiments, how to assemble observations in significant patterns. None of this can be done without facts, certainly, and these can be gathered only by many minds and many hands. But science does more than collect facts; it makes sense of them. Great scientists are virtuosi of the art of discovering the meaning of what otherwise might seem barren observations. An idea that is born and grows in the mind of a great scientist ties together disjointed facts, inferences, and hypotheses to shape a theory that is intellectually satisfying and even beautiful. So it was with Mendel, whose experiments on crossing varieties of peas were in themselves not unlike the experiments of several of his predecessors, who had worked on other species of plants; what Mendel brought to the subject was an insight that made his own experiments reveal how biological heredity is transmitted from parents to offspring. Again, the idea of evolution was not new when Darwin wrote *The Origin of Species*. What Darwin did was to examine critically a great mass of observations, his own and those of other biologists, in the light of an idea that others had not perceived. When T. H. Huxley, who became Darwin's most effective advocate, saw the result, he reproached himself: how stupid he was not to have seen what Darwin made so clear! His self-reproach was unnecessary. Great ideas often seem simple and self-evident, but only after somebody has explained them to us. Then, how interesting they become! The act of insight is among the most exciting and pleasurable experiences a scientist can have, when he recognizes what all the time was there to be seen, and yet he did not see it.

It should not be imagined, of course, that great ideas in science are revealed at once, and that they do, or do not, immediately thereafter become obsolete. Even though the germ of an idea may come suddenly, it must grow and develop. Then it may become the nucleus of a theory that makes sense of a multitude of facts, and that serves to guide others as well as the original investigator in the search for further related facts. The theory of evolution by natural selection is a case in point.

Evolution postulates that the state of the world we observe now has emerged from very different states. In general, the farther back in time we look, the more unlike the present these past states were; slow and imposing as the process is, moreover, the difference between past and present is becoming greater all the time. Evolution is not only a historical event; it is ongoing. The causes that underlie it are still in operation, and, in principle at least, can be made the subject of observation and experiment.

In the widest sense, the term evolution is applicable to cosmic or inorganic, to biological or organic, and to human or cultural development. Cosmic evolution has been going on for somewhere between ten and fifteen billion years, biological for perhaps four billion years, human for a mere two or three million years. The causes that bring about these three kinds of evolution are quite distinct; two of the kinds, the biological and the human, have taken place, so far as we know, exclusively on the planet earth. Yet some philosophers see the three evolutions as parts of a single creative enterprise.

Some historians find germs of evolutionary ideas in the creation myths of various peoples, or in the speculations of ancient Greek philosophers. Whether or not these myths and speculations, often couched in poetic imagery, can be regarded as coming anywhere near to what evolution means in our terms is questionable. Even Herodotus and Thucydides, the ancient Greek historians, while giving well-reasoned, accurate, and critical accounts of events, never put them in the perspective of a developmental process taking mankind from one state to another. Perhaps such a perspective can be seen in the Judeo-Christian world view, which envisages history as a sequence of happenings, from the Creation to Redemption and finally to the Kingdom of God. If so, how ironic it is that the opposition to evolutionary theory in recent times has come mainly from religious circles! In the eighteenth century, the Age of Enlightenment, mankind was conceived to have developed from a primitive state to one that promised eventual perfection. Condorcet, waiting to be executed by revolutionary terrorists, gave an explicit statement of this view in 1793. The evolutionary origin of the sun and the planetary system was postulated late in the eighteenth and early in the nineteenth centuries by Kant and Laplace. The theory of uniformitarianism, according to which the evolution of mountains and seas has been brought about by the same cosmic forces, which are held to be still in operation, stems mainly from Lyell, whose *Principles of Geology* appeared in 1830.

Evolution in the biological sense, the theory that life itself evolves, is the keystone of evolutionary science. Its discovery came last, after cosmic and cultural evolution had been accepted. Although several great thinkers, from Descartes to Buffon, toyed with the underlying idea, it was Lamarck who became the first explicit evolutionist, beginning with publication of his *Philosophie Zoologique* in 1809. His greatness has never been properly recognized, at least not outside France. That is probably so because the term *Lamarckism* has for long been used to indicate only a part of Lamarck's theory, the part that asserts that characteristics acquired during the lifetime of an individual can be inherited, and that is now generally regarded as erroneous. This notion was not original with Lamarck, however, whose main insight, a brilliant one, was that the whole living world is the product of an evolutionary development.

In 1858 and 1859 appeared the works of Darwin and Wallace. From then on, evolution became the great unifying idea in biology. Darwin and Wallace not only affirmed that evolution occurs but also gave a convincing explanation of its main causes. Though they assumed—mistakenly, as we now know—the inheritance of acquired traits as a subsidiary factor, they identified natural selection as the chief source of evolutionary change. This identification has been borne out by biological research during the century and more that has elapsed since their time, though our present con-

has been successfully accomplished. Now a different, and in a sense antipodal, problem has moved to the fore. This is to establish the evolutionary uniqueness of man. In several ways, mankind is a singular, quite extraordinary product of the evolutionary process. Biological evolution has transcended itself giving rise to man, as inorganic evolution did in giving rise to life. All organisms evolve and become adapted to their environments by changing their genes to fit these environments. Mankind evolves chiefly, though not exclusively, by making its environments fit its genes. A single example will suffice as an illustration. Animals adapt to cold climates by growing warm fur, or by winter dormancy, or by genetically fixed drives to migrate to warmer climates. Man adapts to cold by dressing in warm garments and building heated dwellings. Like all other biological species, mankind has a biological heredity transmitted by Mendelian genes. Mankind has also a cultural heredity, transmitted by instruction and learning. In this transmission, symbolic languages, which are also unique to man, play key roles.

Culture is not inherited through genes. It is acquired, by every person for himself, through contacts with other people, who may or may not be biological relatives. Difficult and controversial questions arise concerning the interrelationships of the biological and cultural "heredities." What are the causes of the variations in the expression of cultural characteristics among humans? At one extreme are those who think that the biological evolution of mankind had been completed when culture first appeared, that all humans have essentially the same genetic endowments, and that the domain of culture is wholly separate from biology. At the opposite pole is the view that race, class, and individual cultural differences originate in the genes. The scientific controversy over these matters is all too often linked with political convictions and biases of the exponents of the different views. But a few very general statements may appropriately be made here about the whole question.

It is certain that a human genetic endowment is requisite for acquisition of any human culture. It is also certain that no two persons (so-called identical twins excepted) have the same genes. Every nonpathological human genetic endowment confers upon its carriers the capacity to acquire a culture, but the genes do not predetermine which one of the many existing cultures is to be acquired. An analogous situation is found with human language: human genes are required for learning a human language, but they do not decide which language will be learned, still less what a person will say when he learns it. Natural selection has always favored in mankind the development of educability, i.e., of a capacity to learn what a given culture makes necessary in its members, to profit by experience, and to modify and adjust one's behavior in the light of circumstances. Educability is a fundamental trait of the species *Homo sapiens*. It is what makes human behavior different from that of nonhuman animals. And yet this trait is

454

individually variable. Some individuals learn more easily and successfully certain things, and other individuals other things. Every individual is unique and unrepeatable; people are not interchangeable.

Science has been called "the endless frontier." The more we know, the better we realize that our knowledge is a little island in the midst of an ocean of ignorance. There will always be plenty of problems to invite study, thought, and research. Yet from time to time some people conjecture that a branch of science is essentially complete. Some outstanding physicists claimed this at the turn of the current century, at the very time when the discovery of radioactivity was opening a new era of atomic physics, making possible the atomic age! Spectacular advances of molecular biology in recent decades induced more than one scientist to make similar claims. Allegedly, the greatest ideas have already been advanced, and the fundamental discoveries have all been made. There are supposed to remain only some details to be filled in. Science is not endless, it is said: the limit can already be seen.

It is hard to confute this opinion, but not necessarily because it is true. Who knows what great ideas are to be conceived of, and what fundamentally new discoveries are waiting to be made? A new idea is unforeseeable until it has germinated in somebody's mind, and a new discovery is not guaranteed until at least a glimmer of it is seen. In short, ideas and discoveries that will open new paths to knowledge are unpredictable. Whether or not the epoch of great discoveries in science is past is a matter of personal faith or intuition. I, for one, believe that the limits of human knowledge are nowhere in sight.

455

History and Tradition

J. H. Plumb

J. H. Plumb, who is among the most distinguished of contemporary historians, is known to the general public chiefly through such books as *The Horizon Book of the Renaissance* (1961), *Men and Centuries* (1963), and *The Death of the Past* (1970). But his professional reputation is based on his studies of the eighteenth century. Among these are *England in the Eighteenth Century* (1950), *The Growth of Political Stability in England, 1675–1725* (1967), and a monumental life of Sir Robert Walpole, still to be completed, of which the first two volumes have been published.

Although he received his B.A. with first class honors in history from the University of London in 1933, Professor Plumb has made the greatest part of his academic career at Cambridge, where he is now professor of modern English history. He was visiting professor at Columbia University, New York City, in 1960 and distinguished visiting professor at the City University of New York in 1971–72. Awarded a D.Litt. from Cambridge in 1957 for his work in eighteenth-century English history, he is a fellow of the British Academy and an honorary foreign member of the American Academy of Arts and Sciences.

H istory is Janus-faced, but the faces are far from being identical. One is wrinkled with deep lines, as old as the distant ages of mankind; the other is youthful, vigorous, and in the full flood time of early maturity. These faces represent two very different types of history. The former is obviously riddled with traditional attitudes enshrined in works whose fame has lasted for milleniums. The latter, too, is old enough to have established traditions of working and methods of expression, some of which, though not all, continue to be powerful. Two types, therefore, of history need to be considered. One is the way man has always looked at his past. He has turned to it to explain the roots of his society, to tell him its story, he searches it, as his forebears did, for examples of human behavior, and often he scrutinizes the past in the hope that it will enlighten him about the future. This is basically what Voltaire called philosophic history, whose truth may lie deeper than facts. And this for centuries on end was the totality of historical practice—sometimes simple, sometimes sophisticated and complex—not only in the West and throughout Islam but also in China and in Japan. As we shall see, this type of history persists, and rightly so, though the part tradition plays in it has grown at once more complex and weaker with time.

But the more youthful variety of history is easier to deal with and should be taken up first. When Chinese historians of the T'ang period looked back on the Han, or when Livy contemplated Roman history or Herodotus delved into the history of Egypt or of Persia, they were largely concerned to discover moral truths; although they had some concern for factual accuracy, it was not their prime concern. Herodotus, like Thucydides after him, thought nothing of inventing speeches and putting them in dead men's mouths. Similarly, the Chinese historians would deliberately switch the semi-miraculous happenings necessary for the birth of an emperor from father to son without any compunction, because they were necessary for moral emphasis, to demonstrate clearly that Heaven itself supported the new emperor, this being presumed in light of the fact that the emperor had successfully established a dynasty. And so, in the Middle Ages, the monastic chroniclers accepted, not incredulously but because of their belief in God's will and purpose, the miracles of founding abbots or

457

of the saints who had embellished their orders. At the same time, all of these historians put into their works a great deal that was accurate—factual truths about the lives of men and women and events of their societies and communities. But the pursuit of factual truth was not their primary aim. They were illustrating the purpose of God, the truths of morality in which fables, miracles, or myths are as valuable as facts.

The development of critical history—the youthful face of Janus—was highly complex, with slow beginnings, and had, like all mighty rivers, many tributaries. And it is a purely Western phenomenon. As I have written elsewhere, "The Chinese pursued erudition, but they never developed the critical historiography which is the signal achievement of Western historians over the last two hundred years. They never attempted, let alone succeeded, in treating history as objective understanding."*

Probably one of the basic reasons why Europe developed critical history was because its past had been badly fractured. There was a pagan past of Greece and Rome and the Christian past of the Bible that interlocked but did not properly fit, leaving for the critical mind a wealth of problems, chronological and technical as well as interpretative. Also, the half-obliterated pagan past was a wonderful hunting ground for antiquarians, those who were searching for categories of facts and so were discovering facts themselves. There was so much to collect and put in order: chronicles, literature, plays, poems, epigrams and epigraphs, medals, coins, wonderful fields of antiquarian specialization that, from the fifteenth century onward, began to be ever more precise and accurate. The earliest traditions of exact historical scholarship began with the antiquarians and with the critical examination of texts—for example, Lorenzo Valla's famous proof that the Donation of Constantine was a forgery—in the fifteenth century. Valla belonged to a school of lawyers, a school that grew and strengthened over the next hundred years, and that was concerned to discover precisely what legal phrases, even words, meant at the time they became inscribed in law. These lawyers realized that time itself eroded and changed meanings, and that to understand legal concepts of Rome one needed to use historical criticism, to learn how to strip off the coruscations of time. Both processes encouraged the growth of erudition; the recovery and ordering of more facts about the past and the spread of critical methods of handling words and documents within their own special frameworks of time grew steadily throughout the sixteenth century, primarily in Italy and France but also, during the seventeenth century, in England. In France particularly this gave rise to the establishment of techniques—paleographic and diplomatic—that have become a traditional part of scholarship. Similarly, some of the great works of scholarship—the *De Re Diplomatica* of Mabillon or the *Acta Sanctorum* of the Bollandists (still in course of publication after three hundred years)—remain important books for the medieval historian. Here

---

* J. H. Plumb, *The Death of the Past* (Boston: Houghton Mifflin, 1970), p. 13.

the tradition is firm; the growth of knowledge, through established techniques, steady.

Even so, there were rapid improvements in the eighteenth century, and the spearhead of critical history passed to Germany, particularly to the University of Göttingen. Elsewhere there was great improvement. Always historians had embedded charters, letters, and documents in their histories and annals to help give veracity to their argument. But instead of being occasional embellishments, often now the volumes of the documents supporting a history were longer than the history itself. This was particularly true of a great but neglected English historian, Archdeacon Coxe, whose exceptional documentation, accurately presented (at least for his age), not only has given his books enduring value but has also influenced generations of English historians. From Coxe's day, the editing and publishing of documents became an intense preoccupation of the growing number of professional historians of the nineteenth century. The *Monumenta Germaniae Historica,* whose first volume, edited by the great scholar G. H. Pertz, appeared in 1826, induced scholars in other countries to follow Pertz's lead (notably in the case of the Rolls series in Britain), and so was created a tradition of editing, and publication of fundamental sources, that is still assiduously followed. Indeed, one may say that a tradition of editing historical sources was established, if constantly refined, from 1826 until the present day. However, two factors have placed this tradition in jeopardy. One is the soaring costs of printing a text with elaborate critical appendixes; the other is the ease with which nowadays any scholar can get a reproduction of almost any document that he may want. Even so, such editing, like its counterparts in historical erudition, the creation of historical dictionaries and collation of varied historical materials, remains a fundamental part of the historical profession; in essence, the rules laid down by Mabillon, and developed by the great German textual editors, are still followed. Here the traditional methods of scholarship endure.

*   *   *   *   *

The ambitions of the early professional historians were vast, however, and not confined to the editing of thousands of texts. The range of Leopold von Ranke was enormous; he planned a Universal History at the age of ninety. His work still retains considerable value, through the care with which he used sources, the lucidity of his writing, and the sharp intelligence that he exercised, particularly in diplomatic history. Before Ranke, historians such as Gibbon—in a sense the first great critical and professional historian—had taken immense themes for their subjects, and historians continued to do so throughout the nineteenth century. In America (one has only to think of Bancroft, Prescott, and Motley) they all happily embraced great periods of time, rich with complex and multitudinous sources. Multivolume narrative histories or biographies were a common-

460

place of historical literature by the mid-nineteenth century. Yet what seemed to be an established tradition by the 1870s had almost vanished by 1914.

The vast outpouring of archival material in the nineteenth century, combined with stronger professional standards of scholarly care and mastery of sources, naturally increased specialization. This in turn was encouraged by the great national historical reviews that were established. Germany, not surprisingly, was the first in the field with the *Historische Zeitschrift* in 1859; France followed in 1876 with the *Revue historique*. Both England and America were much tardier. The *English Historical Review* was first published in 1886, and the *American Historical Review* in 1895. They were all symptoms of a development in the discipline of history that is now so deep-rooted as to be the most traditional aspect of academic or professional history. From 1900, journals for academic history of every kind proliferated rapidly and still continue to increase. In these journals a professional historian can treat of a small historical problem or throw new light on an aspect of a large one. It permits him to establish a reputation without the need to produce a book. And these journals have profoundly influenced the whole nature of historical investigation, for they are largely concerned with the "whys" of history, concepts about how history happened, rather than a relation of events. This, too, is reflected in the books that great professional historians, bred in this new style of history, began to write at the turn of the century. They ceased to write great narrative histories on large historic themes and turned to more specialized concepts: the nature of feudalism, the origins of parliamentary government, the nature of the Renaissance, the causes of the Reformation, the influence of the frontier on American history. Indeed, Frederick Jackson Turner's famous essay on the frontier, published in 1894, was a turning point in American historiography. Then came the first light of the dawn of that "new history" publicized and promoted by James Harvey Robinson and Charles A. Beard, who taught the methods, the techniques, and the attitudes toward the past that had been established in European historiography. From these and other points stems the great river of professional history, as wide and as long as the Mississippi, that flows through the universities and colleges of America. The influence of these men, and their pupils' influence, is still paramount.

The establishment of high professional standards bred specialization, both vertical and horizontal; that is, aspects of human activity were easier to isolate and study than their complex relationships, so scholars devoted their lives to economic history, or ecclesiastical history, or the history of ideas, or the history of politics or law. And, of course, it was easier to deal with a short period such as that covered by the agrarian revolution in sixteenth-century England, or the role of the lawyers in seventeenth-century Toulouse, or the origins of the meat-packing industry in Chicago. This vertical and horizontal slicing of history has now hardened into a tradition, and is dominant in professional academic circles. Naturally, the strength of its hold varies from country to country. It dominates English academic life, where the work of Sir Lewis B. Namier, which was, in essentials, confined to a segment of political history of the 1760s, is regarded as one of the great achievements of professional history. His work on the history of parliament has spawned a host of imitators. In America this tradition is also very powerful, as it is in France and the rest of Europe. However, among some of the most gifted historians writing today there is a growing disenchantment with specialization that is too rigid in the orientation of the subject or too confined in time.

Many of the greatest academic historians of this century have always been deeply concerned by the limitations of high professional specialization. Lord Acton, who believed this could be overcome by great cooperative enterprises, planned the *Cambridge Modern History*, by which he hoped to create a synthesis from the best specialists. The result was useful but dull, a fourteen-volume work of reference, of exceptionally varying quality; yet some chapters were brilliant, some volumes even admirable. And so the cooperative history of specialists established itself, whether dealing with all human history, such as the wholly admirable Columbia University's *History of the World*—perhaps the finest achievement of this tradition —or significant and large sections of the human story that the great Cambridge histories have covered. It is a method, however, that is less widely practiced in Europe, and though now firmly established as a practice of the professional historians, and still dominated by the tradition established by Lord Acton, it has never proved wholly satisfactory, nor satisfied those historians who wish for closer contacts with the culture of their day.

Historians, since Gibbon's day, have been well aware of its Janus-faced nature. History has possessed since the earliest times of mankind a social purpose and yet, by its very nature, professional and highly specialized history can play only a very limited role. It is excellent for training the critical faculties; on occasion it can stimulate sympathy and understanding of societies and people different from ourselves; but most of it, perhaps 90 percent of it, is uninteresting, even unreadable, except for those involved in its academic disciplines.

Fortunately, men and women since Homer's day and beyond have craved to know about the past. Who made the world? Why is there evil? How is good achieved? Questions as to how and why have always haunted generations of men and women whose curiosity about the past is insatiable, giving us works whose role has long endured—among them, and above all, the Bible, which in essence is a history. There is, indeed, a great constellation of epics—Homer, the Sagas, the Vedas, the early annals of China—that no amount of historical criticism can ever destroy, that remain to delight and to instruct the intelligent and curious reader. These

462

"The half-obliterated pagan past was a wonderful hunting ground for antiquarians.
. . . There was so much to collect and put in order."

epics merge in times closer to our own into the great traditional histories —Gibbon, Hume, Macaulay, Ranke, Michelet, Prescott, Motley—that so delighted our grandfathers and that are still read more by nonhistorians, perhaps, than by trained professionals. And so we have a curious anomaly, a traditional historical literature that is rarely read by the professional historian for its own sake. When the professional historian studies Herodotus or Gibbon, he does so historiographically, that is, to understand either what the author's vision of history was and why or the way he reflected the intellectual forces of his day. Whereas the bulk of the readership of these works, which is nonprofessional, goes to them for entirely different reasons. These traditional works—particularly historians such as Prescott or Gibbon or Macaulay—are read because they are excellent narratives, telling, with excitement in pungent prose, what happened. The stories of the conquest of Mexico, or the decline and fall of Rome, or the English revolution are magnificent in themselves. And as well as stories, there are the historical characters—larger than life, who in their day dominated the human scene—from Alexander the Great to Napoleon. About all these books there is what the French call the "odor of man," the smell of life. We can, through these books, project ourselves into the lives of men who once walked this earth as we do and have now vanished, whereby we participate in what may be called the poetry of time, which is the poetry of history. It is because it affords us this opportunity that history is so enduring a part of literature, a part of the great tradition.

And that tradition still exists, but it has tragically weakened. Where today are the Michelets, the Prescotts, the Macaulays? Few remain, if any, even though history as literature, history to entertain, pours from the presses as never before. Much of it is effective, a delight to read. Sometimes a professionally trained historian wanders into the field of traditional historical writing, almost uniformly with excellent results. For example, Sir John Neale wrote a biography of Queen Elizabeth that is certainly open to technical criticism, as it idolizes the queen; but, nevertheless, it is a remarkable literary tour de force that millions of people have read with delight. The same is true of a young American scholar, Lacey Baldwin Smith, whose *Mask of Royalty,* a book about Henry VIII, like Garrett Mattingly's *Defeat of the Spanish Armada,* will become a part of the classical tradition and endure as a work of art. Yet there are few professional historians at work in traditional history—studies of great events, biographies, and the like—and the reasons are not hard to find.

Traditional history, to be effective, requires great literary gifts—mastery of narrative structure, analytical insight into the vagaries of human behavior, a capacity to evoke through the magic of words, landscape, the way life was lived—all of which are not in the least necessary for a professional historian engaged on precise and narrow issues. And traditional history cannot often be written within a small compass about a narrow issue, so the writer of traditional history has to take great risks. He can never master all of the sources; there will be too many documents, too many letters, too many monographs. No one now can read all that has been published about the conquest of Mexico or the rise of the Dutch Republic. Therefore, the professional historian is naturally shy of attempting to do what his whole training has conditioned him not to do: to use his imagination, his sense of human reality, to bet on his hunches without having full documentary proof.

The reluctance or inability of professional historians to write traditional history means that the writing of it is largely in the hands of amateur historians, working outside the universities and the professional bodies. The last great academic figure who insisted passionately on the premise that history was literature or nothing and indeed wrote great traditional histories throughout his long life was G. M. Trevelyan. But his influence within the professional faculties of history was almost negligible. Lacking professional training, somewhat daunted by the bibliographical and archival expertise that a professional would have entirely at his command, the traditional historian, almost always an amateur, moves insecurely and often disastrously. Never before have so many books of a traditional historical kind been written. Most of them are sitting targets for professional criticisms. Within a year or two they pass into oblivion.

So we have a sad situation: a public demand for traditional history, an extraordinarily large response in terms of books (indeed, not only books; historical television series also meet with vast acclaim in both America and England), and yet an almost complete decline in quality, scarcely a book worthy to sit on the same shelf as the great old masters. To be fair, the decline is not in literary skill. Many recent books—Gene Smith's *Maximilian and Carlota,* Stanley Loomis's *Paris in the Terror,* or Robert Lacey on *Sir Walter Ralegh*—are beautifully constructed and written with the verve and panache worthy of a Prescott or Trevelyan. They fail to establish themselves permanently in the great tradition of historical writing.

One obvious reason for this is their lack of scholarship in depth. The great old masters—under less economic necessity, perhaps, as well as under less social pressure—tended to limit themselves to a few works on great themes. Gibbon spent his lifetime on the *Decline and Fall,** Macaulay, a man of monumental vigor, decades on his history, and even the output of a Motley or a Prescott was not large. In consequence, they had time to delve as deeply as any professional of their day into the sources of their work. Now, sources are more multitudinous than they were, yet the pressure on literary historians is to write quickly, to produce salable one-volume works as frequently as they can. Hence, even to the untrained reader of history, there is often a sense of a lack of depth, of profound knowledge, no matter how skillful the literary craftsmanship.

There is, however, I think, a more subtle reason. There has been a

---

* *The Decline and Fall of the Roman Empire; GBWW*, Vols. 40 and 41.

sharp decline in the role that traditional history plays in modern society. History has been the great interpreter of the human destiny, the pantheon in which mankind has enshrined its heroes, the majestic story of the conflict of good and evil, or the more mundane tale of progress, both material and moral. And furthermore, in the nineteenth century, history became even more closely associated with national destiny—a national destiny, however, that was also providential. The great American historians saw America, freed from the corruptions of Europe, as the great torchbearer of freedom. And whether they were writing about the Dutch Republic or the Conquistadores, there is, in their works, a deep sense that the tidal forces of history led inevitably to the freedom, the maturity, and the intellectual life that nineteenth-century New England, at least, enjoyed. The same is true of the great English historians, who saw English history as a slow but successful struggle for political freedom and representative institutions. If we turn to France or Italy or Germany, we find the same deep chord of national destiny struck. Hence, when these historians were read by tens of thousands of their fellow countrymen, the response went far deeper than entertainment; they fortified belief in their nation's destiny, strengthened social confidence. And that, of course, is why historical studies spread so rapidly in schools and universities in the late nineteenth and early twentieth centuries, and why all governments felt that the history of their nation must be an essential part of education at every level. History had an immediate, an urgent social purpose.

That situation has ended. The time given to history in schools shrinks every year. The enrollment of students in universities for historical studies has ceased to grow, and in many countries has begun to decline sharply. If we turn to other social studies—from economics to sociology—there is far less concern with historical roots of problems than there was. Indeed, it is rare now for scholars, let alone the public at large, to look to history for an explanation of the problems of our time. And nothing is more in ruins than the tradition that the past explains the present, sanctifies its institutions, and indicates the future. That ordinary men and women still hunger for such explanations and such prognostications is apparent from the popularity of Arnold Toynbee's great work on *A Study of History,* and nothing indicates the decay of such an attitude better than the lack of any imitators or even rivals to that work.

And yet this is true only of the West. In the nineteenth century, Marx and Engels forged an interpretation of history—materialist, dialectic and inevitable—that, as developed by Lenin, has become a rigid tradition not only in the Communist countries of Eastern Europe and of China but also among Marxist scholars or politicians in the rest of the world. This interpretation is now as absolute, as revered, as the old Chinese historical interpretation of the Mandate of Heaven. Indeed, it is a curious paradox that as traditional history has begun to crumble, not only in democratic societies of Europe and America but also in Islam and in the less developed

467

Each year North Carolina residents recreate a part of their history by making a wagon train journey from North Wilkesboro to Boone in much the same manner as early settlers of the region. *"Men and women since Homer's time and beyond have*

craved to know about the past. . . . Questions as to how and why have always haunted generations of men and women whose curiosity about the past is insatiable."

countries of Africa and the East, interpretations of history in Marxist countries have hardened into a steel-like dogma. At times this has odd consequences, for human events and indeed human beings have a Houdini-like capacity to escape the clutches of an inevitable historical interpretation; one needs only to recall the problems created by a rigid Christian interpretation of history not merely in the nineteenth century but even in the far distant days of Eusebius to see the point. And so, events—the denunciation of Stalin by Khrushchev—create a constant need for revision of the accepted Marxist tradition, all creating cracks in the edifice, making for cynicism, perhaps the most powerful corroder of tradition of all.

History, therefore, and the practitioners of history are entangled in complexities and paradoxes. As the professional methods and attitudes to history harden into even stronger traditions, the old social purposes of history that stretch back to the very beginnings of written records lose their force. The traditional power of history weakens, even as curiosity about the people and the events of the past grows. This situation is, of course, dangerous—more dangerous than many professional historians realize—for no discipline can survive for very long or be the recipient of vast funds, unless it fulfills an obvious social purpose. What is needed is what happened to history in the eighteenth century, when antiquarianism and philosophic history fused. The result of that fusion was the great historical literature of the nineteenth century. If only professional history could break with some of its traditional attitudes and take upon itself the burden of the history that society needs, the prospect for academic historians and for history in the service of mankind would be brighter than it is.

The Idea of Tradition in Great Books of the Western World

Tradition is not one of the Great Ideas in the *Syntopicon*. It is, however, included in the Inventory of Terms, where we find it noted as a subject of discussion in topics belonging to half a dozen of those ideas, and at least implied in topics related to eight or nine more. This does not mean that the word itself always appears in the passage referred to. The discussion is sometimes carried on in the name of "custom," "convention," "habit," or "example." Nor are such related terms without their differences of meaning. They have, nevertheless, a common connotation, which is the preservation of the past that the idea of tradition necessarily involves, and they may fairly be said to indicate a common concept, as to the definition of which there is no serious dispute in *Great Books of the Western World*, but only some disagreement over the question whether that preservation is a good or a bad thing, considered in all its aspects.

One such aspect appears in the idea that the Past claims some authority in the Present, where it may or may not be regarded with deference. This is taken up in the texts under History 2, which deal with the role of history in education and the guidance of human conduct; it is considered also, with respect to the intellectual tradition, in passages noted at Progress 6c; it figures again, more generally, in writings listed at Time 8b, which deal with historical epochs, the ages of man, and the relative character of modernity.

A second aspect of the past as something that extends into the present appears in the form of particular customs or creeds that are handed down in the expectation of obedience or belief. This is discussed in the texts at Custom and Convention 8, dealing with custom in relation to order and progress; it appears also in writings listed under Custom and Convention 2, which have to do with the transmission of customs, and in Law 8, where passages dealing with the historical development of law are noted.

Still a third aspect of the subject, the most interesting one for a reader of the great books, seems to reveal a community of discourse in the accumulation of human knowledge. We find this considered in the chapter on Truth at topic 6, which lists writings that have to do with the progress of human learning; it is of some concern also in the texts at Philosophy 7, which deal with the history of philosophy and the lives of philosophers in relation to their thought; it is a notion basic to the discussion in the texts noted under Memory and Imagination 4b, which have to do with what is remembered, through instinct, legend, and tradition, in the life of the group or race.

The idea of a surviving past appears also in writings mentioned in the chapter on Art at topic 12, which are devoted to the history and progress of the arts, and by texts at Poetry 2 and 3, which are concerned with the origins of poetry in myth and legend and the influence on the poet of the poetic tradition. And the passages listed variously at Education 9, Family 7*b*, and Language 3*c* all point to the further fact that some, perhaps all, human arts and institutions are to some extent conservative of the past.

We can divide these many texts, which range beyond the concern of this year's symposium, into two groups. In one group, "tradition" or one of its related terms is used or intended generally and reflects a preoccupation with human development or human character. Such is the case in certain discussions of custom that occur, for example, in the *Essays* of Montaigne. The same preoccupation appears in William James's account of habit in the *Principles of Psychology*. We see it also in Freud when he speaks of the role of the superego in the unconscious. What is said about "tradition" on these occasions extends to all human orders—everything that men do, or make, or think—and is applicable perennially, without respect to time or place. Thus Robert M. Hutchins in volume 1 of *Great Books of the Western World* speaks of the tradition of the West as a Great Conversation, recognized by "the common voice of mankind,"[1] which has endured from epoch to epoch. The *Syntopicon* itself is, of course, a monument to this conception, without which it could never have been made.

In the second group of texts, "tradition" or one of its related terms is used with respect to a particular human order or preoccupation, such as art, philosophy, or government, and is often limited to a particular time and place. Hence the application is frequently one in which a custom or tradition is noted as having come or gone, grown stronger or weaker, perhaps even disappeared. In the *Iliad*, Nestor laments the vanished days of his youth when, he says, men were equally accomplished in counsel and the arts of war. Dante speaks of a change that has come about in art, where "Cimabue thought to hold the field in painting, and now Giotto has the cry";[2] he mentions also a "sweet new style" that has emerged in the poetry of his age.[3] Of course there is more than mention in *Don Quixote* about the passing of knight errantry. There is more than mention, too, in Plato's *Dialogues* of Athenian education, with its literary bent and rote learning, of which the *Dialogues* may be read as a critique, and for which Plato in his Academy substituted the mathematics and speculative inquiry that laid the basis of Western thought. As great a change was later brought about by Saint Augustine in Roman education, of which it may be said that he found it pagan and left it Christian, through the example and influence of his writings. And comparable changes were accomplished still later by

Copernicus—first, perhaps, among those whose work has altered the traditional understanding of things—by William Harvey, who revolutionized Galenic medicine, and by Lavoisier, who laid the foundations of modern chemistry.

The role of tradition in a particular human order is judged to be bad by some of these authors, by others is thought to be good. Among the first, those whose concern is with science tend to be most cogent and most critical. In this order, the weight of tradition is usually protested on the ground that it inhibits or prevents the progress of learning. Bacon, for instance—noting "the overmuch credit" that is given to the authority of the ancients, "making them dictators, that their words should stand, and not consuls to give advice"—says, "the damage is infinite that the sciences have received thereby, as the principal cause that hath kept them low at a stay without growth or advancement."[4] In another passage, speaking of "idols [that] beset the human mind," he mentions the "many elements and axioms of sciences which have become inveterate by tradition," and which he includes among what he calls the "idols of the theatre," because they, like "all the systems of philosophy hitherto received or imagined, [are] so many plays brought out and performed, creating fictitious and theatrical worlds."[5] And still later he complains that not experience but "mere reports of experience, traditions as it were of dreams," are the basis of the still-medieval science that he sees, which must be "built anew" if the mind of man is to be purged of "credulity and accident, and the puerile notions it originally contracted."[6]

Hobbes is even more severe, condemning deference to the past not only in science but in nearly everything else. "There is nothing so absurd that the old philosophers (as Cicero saith, who was one of them) have not some of them maintained," he writes. "And I believe that scarce anything can be more absurdly said in natural philosophy than what now is called Aristotle's *Metaphysics;* nor more repugnant to government than much of what he saith in his *Politics;* nor more ignorantly than a great part of his *Ethics.*"[7] Pascal, in his "Preface" to the *Treatise on the Vacuum*—an important text, about which there will be occasion to say more later on—is unwilling to condemn ancient authority in the same broad way, but he too notes the bad effect it has had in what we would now call physics, where, accepting the ancient dictum that nature abhors a vacuum, men had not until his time troubled to find out whether it was, in nature, actually so.[8] Galileo's account of his experiment with falling bodies in effect makes the same point, but it is not accompanied by any general remarks about the pernicious effects of traditional ways of thought.[9] We find such remarks, however, in Lavoisier, who in establishing that water is a compound and not a simple substance observes:

> *It is very extraordinary that this fact should have hitherto been overlooked by natural philosophers and chemists: indeed, it strongly proves that, in chemistry*

473

*as in moral philosophy, it is extremely difficult to overcome prejudices imbibed
in early education and to search for truth in any other road than the one we
have been accustomed to follow.*[10]

And to this may be added the passage, of more extended application, that
occurs in the second chapter of *The Decline and Fall of the Roman Empire*,
where Gibbon notes the intellectual stagnation that had overtaken the
Empire in the age of the Antonines, when, he says,

> *the authority of Plato and Aristotle, of Zeno and Epicurus, still reigned in the
> schools; and their systems, transmitted with blind deference from one generation
> of disciples to another, precluded every generous attempt to exercise the powers,
> or enlarge the limits, of the human mind.*[11]

As the focus of texts that are critical of tradition is chiefly on science,
though it is not confined to that (Gibbon goes on to observe that in the
same period of the Empire "the beauties of the [ancient] poets and orators,
instead of kindling a fire like their own, inspired only cold and servile
imitations: or if any ventured to deviate from those models, they deviated
at the same time from good sense and propriety"[12]), so the focus of texts
that approve the role of tradition tends to be on politics, morals, and
religion, though authors can be found who judge that the weight of the
past is a bad thing even in those orders. ("Prudence," said Jefferson, ". . .
will dictate that governments long established should not be changed for
light and transient causes,"[13] but the authors of *The Federalist* ask, "Is it not
the glory of the people of America, that, whilst they have paid a decent
regard to the opinions of former times and other nations, they have not
suffered a blind veneration for antiquity, for custom, or for names, to
overrule the suggestions of their own good sense, the knowledge of their
own situation, and the lessons of their own experience?"[14]) As the ground
for objecting to the role of tradition in science is chiefly that it prevents or
inhibits progress, so the ground for supporting it in politics, morals, and
religion is that it prevents or limits change. Montesquieu, for example, says
that a democracy ought to have "a permanent body . . . to serve as a rule
and pattern of manners; a senate, to which years, virtue, gravity, and eminent services procure admittance," which will "steadily adhere to the ancient institutions, and mind that the people and the magistrates never
swerve from them."[15] And as the texts that oppose the role of tradition in
science and certain other orders do so from the conviction, expressed or
implied, that the past is inferior to the present, so the defenders of tradition do so from a conviction that at least in some orders the reverse is true.
Again, it is Montesquieu who says,

> *The preservation of the ancient customs is a very considerable point in
> respect to manners. Since a corrupt people seldom perform any memorable
> actions, seldom establish societies, build cities, or enact laws; on the contrary,*

474

since most institutions are derived from people whose manners are plain and simple, to keep up the ancient customs is the way to preserve the original purity of morals.[16]

A regard for "ancient institutions" is as much needed when "by some revolution the state has happened to assume a new form" as in other circumstances, Montesquieu adds. For "even those who have been the instruments of the revolution were desirous it should be relished, which is difficult to compass without good laws."[17]

Authors who disapprove of tradition because of its effect on the progress of some human order such as science usually do so in the name of reason, which they oppose to it. This still allows tradition some room. Gibbon, observing how the Romans continued to worship the Greek gods as long as the Empire prospered, without any real belief that there was a connection between their fortunes and their faith, justifies such practice on the excuse—ironically intended, as to be sure it is—that "where reason cannot instruct, custom may be permitted to guide." Montaigne, however, finds reason *in* custom, insisting that there is "no so absurd or ridiculous fancy can enter into human imagination, that does not meet with some example of public practice, and that, consequently, our reason does not ground and back up."[18] What we regard as reasonable in this world is merely what we are accustomed to, he argues,

> *and the common fancies that we find in repute everywhere about us, and infused into our minds with the seed of our fathers, appear to be the most universal and genuine: from whence it comes to pass, that whatever is off the hinges of custom, is believed to be also off the hinges of reason; how unreasonably for the most part, God knows.*

Even "the laws of conscience, which we pretend to be derived from nature, proceed from custom," Montaigne says, so that "everyone, having an inward veneration for the opinions and manners approved and received amongst his own people, cannot, without very great reluctance, depart from them, nor apply himself to them without applause."[19] Such a doctrine, which denies that one custom is more reasonable than another, denies equally, of course, that reason can refute them. It is not therefore a surprise to find Montaigne saying, with respect to the political order, that men ought never to attempt to change their form of government so as to conform to some idea of what the best government is. Whatever plan is then conceived will be inferior in Montaigne's view to the wisdom embodied by time and trial in the government that exists, however bad that government is from an ideal point of view. "Not according to opinion," he insists, "but in truth and reality, the best and most excellent government for every nation is that under which it is maintained: its form and essential convenience depend upon custom." If we are displeased with our condition, yet we shall seek to alter it at our peril, for "nothing presses so hard

475

upon a state as innovation: change only gives form to injustice and tyranny."[20]

Pascal disagrees with part of this. "Montaigne is wrong," he says, in offering such a rationale for custom. "Custom should be followed only because it is custom, and not because it is reasonable or just."[21] As we have seen, that for Pascal does not mean in science, where reason must rule and where men cannot accept any authority that is prejudicial to it. Customary beliefs, the authority of books, ancient teachings—these things belong in Pascal's view rather to history, to languages, and above all to religion, or more precisely to theology. For he says,

> *it is in theology that authority has its chief weight because there it is inseparable from truth, which we know only through it; so that to give absolute certainty to things which reason can grasp, it is sufficient to point them out in Holy Scripture (as, to show the uncertainty of the most probable things, we need only point out that they are not included there); because the principles of theology are above nature and reason, and the mind of man, too feeble to reach them by its own efforts, can arrive at this highest knowledge only if carried there by an all-powerful and supernatural force.[22]*

Because the tenor of these remarks is so very different from that with which Gibbon justifies the religion of Rome in the age of the Antonines, we may overlook the fact that they say the same thing. Of course Gibbon means that in matters that lie beyond the scope of reason, since no belief can be either true or false, any belief will do, or none; whereas for Pascal there is an order of things that includes a transcendent truth that reason cannot reach, that only faith can find. For both men, however, it is not in the order of reason and nature, but only in what lies beyond or above it, that what they call variously custom, tradition, opinion, or authority, in these and other texts, has its proper place.

The texts we have considered in which "tradition" or one of its related terms is said to be either a good or a bad thing in a particular human order are for the most part qualified, at least by implication, as expressions of the goodness or badness of "tradition" in general. Authors who approve or disapprove of custom or traditional authority in one order may accept or reject it in another, or in all others. Pascal, as we have seen, regards such authority as wrong in science but not in religion. Montaigne, who will not allow that any established government—that is, one sanctioned by custom—should be overthrown, even where the strongest reasons appear to exist for doing so, is eloquent on the folly of those who in dress or manners, "blinded and imposed upon by the authority of present usage," condemn any fashion but the current one, forgetting how often such things change.[23] And Bacon, who protests the authority of ancient learning in the experimental sciences, by no means rejects the means by which such learning survives. Indeed, he writes, "knowledge, whether it descend from divine inspiration, or spring from human sense, would soon perish and vanish to oblivion, if it were not preserved in books, traditions, conferences, and places appointed, as universities, colleges, and schools."[24]

There are, to be sure, a number of texts in which such qualifications do not appear, which take what may be called a comprehensive view of the subject. In some of them the role of "tradition" is regarded as beneficial in human character and circumstances generally, or in respect of some human order that is fundamental to such character and circumstances. These texts indicate that tradition, or custom, or whatever seems to convey the past into the present with authority, is an indispensable ingredient of human life considered as a whole, and therefore cannot or should not be denied.

One of these texts is in the *Laws* of Plato, who speaks in terms of custom and habit as well as of tradition itself. Elsewhere in that long dialogue, Plato asserts the importance of "unwritten customs, and what are termed the laws of our ancestors," which he calls "the bonds of the whole state";[25] he insists also upon the importance of religious traditions, "the least part of [which] ought not to be disturbed by the legislator";[26] he argues, as in *The Republic*, that no changes should ever be allowed in music and the forms of dance when they are expressive, as they ought always to be, of virtue;[27] and so forth. But in one particular passage he goes farther and maintains that

> *any change whatever except from evil is the most dangerous of all things; this is true in the case of the seasons and of the winds, in the management of our bodies and the habits of our minds—true of all things except, as I said before, of the bad. He who looks at the constitution of individuals accustomed to eat any sort of meat, or drink any drink, or to do any work which they can get, may see that they are first disordered by them, but afterwards, as time goes on, their bodies grow adapted to them, and they learn to know and like variety, and have good health and enjoyment of life; and if ever afterwards they are confined again to a superior diet, at first they are troubled with disorders, and with difficulty become habituated to their new food. A similar principle we may imagine to hold good about the minds of men and the natures of their souls. For when they have been brought up in certain laws, which by some Divine Providence have remained unchanged during long ages, so that no one has any memory or tradition of their being otherwise than they are, then everyone is afraid and ashamed to change that which is established.*

Therefore, Plato says, "the legislator must somehow find a way of implanting this reverence for antiquity," lest there be "frequent changes in the praise and censure of manners," which constitute "the greatest of evils."[28]

477

A second text in which "tradition" or one of its related terms is held to be good in a general sense is the famous passage in *The Principles of Psychology* where William James discourses on the subject of habit, which he calls "the enormous fly-wheel of society, its most precious conservative agent." The force of habit is such that no man can escape its effects, James asserts. And "on the whole," he adds, "it is best" that we should not escape. "It is well for the world that in most of us, by the age of thirty, the character has set like plaster, and will never soften again."[29]

Still a third text of the sort we are discussing is that in the *New Introductory Lectures on Psycho-Analysis* where Freud speaks of the superego as formed by the child's parents and thus as constituting "the vehicle of tradition and all the age-long values which have been handed down ... from generation to generation." In conveying this tradition, Freud adds, the superego is "the representative of all moral restrictions, the advocate of the impulse towards perfection, in short ... as much as we have been able to apprehend psychologically of what people call the 'higher' things in human life."[30] Similar statements appear later in the *Outline of Psychoanalysis*, where Freud again makes the point that the superego reflects the influence of the parents on the child's mind, and "includes not merely the personalities of the parents themselves, but also the racial, national, and family traditions handed on through them."[31] The same work contains a further interesting passage in which Freud adds:

> *In spite of their fundamental difference, the id and the superego have one thing in common: they both represent the influences of the past (the id the influence of heredity, the superego essentially the influence of what is taken over from other people), whereas the ego is principally determined by the individual's own experience, that is to say by accidental and current events.*[32]

There are also texts, however, quite as comprehensive as any of these, that take the opposite view, disputing the necessity and the worth of tradition in human affairs with the same lack of qualification. They regard tradition as inhibiting or as being otherwise detrimental to the progress of knowledge, the formation of human character, or the arrangement of human circumstances, and they argue or appeal for a reduction of its influence if they do not absolutely defy it.

One such text consists of the chapter called "Of Darkness from Vain Philosophy and Fabulous Traditions" in Part IV of Hobbes's *Leviathan*, from which a portion has already been quoted. In this chapter, Hobbes reviews with massive scorn a variety of errors or illusions that have survived by tradition through books and other means from ancient or medieval times. The defect of these errors or illusions—among which Hobbes lists the teachings of Aristotle, the commentaries of the Jews, and the dogmas of the Roman Church—is that they are based, or at least our acceptance of them is based, not on what Hobbes calls "reasoning," by

which he means proceeding from "the manner of the generation of anything, to the properties; or from the properties, to some possible way of
generation of the same," so as to be able to produce, "as far as matter and
human force permit, such effects as human life requireth,"[33] but on suppo-
sitions and distinctions that were faulty to begin with and have been
handed down in books that neither understood the errors nor corrected
them. All of which Hobbes rejects as tending to keep men in intellectual
and spiritual darkness, ignorant alike of reason and the gospel, unfitted
for the duties of a human Commonwealth and unready for the Kingdom
of God to come.

To this may be added the statements in the *Discourse on Method* that tell
how Descartes came to rely on his own intellectual resources rather than
those of other men—statements purely personal in their intention, and
significantly so, yet symptomatic of a cast of thought that has become widespread. For, Descartes says, after his experience of schools had convinced
him that nothing was certainly known by the philosophers, and that the
sciences grounded on their writings could therefore not be trusted, he
resolved to seek no other knowledge than that which could be found in
himself, on the assumption that

> *as regards all the opinions which up to this time I had embraced, I . . . could
> not do better than endeavour once for all to sweep them completely away, so
> that they might later on be replaced, either by others which were better, or by the
> same, when I had made them conform to the uniformity of a rational scheme.
> And I firmly believed that by this means I should succeed in directing my life
> much better than if I had only built on old foundations, and relied on prin-
> ciples of which I allowed myself in youth to be persuaded without having
> inquired into their truth.*[34]

On top of this must be added the remarks of John Stuart Mill—as
strong an antitraditionalist in his way as Hobbes, though his tone is very
different—who addresses himself to the subject in the essay *On Liberty*.
There, in the chapter called "Of Individuality, as one of the Elements of
Well-being," Mill asserts that

> *Where, not the person's own character, but the traditions or customs of other
> people are the rule of conduct, there is wanting one of the principal ingredients
> of human happiness, and quite the chief ingredient of individual and social
> progress.*[35]

The defect that Mill sees in the human society of his time is just its tendency to insist upon such sources of conduct and, as a result, to discourage
individual and social development. "The despotism of custom," he writes,
"is everywhere the standing hindrance to human advancement, being in
unceasing antagonism to that disposition to aim at something better than
customary, which is called, according to circumstances, the spirit of liberty,

or that of progress or improvement."[36] Mill accepts certain limits to this spirit. "Nobody denies," he says,

> that people should be so taught and trained in youth as to know and benefit by the ascertained results of human experience. But it is the privilege and proper condition of a human being, arrived at the maturity of his faculties, to use and interpret experience in his own way.[37]

If this does not happen, Mill argues, there cannot be any human development, for "the individuality is the same thing with development, and . . . it is only the cultivation of individuality which produces, or can produce, well-developed human beings."[38]

It will be noted that in the passages we have considered from Plato, William James, and Freud, the value of tradition (or custom, or habit, as the case may be) is thought to lie mostly in its stabilizing influence, the restraint it provides in the cultural life of the race. For each of these authors, this is only the means to an end. James indicates how that is so in the relatively restricted terms that the idea of "habit" implies, as assuring social stability and making possible individual achievement. The function of the superego, Freud argues, is something greater, binding together not merely the social but what we may think of more comprehensively as the human order, and not only in respect of an individual lifetime, to which, of course, any habit is confined, but of the whole of human experience, which the superego makes available to, and brings to bear upon, the individual psyche. And Plato's frame of reference is larger still, being political and philosophical rather than historical or moral: the well-ordered State requires a "reverence for antiquity" as a body requires health—must, if it loses this reverence, become enfeebled and disordered, as a body without health becomes weakened or diseased—to the end that the laws and public institutions may survive and prosper and the citizens may live wise and virtuous lives.

The texts from Hobbes, Descartes, and J. S. Mill, which are as strongly against tradition as these passages are for it, likewise regard it not as an end in itself but as something intermediate in human affairs. But where Plato, Freud, and William James think tradition is enabling—is, indeed, the indispensable condition of a wise, good, and truly human life—for Hobbes, Descartes, and Mill it serves precisely the opposite function, is rather inhibiting if not absolutely preventive of that kind of life. Or, if some qualification is in order before we reach such a conclusion in the case of Hobbes and Descartes, the focus of whose concern may be said to be intellectual rather than moral—with what we know rather than with what we do (whatever difference that makes)—yet at least in the case of Mill there can be no doubt that we have a disagreement, with respect to Plato,

James, and Freud, that is both direct and profound. And this disagreement is at least implied in many of the other texts we have reviewed, so that it seems necessary to accept that, while the issue is not always exactly joined, when it is, the judgments of the authors of *Great Books of the Western World* on the subject are seriously conflicting.

There are, however, a number of texts in the set that endeavor to reconcile or transcend this disagreement, or that seem to provide grounds on which we may reconcile or transcend it ourselves—texts that indicate the fullest perception of the conflict that has been noted. This means, among other things, that they recognize the deadening effects that tradition can have in human affairs or on human understanding (for their focus is as much on knowledge as it is on action), and that they undertake to defend it only insofar as they can regard it as a vital force.

Such a text is Pascal's Preface to the *Treatise on the Vacuum,* of which some account has already been given. In this remarkable discussion that, brief as it is, seems to say nearly everything that can be said about tradition, Pascal distinguishes between the kind of knowledge that animals have and the kind that is peculiar to man. He observes that the knowledge animals have through instinct is complete but limited: nature teaches them whatever they need to know in order to accomplish their natural purpose, but no more; and as their knowledge does not need to be increased, so it cannot be preserved, being created afresh in each new member of the species. "It is different with man," Pascal says, "made only for infinity."

> *He is ignorant in his life's first age, but he never ceases to learn as he goes forward, for he has the advantage not only of his own experience but also of his predecessors', because he always keeps in his memory the knowledge he has once acquired, and that of the ancients is always at hand in the books they have left.*

In terms we have been using, this is to say that as man learns by reason rather than instinct, so the source of his knowledge is not nature but experience, both his own and that of his ancestors. The latter cannot limit us, Pascal insists, unless we make the mistake of treating it with reverence, as if, once the opinions of the ancients had been expressed, there were "no more truths to know." When we do this, in effect we treat such opinions as if they *were* instincts, and thus can learn nothing from them. The right way for man to regard the matter, Pascal argues, is to realize that "since he keeps his knowledge, he can also easily increase it," and that the men of any given time are, as one may say, in the same condition as the ancients would be if they had been able to continue their studies. For "the same thing happens in the succession of men as in the different ages of an individual," Pascal goes on, "so that the whole series of men during the course of so many centuries should be considered as one self-same man, always in existence and continually learning."[39]

481

A second text that seems to reconcile or transcend the conflict we have noted is from *The Critique of Judgment*, where Kant considers how an aesthetic judgment—that is, a judgment of taste, having to do with the excellence or beauty of a thing—can be arrived at. Such a judgment has no objective basis, yet lays claim to the agreement of everyone; can be verified only in the sense, and to the extent, that it agrees with the judgment of others, yet lays claim to autonomy, denying that other judgments are its source. "The fact that we recommend the works of the ancients as models," Kant says, "and rightly, too, and call their authors *classical*, as constituting a sort of nobility among writers that leads the way and thereby gives laws to the people, seems to indicate *a posteriori* sources of taste and to contradict the autonomy of taste in each individual."

> But we might just as well say that the ancient mathematicians, who, to this day, are looked upon as the almost indispensable models of perfect thoroughness and elegance in synthetic methods, prove that reason also is on our part only imitative, and that it is incompetent with the deepest intuition to produce of itself rigorous proofs by means of the construction of concepts.[40]

Kant allows that when we come to judge of anything, without considering what others have said before us, we are likely to blunder. It is not, however, "that predecessors make those who follow in their steps mere imitators, but by their methods they set others upon the track of seeking in themselves for the principles, and so of adopting their own, often better, course." They serve as examples rather than as rules, and the difference is that in judgments based on reason, such examples only reinforce the authority of concepts, whereas in aesthetic judgments, which are not based on concepts but are only expressions of taste, examples are our only guide, indicating "what has in the course of culture maintained itself longest in esteem." We follow such examples as precedents, Kant says, and this, so far as the influence of a particular author extends, "means no more than going to the same sources for a creative work as those to which he went for his creations, and learning from one's predecessor no more than the mode of availing oneself of such sources."[41]

To these observations of Kant's we may add the text—the last we have room to consider—provided by T. S. Eliot's essay "Tradition and the Individual Talent," which appears not in *Great Books of the Western World* but in *Gateway to the Great Books*, volume 5. For this essay, too, seems to reconcile or transcend the conflict we have observed. That is, it seems to rescue the idea of tradition from its deadening implications—not, as Pascal does, by asserting the continuity of humankind, and not as Kant does by invoking the notion of example or precedent, but with its perception that there is a particular order of human experience to which tradition belongs, and which may be said to comprise just that portion of the historical order that is always present and alive.

The context in which this perception of Eliot's occurs is that of art, in particular of poetry, as Pascal's context is scientific and Kant's is philosophical. But it is an idea with wider applications than Eliot gives it. It recognizes that there is a difference between the purely historical order and the order—the ideal order, as Eliot suggests it is—that is formed by "the existing monuments." This order is both temporal and timeless; it occurs within the historical order, but the parts of it, the achievements that comprise it, have a simultaneous existence. As such they constitute a tradition, Eliot says, that cannot be inherited, but can be obtained, if we chose, by great labor. If we are willing to put forth this labor, he adds, we acquire a historical sense that makes us conscious that as whatever work we undertake is affected by the tradition of which we have become aware, and in which our work takes its place, so the tradition is affected by that work, if ever so slightly—affected in the relationship that is thus established between the part and the whole, in the new intelligibility that each thereby acquires, and in the new value they take on in being measured by each other. For none of the works of man has its meaning alone, but each is significant in relation to the rest.

What we discern in these observations of Eliot's, as in Kant's remarks and those of Pascal, is an endeavor to distinguish between what may be called traditionalism, which forces the present, for good or ill, to adapt itself to the past, and a different sort of influence that places the present in a context that allows for—that requires—development. It is this latter meaning of tradition, implicit in many other texts besides those we have discussed, that a careful reading of *Great Books of the Western World* seems to bring out, as being the wisdom of the subject when it is squarely contemplated. That this should be so is consistent with the kind of tradition that the books themselves are thought to embody, of which Eliot in particular, though he has in mind a somewhat different order, gives such a good account. It is as if we had discovered in them the principle of their own vitality, which they had not often or lengthily troubled to explain, but which, when necessary, they could articulate and make manifest. "For books," as Milton says, "are not absolutely dead things, but do contain a potency of life in them to be as active as that soul whose progeny they are; nay, they do preserve as in a vial the purest efficacy and extraction of the living intellect that bred them."[42] In respect to the idea of tradition, as with so many other subjects, the *Great Books* seem able to show with special force how this is so.

483

[1] *GBWW*, Vol. 1, p. xi.
[2] *GBWW*, Vol. 21, p. 69d.
[3] Ibid., p. 90.
[4] *GBWW*, Vol. 30, p. 14c–d.
[5] Ibid., pp. 109, 110.
[6] Ibid., p. 126.
[7] *GBWW*, Vol. 23, pp. 268–69.
[8] *GBWW*, Vol. 33, p. 358.
[9] *GBWW*, Vol. 28, pp. 157 ff.
[10] *GBWW*, Vol. 45, p. 33.
[11] *GBWW*, Vol. 40, pp. 23–24.
[12] Ibid., p. 24.
[13] *GBWW*, Vol. 43, p. 1.
[14] Ibid., p. 62.
[15] *GBWW*, Vol. 38, p. 22a.
[16] Ibid., p. 22.
[17] Ibid.
[18] *GBWW*, Vol. 25, p. 44.
[19] Ibid., p. 46.
[20] Ibid., p. 463.
[21] *GBWW*, Vol. 33, p. 230.
[22] Ibid., p. 355.
[23] *GBWW*, Vol. 25, p. 143.
[24] *GBWW*, Vol. 30, p. 29.
[25] *GBWW*, Vol. 7, p. 716.
[26] Ibid., p. 692.
[27] Ibid., p. 654.
[28] Ibid., p. 718.
[29] *GBWW*, Vol. 53, p. 79.
[30] *GBWW*, Vol. 54, p. 834b–c.
[31] *An Outline of Psychoanalysis*, trans. James Strachey (New York: W. W. Norton & Co., 1949), p. 17.
[32] Ibid.
[33] *GBWW*, Vol. 23, p. 267.
[34] *GBWW*, Vol. 31, p. 45b–c.
[35] *GBWW*, Vol. 43, pp. 293–94.
[36] Ibid., p. 300.
[37] Ibid., p. 294.
[38] Ibid., p. 297.
[39] *GBWW*, Vol. 33, p. 357.
[40] *GBWW*, Vol. 42, pp. 513d–14a.
[41] Ibid., p. 514.
[42] *GBWW*, Vol. 32, p. 384.